Essays on Rhetoric

Essays on Rhetoric

Edited by DUDLEY BAILEY

UNIVERSITY OF NEBRASKA

NEW YORK

OXFORD UNIVERSITY PRESS

1965

Preface

This book is intended for students in composition and speech courses in which the tradition of rhetoric plays a vital part. This collection of essays is intended to bring to such students an opportunity to read in some depth from the venerable tradition of Aristotelian rhetoric and something at least of interesting and important modern observations upon the art of persuasion. Though rhetoric is one of the most widely taught of subjects, the theoretical substance of the subject remains largely unknown to contemporary college students. Yet its importance to composition, oral or written, is rarely questioned, and its importance to the understanding of our literary and forensic heritage is unquestionable. At present, instructors in composition and speech, if they intend that their students shall gain firsthand knowledge of the rhetorical tradition, are forced to make sizable library assignments. This text is put forth to meet the need for readings in this tradition.

I have attempted to give a fair sampling of the tradition of rhetoric known to the ancient, medieval, and Renaissance world, by dovetailing selections from Plato, Aristotle, Cicero, Quintilian, Blair, and Campbell. This tradition, though by no means so popular today as in former times, is still the only acknowledged rhetorical tradition we have. No genius of the stature of Aristotle has given his attention to the science of persuasion and brought together the widely variant applications which the modern world has provided. Until such a genius appears, we must be content with a comparatively heterogeneous set of ideas bearing upon various aspects of the problems of writing and speech.

In short, the second half of this collection is by no means so cohesive as the first half. It does not follow that the second half is less interesting; students will find much in it that is stimulating and provocative. But I do not pretend that the modern essays are organized in the way that the earlier pieces are.

I have restricted the apparatus of the text to some notes for some of the essays, which are intended to help the student through the more difficult selections. I have not invaded the proper realm of the teacher by posing study questions or assigning student papers; my intention is to aid the teacher, not supplant him. Many of the modern selections are printed without supplementary notes: there is no need to 'clarify' such lucid writers as Richard Weaver and Gilbert Ryle.

This is not to say that the readings in this collection are easy. They require close attention and study by the student. College courses which do not demand intellectual rigor of students will find little use of this text, in all likelihood. But the majority of college undergradautes are now capable of dealing with difficult intellectual problems, and as soon as the products of a considerably enriched English curriculum in the schools reach the colleges, they will demand such substance of college courses in writing and speech as this book provides in part.

A faculty fellowship granted by the Woods Charitable Fund freed me to begin work on a modern rhetoric; this collection of essays is a by-product of the initial reading for that task.

I owe thanks for aid and encouragement to Professors Paul A. Olson and Gene B. Hardy of the University of Nebraska, James E. Miller, Jr., of the University of Chicago, Royal A. Gettmann of the University of Illinois, G. Thomas Fairclough of the University of Cincinnati, Daniel W. Bernd of San Fernando Valley State College, and Edward P. J. Corbett of The Creighton University. Mrs. Butler Shaffer helped with the preparation of the text. On behalf of the publisher, Professor Scott Elledge of Cornell University made keen and valuable suggestions. Neither he nor others mentioned are responsible for the shortcomings of this book.

Lincoln, Nebraska   Dudley Bailey
15 October 1964

Contents

The Great Tradition

Phaedrus

SOCRATES AND PHAEDRUS [IN DIALOGUE.]

SOCRATES. Whither bound, dear Phaedrus? And whence come you?

PHAEDRUS. From Lysias son of Cephalus I come, sir; and I'm off for a walk beyond the city-wall, for I've sat by him all the while since early morning. I take the advice of your medical friend and mine, Acumenus, about walks on the open roads; he says they are better than foot-racing for the constitution.

SOCRATES. He is right, too, my friend.—And so Lysias was in town, was he?

PHAEDRUS. Yes, indeed; visiting Epicrates at the house 'Moruchia' near the temple of Olympian Zeus.

SOCRATES. Well, what had you by way of entertainment there? Lysias, no doubt, regaled you all with discourse?

PHAEDRUS. You shall learn, if you have leisure to go along with me and hear.

SOCRATES. Why not? In the words of Pindar, fancy my not 'setting above' any 'matter I had in hand' the chance to hear what passed between Lysias and you.

PHAEDRUS. Come on.

SOCRATES. Tell on.

PHAEDRUS. No question, Socrates, but the matter is of special interest to you; for the subject we discussed was, in its way, the subject of Love. Lysias, in fact, has written something on this theme: A beautiful youth is solicited in love, but not by a man in love with him; that is the dainty point of it, in the argument that the non-lover is to be accepted instead of the lover.

SOCRATES. O admirable Lysias! If only he would write that a poor man must be accepted before a rich one, and an old man before a young one, and so

From *Plato: Phaedrus, Ion, Gorgias, and Symposium, with passages from the Republic and Laws,* trans. by Lane Cooper, New York, Oxford University Press, 1948. Copyright, 1938, by Lane Cooper. Used by permission of Cornell University Press.

on, how that would hit the case for me and so many of us! There you would have urbane arguments, and utterances for the public welfare! I am now so eager to listen that you might walk as far as Megara, turn at the wall there, as Herodicus advises, and come all the way back, with me at your side.

PHAEDRUS. What can you mean, O best of men? Lysias, the most amazing writer of the time, has spent his leisure for many a day on the composition of a work; and you think me able, Socrates, unskilled as I am, to reproduce it all from memory without injustice to him? I am far from having such ability. What wouldn't I give to possess it!

SOCRATES. Phaedrus! either I know Phaedrus, or I no longer know myself. But there is no doubt at all on either point. And well I know that the man who listened to that speech of Lysias did not hear it only once; no, he bade the author repeat it to him over and over again, and the author readily consented. And if that was not enough, at last he got hold of the copy itself, and examined the points in it that he most longed to see; and thus he sat and worked all morning, until he was tired and went for a walk. So now, I swear by the Dog, he has the speech by heart, if it wasn't over-long; and he was going outside the city-wall to perfect himself in the delivery. Then he met a pining man who was frantic to hear speeches; him he saw, and, seeing, he rejoiced for that he would have a fellow enthusiast, and he bade this man come with him. But when the pining lover of discourse besought him to begin, that other man put on coy airs, and said: 'I have no desire to speak'; though in the end he meant to do it, and, if the listener proved unwilling, would have forced him to hear against his will. So, Phaedrus, beg him to do now what he will shortly do in any case.

PHAEDRUS. Evidently the best thing for me, by far, is to go ahead as well as I can. You clearly will not let me off until I give the speech no matter how.

SOCRATES. There you show true penetration.

PHAEDRUS. Then here goes as I said. Actually, Socrates, I did not learn the whole thing word for word. However, I can begin at the beginning, take up the main heads in their order, and pretty well give the gist of all the differences Lysias brought out between the lover and the non-lover.

SOCRATES. You can begin, sweet friend, by showing what it is you have in your left hand underneath your cloak. I'll guess that you have there the discourse itself. If that is so, then don't mistake me. Much as I love you, with Lysias present I am not prepared to let you exercise your memory of him on me. Come now, show it!

PHAEDRUS. I surrender! You have dashed the hope I had of practising on you. Now, then, since we are going to read it, where would you like to have us sit?

SOCRATES. Let us turn off the road, and follow the Ilissus. Along the stream we shall find a quiet spot that you like, and there sit down.

PHAEDRUS. That's a timely suggestion, I think, for to-day I go barefoot. You always go barefoot. Let us walk in the brook, and bathe our feet; it's the easiest way, and pleasant, too, at this time of year and this hour of the day.

SOCRATES. You lead on, and keep looking for a place where we may sit.

PHAEDRUS. Do you see that lofty plane-tree yonder?

SOCRATES. What about it?

PHAEDRUS. There we shall have shade, and a gentle breeze, and grass to sit on, or lie on if we like.

SOCRATES. Keep on towards it.

PHAEDRUS. Tell me, Socrates, wasn't it here or hereabouts that Boreas, in the story, carried off the nymph Orithyia from the banks of Ilissus?

SOCRATES. So they say.

PHAEDRUS. From this very spot, maybe? The brook is so bright, so pure, so clear to see, and the banks so fit for maidens to play on.

SOCRATES. No; not just here, but a quarter of a mile or more downstream, where we cross over to the temple of the Huntress. The place is marked by some sort of altar to Boreas.

PHAEDRUS. Well, I never noticed that. But I swear I wish you'd tell me, Socrates, do you think the old tale is true?

SOCRATES. Suppose I had my doubts, as the wise have had them, then I shouldn't seem absurd if I rationalized the tale, and said that this maiden was at play with Pharmacia by the neighboring cliff, when a gust of the North wind took them over to their death, and so the tale arose that she had been carried off by Boreas—either hence or from Mars Hill, for according to another version of the story she was snatched from there and not from here. For my part, Phaedrus, I like such explanations well, only they demand too much ingenuity and pains of the one who is to give them; once he begins, the luckless man must go on to straighten out the Hippocentaurs, and after that the Chimera. Of their sort then come flocking Gorgons, and Pegasuses, and a vast train of other incredible beings, prodigies fabulous and strange. If you are sceptical, and try to reduce them one by one to the rules of probability, the task must needs employ your rustic wisdom for many an idle hour. And I, I have no leisure for the purpose. Why not? Because, my friend, I cannot otherwise obey the Delphic motto, and *know myself*. To be ignorant of this, to inquire first into extraneous matters, I take to be absurd. And hence I say farewell to such inquiries; content with everyday opinion on these matters, I investigate, not them, but, I repeat, myself. What am I? Perchance a serpentine monster more knotted in manifold coils than Typhon, and surging with passion more than he? Or a creature of a gentler, simpler sort, sharing somehow in a lot divine, and of a nature not puffed up?—Meanwhile, my friend, as we go arguing, isn't this the tree to which you were to lead us?

PHAEDRUS. Yes, this is it.

SOCRATES. By Hera! What a lovely resting-place! This plane-tree, how it spreads abroad and towers up; and there the tall agnus castus, how it lifts its grateful shade, in fullest bloom! The whole spot is laden with the fragrance. And then the water, how delightful, how cold it runs beneath the plane-tree, as my foot reports! This would seem to be a place that is sacred to Nymphs, and to the river-god Achelous, for see the little images of maidens and the votive statuettes. And please to note the motion of the air, how delicate, here how exceeding sweet. The shrill music of the summer breeze gives undersong to the insect-chorus of cicadae. Rarest of all is the grass, with the gentle slope where we may find repose and a natural pillow for the head. In sum, my Phaedrus dear, you are the prince of guides for the stranger.

PHAEDRUS. Amazing man, how very odd you do appear. It is actually as you say; you are like some stranger with a guide, away from your native land. I judge that you never roam out of the city into the countryside beyond; as far as I can see, you never so much as set foot outside of the wall.

SOCRATES. Forgive me that, my best of friends. I am a lover of learning; the countryside and the trees will not instruct me; 'tis the people in the city are my teachers. Still you, I do declare, have seemingly found the drug that can draw me forth. As hungry creatures follow those who wave before them a leafy branch or a piece of fruit, so with me and a discourse. Only hold a book before my nose, and you may lead me all round Attica, and wherever else you care to. At the moment, now I have come as far as this, I think I shall lie down. You choose any posture you think easiest for reading, and when you are settled, read.

PHAEDRUS. Now listen:

How matters stand with me, you know; and that I think it would advantage both of us if this and that took place, you have heard. I deem it meet I should not fail of my desire on the pretext that I am not your lover; for lovers later rue their acts of kindness, then when their passion is spent. To the other sort there comes no time when they feel regret; for nothing compelled them. Free and unconstrained they plan for the best in view of their own concerns, and bestow their largess according to their power. And then, lovers review the damage they have done through love to their own concerns; calculate the services they have rendered; add on the troubles they have borne; and so conclude that the beloved long since received an ample guerdon. But the non-lover can plead no excuse like that; allege no neglect of his concerns for love; count up no troubles he has undergone; make no complaint of differences the love has caused twixt him and his relations. Accordingly, so many ills dismissed, nothing remains but that with ardor he shall do what when 'tis done he thinks will gratify the loved one. And then, if you say that the lovers deserve more esteem than non-lovers, because it is held that the lovers feel most deeply for those whom they love, and are ready with words and with deeds to offend any other so long as it pleases the loved one; then, if it be so, it is easy to see that in future the lover will care for the next one he loves, and prefer him to this one—if it pleases the next one, will clearly do mischief to this one. And what! How could it be proper to grant the highest of favors to a person afflicted in such wise that no man of discretion would ever essay to relieve him? And the victims themselves admit they are sick rather than in their senses, confess that they know they are out of their heads and can exercise no self-restraint. Now suppose they were come to their senses, would they ever conceive to be good those resolves which they took in their previous state? And if from lovers you must make your choice, to take the best, your choice will be restricted: the lovers are few. But if from all the rest you choose the most congenial man for you, the choice is large, for they are many. Far greater, then, the hope that you will find among the many the man who merits your love.

But say you shrink before public opinion, for shame at what people may think when they learn; then what are the chances? The likelihood is that the lover will blab; for the lovers, who think that the rest envy them as they envy others, exultantly tell, and glory in blazing abroad that their suit was not fruitless. The non-lovers keep themselves better in hand, and so choose the highest reward instead of what men may think. And then, of necessity many must learn and observe that the lover pursues the loved one, that he makes it a business, and hence when they see the two conversing together, then they think that the meeting concerns some affair of desire accomplished or coming. But no one proceeds to accuse the non-lovers for coming together; all know that two people must meet and talk out of friendship or casual pleasure. And now, perchance a fear has come to you as you think how hard it is for love to be lasting; and if somehow there came a dissension, you think that it would be a mishap of equal import to both, but that once you have yielded that which you prize above all, the great harm of the discord then will be yours. In such case, methinks, how much more should you quail at the lover; for lovers are vexed at numberless things, and when anything happens they think all is done in order to injure them. And hence too they try to keep the loved one from mingling with all other men; the lover fearing the rich lest they win over him with money, fearing men of education lest they get the mastery through wit; whoever else has any good possession or acquirement, against the influence of each the lovers are on their guard. If they induce you to offend all these, they leave you utterly bereft of friends; if you have more sense than they, and act with an eye to your own advantage, you will have to quarrel with them. But those who are non-lovers, who because of their desert have accomplished their desire, these would not be jealous if you had companions, rather would they hate the men who did not wish to be such; they would think you slighted by these last, benefited by companions. Far greater, then, the hope of amity, far less the chance of enmity, for you from the affair.

And now, many of the lovers have desired the body ere they knew the bias, and before they learned the other matters appertaining to the loved one. It is dubious if such will care to stay your friends, then when their passion is spent. But the non-lovers, who were friends of the beloved before they did these things, will not be prone, for benefits received, to lessen their affection towards the loved one; rather will the memory of favors past remain as pledge of favors yet to be. And now, it will be better for your soul if you will rather yield to me than to a lover; for lovers praise the loved one beyond best measure for his words and for his actions, partly since they fear they may offend him, partly that through passion they mis-judge him. Such are the manifestations of Eros; 'tis he that makes unlucky lovers think things grievous that cause no pain to any but them; and he compels the lucky ones to praise when things should give no pleasure. And so, far rather must we pity those who are beloved than envy them. Do you but yield to me, and, first, my intercourse with you shall have in view, not present pleasure only, but future gain as well; I, not enslaved by passion, but master of myself, shall not on small occasion give way to violent hate, but for transgressions great shall slowly gather anger small; unintentional offence I shall forgive; intentional ones, endeavor to prevent. These are the certain marks of an affection that will last for a long time. Perhaps a thought has come to you like this, that there can be no firm affection unless one is in love? But reflect! If so, we should not set much value on our sons, nor yet on our fathers and our mothers, nor could we have loyal friends; they all are dear to us, not out of passion such as this, but from associations of another sort.

And then, should one grant favors above all to those who crave them? If so, with other folk we ought to do our best not for the most deserving but the most lacking; these are the ones who will be released from the greatest ills, and hence they will most thank us. And now, when you shall give a private dinner, you should invite the beggars and those who need to fill their bellies, but not invite your friends. The others will love you and pursue you, and gather at your door, and be most pleased and very grateful, and call down many a blessing on your head. But come; perhaps one should not grant one's favors to those who crave them so. Perhaps the favors should be granted above all to those who are most able to repay you; and not to those who importune you, merely, but rather to such as merit what is granted; and not to those who will enjoy the brief hour of your youthful beauty, but to those who will share their good things with you when you are grown older; and not to those who after they succeed with you will boast of their success to others, but to those who modestly keep their secret before all; and not to those who will be eager for a little while, but to those who will stay friends with you through life; and not to those who when their passion wanes will seek a pretext for a quarrel with you, but to those who, when your hour of youth has passed, will then make manifest their solid virtue. Now therefore, bear in mind what I have said, and remember also this: the lover's friends admonish him about his way of life, that it is bad; but never yet has non-lover been blamed by his relations for harmful inattention to his own affairs because he was non-lover.

Perhaps you now would ask me if I counsel you to gratify all the non-lovers. But I think the lover would not bid you to have this intent to all the lovers either; for the favor quite impartial is not so well esteemed by the receiver, and the favor given one man cannot be kept secret from the others, if you wish this. No harm should ever come from it to either man, but benefit should come to both. And now I judge what has been said to be enough. But you, if you find any lack, and think that aught has been omitted, question.

PHAEDRUS. What say you, Socrates? Isn't the speech a marvel every way, and especially in the use of language?

SOCRATES. Simply amazing, my friend! I was transported with it! And this effect I owe to you, Phaedrus, for as you read, and I kept gazing at you, I saw you in an ecstasy with the speech. So, as I thought you more of an adept than I in matters of the sort, I followed your example, and in your leading, dear head divine, I fell into a frenzy.

PHAEDRUS. Come, now. You are pleased to jest about it.

SOCRATES. You make me out a jester, not in earnest?

PHAEDRUS. No, no, Socrates. But, in the name of friendship, tell me truly what you think. Do you believe there is a single Greek besides that could treat the subject in another way, and treat it better or more fully?

SOCRATES. How now? Are you and I to praise the speech because the author has said what was called for, or is the sole point whether the expressions, taken singly, are clear, compact, and finely turned? If we must judge it by the substance, I readily give way to your opinion; the substance, because of my ineptitude, escaped me. I paid attention to the rhetoric of it only, and this I doubted whether Lysias himself would consider adequate. If you will let me say so, Phaedrus, it seemed to me he said the same things over twice or thrice, perhaps because he wasn't very well supplied with things to say on a given subject, or perhaps he didn't bother about a point like that. And then it seemed to me that he was showing off in youthful fashion how well he could say the same thing over in two different ways.

PHAEDRUS. Nonsense, Socrates! What you call repetition is the peculiar merit of the speech. Of all the pertinent sentiments to be uttered on the subject, not a single one has he omitted; consequently no one ever could surpass what he has said, or treat the subject in another way more fully and more justly.

SOCRATES. There I can no longer follow with you. Ancient sages, men and women, have spoken and written on these matters; they will rise up in judgment and confute me if I, through a desire to please, agree with you.

PHAEDRUS Who are they? And where did you ever listen to better things than these?

SOCRATES. Off-hand I cannot say. But clearly something, somewhere, I have heard, it may be from the lovely Sappho, or from Anacreon the wise, or it might be one of the writers in prose. What ground have I for saying so? My breast, dear friend, is somehow full; I feel that I could make another speech, not like this speech of Lysias, nor worse. And well I know that what I have to say is not my own invention, for I am conscious of my ignorance. So I am left to think that I have been filled through the ears, like a pitcher, from the fountains of another; whose, I know not. Here, again, stupidity has led me to forget how and where I heard it.

PHAEDRUS. O how splendid! How noble of you! Never mind from whom or how you heard it; you need not tell even if I beg you to. Only do as you say; promise to make a speech better than this in the book, and just as long, and different in its handling of the subject; and then I'll promise you, like the nine Archons, to set up at Delphi, large as life, a golden statue, not only of myself but of you as well.

SOCRATES. You are a darling, Phaedrus, and actually as good as gold, if you think I mean that Lysias has failed at every point, and think that I can make a speech from which his arguments are all to be rejected. I fancy that would not occur even with the worst of writers. Take the present theme, for instance. What speaker, do you think, in saying that you ought to favor the non-lover rather than the lover, would fail to praise the discretion of the non-lover, and to censure the indiscretion of the lover? These are inevitable points, so what could one say in their stead? No; I think we must allow and excuse the use of such points by the speaker. And when he uses them, we shall praise, not his invention, but his arrangement of them; when he says things that are not inevitable, not so easy to think of, then besides the arrangement we may praise his invention.

PHAEDRUS. I grant you that; it all sounds reasonable to me. So I'll do thus: I shall let you start with the assumption that the lover is more distraught than the non-lover. If you, now, can produce a different speech, more copious and better, then beside the Cypselids' huge oblation at Olympia shall your colossus stand, like it of beaten gold!

SOCRATES. You take my jest in earnest, Phaedrus? Because, to tease you, I laid hands on your beloved? And do you really think that I shall try to make a speech that will outdo the ingenuity of Lysias?

PHAEDRUS. There I have you, my friend, as you had me. You certainly will have to speak 'as best you can,' or else we shall perforce resort to silly comic repartee. Watch out; don't make me say, please, what you said to me: 'Socrates, either I know Socrates, or I no longer know myself'; and 'He wished to make a speech, and then put on coy airs.' No; make up your mind that hence we do not stir until you give the speech which you said was in your bosom. Here we are, alone, in a deserted place; and I am the younger man, and stronger. Accordingly, 'Make no mistake as to my meaning!' Speak willingly, and don't compel me to use force.

SOCRATES. But, blessed Phaedrus, I shall make myself a laughing-stock if I, an amateur, compete extempore with Lysias, a master of his art.

PHAEDRUS. Do you know what? You stop your coy pretending with me. I guess I have a word I can say that will start you speaking.

SOCRATES. Then never say it!

PHAEDRUS. But I will, too; and my word shall be an oath! I swear to you by —let's see, by which of the deities? By this plane-tree, say. By her I swear that if you do not speak the speech here in her presence, never will I unfold to you another speech, never tell you of one, by any man.

SOCRATES. Ah, villain! How well you have found the way to catch the man with a foible for discourse, the way to make him speak!

PHAEDRUS. Why, then, keep twisting?

SOCRATES. I stop. I heed your oath; for how could I renounce so rich a feast?

PHAEDRUS. Proceed, then.

SOCRATES. Do you know what I shall do?

PHAEDRUS. How do you mean?

SOCRATES. I am going to cloak my face while speaking, and to gallop through the speech as fast as I can, for if I looked at you, my embarrassment would get me confused.

PHAEDRUS. If you will only speak! For the rest you may do whatever you like.

SOCRATES. Come then, ye tuneful Muses, whether ye have this name from your tuneful song, or take it from the tuneful race of the Ligurians! Come give me aid in the tale this matchless friend of mine compels me to rehearse; that so his friend, whom he till now has deemed a wise man, here-after may seem wiser to him than before.

Once upon a time there was a boy, a stripling rather, very beautiful; and he had many, many lovers. Among them there was one, a man of guile, as much in love with him as any of them, who had convinced the boy it was not so. And once when the man was wooing him, he tried to prove this very thing, to wit, that one should grant one's favors to the non-lover before the lover; and thus he spoke:

For every case, my lad, the counselor who would counsel well has only one way to begin. He has to know the thing concerning which he gives advice, or the advice will wholly miss the mark. But people mostly fail to see that they do not know the nature of the individual thing. Now, since they think they do know, they fail to reach an understanding at the start of their inquiry, and therefore they go on to the natural result. That is, they end by contradicting both themselves and one another. Now you and I must not be guilty of the error we condemn in others, but since we two are going to discuss the question whether one should rather choose to enter into friendship with the lover or the non-lover, let us first of all agree upon a definition of love. What is it, and what power has it? With our definition kept in view, and constantly referring to it, let us inquire whether love brings benefit or harm. That love is a desire is clear to all; again, that non-lovers too desire the beautiful, we know. Then by what shall we dis-tinguish the lover and non-lover? Observe, again, that in each of us there are two ruling and leading principles which we follow according as they lead us; one the innate desire for pleasure, the other an acquired conviction which has for its mark the best. The two sometimes are in harmony within us; at times, again, they are at war; and sometimes the one, sometimes the other, has the mastery. When opinion by the aid of reason leads us to the best, and is the victor, we call the victory self-restraint; but when desire, devoid of reason, drags us toward pleasure, and rules within us, we call this the rule of excess. Excess, indeed, has many names, for it has many mem-bers, many shapes; and whichever of its forms predominates in a given case, this lends its name to the possessor, a name not fair nor honorable either. For instance, if desire of food gets the mastery of reason and the best, and the other desires, we call it gluttony, and the man who has it gets the name of glutton. Again, if the desire for strong drink becomes tyran-nical, and leads the victim on this path, what epithet he gets is obvious. And so with other members of the family of desires, when a desire con-stantly obtains the upper hand, the man acquires the corresponding well-known name. The drift of all that has been said thus far, I take it, is by this time clear; yet a thought expressed is surely clearer than a thing un-said. Accordingly: the irrational desire that conquers the conviction which strives after the right; that is borne towards pleasure from beauty; that, again, with force recruited from desires akin to it is rapt towards beauty of the body; this desire, when it is master in the leading, takes its name from force itself, and is called *eros,* love.

How now, dear Phaedrus? Do I seem to you to be inspired? To me it would appear so.

PHAEDRUS.   Assuredly, Socrates, you have had an unusual attack of fluency.

SOCRATES.   Listen to me, then, in silence, for of a truth the place seems holy. And so you must not wonder if, as I proceed, I often seem to be possessed, for even now my utterance is well-night dithyrambic.

PHAEDRUS.   You say most truly!

SOCRATES.   The responsibility is yours; but hear what follows, and perchance the fit may be averted. But all is in the hands of God! Return we to our boy:

Well then, O best and bravest! The matter about which we must consult has now been stated and defined. With our eyes upon the definition, in what remains let us inquire what benefit or damage is likely to result from the lover and non-lover for him who grants the favor.

The man who is ruled by desire, who is a slave to pleasure, will surely try to make the loved one as pleasing to him as may be. Now to a man of unsound wits all that is pleasant which is not against him; anything superior, or equal to him, he finds hateful. So the lover will not readily endure to have a loved one who is better than himself, or made equal to him, but is always busy rendering him inferior and weaker. Now, the ignorant is inferior to the wise, the coward to the brave, the feeble speaker to the eloquent, the slow of wit to the acute. Mental defects like these, and more of them, whether natural or acquired, are sure to please the lover in the loved one, in whom, if they are not implanted, the lover must implant them, or be deprived of his momentary satisfaction. And he is certain to be jealous; he will prevent the loved one from associating with many other men, in associations that would benefit the loved one, and would distinctly tend to make a man of him—there you have great cause of harm; and, greatest harm of all, will keep him from society that would give him the highest wisdom. This is divine philosophy; from it the lover certainly will keep the loved one far away, in the utmost fear of incurring his disdain. For the rest, he will contrive to keep the loved one ignorant every way, and to look for everything to him, the lover, so that to him the loved one may be most pleasant, most harmful to himself. Accordingly, in what concerns the mind, a man in love is no wise a helpful guide and comrade.

Take next the bodily state, and the care of the physique. What will the condition be, and what the care of the body, when he becomes its master who perforce is following pleasure instead of good? Let us see. He will be observed pursuing one of the effeminate sort, not sturdy, reared not in the clear sunlight but rather in commingled shade, unused to manly toil and dusty sweat; of the sort addicted to a soft and ladylike existence, decked out with borrowed paints and perfumes for want of natural health and color. To these details add all the others; they are obvious, and not worth going into further. The whole we may outline in a word, proceeding then to something else. A body such as this, in war and other serious times of need, will give the enemy reason to rejoice, and give one's friends, and even lovers, cause for fear.

We let that pass for obvious, and turn to what comes next in order: that which we possess. What benefit or harm to this will result for us through the fellowship and management of the lover? To each and all, but above all to the lover, it is clear that he would wish the loved one, before all else, to be bereft of his dearest and truest and holiest possessions. He would desire to see him fatherless and motherless, without relations, lacking friends, for he views them all as persons who would check and blame his intercourse most sweet with the beloved. If, however, the object of his love has property, whether gold or other valuable holdings, the lover will regard him as less easily caught, or, when caught, less easy to be handled; wherefore the lover is certain to begrudge the loved one his command of property, and certain to be glad when it is lost. Nay more, he would wish the loved one to remain as long as possible unmarried, childless, homeless, since he desires the utmost prolongation of his own sweet joy.

There exist in nature other evils that are bad enough, and yet in most of them some power has interfused a momentary grace. Take the flatterer, a fearsome animal that does great harm, and yet with him has nature intermingled a sort of pleasure that is not without its charm; and so the courtesan, whom one might blame for an injurious creature; and there are many other creatures and pursuits of a similar bias that afford a very great ephemeral pleasure. But the lover is not only hurtful to the loved one; he is extremely disagreeable to live with also. According to the ancient proverb, 'Mates of an age delight each other'; I suppose equality of years brings them to the same amusements, and the similarity produces friendship. Yet even they will tire of one another's company. And verily 'constraint of every sort' is said to be 'grievous to all.' But now, besides this inequality, the lover has constraint upon the youth, and to the utmost. He, the older, stays with the younger, and will not leave him, day nor night, if he can help it; constraint and mad desire drive him onwards; the sting of love allures him with the gift of constant joy in seeing, hearing, touching the beloved, of feeling him with every power of sense. So he clings to his beloved, and gladly serves him. But what of the beloved one? What consolation or what pleasure will he be receiving all this time? The intercourse will bring him to the uttermost repugnance? To see the aging, faded countenance, and the rest of the person to match, things unpleasant even to hear described, let alone being daily forced into actual contact with them! And meanwhile to be jealously watched and guarded against everything and everybody, and to hear his praises sung, inept, extravagant, likewise to hear reproaches that could not be tolerated from a sober man, but from a drunken not merely unendurable but indecent, as the man gives way in public to his endless gabble!

Is he hurtful and repulsive while he loves—then what later? When his love is gone, ever after he is false; false to him whom with many oaths and great, and prayers, and promises, he had of yore scarcely brought to bear the tedium of his company through hope of benefits to come. The day of payment has arrived, but now he has, within, another master, a new guide, namely reason and good sense instead of love and madness; is in fact another person. Yet the beloved knows nothing of the change; he begs of the lover a return for favors past, reminding him of what was done and said, as if he still were dealing with the same man. But the latter for shame does not dare say he has become another, and neither is he able to make good the vows he swore and the promises he gave when he was ruled by folly. He dare not do so, now he has regained his mind and self-restraint, for fear that, if he did again the things he did before, he would become again the man he was before. He runs away from these things, and must perforce be a defaulter. The clam-shell falling t'other side up, the erstwhile lover from pursuing turns to flight; and now the other must pursue, fuming and with curses, wholly unaware from the beginning that he ought never to have granted favors to a lover, to one perforce demented, but far rather to a non-lover, to a man possessed of reason. Else must he yield himself to a disloyal, shrewish, jealous, odious, creature, hurtful to him in estate, hurtful to his bodily welfare, very hurtful, above all, to the cultivation of his spirit; than which there neither is nor ever will be, truly, anything of higher value in the eyes of gods or men. These are things to keep in mind, my boy; and you must know the fondness of the lover, what it is. Its nature is not that of kindness. No, it comes to satisfy its appetite, to devour you as a sort of food:

Like as wolves adore a lamb, thus do lovers love a boy.

There you have it, Phaedrus! You are not to hear me speaking further, but now let my discourse to you be ended.

PHAEDRUS. But I imagined you were only half-way through. I thought you would go on to give as much on the non-lover; would say one ought to grant one's favors rather to him; and would discuss his points of excellence. Why stop now, Socrates, so soon?

SOCRATES. Did you not mark, O friend, that already I am chanting in heroic measure, no longer uttering mere dithyrambics? And this was blame! If I begin to praise the non-lover, what style of composition, think you, shall I use? The Nymphs to whom you wittingly exposed me, do you not see it is by them I clearly am inspired? And hence I say, with one word, that, in every point at which we have vilified the lover, the non-lover has just the opposite advantage. And what need of an extended speech? Suffice for both of them what has been said. So now my tale may fare as fare it will. And I shall wade across this stream, and go my way ere you compel me to do something harder.

PHAEDRUS. O Socrates, not yet!—Not till the heat of the day is past! Don't you see that it is almost noon, that the sun is standing in the zenith, as they call it? Do let us wait, and, while we wait, discuss the speeches; and as soon as it grows cooler we'll be off.

SOCRATES. You are superhuman, Phaedrus, in regard to speeches; simply marvelous! There is no one of your generation, I think, who has produced more speeches than have you, whether through making them yourself or somehow forcing other people to make them—apart from Simmias of Thebes. Him I except. But you are head and shoulders above all the rest. And now, it seems, for me you are become the reason why yet another speech must be delivered.

PHAEDRUS. That is scarcely a declaration of war! But how am I the reason, and for what speech?

SOCRATES. Just as I was going to wade the stream, good friend, there came to me the spirit and the customary sign—the visitant that ever checks me on the brink of an intended action; and methought I heard from it a voice forbidding me to go away before I made atonement, as if I had done wrong to the divine. Now then, I am a seer, no very deep one, but, like those who write a poor hand, good enough for all I personally need; and hence I am already well apprised wherein I erred. O how prophetic is the soul, my friend! I had misgivings even a while ago when I was uttering the speech, and, like Ibycus, I was somehow troubled with a fear of sin against the gods, lest

At the price of sinning I should purchase honor among men.

Now I know my error.

PHAEDRUS. What error can you mean?

SOCRATES. Dreadful, Phaedrus, dreadful was the speech that you brought with you, and what you made me utter was as wrong.

PHAEDRUS. How so?

SOCRATES. It was foolish; and it verged upon impiety. Could anything be more terrible than that?

PHAEDRUS. Nothing, if the speech in reality was as you say.

SOCRATES. Well, what do you believe? Is not Eros the son of Aphrodite, and a god?

PHAEDRUS. So men say.

SOCRATES. Yes, but it was not said by Lysias, nor yet in that speech of yours that you drew from my lips bewitched by you. If Love be, as indeed he is, a god or a thing divine, he can be nothing evil; but our two speeches just declared him, both of them, to be so. Therein they both transgressed concerning Love; and, besides, the fatuity of both was absolutely droll, for, while neither of them contained a thing that was sound or true, they both assumed a solemn air of being somewhat, in the hope of cheating manikins and winning their applause. Wherefore, my friend, I must purify myself; and for those who have transgressed in the telling of a myth there is an ancient mode of cleansing that was not known to Homer. But Stesichorus knew of it, since when he was bereft of eyesight for his tale abusing Helen, he did not, like Homer, fail to understand the reason; no, being a learned artist, he knew what was the matter, so he straightway writes the poem:

> No truth is in that tale:
> Nor didst thou go in well-oared ships, nor reach the citadel of Troy.

And when he had done all the poem, which is called *The Recantation,* forthwith he saw again. Now I am going to be wiser than the poets in just this: before I suffer aught for my abuse of Eros, I shall strive to make atonement to him by my Recantation, bare-headed, and not speak covered as before for shame.

PHAEDRUS. O Socrates, nothing you could say would give me more delight than that!

SOCRATES. You see, good Phaedrus, you are aware what a lack of delicacy was shown in both the speeches, this last as well as the one that you recited from the book. Suppose some man of gentle, noble nature had happened to be listening to us, one who loved another of his sort, or one who ever had been thus in love; suppose he heard us saying that lovers out of trifling causes engage in mighty hates, are jealous of their loves, and do them harm; how, think you, could he help imagining that he was listening to people who had been brought up somewhere among sailors, and who never had seen a generous love. Would he not utterly deny the justice in our censure of Eros?

PHAEDRUS. Why Socrates, I swear, perhaps he would.

SOCRATES. Now therefore I, because the thought of him makes me ashamed, and because I am afraid of Love himself, desire to wash the brine out of my ears with the water of a sweet discourse. And I counsel Lysias also without delay to write a speech in which he shows that, when other things are equal, the one who loves should be accepted in place of the non-lover.

PHAEDRUS. Be assured that he will do so. You shall speak the praises of the lover; and then Lysias must by all means be compelled by me to write in turn on the same theme.

SOCRATES. That I can well believe, so long as you are what you are.

PHAEDRUS. So pluck up heart, and speak.

SOCRATES. Where is the boy I was addressing? He must listen to this speech also; for if he failed to hear it he might accept a non-lover before any one could stop him.

PHAEDRUS. Here he is beside you, close at hand, always at your service.

SOCRATES. Know then, O lovely boy, that the former speech was the work of Phaedrus, son of Pythocles, from Myrrhinus, but the one I am about to give is a speech of Stesichorus, Euphemus' son, from Himera. And it must go as follows:

'No truth is in that tale' which says that, when a lover may be had, one ought to accept the non-lover, rather than the lover, because the lover is mad, the non-lover in his senses. It would be right enough, if to be mad were simply and solely an evil. But in reality the greatest blessings come to us through madness, for there is a madness that is given from on high. The Delphic priestess, and the sacred women of Dodona, with their madness have wrought many noble things for many a house and many a state in Hellas, but when in their senses have accomplished meagre things or none. And shall we tell of the Sibyl, and the rest, who, employing a prophetic inspiration, have foretold, to many, manifold things, and saved them from impending downfall? It would lengthen out our speech with instances known to all.

But here at least is worthy evidence from the men of old who invested things with names, and did not judge madness to be something base, nor shameful either; else they would not have linked this very word mania with the noblest art, the one by which the future is discerned; for they called it the 'manic' art. No, as something good, when madness comes by lot divine, so they applied the name. But the men of our time ineptly inserted the letter *t*, and called the art 'mantic.' So also when the ancients gave a name to the study of the future as conducted by sane men through observing birds, or through other signs, things that from the reasoning faculty [*dianoia*] supply intelligence [*nous*] and information [*historia*] to human thought [*oiesis*], they called the art *oio-no-istic*. This art is now called *oiōnistic* [augury from birds]; the long *ō* is a modern affectation. The ancients, therefore, testify to this: In such degree as the mantic art surpasses the art of augury, alike in name and in function, in that degree does mania, which is sent of God, excel in perfectness and worth the sanity which proceeds from men. Moreover, where the direst maladies and woes have fallen upon certain houses through ancestral guilt, there madness has intervened, and with oracular power has found a way of deliverance for those who are in need, taking refuge in supplications to the gods and worship of them; and thus, through cleansing and mystic rites, he who has part in this madness finds safety now and for the future; to him who is rightly mad, rightly possessed, the madness brings release from his present ills.

Third is the kind of madness and possession coming from the Muses. It seizes on a delicate and virgin soul, awakes it, sets it raving in songs and every form of poetry, and thus, adorning countless deeds done by the men of old, provides instruction for posterity. But he who, wanting madness from the Muses, comes to the doors of Poesy, trusting to enter in, who thinks forsooth that art is adequate to make him poet, he remains outside, a bungler, and his poetry of common sense fades into nothingness before the poetry of the madmen.

Of thus many noble works I can make mention to you, effected by the madness that cometh from on high. Therefore, neither let us fear the thing itself, nor let any speech disturb and frighten us by holding that the man of sense is to be chosen for a friend before the man inspired. No; let the speaker, if he can, show moreover that love is not sent from heaven for the weal alike of lover and beloved, and so carry off the palm! Be it our part to prove the very opposite, that madness such as this is given by the gods for our highest blessing; and our proof will be rejected by the very clever, accepted by the wise. Accordingly, first of all we must apprehend the real nature of the soul, divine as well as human, by observing how it operates and how it is affected. And thus begins our proof:

Soul, wherever found, is immortal; for the ever-moving is immortal. But that which lends its motion to another thing, or receives its motion from another, when the motion ceases ends its life. Only the self-moving, since it never leaves itself, never ceases from its motion, and this is also the source and origin of movement for all other things that are in motion. But the beginning is unbegotten; for everything that is begotten must arise from a beginning, while this beginning cannot proceed from something. If it arose from something else, then it could not be a beginning. And as it is unbegotten, it must also be indestructible; for if the beginning were destroyed, it never could arise from anything, nor aught else from it; and we must grant that all things have to come from a beginning. Thus the origin of motion is the Self-moved, and this can neither be destroyed nor begotten, else all the heavens and the whole creation must collapse, stand still, and never again have any source of birth or movement. But we have seen the Self-moved to be immortal; then if one argues that the essence of the soul, the very concept, lies in this, one will not be put to shame; for each and every body that derives its motion from without is soulless, but that which has its motion in and from itself, that has soul, since this is the very nature of the soul. If this be true, if that which is self-moved be nothing else than Soul, then of necessity the Soul would have to be both unbegotten and immortal.

Upon her immortality we have said enough. Upon her essential form we must speak as follows. What it really is would be matter for a large discourse in every way far beyond the power of man. What it is like can be discussed in human wise more briefly, so let us discuss it in this fashion. Let the soul be likened to the conjoint nature of a team of winged horses and a charioteer. Now with the gods the horses and the charioteers are noble, all of them, both in themselves and by descent, whereas with other races there is a mixture. With us, note first, the driver has to guide a pair of horses, and, secondly, one of them is beautiful and good, the other the reverse in character and stock. And hence for us the driving must needs be difficult and vexing. Now comes the question why a living creature is called mortal or immortal, and this we must try to explain. Soul in its totality has the care of all that is inanimate, and traverses the whole heaven, appearing now in one shape, now in another; when it is perfect, and fully winged, it soars on high, and regulates the entire world. But the soul that has lost its wings is borne along until it fastens upon something solid, and there finds a dwelling-place, taking on an earthly body which seems to be self-moving—but the cause of motion is the power of the soul. The conjoint whole, soul and the body thereto knit, is called a living creature, and has the added name of 'mortal.' Immortal it could not be called by any process of reason; and yet, though we never have seen a god, nor adequately conceived of one, we imagine an immortal creature, having a soul, and having a body, which are conjoint in one for ever. Let that, however, be, and our words concerning it be, as is acceptable to God. And let us now consider why the wings are lost, the reason why the spirit sheds them. It is like this:

The natural office of a wing is to carry weight aloft, soaring upward to the region where dwells the race of the gods. Of all the bodily elements it is most akin to the divine. Now the divine is beauty, wisdom, goodness, and the like; and above all by these it is that the wings of the soul are nourished and grow strong; and the opposites such as ugliness and evil cause them to dwindle and vanish away. In heaven the mighty leader Zeus goes forth, driving a wingèd car, disposing all things orderly, overseeing all. Him there follows a soldiery of gods and spirits, arrayed in eleven bands;

for Hestia only abides at home in the dwelling of the gods; but all the rest who rank among the number of the Twelve go forth, and lead each one as captain according to his place in the appointed order. Many are the blessed sights, many the glorious processions, as the blest race of gods come and go within the heaven, each doing his allotted work, while whosoever will, and can, follows in their train, for in the celestial choir Envy finds no place. But as often as they go to feast at the banquet, then they mount up the steep to the utmost summit of the vault of heaven; and there the chariots of the gods in even poise, obedient to the driver's hand, advance with ease. The others lag; for the horse of evil mixture sags downward; unless he has been chastened by his driver, he drags him down and sinks him to the earth. It is the hour of agony and sternest conflict for the soul. But the souls that are called immortal, these when they attain the summit pass outside, to stand upon the roof of heaven; here stationed, they are carried round in the celestial revolution, and behold what lies beyond.

But that realm above the heaven no poet here below ever has worthily sung, nor poet ever will sing. After this wise is that realm—for one must dare to speak the truth when truth is all one's theme. There abides that Substance which has veritable being; Essence colorless, without a shape, intangible; apparent only to the pilot of the soul, the Mind. This is it, in that place, with which all true knowledge is concerned. And hence divine intelligence, fed with reason and pure knowledge, and intelligence in every soul that cares to take the food befitting it, in course of time beholding the Reality, loves it, and in contemplation of the truth is nourished and made glad, until the revolution is complete, and the soul brought back to its original station. In the journey round, the soul contemplates Justice absolute, contemplates Temperance, contemplates Knowledge; not such knowledge as may have beginning, nor such as changes with a changing object among the objects we call 'present'; but that knowledge which abides in existence absolute. And so it views the other real verities, and feeds on them; and having feasted, it sinks down again into the inward part of heaven, and goes homeward. And when the soul comes home, the charioteer makes the horses stand at the manger, casts ambrosia before them, and then gives them to drink of nectar.

Such is the life of the gods. The other souls fare thus. The soul which best follows God, and is most like to Him, rears up the head of the charioteer into the outer realm, and is borne round in the revolution, but is troubled by the horses, and hardly beholds those things which are. Another soul now rises up, now plunges down, now sees realities, now fails to see, for the violence of the horses. The rest come following, yearning all for that which is above, but cannot reach it. They are borne about below; they trample on each other, they collide, each straining to outstrip his neighbor. Now is there tumult, struggle, utmost sweat, when through the bungling of the charioteers many a soul is crippled, full many the wings that are crushed. And, wearied with the toil, they all depart untutored in the vision of reality, and go away to feed upon the fodder of opinion. But why that vehemence to see the realm where lies the plain of truth? Because in the meadow there the pasturage is found which suits the highest part of the soul; and on this food is nourished the power of wing by which the soul is borne aloft.

Besides, the law of Adrasteia [Destiny, Heavenly Justice] is this. The soul which in the retinue of a god has had any vision of the verities is safe from harm until the following revolution, and if always it can do this always remains unharmed. But when a soul has lacked the power to follow, and has not seen; when through some chance misused it is filled with forgetfulness and evil, and made heavy; when, weighted down, it sheds its wings and falls to earth, then the law is this. In its first birth the soul shall not be implanted in the physique of any beast, but only in a man. The soul that had the amplest vision shall enter into the birth of one who is to be a lover of wisdom or a lover of beauty, or a servant of the Muses and of Eros. And the next shall enter into the birth of an upright king, or a martial one, a ruler. And the third in order into that of a statesman, or some overseer or merchant. The fourth into that of an ardent athlete, or a hygienic trainer. The fifth is to have the life of a diviner or attendant in the mysteries. To the sixth belongs the life of a poet or some other of those who are concerned with imitation; to the seventh that of an artisan or farmer; to the eighth that of a sophist or a demagogue; to the ninth the life of a tyrant.

Among all these, whoever leads a righteous life obtains a better lot; whoever leads a wicked life, a worse.

Before the individual soul returns to the place from which it comes there must elapse ten thousand years. In briefer time it is not fledged with wings—save only for the soul of him who without guile has followed after wisdom, or who in the love of wisdom has been enamoured of a youth. These, when for three successive revolutions of a thousand years they have thrice in order chosen such a life, in the three-thousandth year get wings, and go their way. The rest, when they have ended their first life, are brought to judgment; and, after judgment, go, some of them, to the subterranean places of correction where they suffer the just penalty, while the others are by justice rendered light, and carried up to a heavenly place where they lead the existence they merit for the life they led in human shape. But in the thousandth year the time arrives for both to come and draw lots, and to choose their second life; and they choose, each soul, the life which each one wills. And now it is that a human soul may pass into the existence of a beast, and also from a beast he who once was human may pass back again into a man; for the soul that never had a vision of the truth, never can it pass into our human shape. Why not? Because Man necessarily has intelligence according to 'ideal form' as it is called, which proceeds from many sense-perceptions into one concept of reflection. But this act of thought is recollection, a remembrance of those things which once our soul beheld when it went in the procession with its God, when on high it viewed the things we now say *are,* when it lifted up its head towards true existence. Wherefore rightly is the mind of the lover of wisdom only winged; for with all the power he has he gives himself in memory to those things by communing with which God is divine. And a man who makes right use of memories like these is ever being initiated into perfect mysteries, and he alone becomes truly perfect. But since he turns away from the concerns of men, and cleaves to the divine, the world rebukes him for a madman; the many see not that he is a man inspired.

Here, then, is the point we have reached with our whole discourse on the fourth kind of madness. This kind it is that causes a man to be held for mad, who, when he sees the beauty here below, in remembrance of the veritable beauty is fledged with wings, and, quivering, would fain mount upwards; but he cannot, and only gazes up, like a bird indifferent to everything below. And so, of all the kinds, this kind of inspiration is the best, and comes from the best sources; is best for him who has it, and for him who has to do with it. And we see that a partaker of this madness, one who is enamoured of youthful beauty, is called 'lover.' It is as we have said. By very nature, every human soul has viewed the things which are, else would it not have entered this sort of living creature. But from things here and now to recollect those real things is not for every soul an easy matter; not easy for those that then and there had only a brief vision, nor for those that, fallen hither, suffered evil hap, through dubious associations were turned to wickedness, and thus forget the holy things which then they saw. Small is the remnant of the souls in whom is present the needful share of memory; but these when they behold some semblance of the things that are yonder are amazed, and lose possession of themselves, but what it is so moves them, that they do not know, because they cannot clearly make it out.

Now as for justice, temperance, and whatever else is precious unto souls, no gleam of them appears in their semblances here below; with groping faculties hardly do some few of us by recourse to images have glimpses of the generic form which is imaged. But then was there beauty to see, brightly shining, when with the blessed choir—we in the train of Zeus, others following other of the gods—the souls beheld the beatific spectacle and vision; and were perfected in that mystery of mysteries which meet it is to call most blessed. This did we celebrate in our true and perfect selves, when we were yet untouched by all the evils awaiting us in time to come; when as initiates we were allowed to see perfect and simple, still and happy Phantoms, pure as we were pure; when we had no mark upon us of this tomb we call the body, our prison which we bear about, shackled to it like a shell-fish to its shell.

Therewith farewell to Memory; our homage to it now has been lengthened for our yearning after the visions we had then. Our concern is Beauty. We were telling how the essential beauty shines among the realities yonder; and after our arrival here we apprehended it, most clearly gleaming, by that sense which is most clear in us, the eyesight; for sight comes to us as the most piercing of our bodily sensations. But the eye does not see Wisdom. O what amazing love would Wisdom cause in us if she sent forth an image of herself that entered the sight, as the image of Beauty does! And the other Verities, what love they would awaken! But now has Beauty alone obtained this lot, to be most clearly seen, most dearly loved.

Now he who has not lately shared the mysteries, or has been corrupted, is not quickly carried hence to yonder region, to authentic beauty, when he sees what has the name of beauty here below; and hence when he looks at this he does not revere it. Instead, giving himself over to sensual enjoyment, he goes leaping on beauty like a quadruped, and copulating, consorts with wantonness, and fears not nor is ashamed, in spite of nature, to make pleasure his pursuit. But he who has lately partaken—who saw much that was then to be seen—when he beholds a face of aspect divine well copying the Beautiful, or an ideal bodily form, first he shudders, and something of the terror he then had comes over him; anon, as he gazes at the object, he reveres it as if it were a god, and if he were not afraid that men would think him downright mad, he would bow down to his love with offerings as if it were a graven image and a god indeed. While he looks, the shuddering passes, and he is taken with sweating and unwonted heat; for he has received the effluence of beauty through his eyes, and is made hot, and with that effluence his wing is bathed to life. And with the warmth are melted the parts where sprout the wings, which parts, long since grown hard, were tightly sealed, and kept the plumes from budding forth. And as the nourishment streams in, the quills of the feathers swell, and begin to grow from the root, underneath, all over the form of the soul—for of yore the entire soul was feathered. While this goes on, the soul throughout is seething and throbbing, and has precisely the sensation we experience in teething; when the teeth are just emerging, there is a tickling irritation and discomfort round them. Even so with the soul when the feathers begin to sprout; it seethes, is in discomfort, tingles.

Well, then, let the soul be gazing at the beauty of the youth; from then there *hies* a *rush* of *particles* [*mĕrē*], which in consequence is called *desire* [*himeros*]. The soul, when it receives this, is thereby bathed in vital fluid, and is warmed; has relief from the distress, and is in joy. But when it is all alone, and is grown dry, then the mouths of the ducts whence the plumage shoots forth dry up and are sealed, so that the growth of the plumage is blocked. But the germs of the plumage, shut in with desire, throb like beating pulses, each individual sprout prickling in its duct, so that the entire soul, encircled with the stinging, bounds in frenzied pain. Yet again, in the memory it has of the beautiful one it rejoices. And from the dual mixture the soul is sore bewildered with its incredible experience; in its perplexity it rages, and for raving cannot sleep by night nor abide anywhere by day, but runs wistfully wherever it imagines it can see the possessor of the beauty. Once it sees him, once it has drawn upon it the waters of desire, the orifices that before were sealed are opened, the soul recovers breath, and it has respite from its pangs and agonies; and this delight, which it has instead, is the sweetest of all pleasures in this present time. Wherefore the soul is unwilling to be parted from the beautiful one; esteems him above every other; yes for his sake forgets mothers, brothers, comrades—all; neglects its property, makes nought of losses through neglect; the rules and decencies of life in which it heretofore took pride, all these it now despises. It is ready to live as a slave, to sleep wherever they let it, as near as possible to the object of its yearning; for not merely does it worship the possessor of the beauty, but in him it has found the one and only healer of its greatest woes.

This is the state, my lovely boy—you to whom my speech is addressed —this is the state which men call Love. What the gods call it, if you heard that, the audacity doubtless would make you laugh. There are two verses which, I think, some disciples of Homer recite out of their own private stock; two verses in honor of Eros, the second quite exuberant, and not very strict in the metre. They are chanted as follows:

> 'Eros volant' is he called by mortals;
> By immortals 'pteros' ['Winged'], for his force in causing wings.

Believe all that or not; but just the same, for cause and for effect, there you have what happens in the case of lovers.

Well then. When one from among the retinue of Zeus is seized with love, he can with greater power bear up the burden of the 'Winged' one; but they who are attendant upon Ares, who made the revolution in his train, when one of these is caught by Eros, and thinks he has in any wise

been wronged by his loved one, he grows murderous, and is ready to
immolate himself as well as the beloved youth. And so with each of the
choir that follows a particular god; each one with all his power lives
his life in honor, and in imitation, of that God; each one, that is, so long
as he is uncorrupted, and is living the first earthly life he is born into;
and in such fashion he consorts with the objects of his love, and conducts
himself towards others. As for the love one picks among beautiful boys,
each lover chooses in accordance with his bias; to each the object chosen
is like deity; and so each fashions and adorns for himself as it were an
image, to the end that he may honor and secretly adore it. Thus they
who are of Zeus, in seeking their loved one, look for a soul that shall
resemble Zeus. Accordingly, they mark his nature to see if he be fond of
wisdom and like a leader; and when they find the one they seek, and
come to love him, they do everything to have him really such. If they
have not had already the necessary training, they now set out to get it,
learning from whatever source they can, and pursuing their own researches,
too; they trace the nature of their own particular deity within, and are
successful in their quest because they were forced to fix their gaze steadily
upon their god. And as with the memory they reach after him and grasp
him, filled with inspiration they take traits of character from him, and
ways of action, so far as men ever can participate in deity. All this, now,
they attribute to the loved one as the cause, and so they love him more
than ever. And if the source from which they draw be Zeus, then, like
the Bacchantes, they drench the soul of the loved one, doing all they can
to make him likest their divinity. Those, again, who followed in the
train of Hera seek one with a royal nature, and, when they find him,
they do just the same with him. So they who are of Apollo, and similarly
for each particular god; they walk in the way of their god; they seek a
love with the corresponding nature. And when they have obtained one,
they imitate their deity, persuade their loves to do the same, and give
them discipline; each lover so far as he has power will draw his love
into the way of life and visible likeness of that deity. They are not en-
vious of their loves, and indulge in no trivial animosities with them;
instead, they do their utmost in every way and with all their force in the
effort to bring the loved one into absolute likeness with themselves and
with the god they honor. Thus fair and blissful to the beloved is the
desire of those who truly love; and the initiation into the mysteries of
love of those who are inspired by it, if they attain to their desire in the
way I have described, is a boon bestowed upon the beloved by the lover
who has won him.

When the one is caught, the manner of the winning is as follows. You
recall how at the opening of this tale we divided every soul in three,

two parts horselike in formation, and the third in function like a charioteer. So now let us hold to this distinction. Now of the horses one, we
say, is good, the other not. But wherein consists the merit of the good
horse, the vice of the bad one, that we did not fully enter into, so we
must discuss it now. Well then, take the first of the pair, the one in
splendid trim. His form is erect; he is finely put together; with stately
neck; nose aquiline; his color white; dark-eyed. He is a friend of honor
with temperance and modesty conjoint; a comrade of true glory; needs
not the whip; is guided by command alone, and reason. But the other!
He is built awry; is gross; limbs put together anyhow; his neck is short
and thick; face squat; his color black; with glaring, bloodshot eyes;
comrade of lust and boasting; with shaggy ears—uncomprehending;
hardly submissive under lash and goads. Accordingly, when the charioteer
has sight of the beloved object, when all his soul is warmed throughout
with the sensation, and full of tingling and the prickings of desire; then
the horse obedient to the charioteer, now as always holding back for
shame, refrains himself from rushing at the loved one. But the other
heeds no longer the goadings of the charioteer, nor the lashing; he plunges
violently and charges, giving infinite annoyance to his fellow and the
charioteer, and compels them to approach the loved one and remind him
of carnal satisfaction. At first the twain resist, indignant at their being
forced toward acts which must be horrid and illicit; but in the end, when
there is no cessation of the evil, they go whither they are drawn, yielding
and consenting to do what is demanded.

And now they are gone near, and they behold the image of the loved
one radiantly flashing. But when the charioteer has gazed at the vision,
his memory is carried to the eternal form of beauty, and again he sees
that form, conjoint with wisdom, borne erect upon its hallowed pedestal.
And at the sight he is afraid, and in awe falls backward, and therewith
jerks, perforce, so violently back upon the reins as to bring both horses
squatting on their haunches, one readily because he was not tugging,
the turbulent one bitterly against his will. Now see both horses retired
and at a distance. The one through shame and consternation has bedewed
the entire soul with sweat; but the other, released from the pain he had
from the bit and his tumble, hardly has got his breath before he begins
reviling, heaping curses on the charioteer, and on his mate, for their
cowardice and lack of manhood in breaking ranks and breaking the
agreement. And once more he would compel them, all unwilling, to go
near, and hardly would he yield to their beseeching that the matter be
deferred to another time. And now this time agreed upon has come,
and the two pretending not to recollect, he reminding them, he struggling,
neighing, tugging, again compels them to go near the beloved boy to

make the same proposals. And when they are come near, he lowers his head, sticks out his tail, takes the bit in his teeth, and pulls shamelessly. But now the charioteer has felt the same emotion as before, more deeply; has recoiled as from the barrier athwart a race-course; with a more violent wrench jerked back the bit from the teeth of the unruly horse; covered his scurrilous tongue and his jaws with blood; forced him, legs and hams, to the ground; and delivered him up to anguish.

But when the evil horse repeatedly has suffered the same torment, he ceases from his turbulence, is humbled, and henceforth follows the guidance of the charioteer; and, when he sees the beautiful one, is perishing with terror. And so it comes about that the soul of the lover from that time on follows the beloved in modesty and awe.

Now take the beloved, who has been met with every service on the level of a god, from a lover that is not feigning but is truly having this experience. And the beloved, on his side, is by nature friendly to the one who serves him. Well, suppose by chance, and even therefore, he has by schoolmates, or by others, been prejudiced through their calling it disgraceful to be intimate with a lover, and suppose he therefore gives his lover a repulse. Still, as time goes on, his ripeness and the force of circumstance will have led him to enter into comradeship; for surely it never yet has been ordained that bad shall be friend to bad, or good not friend to good. And when the lover is admitted, when his converse and companionship have been accepted, the good will of the lover, coming very close, is amazing to the loved one, who perceives that all the others —friends and kinsfolk—put together offer not a moiety of friendship in comparison with the friend inspired of God. And as this intimacy continues, as the loved one comes in close, with bodily contacts in gymnasia and the other places where they meet, then and there the fountain of that stream which Zeus, in love with Ganymede, called 'himeros' [desire], thus naming it, begins to flow abundantly towards the lover. One part of it is taken into him; the other, when he is filled to overflowing, runs without; and just as wind, or any echo, bounds back again from a surface smooth and hard, returning to the source from which it issued, just so the stream of beauty goes back into the beautiful one through the eyes. When by this natural conduit it goes to the soul, and, arriving, fills it full, it wets the ducts of the plumage, and now the wings have been quickened. The soul of the loved one in turn has been filled with love!

So now he loves—but knows not what. He does not know, cannot explain, what has come over him; nay, is like a man who has caught an ailment of the eyes from some one else, and cannot tell you how he got it. As in a glass he sees his image in the lover, and does not know it is himself. And in the lover's presence, like him he ceases from the pangs of love; and in his absence, is filled with longing as he again is longed for, and holds love's image, Love for Love [*Anteros*], which yet he calls, and takes to be, not love, but friendship. With parallel desire, yet not so vehement, he yearns to see, touch, kiss, lie down beside, the lover. And these things, it is likely, he will thereafter quickly do. Accordingly, as they are couched together, the wanton horse of the lover will have a thing to say to the charioteer, and will demand, as just reward for all his pains, some small enjoyments. But the horse of the sweetheart has not a thing to say. He is bursting with desire, and utterly confused; embraces the lover, and kisses him, caressing him as benevolent out of measure. So when they lie thus, side by side, for his part he would not, it seems, deny the lover any boon he might happen to ask for; only, the fellow horse, together with the charioteer, resists all that with modesty and reason.

Suppose, now, that the better elements of the mind prevail, leading the lover and beloved into well-ordered ways, into philosophy; then blissful is the life they live on earth, and full of harmony, masters of themselves, decorous; when they hold in bondage that from which the evils of the soul arise, and have set free its source of power. And when this life is ended, they soar up on wings, unburdened; they have conquered in one strife of the three successive, true Olympic, contests; and there is no greater good that either human wisdom or madness from above can bring to man. But, again, suppose their way of life to be less fine; suppose their aim in life is not philosophy, but honor. Then doubtless, some time, in their cups, or at some other careless moment, their two unruly horses will catch the souls off guard, will join in bringing them together to the same intent, will make the choice which the many deem most blissful, and will accomplish it. And having done it, thereafter they maintain this choice, yet indulge it sparingly, the act being one which lacks approval from the mind as a whole. The two, accordingly, are friends indeed, these also, if in less measure than the first; friends both in the time of love and when later they are out of it; and believe that they have given and received pledges the most sacred, never to be broken, never without wrong to let them come to hatred. At the end they issue from the body, wingless indeed, yet they have had an impulse to get wings, and hence they have no trifling recompense from the madness of Love; they are not ordained to enter darkness and make the subterranean journey, for already they have begun the journey beneath the arch of heaven. No, they spend a life of light, journey blissfully together, and, for their love, together acquire the wings when their time for wings is come. Such are the golden gifts, my boy, and thus divine, which the affection of a lover will bestow upon you. But the intimacy starting from the non-lover is alloyed with mortal judgment, is mortal also in its calculating thrift, and engenders in the soul of the beloved an illiberal way which is lauded for a virtue by the mob. And later? It will send the soul gyrating for nine thousand years around the earth, and under earth, a thing without a mind.

There, Eros dear, you have our recantation, the loveliest and best within our power, at once for offering and atonement. In 'everyway, and especially in the use of language, the speech' was forced to be somewhat poetical, because Phaedrus would so have it. Forgive the previous speech, accept the present one; be gracious, merciful; do not take away the art of love you gave me, do not in anger cripple it. Rather grant that more than now I may win esteem with the beautiful. If when we spoke before, Phaedrus and I, we said aught that was harsh toward thee, blame Lysias, the father of the speech, make him cease from speeches of the sort, turn him towards philosophy, as his brother Polemarchus has been turned; so that his lover, present here, may no longer halt, as now he does, between two stools, but wholly dedicate his life to Eros along with philosophical discourse.

PHAEDRUS.   I join in the prayer with you, Socrates, and say: If this is best for us, may it all come to pass. But I have been wondering all along at this speech of yours—you worked it out so much more finely than the one before. Indeed, I have my fears that Lysias will make but a sorry showing, if ever he consents to submit another speech in competition with it. And, do you know, amazing man? Lately a man in public life was railing at him for this very thing, and throughout the tirade kept calling him *logographer* ['speech-writer']. So perhaps from a feeling of pride he may refrain from writing for us.

SOCRATES.   What an absurd idea, my young man. You are much mistaken in your friend if you think he can be frightened by a little hubbub. And perhaps you fancy that his assailant meant what he said in his taunt?

PHAEDRUS.   He seemed to, Socrates. And you yourself are aware that the greatest and most influential statesmen are ashamed of writing speeches, and leaving things in written form behind them, for fear posterity will call them Sophists.

SOCRATES.   'Sour grapes,' Phaedrus; you forget them. And, apart from that, you fail to see that, among the politicians, those who have the best conceit of themselves are fondest of writing speeches, and of leaving compositions to posterity. And note this, too. When one of them writes a speech, he dotes so on the men who praise it that he heads it with their names; adds to it the names of those who praise him in each particular case!

PHAEDRUS.   What do you mean? I do not see.

SOCRATES.   You don't see how, at the outset of a writing by an honorable politician, the one who praises it is mentioned first?

PHAEDRUS. How so?

SOCRATES. Approximately thus. 'It was voted by the Senate,' or 'by the people,' or by both, 'on the motion of So-and-so'; here the writer, with great dignity, comes to mention his own name, and hence the praises; and thereafter he goes on, displaying his own wisdom to the praisers, now and then producing a very lengthy document. Well, does that kind of thing appear to you to be aught else than a written composition?

PHAEDRUS. To me, naught else.

SOCRATES. Well, then, if this composition holds the stage, its author leaves the theatre in great delight; but if it is suppressed—if he does not win the privilege to write a speech, is not accounted worthy to compose a document—he is grieved, and all his partisans grieve with him.

PHAEDRUS. So they do.

SOCRATES. And obviously not because of their disdain for the profession, but because they admire it.

PHAEDRUS. Surely.

SOCRATES. What, then! When an orator, or, say, a king, becomes so able as to vie with Lycurgus, or Solon, or Darius, to attain to immortality as a *logographer* in the State, does he not while living think himself an equal of the gods, and have not posterity the same opinion of him when they behold his writings?

PHAEDRUS. Surely, surely.

SOCRATES. What think you, then? Will any one like that, no matter what his animosity to Lysias, actually condemn him for his writing?

PHAEDRUS. It is not a likely inference from what you say. He would seem, in fact, to be condemning his own personal desire.

SOCRATES. The matter, then, is clear to each and all. There is nothing in itself disgraceful about writing speeches.

PHAEDRUS. Why should there be?

SOCRATES. The disgrace, methinks, begins when some one speaks and writes, not well, but basely, badly.

PHAEDRUS. That is clear.

SOCRATES. What, then, is the method of writing well or not? Phaedrus, on these points do we need to examine Lysias or any one else who has written, or ever will write, a composition on affairs of State or on a private matter, in metre as a poet or without it as an ordinary man?

PHAEDRUS. You ask if we have *need* of that? What would be the use—may I say, of life?—if not for pleasures such as these? Surely we do not live for the pleasures that call for suffering in advance before we can enjoy them; a quality almost all those pleasures have that appertain to the body, and that is why they rightly are called 'servile.'

SOCRATES. At all events, we seem to be at leisure. And meanwhile it appears to me as if the cicadae, chanting and conversing over our heads as is their wont in the heat of the day, were actually watching us below. Now if they saw us, just the two of us, doing as most people would at noon, not discussing, but nodding and lulled to sleep by their song through mental indolence, rightly would they laugh at us, and fancy that some pair of slaves had turned in by them for a resting-place, like sheep to sleep away the noontide by the fountain. But if they see us in discussion, and coasting past them unbewitched by their Siren voices, perhaps in their delight they will bestow on us the guerdon they have from the gods as a gift for men.

PHAEDRUS.   What is it that they have? The gift you mention I seem never to have heard of.

SOCRATES.   And you a lover of the Muses! It ill befits one never to have heard the like. This is the story. The Cicadae were human beings once, in an age before the birth of the Muses. And when the Muses came, and song appeared, some of the human beings then were so ravished with delight that they sang and sang, forgetting food and drink, until, all unknowingly, they passed away. From them thereafter sprang the tribe of Cicadae; and the gift which they have from the Muses is this. From their birth they have no need of nourishment, but chant on everlastingly, without eating, without drinking, until they die; whereupon they come to the Muses to report which of the dwellers here below honors each several Muse. To Terpsichore they make report about the men who have honored her in choral dances, and render them more endeared to her; to Erato they tell of those who honor her by dealing with love; and similarly to all the rest, to each according to the kind of tribute paid her. To Calliope the eldest, and to Urania who is next to her, they report concerning those who live the philosophic life, and who honor the music of these two; for among the Muses these above all are concerned with heaven and problems both divine and human, whereon their voices it is that sing most sweetly. For many reasons, then, at midday one ought to be conversing, and not asleep.

PHAEDRUS.   Yes, indeed. To be conversing!

SOCRATES.   Well then, take the subject we were just now proposing to examine, how a discourse should be formed in order to be written well, or the reverse. This matter ought to be looked into.

PHAEDRUS.   Surely.

SOCRATES.   Come, now. What is needed in advance if an utterance is to be good and fine? Must not the mind of the one who utters it be cognizant of the truth about the matters he is going to discuss?

PHAEDRUS.   And yet, friend Socrates, on that point I have heard differently. I have heard that one who plans to be an orator lies under no necessity of learning what is actually right, but must learn what seems right to the crowd who are to pass judgment, nor yet what is really good and beautiful, but what is going to seem so. From these appearances, they say, comes persuasion, and not from the truth.

SOCRATES. What 'they say,' Phaedrus, 'must not be cast aside,' if they who say it are indeed wise, but must be examined on the chance that there may be something in it; so we must not hastily dismiss this statement now.

PHAEDRUS. Quite right.

SOCRATES. Let us examine it in this way. . . .

PHAEDRUS. How?

SOCRATES. Well, suppose I were trying to persuade you to secure a horse and go against the enemy, and neither of us knew what a horse was like, but I happened to know so much about you, namely, that Phaedrus thinks a horse to be that one of the domestic animals which has the longest ears. . . .

PHAEDRUS. That, Socrates, would be ridiculous!

SOCRATES. Wait! Suppose I were in sober earnest trying to persuade you with a speech I had composed in honor of an ass, which I called a horse, where I said he was invaluable as a beast to own at home and on campaign—you could use him as a mount in battle, he would serve to carry baggage, he would be helpful in a great variety of ways. . . .

PHAEDRUS. The whole thing would be utterly absurd.

SOCRATES. Yes, but isn't absurdity in a friend better than crafty speaking in a foe?

PHAEDRUS. It would seem so.

SOCRATES. Well then, take the artful rhetorician who does not know what good and evil are, and essays to persuade an equally ignorant State, not by an encomium on 'the shadow of an ass,' instead of 'horse,' but by recommending evil as if it were good. When, having studied the opinions of the crowd, he persuades them to do evil deeds instead of good, what sort of harvest, think you, will the art of rhetoric thereafter reap from the seed it has sown?

PHAEDRUS. No welcome harvest, surely.

SOCRATES. Come now, good friend. Haven't we been too harsh in condemnation of the Art of making speeches? She might well say: 'Strange creatures, why do you talk such nonsense? I never force a man to take up speaking when he is ignorant of the truth, but, if you grant that my advice has any value, he will acquire the knowledge first, then come to me. The one great point I make is this, that, without me, the man who knows the actual truth of things is not thereby a whit the nearer to a mastery of persuasion.'

PHAEDRUS. And will she not be right in saying that?

SOCRATES. I grant you, yes—if the arguments that come to her trial bear witness that she is an art; for I seem as it were to hear some arguments approaching and protesting that she lies, and that Rhetoric is no art, but a trade devoid of art. 'A solid art of speaking,' says the Spartan, 'without a grip on truth, there is not nor will be hereafter, ever.'

PHAEDRUS. These arguments, Socrates, we need them! Bring on the witnesses, and examine them for the matter and the manner of their telling!

SOCRATES. Come hither, noble creatures, and persuade our Phaedrus, sire of lovely offspring, that unless he has paid due attention to philosophy, he never will be competent to speak on any subject. And let Phaedrus answer.

PHAEDRUS. Ask on!

SOCRATES. Now then. Taken as a whole, is not Rhetoric the art of winning the soul by discourse, which means not merely argument in the courts of justice, and all other sorts of public councils, but in private conference as well? Is it not one thing, and the same, whether it has to do with matters great or small; always intrinsically honorable—I mean, of course, *right* Rhetoric—whether the points at issue are serious or not? Is that approximately what you have heard?

PHAEDRUS. By Zeus, no! Not just that! Rather I have heard the art of speaking and writing connected with cases at law, although speaking has its place in public assemblies also. Beyond that my information has not gone.

SOCRATES. So then, you are acquainted only with the *Arts of Speaking* by Nestor and Odysseus, which they composed in their leisure hours at Troy, and have not heard of that by Palamedes?

PHAEDRUS. Not I; nor, I vow, of Nestor's either—unless by 'Nestor' you allude to Gorgias, and by 'Odysseus' to Thrasymachus or Theodorus.

SOCRATES. Perhaps I do. No matter; let them go. Tell me this instead. In a court of justice, what are the adversaries at? They are in a speaking duel? Or how shall we put it?

PHAEDRUS. Put it just so.

SOCRATES. A duel about right and wrong?

PHAEDRUS. Yes.

SOCRATES. And the man who thus contends, employing art, will make the same thing appear to the same jury at one time right, and, when he wishes, wrong?

PHAEDRUS. Why not?

SOCRATES. And, speaking now in the assembly, he will on this occasion make the same things appear to the City good, on that occasion just the opposite?

PHAEDRUS. Precisely.

SOCRATES. Now take Palamedes [i.e. Zeno] of Elea. Don't we know about his art of speaking, by which he made the same things seem to the same persons alike and different, single and manifold, and, again, at rest and also in motion?

PHAEDRUS.   I quite believe it.

SOCRATES.   Well then, the art of disputation is not confined to courts of justice and political assemblies, but apparently, if it *is* an art, must be one and the same art for every kind of speaking; and must be the art that enables a man to find resemblances between one thing and another in every case where resemblance can be found, and for those for whom it can be done, and, when another man deceptively makes the same assimilations, to bring the matter into the light.

PHAEDRUS.   Just what do you mean by that?

SOCRATES.   I think my notion will be clear if we inquire as follows. Does deception more readily occur in things that greatly differ, or when the difference is slight?

PHAEDRUS.   In things where the difference is slight.

SOCRATES.   Yes indeed. In passing over from one thing to the opposite, you will more readily escape detection if you move by small graduations than by leaps.

PHAEDRUS.   Certainly.

SOCRATES.   Then he who is going to deceive another, and not himself to be deceived, must have an accurate and thorough knowledge of the basic similarities and differences of things.

PHAEDRUS.   So he must.

SOCRATES.   Now if a man is ignorant of the truth about a given thing, how can he discern in other things the similarity, great or small, which they have to the thing unknown?

PHAEDRUS.   He can't.

SOCRATES.   Clearly, therefore, when people form opinions at variance with reality, and are duped, the deception filters in through resemblances.

PHAEDRUS.   That surely is the way it comes about.

SOCRATES.   Then he who has not gained a knowledge of the real nature of individual things will not possess the art of leading men by gradual transition, through resemblances, from the reality in each several case to its opposite, nor of avoiding this deception?

PHAEDRUS.   No, he never will.

SOCRATES.   Then, comrade mine! this art of speaking which he displays who does not know the truth, and has only hunted opinions—it seems to be a ridiculous art, and in fact no art at all.

PHAEDRUS.   I fear so.

SOCRATES.   How would you like, now, to take the speech of Lysias which you have by you, and the speeches I delivered, and to look in them for instances of what we term 'inartistic' and 'artistic'?

PHAEDRUS. I should like that above all, for our talk at present is too abstract because we lack examples.

SOCRATES. And by some good fortune, it would seem, two speeches have been given which illustrate how a man who knows the truth may play with words and lead his audience about. And, Phaedrus, of this I judge the local deities to be the cause. Perhaps, indeed, the prophets of the Muses, our singers overhead, have granted this boon to us through their inspiration; for I, at all events, am not possessed of any art of speaking.

PHAEDRUS. So be it; only make your point.

SOCRATES. Come now; read me the opening of Lysias' discourse.

PHAEDRUS. 'How matters stand with me, you know; and that I think it would advantage both of us if this and that took place, you have heard. I deem it meet I should not fail of my desire on the pretext that I am not your lover; for lovers later rue . . .'

SOCRATES. Stop there. The point is, wherein the speaker errs, and composes without art? Am I right?

PHAEDRUS. Yes.

SOCRATES. Well now, is not so much clear to all, that, in a question of this sort, on some matters we are in accord, but at variance on others?

PHAEDRUS. I think I understand what you are saying, yet make it clearer.

SOCRATES. When any one uses the word 'iron' or 'silver,' we all of us think of the same thing?

PHAEDRUS. Why certainly.

SOCRATES. But what occurs when the word is 'right' or 'good'? Every one's mind is borne in a different direction, and we dispute about what is meant, not only with each other, but even with ourselves?

PHAEDRUS. Absolutely.

SOCRATES. So there: on some points we agree, on others we do not.

PHAEDRUS. So it is.

SOCRATES. Now then, in which of the two are we more easily deceived, and in which has Rhetoric the greater power?

PHAEDRUS. Obviously in the class of things that are doubtful.

SOCRATES. If so, then he who is to cultivate the Art of Rhetoric must first of all methodically distinguish these two classes, and acquire a clear impression of each of them, the class of things in which most persons waver, and the class where they do not.

PHAEDRUS. The man who has acquired that, Socrates, will have grasped an excellent principle of art.

SOCRATES. And thereafter, I think, as he meets each individual case, he will not miss the point, but must clearly see to which class the thing he is to speak on appertains.

PHAEDRUS. No doubt he will.

SOCRATES. What, then, shall we say of love? Does it belong in the class of debatable things, or to the class about which there is no dispute?

PHAEDRUS. Surely to the class of things that are in dispute. Otherwise do you think it would have been possible for you to say what you just now said of love?—that it is a source of injury to the loved one as well as the lover, but, again, that it is the greatest of all blessings!

SOCRATES. Excellently put! But go on, and tell me this, for since I was in an ecstasy I don't quite recollect. In beginning my discourse did I give a definition of love?

PHAEDRUS. Indeed you did, and with amazing rigor.

SOCRATES. Ah me! How much superior in art you make the Nymphs, the daughters of Achelous, and Pan the son of Hermes, to Lysias son of Cephalus, with regard to speeches! Or am I wrong, and did our Lysias in beginning his erotic speech compel us to conceive of Eros as the particular reality which he wished us to retain? And did he then proceed to order all details with reference to this notion, and finish off with it in view? Would you mind if we read his opening again?

PHAEDRUS. If you like; but what you seek for is not there.

SOCRATES. Read, that I may hear his very words.

PHAEDRUS. 'How matters stand with me, you know; and that I think it would advantage both of us if this and that took place, you have heard. I deem it meet I should not fail of my desire on the pretext that I am not your lover; for lovers later rue their acts of kindness, then when their passion is spent.'

SOCRATES. There seems to be no doubt at all about it; he is very far from doing the thing we require. He does not begin at the beginning of his speech, but at the end. He tries to swim up-current on his back, and starts with what the lover would say to his loved one in closing. Or am I utterly wrong again, my darling Phaedrus?

PHAEDRUS. It certainly is a topic to end with, Socrates, this matter of which he is speaking.

SOCRATES. And what about the rest? Doesn't it look as if the parts of the speech had been tossed off topsy-turvy? Or *is* there some obvious and cogent reason why the second thing he says comes second instead of any other of his statements? For myself, in my ignorance I cannot help believing that the writer just boldly uttered whatever came into his head; but you —you have some rhetorical necessity to adduce, which made him put these utterances in this side-by-side arrangement?

PHAEDRUS. You are very good to think me capable of so keen an insight into his procedure.

SOCRATES. Here, at all events, is something which you will allow, that every discourse is put together like a living creature—it has a kind of body of its own, and hence lacks neither head nor foot, but has both middle and extremities, all composed in such sort that they suit each other and the whole.

PHAEDRUS.   Could any one deny it?

SOCRATES.   Well, then, examine the speech by your friend, and see if it is like that or otherwise. You will actually find it nowise different from the inscription which some say was put on the tomb of Midas the Phrygian.

PHAEDRUS.   What about that? And what is the trouble with it?

SOCRATES.   It runs like this:

> A maiden of bronze am I; on the tombstone of Midas I lie.
> So long as waters flow, and tall trees blow,
> In this spot abiding, here on much-lamented tomb,
> I shall declare to all who pass: 'This is the grave of Midas.'

And it makes no difference at all whether any bit of it is uttered first or last. I am right in thinking you can see that?

PHAEDRUS.   You are poking fun, Socrates, at our speech.

SOCRATES.   To spare your feelings, then, let us say no more of it. And yet I think it contains a wealth of examples from which any one who looked at them might profit—by aiming not to imitate them in the least! Let us rather go on to the succeeding speeches; for to my mind there was something in them that is worth examination by those who wish to make inquiry about speaking.

PHAEDRUS.   What sort of thing have you in mind?

SOCRATES.   The two discourses were in some sort opposites; the one maintained that the lover, the other that the non-lover, should be favored.

PHAEDRUS.   And maintained it manfully!

SOCRATES.   I thought you would utter the truth, and would say 'madly.' In fact that was precisely what I had in mind. We said that love was a kind of madness, did we not?

PHAEDRUS.   Yes.

SOCRATES.   And said there were two sorts of madness? One has its cause in human illness; the other comes by a divine release from the ordinary rules of life.

PHAEDRUS.   Certainly.

SOCRATES.   And of the madness from on high we made a quadruple division, corresponding to these four divinities?—to Apollo we ascribed prophetic inspiration; to Dionysus, mystic madness; to the Muses, the poetic; and to Aphrodite and Eros, the fourth, the madness of the lover, and this we declared was the best. And—I know not how—we drew the passion of love in a figure, perhaps laying hold upon some truth, but possibly in another direction led astray; and so we poured out a commingled speech, which did not wholly lack persuasive force. And thereupon we chanted a kind of myth-like hymn, and sportive, yet in measured strain and pious, a hymn in honor of my lord as well as thine, O Phaedrus! to Eros, guardian of lovely boys.

PHAEDRUS. And to me, I know, the listening was not unpleasant!

SOCRATES. Accordingly, from this example let us learn the method of transition, in discourse, from blame to praise.

PHAEDRUS. Just what do you mean by that?

SOCRATES. Just this. It seems to me that in reality the rest was done in play, for pastime, yet, in what by lucky chance was uttered, two principles were at work which it would not be unwelcome to seize upon if any one could seize on their artistic function.

PHAEDRUS. And which are they?

SOCRATES. First, the synthesis of manifold and scattered items, through a comprehensive view of them, in one idea, to the end that, by defining each particular, a man may render clear, every time, the thing about which he wishes to instruct us. For example, in what we just now said of love, our defining what it is; the formulation may have been well done or ill, but certainly the speech thereby had self-consistency and clearness when delivered.

PHAEDRUS. What is the other principle you mention, Socrates?

SOCRATES. The reverse: one must be able to divide by species, according to the natural formation, where the joints are, and not attempt to fracture any part after the fashion of a clumsy butcher. No, we must do as our two speeches just now did when they alike assumed a single concept, of unreason; then as a body which is one is by nature thence divided into parallel members with like names, and these members are termed right and left, so with the derangement which the speeches both regarded as a form by nature one in us. One speech severed the left-hand part, and severed this again, and did not desist until among the members it hit upon a kind of sinister [left-hand] love so-called, which it condemned—and very justly, too. The other speech drew us to the members on the right-hand side of madness, and likewise hit upon a kind of love—the same word as before—a godlike love which it held up to us, and lauded as the source of our greatest blessings.

PHAEDRUS. You speak with the utmost truth.

SOCRATES. I am myself a lover, Phaedrus, of these methods of analysis and combination; I cherish them in order that I may be able to speak as well as think. And if in any other man I find the power of insight into the One and Many as naturally conjoint, him I follow 'after,' treading 'in his footsteps as in the footprints of a god.' And furthermore, for those who exercise this power I have a name, and whether I am right or not God knows, but up to this I call them 'dialecticians.' Come, tell me now what one should call the students of your art and Lysias'. Or is it, perhaps, the same thing as that art of discourse by the use of which Thrasymachus and the rest have grown skilful at speaking themselves, and also make others skilful, whoever is willing to bring them golden tribute as to kings.

PHAEDRUS. And kingly men they are, but not through competence in the matters you ask about. Now for this kind of thing which you call 'dialectic,' to my mind you are right when you so call it; but what the thing called rhetoric is, I think that still escapes us.

SOCRATES. What are you saying? In our two processes there is something lacking, which yet must be included in the art? It must be something fine! By all means let us not make light of it, you and I. Account must yet be taken of that part of rhetoric which has been omitted.

PHAEDRUS. And, Socrates, that means, no doubt, a wealth of things, all those that are in the books that have been written on the art of rhetoric.

SOCRATES. Yes; thank you for reminding me. I think you mean the 'Proem' first—how one should make the opening of the speech. Those are the things you refer to, isn't it so?—the 'niceties' of the art.

PHAEDRUS. Yes.

SOCRATES. And secondly comes the 'Narrative,' and after it the 'Testimony'; and thirdly 'Evidence'; and fourthly 'Probabilities.' And, if I don't mistake, that best of word-smiths, from Byzantium, adds 'Confirmation' and 'Sur-confirmation.'

PHAEDRUS. You mean the very eminent Theodorus?

SOCRATES. Who else? And he has 'Refutation' and 'Sur-refutation'—how to do them in accusation as well as in defence. But the illustrious Parian, Evenus, shall we not bring him to the centre? The inventor of 'Insinuation' and 'Praise Indirect'! And 'Censure Indirect,' which some maintain he put into verse to help the memory! What a savant! And Tisias and Gorgias, shall we let them slumber? They who saw that probabilities are more to be desired than truth, and who, again, make what is little seem large, and what is large seem little, all through the force of logic, give new things an air of being old, give old things novelty, and discovered how to speak with brevity, or lengthen out for ever, on each and every subject. I once told Prodicus about this last. He laughed and said: 'I am myself the sole inventor of the art of speaking as one should. The rule is, "Speeches should be neither long nor short, but meet." '

PHAEDRUS. Ah, Prodicus, how very clever!

SOCRATES. Are we not to mention Hippias? Methinks he too, our friend from Elis, would vote with Prodicus.

PHAEDRUS. And why not?

SOCRATES. And Polus, with his *Muses' School of Speech!* What shall we say of chapters like his 'Duplicate Expression,' 'Art of Maxims,' 'Art of Imagery,' and 'Vocabulary of Licymnius,' which the latter donated to Polus for his work on *Beauty of Language?*

PHAEDRUS. What about Protagoras, Socrates? Didn't he have some things like that?

SOCRATES. Yes, indeed, my boy. Something on *Propriety of Language,* and many other elegant inquiries. But truly, for piteous speeches bearing on the themes of Age and Poverty the Chalcedonian giant [Thrasymachus] seems to me to carry off the prize in art; while, as he declared, he was a veritable genius at first rousing a great crowd to anger, and again, when they were raging, with his enchantments soothing them, and was past master at devising calumnies and disposing of them, whatever the situation.

With regard to the conclusion of a speech, all seem to be agreed in their opinion, though some call it 'Recapitulation,' and others apply to it some other name.

PHAEDRUS. You mean the Summary of individual points, with which to remind the listeners, at the end, of all that has been said?

SOCRATES. There you have what I had to say. And now, if you have anything to add about the art of rhetoric—

PHAEDRUS. Nothing but small details, not worth discussing.

SOCRATES. We may dismiss the small details. Let us take these major matters, examine them more fully by the light of day, and see what value they have, what artistic force, and when they have it.

PHAEDRUS. They have the utmost force and value, Socrates—at all events in popular assemblies.

SOCRATES. Well, they have it. But, my enthusiast, look you, and see if their web does not really appear to you as full of holes as it does to me.

PHAEDRUS. Show me once.

SOCRATES. Well, tell me now. Suppose a man were to go to your good friend Eryximachus, or to his father Acumenus, and were to say: 'I know what sort of drugs to give the body so that, according as I will, I can warm it up, and cool it off, and, if I choose, can make it vomit, or, if I change my aim, can evacuate it downwards; together with all sorts of things like that. And, since I know these things, I claim the right to be called doctor, and to make any one else a doctor to whom I impart the knowledge of them.' What do you think your friends would say to that?

PHAEDRUS. What could they do but ask him if he knew, besides, what persons one should treat thus, also when one ought to give each treatment, and to what extent?

SOCRATES. Now suppose he answered: 'Of that I know absolutely nothing. Still I maintain that he who learns from me the things in question will be fit to do what you inquire about.'

PHAEDRUS. In that case, they would say, I think: 'The man is crazy. He has picked up somewhere from a book, or got by chance, a hearsay knowledge of some drugs, and thinks he has become a doctor, without the slightest understanding of the art.'

SOCRATES. Well then, suppose, again that one went to Sophocles and to Euripides, and said that he knew how to make very extended speeches on a little matter, and very little speeches on a great one, and pitiful speeches when he chose, and the reverse again, speeches terrible and menacing. Suppose he went on like that with all the rest, and thought by teaching it he could transmit the art of writing tragedies?

PHAEDRUS. They likewise, Socrates, I fancy, would laugh at a man who thinks that tragedy is aught else than the proper combination of these elements in such a way that they harmonize with one another and with the whole.

SOCRATES. But methinks they would not be uncivil, or abuse him; rather, would behave as a musician would on meeting a man who thought himself a master of harmony because he could strike the highest and the lowest note. The musician would not rudely say: 'Villain, your wits are addled.' No, being a musician, he would say, quite gently: 'Dear Sir, a man who is to be skilled in music must indeed know what you mention, but there is nothing to prevent a man who has what you possess from not possessing the slightest grasp of music. You know what must be learned before one takes up harmony, but harmony you do not know.'

PHAEDRUS. Absolutely right!

SOCRATES. So that would be the answer Sophocles would give their man for his display: 'Preliminaries to the tragic art, but not the art itself.' And so Acumenus: 'Preliminaries to the art, but not the art of healing.'

PHAEDRUS. Right, right, in every way!

SOCRATES. But what do we think 'Adrastus of honeyed speech' would say, and even Pericles, if they heard of the admirable devices we just now ran through—'Arts of Brevity,' and 'Arts of Imagery,' and all the rest, of which, after we went through the list, we said that they ought to be examined by the light of day? Would they be harsh, as I have been, and you? Would they be so rude as to apply a discourteous epithet to those who have written and taught these matters for an 'art of rhetoric'? Or, being wiser men than we, would they perhaps admonish us two as well, and say: 'Phaedrus and Socrates, instead of being angry, we ought rather to be lenient with persons who are ignorant of dialectic, and hence have not been able to define what Rhetoric is. Through this infirmity it was that, possessing the preliminaries which are needed for the art beforehand, they thought they had discovered Rhetoric. And, going on to teach these things to others, they imagine they have taught them Rhetoric in perfection; and think the effective use of these devices, and the organization of the whole, to be a work of no importance, something which their pupils themselves, and by themselves, must furnish in the speeches.'

PHAEDRUS. I quite admit the danger, Socrates, that the art which these men teach for Rhetoric, and on which they write, has the character you give it; to me, you seem to have described it truly. And still I wish to know about the art of the really eloquent and persuasive speaker. How and whence can one acquire it?

SOCRATES. The possibility of becoming a complete adept, Phaedrus, seems probably here to be, perhaps it must here be, dependent on the same conditions as it is elsewhere. If by nature it lies in you to be eloquent, you will be an orator of repute if first you get understanding and practice. If you lack on either side, to that extent you will be wanting. But, so far as the result depends on art, the way in which both Lysias and Thrasymachus proceed does not appear to me to be the method.

PHAEDRUS. What is the right way, then?

SOCRATES. The chances are, my best of men, that Pericles became the most finished of them all in the art of eloquence.

PHAEDRUS. And why say that?

SOCRATES. All the arts that are of great importance call for accessory discussion and high speculation about Nature. From this, it would appear, come, somehow, loftiness of thought and completeness of execution; which Pericles acquired in addition to his natural gifts. And the acquisition came, I think, from his falling in with Anaxagoras, a man of this description, with the result that Pericles was occupied with lofty speculations, and attained to know the nature of mind and its negation, both—subjects upon which Anaxagoras discoursed at length. That was the source from which he drew from the art of Rhetoric what could be brought to bear on it.

PHAEDRUS. What do you mean by that?

SOCRATES. The method in the art of healing is pretty much the same as that of Rhetoric.

PHAEDRUS. How so?

SOCRATES. In both arts you have to analyze a nature, in one the nature of the body, in the other the nature of the soul; that is, if you are going to apply, not by routine and empirically, but by art, drugs and diet in order to produce health and vigor in the body, arguments and systematic training for the soul so as to give it the conviction you desire to give it, and the power.

PHAEDRUS. That seems altogether likely, Socrates.

SOCRATES. But the nature of the soul—what is your opinion? Do you think one can conceive of that, in a way worth mentioning, apart from universal nature?

PHAEDRUS. If we are to trust Hippocrates—and he is an Asclepiad—you cannot even think about the body in any other way.

SOCRATES. And he does well, my friend, to say so. But besides consulting Hippocrates we must appeal to reason, and see whether it chimes in.

PHAEDRUS. So say I.

SOCRATES. Well then, concerning Nature inquire what Hippocrates and right reason, both, may have to say. Concerning the nature of anything whatsoever, is not the proper line of thought as follows? First, is it simple or multiform, the object, namely, concerning which we wish ourselves to be expert, and able to make another so? And next, supposing it be simple, we must inquire about its function: what is its natural capacity of acting upon something, or of being acted on by something? But if it has a plurality of forms, these must be listed, and then what we saw for the simple object we must see for each of the forms: what does it naturally do to what, or what is naturally done to it by what?

PHAEDRUS. That may well be, Socrates.

SOCRATES. Any method that was wanting in these steps would be like the progress of a blind man. But surely one who follows a pursuit with art ought not to be likened to a blind man, nor to a deaf one. Clearly, rather, the man who will teach another speaking, and does so with art, will accurately explain to him the nature of that to which the pupil's words will be addressed. And that, presumably, will be the soul.

PHAEDRUS. Assuredly.

SOCRATES. Then all his energy is concentrated upon this: he aims to produce conviction in the soul. Isn't it so?

PHAEDRUS. Yes.

SOCRATES. Then obviously Thrasymachus, or any one else who is seriously going to teach the art of rhetoric, will first describe the soul with all precision, and make us see whether by nature it is one, and does not vary, or like the bodily shape, is multiform. That is what we mean by explaining the nature of a thing.

PHAEDRUS. Yes, by all means.

SOCRATES. And secondly he will show how it naturally acts on something, or is acted on by something.

PHAEDRUS. Surely.

SOCRATES. Thirdly, having classified the types of speeches, and the types of soul with their emotional reactions, he will go through the list of causes and effects, fitting type to type, and showing why a given type of speech [argument] must effect persuasion in a given type of soul, and do the opposite in another.

PHAEDRUS. Nothing could be more admirable, it would seem, than that.

SOCRATES. Nay more, my friend. If there is to be art, neither any other subject, nor this subject, will ever be discussed in speech or writing, whether exposition or discourse, in any other way than this. But the authors nowadays whom you have listened to, who write *Arts of Speaking,* are cunning ones, and hide their craft, well knowing meanwhile all about the soul. Accordingly, until they treat the subject in this fashion when they speak and write on it, they shall not persuade us that they write with art.

PHAEDRUS.   What fashion do you mean?

SOCRATES.   Just what expressions one should use, it is not easy to say. But I am willing to tell how one should write if the result is to be as artistic as it may be.

PHAEDRUS.   Tell on.

SOCRATES.   The function of a speech, we saw, is to win the soul; and hence the man who aims to be an artistic speaker must necessarily know the soul in all its species. There aie so and so many kinds of souls, of such and such a nature, and hence men severally are of such a sort, and such another. Once these distinctions have been made, we come, in turn, to speeches [arguments]: there are so and so many kinds of them, each kind of such or such a nature. Now then, men of a given sort under speeches of a given nature, and through that cause, are readily brought to such and such convictions; whereas men of another given sort are made incredulous through this and this. When one has these matters well in mind, the next thing needed is to see them as they are in practice, and as they are effected there; a man must have the power to follow up the scent acutely. Otherwise he never will know anything more than what he heard when he attended lectures. But when he is in a competent state to say what sort of man will be persuaded by arguments of given kinds, let us suppose that he has his man at hand, can feel him out, and can tell himself with certainty: 'This is the man, and this the nature, that those lectures dealt with. Now the case is actually before me where I must apply just these arguments, thus, in order to effect persuasion in these definite points.' Suppose that the speaker now can do all this; can add to it a grasp of the proper times for speaking and refraining; can discern, again, with regard to 'Style Concise,' 'Style Pitiful,' 'Style Terrible,' and all the other forms of discourse he has learned, the opportune moments, and inopportune, for using each of them. Then, and not till then, will the art be finished, be beautiful and complete. Nay more, if any one omits a single step, as speaker, or as teacher, or as writer, and avers that he writes with art, the man who disbelieves him wins. 'Well then, Socrates and Phaedrus,' the man who compiles a Rhetoric will say, 'is this the proper view? Or should one entertain some other concept of the art of speaking?'

PHAEDRUS.   I think no other view is possible, Socrates; and yet the labor involved would seem to be no trifling matter.

SOCRATES. That is true. And on that account we ought to turn all the explanations inside out, and see if there appears some other, perchance easier and shorter, way to the art, so as not to wander in vain on a long and rugged road when we have a short and smooth one. No, if you have any help to offer, something you have heard from Lysias or any other, try to recollect and tell it.

PHAEDRUS. If all depended on the trying, I might have it, but at the moment I have nothing at all to offer.

SOCRATES. Well then, would you like me to give an explanation, one that I heard from some of those who treat the subject?

PHAEDRUS. Yes, do.

SOCRATES. You know there is a saying, Phaedrus: 'Even the wolf has a right to be heard.'

PHAEDRUS. You be his advocate.

SOCRATES. Well, they say there is no call to be so solemn in this matter, or to go far afield with the aim of reducing all to principle, because (as we said at the opening of this discussion) a man who is going to be competent as a speaker need not possess the truth at all in questions of justice or of goodness with respect to actions, or indeed to men, so long as men are what they are by nature or through education. In the courts, they say, the truth about such questions is of absolutely no concern to any one; the thing that counts there is what will be believed, and that is 'probability.' To this the man who is going to speak 'with art' must devote himself. What actually took place must sometimes not be mentioned even, if the way in which it happened was not 'probable'; rather, it is the 'probabilities' that must be adduced, alike in prosecution and in defence. In fact, under all conditions the thing to be kept in view is 'probability,' while the speaker often and often says good-bye to the truth. This 'probability,' they hold, if it be kept up steadily throughout the speech supplies the entire art of rhetoric.

PHAEDRUS. Precisely, Socrates. You have given the matter as they state it who profess to be experts in the technique of speaking. I recollect that we briefly touched upon the like in what was said before. This matter would seem to be something of extreme importance to the experts.

SOCRATES. Take Tisias now; you have studied and restudied him with care. Accordingly, let Tisias pronounce upon this question, whether by 'the probable' he means aught else than what the crowd believe.

PHAEDRUS. He means just that.

SOCRATES. And it seems he has thought out the following case, at once a deep discovery and artistic secret, thus recorded: If a feeble and courageous man has beaten up a strong and cowardly one, and robbed him of his mantle or the like, and is brought to trial for it, then neither one of them must tell the truth. Instead, the coward must declare that he was not assaulted by a single man, to wit the brave one, who will counter with the statement that the two of them were alone, and will in turn advance the argument: 'How could a fellow such as I lay hands on one like him?' The coward, now, will not admit his cowardice, but will try to invent some other lie, and thus no doubt give his antagonist the opening to refute him. And so for other cases, the means to artful speaking are pretty much like these. Isn't it so, my Phaedrus?

PHAEDRUS. It is.

SOCRATES. Ah, what a genius he must have been to bring to light a deeply-hidden art, this Tisias, or whoever did invent it, and whichever was the land whence he rejoices to derive his name! And yet, my friend, what shall we do? Shall we say to him, or shall we not?—

PHAEDRUS. Say what?

SOCRATES. Say this: 'For some time, Tisias, indeed before you came along, we have been arguing that this "probability" was, in fact, engendered in the masses because of its resemblance to the truth. As for resemblances, we just now stated that the man who, everywhere, best understands how to discover them is the man who knows the truth. Accordingly, if you have anything else to say about the art of speaking, we should like to hear it. If not, then we shall put our trust in the positions we recently examined. We say: Unless a man has taken to account the different natures of those who are to hear him, and unless he can divide realities according to their species, and can also comprehend particulars, taken singly, under one idea, he never will be an expert in the art of eloquence to the measure which a human being can attain. But this result never will be gained without much diligence. And by a man of wisdom the toil must be endured, not for the sake of eloquence and action before men, but in order to be able to utter what is pleasing to the gods, and in everything, with all one's power, to act in the way that will please them. No, Tisias, you see just how it is; it is just as wiser men than we are say. It is not one's fellow servants that one should care to please, if one has sense, save incidentally, but one's good and noble masters. And therefore, if the way around is long, do not marvel; for, when the ends are great, the circuit must be trod; the path is not as you conceive it. Yet your ends also, as the argument sets forth, will be best attained in this way, if they are what a man desires.'

PHAEDRUS. Most admirably spoken, Socrates, it seems to me, if only one could do it.

SOCRATES. But when you strive for noble ends, it is also noble to endure whatever pain the effort may involve.

PHAEDRUS. Indeed it is.

SOCRATES. So there, on art and lack of art with reference to speaking, let that suffice.

PHAEDRUS. So be it.

SOCRATES. But as for writing, with propriety or impropriety, the question still remains what are the conditions that govern writing well and writing ill. Isn't it so?

PHAEDRUS. Yes.

SOCRATES. Well then, do you know how one will best please the Deity in regard to arguments—how one should do or speak?

PHAEDRUS. Not at all. Do you?

SOCRATES. At all events I have a thing to tell by hearsay from the men of an earlier time. The truth of it they only know. If we ourselves should find the truth, what difference would it make to us what people thought?

PHAEDRUS. The question is absurd. Go on and tell the thing you say you heard.

SOCRATES. Well, I heard there was a god in the vicinity of Naucratis in Egypt, one of the ancient deities—the one who had the sacred bird they call the ibis; and the name of this divinity they said was Theuth. He it was who first discovered number and arithmetic, geometry, astronomy, checkers too, and dice; and he invented writing! But the ruler of all Egypt in those days was Thamus, who dwelt in the great city, of the upper region, which the Greeks call the Egyptian Thebes, and him, the god, they call Ammon [and not Thamus]. To him, accordingly, came Theuth to exhibit his arts, declaring that they ought to be dispersed among all the Egyptians. Then Thamus asked what benefit each invention had to offer, and, as Theuth went through the list, praised some of them and censured others, according as he approved or disapproved of them. Many were the judgments, it is said, which Thamus pronounced to Theuth on either side; it would be too long a story to detail them. But finally the question came regarding letters, and Theuth declared: 'This form of learning, O King, will make the Egyptians wiser and more able to remember; the elixir of memory and wisdom is discovered!' But he replied: 'O most ingenious Theuth, one man can bring an art to birth, but it takes another to judge what share of harm or benefit the art may have for those who are going to use it. And you, now, the father of written letters, are led by your affection to ascribe to them a power exactly the reverse of what their tendency is. The result of your invention will be this: in the souls of those who learn it, forgetfulness will have lodging through a want of cultivation of the memory; they will trust to writing, a thing outside themselves, and effected by external characters, and hence will not remember of themselves and from within. The elixir you have found is not an aid to memory, but to reminiscence.

You provide your pupils with the show of wisdom, not true wisdom. Through you they will learn many things without instruction, and will hence appear to have much knowledge while for the most part they are ignorant, and hardly to be endured because they are grown seeming wise instead of wise.'

PHAEDRUS. Yes, Socrates, you readily make up stories about Egypt or any other land you have a mind to.

SOCRATES. They used to say, my friend, in the shrine of Zeus at Dodona, that the first prophetic utterances came from an oak. To the people then, who were not wise like you young men to-day, it sufficed in their simplicity to listen to the words of 'oak or crag,' if only these told the truth. To you, no doubt, it makes a difference who speaks, and whence he hails; for you do not merely look to see whether the thing is so or otherwise.

PHAEDRUS. Your reproof is just, and I think your Theban has the right of it in what he says of letters.

SOCRATES. And so the man who fancies he has left behind him any art in writing, or the man, again, who receives the like in the belief that something clear and certain will issue from the writing, will be a very simple person. He will, in truth, ignore the prophecy of Ammon, because he thinks that written words avail beyond recalling, to the man who knows, the matter about which they have been written.

PHAEDRUS. Most true.

SOCRATES. A terrible thing about writing, Phaedrus, is this, and here, in truth, it is like painting. I mean, the creations of the painter stand like living creatures, but if you ask them anything, they maintain a solemn silence. And so it is with writings; you might think they spoke as if they had intelligence, but if you put a question with a wish for information on a point in what is said, there is one, one only, invariable reply. Further, once a word is written, it goes rolling all about, comes indifferently among those who understand it and those whom it no wise concerns, and is unaware to whom it should address itself and to whom it should not do so. When it is mishandled, when it is unjustly railed at, it always needs the assistance of its father; it cannot defend itself, nor help itself.

PHAEDRUS. Here, too, your statements are absolutely right.

SOCRATES. What then? Do we not perceive another word, brother to the first, but lawful, and see how genuine it is in the manner of its birth, how much superior and more vigorous by nature?

PHAEDRUS. What word is this, and how, say you, is it begotten?

SOCRATES. I mean the word attended by intelligence, and graven in the learner's soul, able to defend itself, and knowing whom it ought to speak to, before whom it should be silent.

PHAEDRUS. You mean the word of him who knows, the word alive and animate, of which the written word may properly be called a kind of simulacrum?

SOCRATES. Precisely. But come now, tell me this. Suppose a farmer of intelligence has seed he cares for, which he wishes to produce a crop. Will he in all seriousness at the height of summer plant the seed in 'jardinières of Adonis,' and rejoice to see his vases flourishing in a week? Or would he do the like, if ever he did it, only in play and for diversion? When he was in earnest, he would employ the art of agriculture, would sow his seed in proper soil, and would be content if after seven months the seed he sowed attained its normal harvest?

PHAEDRUS. That, Socrates, would be his way, I think. He would do this way when in earnest, while in the other case he would do otherwise, and as you say.

SOCRATES. But what about the man who has a knowledge of the just, the beautiful, the good? Shall we maintain that he has less intelligence about his seeds than the farmer has?

PHAEDRUS. Far from it.

SOCRATES. Then you see he will not earnestly 'write in water'—will not sow his seed in ink by penning words which are unable to defend themselves by argument, nor can they adequately transmit the truth.

PHAEDRUS. The likelihood is he will not.

SOCRATES. No indeed. Rather, as it seems, when he plants his letter-gardens, when he writes, he will do so for diversion. When, however, he does write, he stores up memoranda for himself against the forgetfulness of age, if that should come, and for every one who follows the same track as he. And he will have pleasure as he sees the tender plantings thrive. When other men betake themselves to other recreations, plunging into drinking-bouts and all pleasures of that ilk, then he, it seems, instead, will pass the time in play of the sort I mention.

PHAEDRUS. What a noble pastime, Socrates, as you say, beside the base one! A pastime of the man who can divert himself with literature, composing tales of justice and the other subjects which you mention!

SOCRATES. So it is, dear Phaedrus. But far nobler, in my judgment, is the serious occupation with these subjects, when one employs the art of dialectic; when one takes a soul of fitting kind to plant in, and sows words in it, intelligent words that are prepared to help themselves and him who planted them, that are not without a harvest, but bear seed from which in other natures other words are planted that have the force to carry on in an undying lineage for ever. And they make their possessor happy to the utmost bound of human happiness.

PHAEDRUS. The pursuit you now describe is nobler yet by far.

SOCRATES. Now then, Phaedrus, since these points are settled, we can come to a decision about the other.

PHAEDRUS. What other?

SOCRATES. Why, the point we wished to clarify, which has brought us where we are. We were bent upon inquiring into the clamor against Lysias for his writing speeches, and upon examining discourses in themselves to see which were written with art, and which without. Now it seems to me the question about what has art and what has not has been made fairly clear.

PHAEDRUS. Yes, it seemed so. Go back, however, and remind me how.

SOCRATES. In advance, a man must know the truth about each particular of which he speaks or writes. He must be able to define each one of them in itself. When he has defined them, he must, in turn, know how to subdivide them severally according to their species, to the point where a division cannot be carried further. By the same method of analysis he must investigate the nature of the soul, and must discover what kind of argument is adapted to each nature. This done, he must settle and order his discourse accordingly, addressing to the many-sided soul a varied speech that touches every chord, a simple one to the simple. Not till then can discourses be artistic as far as it lies in the nature of their genus to be made so, to be controlled by art for the purpose of instruction or persuasion. That is what the whole preceding argument has revealed to us.

PHAEDRUS. Most certainly it was in substance thus that the matter did come out.

SOCRATES. But what about the question whether it is fine or base to utter speeches, and to write them, and under what conditions doing so might in justice be called a disgrace or not? Was that made clear when it was said a little while ago . . . ?

PHAEDRUS. What?

SOCRATES. That if Lysias or any one else ever wrote, or shall hereafter write, in private life or in public as a statesman, any document of a political description, and imagines it has in it certainty and clearness in a high degree, then that is a disgrace to the writer, whether anybody says it is or not. Verily, awake or dreaming, to be ignorant of what is right and what is wrong, of what is good and what is bad, cannot escape from being blameful, not even if the entire mob were to applaud it.

PHAEDRUS. No indeed.

SOCRATES. But take the man who judges that in the written word, no matter what the subject, there necessarily is much that is for play; the man who thinks that no discourse, in metre or without it, is ever worth great effort in writing, or in reciting as the rhapsodes do (when all is uttered, not after critical examination, nor for instruction, but just to be believed); the man who, rather, thinks that the best things of this kind really constitute a means of recollection for those who know, while in discourses for instruction, uttered for the sake of learning, words really graven in the soul concerning justice, beauty, goodness, in these alone are clarity, perfection, and value worth the effort; the man who thinks that such discourses only should be called his children, legitimate sons as it were, first among them the word that may be found indwelling in himself, and then its offspring, who are its brothers also, when such are by desert implanted in other souls of other men; the man who lets all other discourses go their way rejoicing. That man, perchance, my Phaedrus, is such a one as you and I would pray we both of us might become.

PHAEDRUS.   What you say is absolutely what I wish and pray for.

SOCRATES.   And now the subject of rhetoric has diverted us long enough. Go you to Lysias, and tell him how you and I went down to the fountain of the Nymphs, and to their shrine, and how we heard a message which they bade us give to Lysias and to anybody else who may compose orations; and to Homer and anybody else, again, who has put together poetry, without musical accompaniment or with it; and to Solon, thirdly, and anybody else who has written documents in the way of utterances for the State, and called them laws. Say: If the author has composed with a knowledge of the truth, and therewith can give assistance when put to the test concerning that which he has written; if he is able of himself, by speaking, to show the inferiority of what is written; then such a man must not be called by any name suggested by his writings. He must receive his title from that to which he gave his effort.

PHAEDRUS.   What title, then, will you accord to him?

SOCRATES.   To call him 'wise,' is seems to me, would be too much, Phaedrus; that seems appropriate to God alone. Either 'friend of wisdom' [*philosophos*] or some name like that would be more fitting for him, and in better taste.

PHAEDRUS.   And not at all beside the point!

SOCRATES.   But, on the other hand, the man who has nothing of more value than what he has composed or written, turning it over and over by the hour, attaching a bit here, excising there, him no doubt you will properly address as 'poet,' or an 'author of orations,' or the 'writer of a law'?

PHAEDRUS.   Why not?

SOCRATES.   Then go and tell this to your comrade.

PHAEDRUS.   And what of you? What are you going to do? Your comrade must not be neglected, either.

SOCRATES.   What comrade?

PHAEDRUS.   Isocrates the fair. What message, Socrates, will you take to him? What shall we say he is?

SOCRATES. Isocrates is young yet, Phaedrus; still I wish to tell what I foresee concerning him.

PHAEDRUS. What is it?

SOCRATES. In natural gift he seems to me too good to be compared with Lysias in point of eloquence, and, further, to surpass him in nobility of character. Accordingly, it would be no marvel if, as he grows older, and in the kind of eloquence he now employs, he were to excel all who ever have attempted speaking, and leave them farther behind than children. Further, I suspect that these activities will not suffice him, and an impulse more divine will drive him to yet greater things; for from nature, my dear friend, there is in the mind of the man a certain *philosophia*. Such is the message I shall carry from the deities of this place to Isocrates, my well-beloved, and do you bear the other to Lysias, who is yours.

PHAEDRUS. It shall be done. And now the heat is more endurable. Let us begone.

SOCRATES. Before we go is it not seemly to address a prayer to the deities of the place?

PHAEDRUS. Yes, surely.

SOCRATES. Beloved Pan, and all ye other gods here dwelling, grant that I may grow beautiful within, and that whatsoever I possess without may be in harmony with my inner man. Let me deem the wise one rich; and may my store of wealth be such as only the man of self-restraint can bear or draw.

Do we need anything more than that, my Phaedrus? The prayer, I think, is enough for me.

PHAEDRUS. In your petition share with me; for friends have everything in common.

SOCRATES. Let us begone!

AIDS TO STUDY

This dialogue between Socrates and Phaedrus falls into seven rough divisions:
1. An introduction, in which Socrates and Phaedrus begin talking about the persuasiveness of Lysias;
2. Phaedrus' recital of Lysias' speech on love, in which one is urged to prefer a non-lover to a lover;
3. Socrates' criticism of Lysias' speech;
4. Socrates' first speech, also urging preference for the non-lover over the lover;
5. Socrates' criticism of his own speech and recantation of the position he takes in the first speech;

6. Socrates' second speech, in which he urges preference for the lover over the non-lover; and

7. A lengthy discussion of the nature of rhetoric, in which Socrates and Phaedrus try to work out an answer to the question of the ethical nature of rhetoric.

The essence of Socrates' criticism of Lysias' speech is that Lysias' 'invention' is weak. By 'invention' is meant the finding of the best argument for one's point of view. Socrates' criticism is that Lysias has used, as the basis of his argument, an obvious point—that non-lovers are more discreet than lovers; a better argument would be based upon a less trite observation. Socrates' first speech, which follows, is an attempt at a more ingenious invention (though he disclaims the basic ideas as his own, but says they are gained from reading and conversation). The basis of Socrates' argument is that love is a case in which desire overcomes reason, and one should shun it as he shuns other unreasonable desires like avarice and gluttony and drunkenness. It is interesting that Socrates' second speech turns on this exact point of irrationality—the nature of madness. His first speech is the view of a 'rational' man; his second speech is the view of a 'wise' man, in his estimation.

Very briefly put, the argument in Socrates' second speech goes as follows: love of the beautiful is a mortal link to the absolute truths of the universe, and hence it is a way to truth and hence holy. Love of the beautiful is the way by which the soul may grow toward truth. If one accepts love as an impetus toward knowledge, he is blessed; if he yields to lust, he misuses love. Socrates explains by way of an analogy of the charioteer (the soul) with two horses, one fine, handsome, and obedient (proper love), the other gross, ugly, and willful (improper love). The charioteer must curb the latter horse if he is to drive toward the truth.

The drift of the dialogue is that ingenious 'invention' is better than dull or commonplace 'invention,' but the best argument is one which proceeds from truth, not falsehood. Socrates is ashamed of his first speech—not that it is less ingenious than Lysias', but rather because it proceeds from a false view of things, in his opinion. In argument, one must, above all else, see things rightly: rhetoric is 'the art of winning the soul by discourse, which means not merely argument in the courts of justice, and all other sorts of public councils, but in private conference as well'; it is 'always intrinsically honorable.' Socrates is trying to persuade Phaedrus that 'right rhetoric' is always based upon truth. He moves to the three speeches to illustrate this basic notion, and he summarizes his view with: 'In advance, a man must know the truth about each particular of which he speaks or writes. He must be able to define each one of them in itself. When he has defined them,' etc.

In short, the well-turned phrases of Lysias are not the real key to good rhetoric, though well-turned phrases have their place in it. And cleverness of argument is not the real key to argument, though it, too, is admirable. The real key to good rhetoric is the fundamental truth of the argument presented. Rhetoric is not a matter of making the best case; it is a matter of finding the most completely truthful case.

From *The Rhetoric*

I.I. [SCOPE AND PURPOSE OF THE ART.] * Rhetoric is the counterpart of Dialectic
[—that is, the art of public speaking and the art of logical discussion are
co-ordinate, but contrasted, processes]; for both have to do with such things
as fall, in a way, within the realm of common knowledge, things that do not
belong to any one science. Accordingly, everybody to some extent makes use
of both Dialectic and Rhetoric; for all make some attempt to sift or to support theses, and to defend or attack persons. Most people do so, of course,
either quite at random, or else merely with a knack acquired from practice.
Success in either way being possible, the random impulse and the acquired
facility alike evince the feasibility of reducing the processes to a method; for
when the practised and the spontaneous speaker gain their end, it is possible
to investigate the cause of their success; and such an inquiry, we shall all
admit, performs the function of an art.

Now hitherto the authors of 'Arts of Speaking' have built up but a small
portion of the art of Rhetoric truly considered; for this art consists of proofs
[persuasions] alone—all else is but accessory. Yet these writers say nothing
of enthymemes, the very body and substance of persuasion, and are concerned
in the main with matters external to the direct issue. Thus the arousing of
prejudice, or pity, of anger, and the like feelings in the soul, does not concern
the facts, but has regard to those who decide. Consequently, if trials were
everywhere conducted as at present they are in some cities—and especially in
those that are best-governed—pleaders who were guided by the handbooks
would have nothing to say; for by common consent the laws should forbid

From *Rhetoric,* translated and edited by Lane Cooper, New York, Appleton-Century-
Crofts, Inc., 1960. Copyright, 1932, by Lane Cooper. Reprinted by permission of Apple-
ton-Century-Crofts, Inc.
* In these selections from Aristotle, brackets enclose explanatory additions made by the
translator to render the rather sparse text more readily understandable to the reader.

irrelevant speaking, and some courts, as that of the Areopagus, actually do forbid it. This certainly is right reason; the man who is to judge should not have his judgment warped by speakers arousing him to anger, jealousy, or compassion. One might just as well make a carpenter's rule crooked before using it as a measure. And obviously in a dispute there is nothing to do beyond showing that the alleged fact does or does not exist, has or has not occurred. The question whether it is important or trivial, the question whether there is justice or injustice, so far as the legislator has not defined these points, that is precisely what the judge is there to decide; he is not supposed to learn his lesson from the disputants.

Naturally it is best that laws enacted on sound principles should, so far as may be, themselves determine everything, leaving as little as possible to the decision of those who judge; first, because it is easier to find one individual, or some few, with wisdom enough, and a capacity for legislative and judicial functions, than to find a large number with the like endowment; and secondly, because legislative acts are the fruit of long deliberation, whereas decisions must be given on short notice, so that it is hard for the judge or the assembly to satisfy the demands of private justice and public expediency. Most important of all, the decision of the legislator concerns no one actual case, but is prospective and general; whereas a member of the assembly or of the court must decide present and individual cases, in which their personal likes and dislikes, and their private interests, are often involved, so that they cannot adequately survey the truth, but have their judgment clouded by their own pleasure or pain.

On other points, then, we say the authority of the judge should be reduced as far as possible; but the decision whether a thing has or has not occurred, will or will not occur, is or is not so, must be left in the hands of those who judge, since for these matters the legislator cannot provide. Such being the case, it is clear that our authors of handbooks, in attempting to define the proper content of the Proem, the Narration, and the other divisions of the speech, and the like, are dwelling upon irrelevant matters, for their rules have to do, simply and solely, with the production of a certain mental attitude in the judge. These authors tell us nothing about artistic proofs—nothing, that is, about the way in which one is to become a master of the enthymeme. [By 'artistic' proofs or persuasions we are to understand systematic proofs by 'enthymeme' and 'example,' as opposed to 'non-artistic' proofs such as 'laws, witnesses, compacts (=documents), tortures (=ordeals, inquisitions), and oaths,' as distinct also from the emotional appeals (already noted) to the judges, and as distinct from evidence drawn from character. Aristotle here anticipates his explanation of 'artistic proofs.' By 'artistic' he means *appertaining to the art of Rhetoric proper;* by 'non-artistic,' what is external to the art—adventitious and adjunct means of persuasion that are not involved in the essential issue which is the subject of the speech. Similarly he anticipates his explanation of 'enthymeme,' the rhetorical syllogism, drawn, not from the principles of the exact sciences, but from propositions, or probabilities, relating to everyday affairs. When he objects so vigorously to existing handbooks for their preoccupation with 'non-artistic proofs,' we are hardly prepared for Aristotle's own attention to them in the present treatise, which probably deals more systematically with the means of arousing emotion in the audience than did any of its predecessors. His extended treatment of the emotions is partly an inevitable concession to practice, for the orator must deal with an audience, and an audience necessarily is emotional; you may work on their emotions in a better way or a worse, but neglect them you cannot. Yet his method is also justified on grounds of perspective since he does subordinate the 'non-artistic' to the 'artistic' proofs, the accessories to the main issue; whereas, he contends, his predecessors wholly neglected what was fundamental. Accordingly, though he owes some actual debt to them, his perspective is good, where theirs doubtless was bad.]

That is the reason why those authors have utterly neglected the deliberative branch of speaking, which is nobler and more statesmanlike than the branch that is concerned with the everyday relations between man and man, and treat only of the latter type, though the right method is the same for both. They all aim at a systematic treatment of the art of pleading, because the forensic type gives a better chance to introduce matters that are foreign to the issue. The deliberative branch, that of the statesman, since it deals rather with communal interests, affords less room for trickery [—that is, for biasing the judges (audience) by playing upon their emotions]. In a debate upon communal interests, the judges decide questions which really touch them as individuals, so that nothing more is needed than to prove that affairs are as the advocate of a given policy states [—since each can see what is advantageous to him, there is no need of arousing their passions]; but in forensic speaking this is not enough, [the judges have not the same interest in the outcome of a given case] and it pays to win the audience over [by working on their emotions]. Here the judges make award regarding interests that are not their own; if they view these in the light of their own feelings, and yield to the gratification of their ears, they lend themselves to the more plausible speaker, and so decide the case. They do not *judge* it. And hence in many places, as we said above, the law forbids irrelevant pleading. In deliberative assemblies, the judges themselves take care of that.

It is clear, then, that the artistic method has to do with proofs [persuasions] in the stricter sense. Now proof [persuasion] is a kind of demonstration; for we entertain the strongest conviction of a thing if we believe that it has been 'demonstrated.' Rhetorical proof, however, [is not scientific demonstration]; it takes the form of an enthymeme, this being, in general, the most effective among the various forms of persuasion. The enthymeme, again, is a kind of syllogism; now every kind of syllogism falls within the province of Dialectic, and must be examined under Dialectic as a whole, or under some branch of it. Consequently the person with the clearest insight into the nature of syllogisms, who knows from what premises and in what modes they may be constructed, will also be the most expert in regard to enthymemes, once he has mastered their special province [of things contingent and uncertain such as human actions and their consequences], and has learnt the differences between enthymemes and logical syllogisms. [The latter are complete, and yield an absolute demonstration.] Truth and likeness to truth are discerned by one and the same faculty; while human nature, let us add, has aptitude enough for discerning what is true, and men in most cases do arrive at the truth. Consequently one who is skilled in discerning the truth can do well in weighing probabilities [matters of opinion].

It is clear, then, that our handbooks have limited the art to extraneous matters; and it is clear, too, why they have leaned to forensic speaking.

But the art of Rhetoric has its value. It is valuable, first, because truth and justice are by nature more powerful than their opposites; so that, when decisions are not made as they should be, the speakers with the right on their side have only themselves to thank for the outcome. Their neglect of the art needs correction. [A proper knowledge and exercise of Rhetoric would prevent the triumph of fraud and injustice.] Secondly, [Rhetoric is valuable as a means of instruction]. Even if our speaker had the most accurate scientific information, still there are persons whom he could not readily persuade with scientific arguments. True instruction, by the method of logic, is here impossible; the speaker must frame his proofs and arguments with the help of common knowledge and accepted opinions. This method has been noted in the *Topics,* in our remarks on popular discussion. [See Aristotle's *Topica* 1. 2.] Thirdly, in Rhetoric, as in Dialectic, we should be able to argue on either side of a question; not with a view to putting both sides into practice— we must not advocate evil—but in order that no aspect of the case may escape us, and that if our opponent makes unfair use of the arguments, we may be able in turn to refute them. In no other art do we draw opposite conclusions; it is characteristic of Rhetoric and Dialectic alone that, abstractly considered, they may indifferently prove opposite statements. Still, their basis, in the facts, is not a matter of indifference, for, speaking broadly, what is true and preferable is by nature always easier to prove, and more convincing. Lastly, if it is a disgrace to a man when he cannot defend himself in a bodily way, it would be odd not to think him disgraced when he cannnot defend himself with reason [in a speech]. Reason is more distinctive of man than is bodily effort. If it is urged that an abuse of the rhetorical faculty can work great mischief, the same charge can be brought against all good things (save virtue itself), and especially against the most useful things such as strength, health, wealth, and military skill. Rightly employed, they work the greatest blessings; and wrongly employed, they work the utmost harm.

We have seen that Rhetoric is not confined to any single and definite class of subjects, but in this respect is like Dialectic, and that the art has its uses; and we see that its function is not [absolutely] to persuade, but to discover the available means of persuasion in a given case. [Not outward success, but a correct method, is the criterion of art; the correct method will bring success in proportion. An unwarranted appeal to the emotions might win an undesirable success.] Herein Rhetoric is like all other arts. Thus the aim of medicine is not, strictly speaking, to restore a sick man to perfect health, but to bring him as near to health as the case admits; people who never can be well may yet be properly treated. Further, we see that it is the office of one and the same art to discern the genuine means, and also the spurious means, of persuasion, just as it is the office of Dialectic to discern the truth, and also the sham, syllogism; for sophistical dialectic, or sophistical speaking, is made so, not by the faculty, but by the moral purpose. [The faculty is the same in both arts.] There is this difference, however: we apply the term 'rhetorician' alike to describe a speaker's command of the art and a speaker's moral purpose; whereas, in the field of Dialectic, the term 'sophist' refers to the moral purpose, while 'dialectician' applies to the faculty [the normal function].

[Having thus made clear that Rhetoric is an art, and when rightly practiced an honest and useful art,] we must now proceed to discuss its method— the mode and the means that will enable us to attain to the proper ends. Accordingly, let us start afresh, as it were, first defining, and then going on to the rest.

1.2. [DEFINITION OF RHETORIC. MODES AND MEANS OF PERSUASION.] So let Rhetoric be defined as the faculty [power] of discovering in the particular case what are the available means of persuasion. This is the function of no other art [save Dialectic]. The others are each instructive or persuasive with regard to some special subject-matter. Thus medicine informs us about the conditions of health and disease; geometry about the properties of magnitudes; arithmetic about numbers; and so with the rest of the arts and sciences. But Rhetoric, it would seem, has the function of discovering the means of persuasion for every case, so to speak, that is offered; and hence we say that the art as such has no special application to any distinct class of subjects.

Proofs [persuasions] are of two kinds, artistic and non-artistic. [Or we might call them 'scientific' and 'unscientific.' Aristotle distinguishes means of persuasion that inherently belong *in* the art, and those that, while associated with it, are really external and adventitious.] By 'non-artistic' proofs are meant all such as are not supplied by our own efforts, but existed beforehand, such as witnesses, admissions under torture, written contracts, and the like. By 'artistic' proofs [means of persuasion] are meant those that may be furnished by the method of Rhetoric through our own efforts. The first sort have only to be used; the second have to be found.

Of the means of persuasion supplied by the speech itself there are three kinds. The first kind reside in the character [*ethos*] of the speaker; the second consist in producing a certain [the right] attitude in the hearer; the third appertain to the argument proper, in so far as it actually or seemingly demonstrates. [Under all three heads, and explicitly under the third, Aristotle makes room, with the scientific branch of Rhetoric, for devices related to those of the sophistical branch. As in the *Poetics,* we see that the artist may use elements that are somewhat external to the art itself, in a more artistic way rather than a less.]

The character [*ethos*] of the speaker is a cause of persuasion when the speech is so uttered as to make him worthy of belief; for as a rule we trust men of probity more, and more quickly, about things in general, while on points outside the realm of exact knowledge, where opinion is divided, we trust them absolutely. This trust, however, should be created by the speech itself, and not left to depend upon an antecedent impression that the speaker is this or that kind of man. It is not true, as some writers on the art maintain, that the probity of the speaker contributes nothing to his persuasiveness; on the contrary, we might almost affirm that his character [*ethos*] is the most potent of all the means to persuasion.

Secondly, persuasion is effected through the audience, when they are brought by the speech into a state of emotion; for we give very different decisions under the sway of pain or joy, and liking or hatred. This, we contend, is the sole aspect of the art with which technical writers of the day have tried to deal. We shall elucidate it in detail when we come to discuss the emotions.

Thirdly, persuasion is effected by the arguments, when we demonstrate the truth, real or apparent, by such means as inhere in particular cases.

Such being the instruments of persuasion, to master all three obviously calls for a man who can reason logically, can analyze the types of human character [*ethe*], along with the virtues, and, thirdly, can analyze the emotions—the nature and quality of each several emotion, with the means by which, and the manner in which, it is excited. Thus it follows that Rhetoric is a kind of offshoot, on the one hand, of Dialectic, and, on the other, of that study of Ethics which may properly be called 'political.' [With Aristotle, Ethics, the science dealing with individual conduct, shades off into Politics (a broader subject), which deals with the conduct and activities of men in groups—of the State.] And hence it is that Rhetoric, and those who profess it, slip into the guise of Politics [and political experts], whether from defects of education, or through quackery [imposture], or from other human failings. As we said at the outset, Rhetoric is a branch of Dialectic, and resembles that. Neither of them is a *science,* with a definite subject-matter; both are *faculties* for providing arguments. On their function, and on their relation to each other, perhaps enough has now been said.

[Let us turn to the instruments of persuasion.] As for real or apparent demonstration, there are in Rhetoric two modes, corresponding to the two modes in Dialectic. As in Dialectic we have, on the one hand, induction, and, on the other, the syllogism and apparent syllogism, so in Rhetoric: the example is a form of induction; while the enthymeme is a syllogism, and the apparent enthymeme an apparent syllogism. 'Enthymeme' is the name I give to a rhetorical syllogism, 'example' to a rhetorical induction. Whenever men in speaking effect persuasion through proofs, they do so either with examples or enthymemes; they use nothing else. Accordingly, since all demonstration (as we have shown in the *Analytics*) is effected either by syllogism [that is, deductively] or by induction, it follows that induction and syllogism [deduction] must be identified respectively with example and enthymeme. [See Aristotle's *Prior Analytics* 2. 23; *Posterior Analytics* 1. 1, 1. 18, 2. 19.] The difference between example and enthymeme may be inferred from the *Topics* [1. 1, 12]. There, with reference to syllogism [deduction] and induction, it has already been observed that to derive a general law from a number of like instances is in Dialectic induction, in Rhetoric example; whereas to conclude from certain assumptions that something else follows from those assumptions (something distinct from them, yet dependent upon their existing) either universally or as a rule—this in Dialectic is called a syllogism, and in Rhetoric an enthymeme. And of the corresponding two types of oratory it is plain that each has some advantage. What is said of Dialectic in our *Methodology* [a lost work of Aristotle] likewise holds true here; for, of the two kinds of speeches, in one the enthymeme predominates, in the other the example; and similarly some speakers are more given to examples, and others to enthymemes. Arguments through examples are not less persuasive, yet arguments in the form of the enthymeme are more applauded. The reason for this, and the right way of using both enthymemes and examples, will be discussed later. At present let us define the processes themselves more clearly.

'Persuasive' means persuasive to a person. To him, a statement may be persuasive and credible by itself, immediately, or it may become so when it seems to be proved from other statements that he believes. No art, however, has regard to the individual case. Thus medicine does not investigate the question what is a cure for Socrates or for Callias—for the individual as such—but asks what will cure a person or persons of such and such a type; the latter inquiry comes within the province of art, whereas, particulars being infinite, the individual fact cannot be scientifically known. And hence Rhetoric will consider, not what seems probable to the individual—to Socrates or to Hippias—but what seems probable to a given class; the same being true of Dialectic. [Conceivably, both Rhetoric and Dialectic might be used to argue any question or problem, but practically both are restricted.] Dialectic does not form its syllogisms out of any chance notions (such as the notions of crazy people), but takes problems that merit discussion; and similarly Rhetoric is applied to recognized subjects of deliberation. It has to do with things about which we commonly deliberate—things for which we have no special art or science; and with the sort of hearers who cannot grasp many points in a single view, or follow a long chain of reasoning. Now we deliberate about such things as appear to admit of two possibilities. [Is a course expedient or inexpedient, a deed just or unjust, a statement true or false?] On matters which admit of no alternative, which necessarily were, or will be, or are, certainties, no one deliberates, at least not on that supposition—for nothing is to be gained by it.

It is possible to construct syllogisms and draw conclusions in a chain, working successively with the results of those that precede; or you may draw upon propositions that have not been thus proved, yet need proof because they are not commonly accepted. But, necessarily, the first of these processes will be hard to follow because of its length, for we assume the judge [audience] to be of but ordinary intelligence; and the second method will be unconvincing because the conclusions are drawn from premises that are not admitted nor commonly believed.

Accordingly, the enthymeme, and likewise the example, must deal with matters which as a rule are variable (the example corresponding to an induction, and the enthymeme being a syllogism); and the links in the chain must be few—seldom as many as the links in a normal chain of deductions. Thus, if one of the premises is a matter of common knowledge, the speaker need not mention it, since the hearer will himself supply the link. For example, in showing that Dorieus was victor in a contest where the prize is a chaplet, it is enough to say, 'He has won a victory at the Olympic games.' The speaker need not add that the prize there was a chaplet, for everyone knows it.

Let us grant that only a few of the premises of rhetorical deductions are necessarily admitted, and that the majority of cases on which we must decide, and into which we must inquire, may lie this way or that; for men deliberate and raise questions about the things they do, and human actions all belong to this class [of uncertainties or mere probabilities]; no human action, so to speak, is inevitable. And we see that, in Rhetoric, for the most part merely usual and contingent conclusions must be drawn from premises of the same sort; just as, in Logic, necessary conclusions must arise from premises that are determined—a matter that has been settled for us in the *Analytics* [*Prior Analytics* 1. 8]. All this being granted, it is clear that the premises from which a speaker derives his enthymemes are sometimes necessarily true, but in the main only generally true. In fact, the materials of enthymemes are (1) probabilities [εἰκότα] and (2) signs [σημεῖα]; so these two terms must correspond respectively with the two terms of the foregoing division. ['Probabilities' correspond to propositions that are generally true (true as a rule), and 'signs' to propositions that are (or seem to be) certain.] A 'probability' is that which usually happens or follows [—as hatred usually attends envy], yet not (as some would define it) *anything* that so happens, for the thing must belong to the class of things that may turn out this way or that. The probable, then, bears the same relation to that of which it is probable as a universal statement to a particular. [Sons tend to love their mothers, is a general statement; it is probable, then, that Orestes will love his mother.]

[A 'sign' (σημεῖον), as distinguished from a 'probable' generalization (one that is in itself likely), affects to be a proposition that is demonstrated by argument.] Signs are of two sorts: one bears, toward the statement it is to prove, the relation of a particular statement to a universal [—representing the inductive method], the other that of a universal to a particular [—representing the deductive method]. Of these, the second, the conclusive sign, is called τεκμήριον, the other, the non-conclusive sign, has no specific name. By conclusive signs I mean the statements from which a syllogism is derived. And hence it is that this sort of sign is called τεκμήριον, for when people take what they have said to be irrefutable, they think they proffer a τεκμήριον, as if the matter were now demonstrated and *concluded;* for in the old idiom τέκμαρ has the same meaning as πέρας [that is, 'limit'].

The sign having the relation of a particular to a universal would be illustrated by saying as an indication that wise men are just: 'Socrates was wise, and also just.' Of course this *is* a sign, yet it can be refuted, even though the statement be true, since the conclusion is not logically required. [You cannot argue: 'Socrates was wise and just; X is wise; therefore X is just.' The syllogism is faulty.] Take, however, either of the following. 'Here is a sign that the man is ailing: he has a fever.' Or, 'She has had a child, for she is in milk.' This kind of sign is infallible, and is the only one to be called τεκμήριον, for this alone, when the statement is true, is irrefutable. The kind having the relation of a universal to a particular would be illustrated if one were to say: 'This is a sign that he has a fever; his breathing is rapid.' Yet here again the point can be refuted, even if the statement [that his breathing is rapid] be true; for a patient may breathe hard without having a fever.

The nature of a probability, a sign, and a τεκμήριον, and the distinctions among them, have now been stated. A more detailed account of them may be found in the *Analytics* [*Prior Analytics* 2.27], with an explanation of the reason why some of the forms are inconclusive, and others are reducible to valid syllogisms.

As for the example, we have already stated that it is a kind of induction, and have noted the sort of materials with which, as an induction, it deals. The example does not concern the relation of part to whole [particular to universal], nor of whole to part, but of part to part, of like to like. When two things fall under the same genus, but one of them is better known than the other, the better-known is the example, [and the less-known is the thing exemplified.] Thus, suppose one contends that Dionysius, in asking for a body-guard, aims to set up a tyranny. The speaker may urge that Pisistratus, with a similar aim, once asked for a body-guard, and, on getting it, established himself as tyrant; and that Theagenes did the like at Megara. And so all the other cases that are known to the audience become each an example with reference to Dionysius, while hitherto we were unaware if he made the request with this design. All these cases [including that of Dionysius] fall under the same generic notion, that a man who aims at a tyranny asks for a body-guard.

So much for the materials from which those proofs are constructed that pass for demonstration. But in the case of enthymemes there is a most important distinction that virtually every one has ignored—a distinction that holds also of the syllogisms employed by Dialectic: some enthymemes, or syllogisms, belong properly to Rhetoric, or to Dialectic; others to other arts and faculties—to disciplines already established, or yet to be formulated. Accordingly, the distinction is overlooked by speakers, who, the more they encroach upon some field of special knowledge, overstep the more the province of Rhetoric and Dialectic.

This point will be clearer if we discuss it at greater length. Let me say, then, that the proper subjects of dialectical and rhetorical syllogisms are those with which the so-called *Topoi* [Common-places, Lines of Argument] are concerned; and by these I mean arguments that are applicable in common to the study of justice and physics, to the study of politics—to a large number of inquiries of divers sorts. Take the topic of *more* and *less*: this is of no greater service when we make a syllogism or utter an enthymeme about matters of right and wrong than when we make one about physics, or about anything else, different though these things are in kind. [Arguments as to degree (*more* just and *less* just, *longer* and *shorter,* etc.) are equally applicable to all subjects.] On the other hand, there are particular arguments, those derived from the propositions relative to a particular species or class of things. Thus there are propositions in physics [natural science] from which it is impossible to form an enthymeme or a syllogism for ethics, and propositions in ethics from which it is impossible to do so for physics, and so on through all the special subjects. The universal *topoi,* since they are not restricted to any special subject, will not give a man intelligence in any one science. As for the particular *topoi,* the better our choice of propositions, the more we imperceptibly glide into some discipline other than Dialectic and Rhetoric; for if we light upon true scientific principles, the art is no longer Dialectic or Rhetoric, but is the discipline based upon those principles. [The rhetorician must not go too far in his use of special or technical knowledge.] However, enthymemes are mostly formed from these particular and special *topoi;* not so many come from the universal *topoi.* Accordingly, in Rhetoric, as in the *Topica,* we must distinguish between the special and the general *topoi* from which enthymemes are to be derived. [See Aristotle, *Topics (Sophistic Elenchi)* 9. 9, and compare *Topics* 1. 10, 14 and 3. 5.] By special topics I mean the propositions peculiar to any given discipline, by general topics those that are common to all. We shall begin with the special.

First, however, let us ascertain what are the several kinds of Rhetoric; their number once determined, we can then ascertain separately the elements and propositions of each.

1. 3. [THE KINDS OF ORATORY.] The kinds of Rhetoric are three in number, corresponding to the three kinds of hearers to which speeches are addressed; for, a speech being the joint result of three things—the speaker, his subjects, and the person addressed—the end or object has reference to this last, namely the hearer; and the hearer must be either (1) a mere observer [critic], or (2 and 3) a judge [decider], and, if the latter, then either (2) a judge of things past or (3) a judge of things to come. One who (3) decides about the future is, for example, an ecclesiast [member of the Assembly]; one who (2) judges about the past is, say, the dicast [juror in a court of law]; while the person who (1) decides about the force and merit of the speech [the 'faculty' or art displayed in it] is the critic [observer, 'theorist']. It follows that there must be three kinds of speeches in Rhetoric, (1) deliberative, (2) forensic, and (3) epideictic. [That is, there are (1) speeches of counsel or advice (deliberation)—as political speeches addressed to an assembly or to the public on questions of State, but also, for example, a speech addressed to an individual (a ruler, or, indeed, any person who is to be advised); (2) judicial speeches, used in prosecution and defence (more generally, in any kind of attack or defence); and (3) panegyrical or declamatory speeches, in the nature of an exhibition or display, eulogies—in general, speeches of praise (or blame).]

(1) The elements of deliberation [counsel] are (*a*) exhortation [encour-

agement], (*b*) dissuasion; for, as advice given in private always has one or the other aspect, so is it with those who discuss matters of State in public —they either exhort or dissuade. (2) The elements of forensic speaking are (*a*) accusation, (*b*) defence, since the parties to a legal action will necessarily be engaged in either one or the other. (3) The elements of an epideictic speech are (*a*) praise and (*b*) blame. As for the divisions of time which severally belong to these several kinds of speakers, to the deliberative speaker belongs the future, for he gives advice about things to come, exhorting or dissuading; to the judicial pleader belongs the past, for it is always with regard to things already done that the one party accuses and the other defends; and to the epideictic speaker, above all, belongs the present, for every one praises or blames with regard to existing conditions [qualities], though a speaker often adds to his resources with reminiscences from the past and conjectures about the future. [See, for example, the *Funeral Oration* by Pericles in the *History* of Thucydides; and compare Shakespeare's Antony in *Julius Caesar* 3. 2. 76–7.]

For these three kinds of Rhetoric there are also three several ends. (1) The aim of the deliberative speaker concerns advantage and injury; for the one who exhorts recommends a course of action as better, and the one who dissuades deters us from it as worse; other considerations—of justice and injustice, of honor and dishonor—he makes subsidiary to this end [of the expedient]. (2) The aim of judicial pleaders concerns justice and injustice, and they in like manner make the other considerations subsidiary to these. (3) The aim of those who praise and blame concerns honor and dishonor, and such speakers likewise subordinate the other considerations to these.

As a sign that the end or aim of each kind of Rhetoric is such as we have stated, we may note that a speaker sometimes does not care to contest the other points. Thus a man on trial may not deny that the act was committed, nor deny that it did some damage; but that he is guilty of injustice he never will admit—if he admitted this, there would be no need of a trial. Similarly, deliberative speakers will often concede the other points, but not that the course they recommend is inexpedient, or the one they deprecate advantageous; while they are often unconcerned about the question whether it is not unjust for one city to enslave another, a neighbor and quite inoffensive. So, too, in praising and blaming, the speakers do not ask whether the deeds of a man were expedient or hurtful; nay, they often set it down to his praise that he performed some noble act at a sacrifice of his own advantage. Thus they praise Achilles for going to rescue his comrade Patroclus, when Achilles knew that it would lead to his own death, and that by refraining he might live on. For Achilles, death on such terms was nobler, while to live was expedient.

From what has been said [cf. 1. 2, p. 65] it is clear that these [expediency, justice, honor, and their opposites] are the subjects, primarily, for which the orator must have a fund of propositions. And for Rhetoric the propositions consist of the demonstrations [τεκμήρια, complete proofs], and the probabilities, and the signs, already mentioned. Every kind of syllogism is composed of propositions, and the enthymeme is the kind that is composed of the propositions we have named.

[Rhetoric deals with human action, past, present, or future.] Now things which are impossible cannot have been done in the past, or be done in the future, but only things which are possible; and things which have not occurred cannot have been done, and things which will not occur cannot be done hereafter. Consequently, the speaker, whether deliberative, forensic, or epideictic must be supplied with propositions [in the general *topoi*] regarding the possible and impossible, and on the question whether a thing has or has not occurred, is or is not to occur. Further, all men in praising or blaming, in exhorting or dissuading, in accusing or defending, try to prove, not merely the facts just mentioned [possibility or occurrence, past or future], but also that the good or evil, the honor or disgrace, the justice or injustice, is great or small, whether absolutely or in comparison with other cases. Obviously, then, the speaker will need propositions [again in the general *topoi*] regarding magnitude and smallness, and the greater and the less, considered generally, and also in comparing individual cases—for example, in arguing which is the greater or less good, the greater or lesser act of injustice; and similarly with the other terms [bad (harmful), just, honorable, and disgraceful]. . . .

. . . Let us now approach the subject in a different way, and get universal topics for enthymemes on all matters. We will indicate the refutative and the demonstrative topics side by side; and also the topics for apparent enthymemes—that is, spurious enthymemes which correspond to spurious syllogisms. . . .

2.23. [A LIST OF TOPICS.] (1) One *topos* of demonstrative enthymemes is from opposites. [If there are two things, one of which (B) is said to be true of the other (A), then] we must observe whether the opposite of A is true of the opposite of B. If it is not, you upset the original proposition [that B is true of A]; if it is, you establish the original proposition. For example: 'Self-control (A) is beneficial (B); for licentiousness is harmful.' Or as in the Messenian oration [of Alcidamas]: 'If war is the cause of our present evils, it is peace that we need to correct them.' Or [an example from (?) Agathon]:

> If, now, it is not fair to grow enraged
> When evil-doers injure us unwittingly,

> Then neither do we owe a grain of thanks
> To him who does us good when forced to do it.

Or [an example from Euripides (*Thyestes,* frag. 396, N.²]:

> But if falsehood is persuasive in this world,
> Be sure now that the opposite holds good:
> In the world there's many a true word ne'er believed.

(2) Another *topos* is from inflections of the same stem. What can or cannot be said of one inflected form [of a word] can or cannot be said of
another. Take, for example, the word 'just.' You may argue that 'just' does
not always mean 'beneficial,' otherwise 'justly' would always mean 'bene-
ficially'; but it is not, in fact, desirable to be justly put to death.

(3) Another *topos* is from correlative terms. If it is the fact that A gave
honorable or just treatment to B, you may argue that B received such
treatment from A; or if A had the right to command, that B was right
in obeying. So Diomedon the tax-collector argued about the farming of
taxes: 'If there is no disgrace in your selling the privilege of collecting them,
there is no disgrace in our buying it.' And if 'well' or 'justly' is true of the
person to whom a thing is done, you may argue that it is true of the doer.
But here the argument may be fallacious; for, granting that the man deserved what he got, it does not follow that he deserved it from you. Accordingly, we must keep the two questions distinct—must see (1) whether
A deserved what he suffered, and (2) whether B was right in so treating
him; and then we can apply our results in whichever way fits the case.
There actually are cases of this discrepancy, where the justice of the punish-
ment does not hinder the act of the man who inflicts it from being wrong.
So it is in the *Alcmaeon* of Theodectes. [Here Alcmaeon is asked whether
no one thought the death of his mother Eriphyle (whom he slew for her
deadly betrayal of his father) to be her just reward]:

> Did none abhor thy mother for her crime?

The son replies:

> Why, the question must be taken in two parts.

And when Alphesiboea asks, 'How?' he rejoins:

> Her they deemed fit to die; me, not to slay her.

Or, again, take the trial of Demosthenes [? the general] and the men who
killed Nicanor; since they were held justified in killing him, he was thought
to have deserved his death. Or take the case of the man [Euphron, tyrant
of Sicyon] who was killed [by Sicyonians] at Thebes; here the spokesman

[of the defendants] asked the judges to decide whether the man deserved to die, arguing that it could not be wrong to kill one who deserved it.

(4) Another *topos* is that *a fortiori* [from degrees of more and less]. Thus you may argue that if not even the gods are omniscient, much less are men; on the principle that, if a thing cannot be found where it is more likely to exist, of course you will not find it where it is less likely. Again, you may argue that a man who strikes his father will also strike his neighbors; on the principle that, if the less frequent thing occurs, then the more frequent thing occurs—for people strike their fathers less frequently than they strike their neighbors. So the argument may run; or it may run as follows. [You may argue that,] if a thing does not exist where it is more frequent, it does not exist where it is less frequent; or that, if it exists where it is less frequent, it exists where it is more frequent—according as you may need to prove that it does not exist [in a given instance], or that it does. And you may also employ this line of argument in a case of parity; so it is used in the lines [from the *Meleager* of (?) Antiphon, where (?) Oeneus says (?) to his wife Althaea whose brothers had been slain by Meleager, and who caused the death of Meleager]:

> Thou pitiest thy sire who lost his children;
> No pity, then, for Oeneus who has lost his gallant son?

Similarly you may argue that if Theseus did no wrong [? in abducting Helen], neither did Paris; or that if the sons of Tyndareus [Helen's brothers, Castor and Polydeuces] did no wrong [? in abducting her], neither did Paris; or that if Hector did well to slay Patroclus, so did Paris to slay Achilles. Or, again: 'If other followers of an art are not bad men, neither are philosophers.' Or: 'If their frequent condemnation to death does not show generals to be bad men, neither does the like show sophists to be bad men.' So, too: 'If it behoves each citizen among you to care for the reputation of your city, it behoves you all as a city to care for the glory of Greece.'

(5) Another *topos* is from considerations of time when. Thus Iphicrates, in the case against Harmodius, said: 'If before doing the deed I had demanded that, if I did it, I should have a statue, you would have given me one. Now that the deed is done, will you refuse me the statue? You readily make promises when you look for a benefit; do not withdraw them when you have reaped it.' Again, to induce the Thebans to let Philip pass through their land into Attica, [his ambassadors argued]: If he had pressed for this [as a condition] before he helped them against Phocis, they would have promised to do it. How monstrous to refuse him a passage now, merely because he let the matter go, and trusted them.

(6) Another *topos* is from utterances made by your opponent against you and turned against him. The turn is singularly effective, as may be seen

in the *Teucer* [of Sophocles]. It was employed by Iphicrates in his reply to Aristophon. 'Would you,' asked Iphicrates, 'betray the fleet for money?' 'Never!' said Aristophon. 'Very good,' was the reply. 'You, who are Aristophon, would not betray it—then would I, who am Iphicrates?' Our adversary, of course, must strike the audience as the more likely of the two to commit such a crime, or our speaker will make himself ridiculous—it would be ludicrous to retort in such fashion to an accuser like Aristides ['the just']. The function of the retort is to discredit the accuser, who as a rule poses for a better man than the defendant, a pretension which it is desirable to upset. But in general the device is absurd if a man upbraids others for doing what he does or would do himself, or urges them to do what he himself neither does nor ever would do.

(7) Another *topos* is from definition. Thus [Socrates in Plato's *Apology* 27 C–E defines his term]: 'What is "the divine"? It must be either a god or the work of a god. Well, then, any one who believes in the existence of a work of a god must needs believe in the existence of gods.' So Iphicrates [in meeting the charge of lowly birth defines and argues]: ' "True nobility" is *goodness*. There was nothing noble about Harmodius and Arisogeiton until they had done a noble deed.' And he argues further that he himself is more akin [to those heroes than his adversary (a contemporary Harmodius) is]: 'At any rate, my deeds are more akin to those of Harmodius and Aristogeiton than yours are.' Another example is found in the [*Apology for*] *Paris* [(?) by Polycrates]: 'We shall all admit that by "incontinent" people we mean those who are not content with the enjoyment of one love.' [And Paris was content with Helen.] Or take the reason Socrates gave for not visiting the court of Archelaus: ' "Ignominy" consists as much in not being able to replay a benefit as in not being able to requite an evil.' Each of the persons mentioned defines his term, gets at its essential meaning, and then proceeds to reason from it on the point at issue.

(8) Another *topos* is from the various senses of a word. See our treatise *On Topics* [1. 15; 2, 3] for the correct use of [ambiguous] terms. [Or perhaps: 'An example, "rightly," is found in the *Topics*.' (Consider the various senses of 'rightly'; establish the sense which fits your case—'rightly' in the sense of 'technically right,' or in the sense of 'with justice'; and then argue from that sense.—But this example is not found in the extant *Topics*.)]

(9) Another *topos* is from [logical] division. Thus you may argue: 'All men do wrong from one of three motives, A, B, C. In my case, the first two of these motives are out of the question; and as for the third, C, the prosecution itself does not allege this.'

(10) Another *topos* is from induction. Thus, beginning with [?Antiphanes'] *Woman of Peparethus,* you might argue that the women everywhere can settle questions touching the legitimacy of the children. This

happened, you may add, at Athens, in the case between the orator Mantias and his son, where the mother established the legitimacy of the son; and happened, again, at Thebes, in the case between Ismenias and Stilbon, where Dodonis proved that Ismenias was the father of her child Thettaliscus, and the latter in consequence was declared to be the son of Ismenias. Another instance of induction may be taken from the *Law* of Theodectes: 'If we do not entrust our horses to men who have mishandled other people's horses, nor our ships to those who have capsized the ships of others, and if this is our way with everything else, then beware of employing for the safety of our State men [mercenaries] who have ill protected the safety of others.' Or take the argument of Alcidamas that all men honor the wise: 'Thus the Parians honored Archilochus, though he had a bitter tongue; the Chians Homer, though he did not reside among them; the Mityleneans Sappho, though she was a woman; the Lacedaemonians even made Chilon a member of their senate, though they are the least literary of people; the Italian Greeks did the like to Pythagoras; and the people of Lampsacus gave Anaxagoras, though an alien, a public burial, and honor him to this very day.' . . . [Or take the argument that states are sure to prosper when they get their laws from philosophers:] 'For Athens grew prosperous under the laws of Solon, and the Lacedaemonians under those of Lycurgus, while at Thebes no sooner did philosophers [Epaminondas and Pelopidas] become the leading men than the State began to prosper.'

(11) Another *topos* is from an existing decision. The decision may be on the point at issue, or on a point like it, or on the opposite point—preferably a decision that has been accepted by all men at all times; but if not that, then a decision accepted by the majority of mankind; or by wise or good men, all or most of them; or by the actual judges of our question; or by men whose authority these judges accept, or by masters of the situation whom they cannot gainsay, or by persons whom it is not fitting to gainsay, such as the gods, or a father, or our teachers. Thus Autocles said, in attacking Mixidemides: 'How! were the Dread Goddesses [the Eumenides] content to submit to the judgment of the Areopagus, and Mixidemides is not?' Or as Sappho said 'Death is an evil; the gods have so judged it, or they would die.' Or take the reply of Aristippus to Plato, who, as Aristippus thought, had said something rather dogmatically: 'Well, our friend,' meaning Socrates, 'never talked that way.' So Agesipolis, having first consulted the oracle [of Zeus] at Olympia, inquired of Apollo at Delphi 'whether he took the same view as his father,' implying that it would be a shame to contradict his father. And so Isocrates [*Helen* 18–38] argued that Helen was a worthy woman, since Theseus decided that she was; and Paris a worthy man [*ibid.* 41–8], since the [three] goddesses preferred him to all others; and Evagoras, again, says Isocrates [*Evagoras* 51–2], was a worthy man, since

Conon, after he 'met with his misfortune' [at Aegospotami], 'went straight to Evagoras,' trying nobody else on the way.

(12) Another *topos* is from the parts of a subject, taken separately. [The whole is the genus, and its parts are the species. What is true, or untrue, of the whole must be true, or untrue, of part 1, part 2, etc.; and you argue from part by part to the whole.] As in our treatise *On Topics* [2. 4; 4. 1]: 'What kind of motion is the soul?' It must be *this* kind, or *this* kind.' The *Socrates* of Theodectes will supply an illustration: 'What temple has he profaned? To which of the gods recognized by the State has he failed to pay honor?'

(13) Another *topos* is from consequences. Since it commonly happens that a given thing has consequences both good and bad, you may argue from these [to their antecedents] in urging or dissuading, in prosecuting or defending, in praising or blaming. For example: education results in unpopularity, a bad consequence, and in wisdom, a good consequence. And so you may argue: It is not well to be educated, since it is not well to be unpopular. Or: It is well to be educated, since it is well to be wise. The *Art of Rhetoric* of Callippus is simply this *topos,* with that of Possibility and the other [two common *topoi*] which we have discussed above superadded.

(14) There is another *topos* when we have to urge or dissuade with reference to contrary alternatives, and have to apply the method just stated to both. The difference between this *topos* and the foregoing is that there any two things are contrasted, while here the things contrasted are opposites. For instance, the priestess urged her son not to engage in public speaking: 'For,' said she, 'if you speak honestly, men will hate you; if you speak dishonestly, the gods will hate you.' [But one may deal with the contrary alternatives thus:] 'Now you *ought* to engage in public speaking; for if you speak honestly, the gods will love you; if you speak dishonestly, men will love you.' There we have in effect the proverbial 'buying the marsh along with the salt' [—the unwholesome marsh with the valuable salt]. And for this form of argument we have the term 'criss-cross' [*blaisosis* = 'knock-knees'—with legs diverging like the extended hind-legs of a frog], when each of two opposites has both a good and a bad consequence opposite respectively to each other.

(15) Another *topos* comes from the fact that men approve one thing openly, and another in their secret thoughts. In public they make a great show of praising what is just and noble; but inwardly they prefer what is to their own advantage. From the premises of your opponent you must try to draw the inference which he does not. [If he assumes a moral tone, you appeal to the inward self-interest of the audience; if he assumes that men act from self-interest alone, you appeal to the motives of justice and

nobility which they openly profess.] No other *topos* of paradox is so effective as this.

(16) Another *topos* is from the proportion between this and that result. For example, when they would compel the son of Iphicrates, a youth under the legal age, to discharge a public duty because he was tall, Iphicrates said: 'If you make big boys count as men, you will have to enact little men into boys.' So Theodectes says in his *Law*: 'You enfranchise mercenaries like Strabax and Charidemus for meritorious service; will you not exile those among the mercenaries who have wrought irreparable harm?'

(17) Another *topos* is the argument from identity of results to the identity of their antecedents. Thus Xenophanes said that to affirm the birth of the gods was as impious as to say that they die; either way, it results that there is a time when they do not exist. [You argue from this identical result (which contradicts the notion, 'the gods are eternal') that the two antecedents are equally untenable.] This type of argument assumes for a general rule that the result of any given thing is absolutely constant. For example: 'You are about to decide upon the value, not of Isocrates [? Socrates], but of philosophical pursuits in general. Or again, 'to give earth and water means slavery [to Persia]; or 'to share in the Common Peace' means obeying [? Philip's] orders. [Of the alternative arguments, positive and negative,] the speaker must take the one that suits his purpose.

(18) Another *topos* depends on the fact that men do not always make the same choice on a later as on an earlier occasion, but reverse it. For example, take the following enthymeme [from Lysias (*Orations* 34. 11)]: 'When we were exiles, we fought to return; now that we have returned, it would be monstrous to choose exile rather than fight.' In the one case, that is, they chose to preserve their homes at the cost of fighting, in the other to avoid fighting at the cost of deserting their homes.

(19) Another *topos* is the treatment of some conceivable motive as the actual motive for an event or state of affairs; for example, the argument that A has given something to B with the motive of paining B by withdrawing it. This is the motive in the lines:

> Heaven to many men gives great prosperity,
> Not out of favor, but that later they
> May come to grief the more conspicuously.

Similarly in the passage from the *Meleager* of Antiphon:

> Not for to slay the boar [the heroes came],
> But for to witness unto Greece the valor
> Of doughty Meleager.

And similarly the argument [of Ajax against Odysseus] in the *Ajax* of Theodectes, that Diomede chose Odysseus [for his companion (cf. *Iliad*

10. 218–54)], not to do him honor, but in order that his companion might be an inferior man to himself. That is a possible motive for the act. [This *topos* belongs rather to forensic speaking.]

(20) Another *topos* is common to forensic and deliberative speaking. Here you consider the incentives and deterrents as the motives people have for doing or avoiding the acts in question. These are the conditions which, according as they are for or against us, make us act or refrain from action. We are moved to act if the thing is possible, easy, and advantageous to us or our friends, or hurtful to our enemies; this is true even if the act is damaging to us, so long as our loss is outweighed by a solid gain. From these considerations a deliberative speaker will urge a course of action; and from the opposite considerations he will argue against it. And from the same considerations a forensic speaker will argue in accusation or defence —arguing from the deterrent motives from the defence, and from the incentives for the prosecution. This *topos* represents the whole *Art of Rhetoric* of Pamphilus as well as that of Callippus. [But see, on Callippus, No. 13, above.]

(21) Another *topos* is from things that are thought to occur though they seem incredible. You may argue that no one would have believed in such an occurrence if the thing had not actually, or almost, happened; even that it is more likely to be true because it is incredible. [That the incredible thing is believed is a proof that it happened;] for the things men believe are either facts or probabilities, and hence, if the thing in question is neither credible nor probable, it must be true, since the reason why it is believed is surely not its credibility or plausibility. An example is the reply made by Androcles of Pitthus when he was arraigning the [existing state of the] law. The assembly was in uproar when he said: 'Our laws need a law to correct them.' [This the audience found incredible; so he added:] 'Why, so do fish need salt [to preserve them], however unlikely and incredible it is that, bred as they are in the brine, they should need salt; and olive-cakes need olive-oil, however incredible it is that the source of olive-oil should need it.'

(22) Another *topos*, useful in refuting an opponent, is this: See what inconsistencies you can find in all the facts—conflicting dates, acts, and statements. And do this under three separate heads. First, with respect to your opponent; for example: 'He says he loves you—yet he conspired with the Thirty.' Secondly, with respect to yourself; for example: 'He says I am litigious—yet he cannot prove that I ever engaged in a single lawsuit.' Thirdly, with respect to you and your opponent together; for example: 'He never has lent one of you a penny, but I ransomed a goodly number of you.'

(23) Another *topos* is useful for persons or causes that have fallen under

odium or slanderous suspicion. Here you state the reason why the facts appear in a wrong light; for then there is something that accounts for the false impression. Thus a mother who had palmed off her son on another woman was thought to be his mistress beause she embraced him; but when the cause was explained, the calumny was quashed. Thus, too, in the *Ajax* of Theodectes Odysseus tells Ajax the reason why he is not thought braver than Ajax, though he really is so.

(24) Another *topos* consists in arguing from the presence or absence of the cause to the existence or non-existence of the effect. If you prove the cause, you at once prove the effect; and conversely nothing can exist without its cause. Thus Thrasybulus accused Leodamas of having had his name recorded as a criminal on the Acropolis, and of erasing it in the days of the Thirty Tyrants; and Leodamas replied: 'Impossible! The Thirty would have trusted me all the more if my hostility to the populace were there on record.'

(25) Another *topos* for the deliberative and the forensic speaker is this: See if it is or was possible to devise a better course than the speaker is recommending, or than is or was taken. If this better course was not taken, the accused obviously has not done the deed; for no one willingly and wittingly chooses a bad method.—This argument, however, is fallacious; for it often becomes clear after the event how an affair could have been better managed, though before the event this was not clear.

(26) There is another *topos* when an intended action runs counter to one's previous actions. Bring them together and compare them. [And, in deliberative speaking, advise accordingly.] Thus, when the people of Elea asked Xenophanes whether they should or should not sacrifice to Leucothea [who as a mortal was Ino,] and mourn for her, his advice was: 'If you think her a goddess, do not sing the dirge; if you think her a human being, do not sacrifice to her.'

(27) Another *topos* is from previous mistakes, which you make the basis of accusation or defence. Thus, in the *Medea* of Carcinus the accusers allege that Medea has slain her children: 'At any rate,' it is urged, 'they have disappeared'—Medea having made the mistake of sending the children away. She defends herself by arguing that it is not her children, but Jason, whom she would have slain; for, supposing her to be capable of the other murder, it would have been a blunder for her not to do this [not to kill him]. This *topos* and species of enthymeme constitute the whole Art of Rhetoric before the treatise of Theodorus.

(28) Another *topos* is from the meaning of names. Thus Sophocles plays on the name [Sidero (*sideros* = hardened iron), in his *Tyro*—the reference being to the cruelty to Tyro of her step-mother]:

Steel, truly, like the name thou bearest.

This type of inference is common in panegyrics of the gods. Thus, too, Conon called Thrasybulus *rash counselor*. And Herodicus said of [the orator] Thrasymachus, 'You are ever *rash in combat'*; of Polus, 'You are ever a *colt'*; and of the legislator Draco that his laws were 'not the laws of a human being, but of a *dragon'*—so cruel were they. So the Hecuba of Euripides [*Troades* 990] says of Aphrodite:

> And rightly the name of the goddess begins as does folly [*aphrosyne*].

And so Chaeremon [? in his *Dionysus*]:

> Pentheus, prophetic name of grief [*penthos*] to come.

Refutative Enthymemes are better liked than the Demonstrative, because the refutative kind brings out, in small compass, two opposing arguments, and the two things, side by side, are plainer to the audience. But of all syllogisms, whether refutative or demonstrative, those are most applauded of which we foresee the conclusion from the outset—so long as it is not too obvious, for part of our pleasure is at our own sagacity—or those that we just keep up with as they are stated.

2.24. [A LIST OF SHAM ENTHYMEMES. Besides genuine arguments (the foregoing) which the honest speaker may use, there are spurious arguments which he must be prepared to meet.] Since the enthymeme is a kind of syllogism; and since there can be syllogisms that look genuine, but are not; it follows that, beside genuine enthymemes, there must be enthymemes that look genuine, but are spurious.

(1) Among the *topoi* of these Spurious Enthymemes the first is from the Diction; and under this head there are two sub-heads.

(*a*) In Dialectic a final statement can be made to pass for the conclusion of a logical process, when no such process has been performed: 'So it is not thus or thus'; 'So, too, it must be thus or thus.' Similarly, then, in Rhetoric a compact and antithetical sentence will pass for an enthymeme. This sort of language is the very habitat of the enthymeme, and it seems that the fallacy resides in the structure of the sentence. In giving their language the air of a logical process, speakers find it useful to summarize the results of a number of their previous arguments; thus [Isocrates (*Evagoras* 65-9)]: 'Some he saved'; 'others be avenged'; 'he liberated Greece.' Each of these points has been proved from something else; when they are brought together, it seems as if we had some novel conclusion.

(*b*) The second head is that of homonyms [equivocal terms, the same or similar names for different things]. Thus [Polycrates] says that the *mouse* is a noble creature, since it gives its name to the most august of all rites— the *My*steries—for such they are. Or you may put into the eulogy of a dog an allusion to the dog-star of heaven; or to Pan, on whom you may quote Pindar:

> Blest one, whom the gods of Olympus
> Call the manifold dog of Cybele;

or you may argue: 'Since it is a great shame to have no dog [*kuna*] in the house, plainly it is honorable to be a dog [i.e., a *Cynic*]. Another example is the statement that'Hermes is the readiest of the gods to go shares [in communicating], for about no other god is there a phrase like "Go shares in Hermes' luck"' [addressed to a lucky finder]. Another, that 'Speech [*logos*] is the best of things, since good men are not "worth money," but "worth esteem"' [*logos*]; the phrase *logou axion* having more than one sense.

(2) Another *topos* consists in asserting of the whole what is true of the parts, or asserting of the parts what is true of the whole. A whole and a combination of its parts seem to be identical, but very often that is not the case. The procedure is to combine, or to disjoin, as may the better serve the purpose. This is the method of Euthydemus, when, for example, he argues: 'You know there is a trireme in the Peiraeus.' The man knows the details separately. [(?) You know there is a trireme; you know this in the Peiraeus.] Similar is the argument that one who knows the letters knows the whole verse, since the verse is the same thing as the letters which compose it; or again that, if a double dose of a thing is harmful, a single dose cannot be called wholesome, since it is absurd that two good things should make a bad one. Put thus, the enthymeme is refutative; put as follows, demonstrative: For one good thing cannot be made up of two bad things. The whole *topos* is fallacious. Take, again, the praise of Thrasybulus by Polycrates, that he 'put down thirty tyrants'; here the speaker adds up the parts. [—An illicit combination; Polycrates argued that Thrasybulus deserved thirty rewards, one for each tyrant.] Or take the argument in the *Orestes* of Theodectes; here you go from the part to the whole [—an illicit division]:

> 'Tis right that whoso slays her spouse should die.

'And it is right that a son should avenge his father. Well, then, these two things are what [Orestes] has done.' [But this is fallacious;] for perhaps the two put together do not form one right act. The fallacy might also be described as one of omission, since the speaker does not say by whose hand she [the mother who slays her husband] should die.

(3) Another *topos* consists in the use of indignation, whether to support a case or to upset it. Such means are used when the speaker, without having proved his case, elaborates on the nature of the deed. If the defence thus amplifies, it produces the impression that the accused is innocent; if the

prosecutor goes into a passion, it produces an impression that the accused is guilty. There is no genuine enthymeme; the listener falsely infers guilt or innocence; the fact has not been proved.

(4) Another *topos* is from a 'sign' [a single instance, used as a logical proof]. Here, too, we have no logical argument. For example, suppose some one says: 'Lovers are useful to their countries; for the love of Harmodius and Aristogeiton caused the downfall of the tyrant Hipparchus.' [The single case does not prove the rule.] Or suppose that one calls Dionysius a thief 'because he is a rascal.' Here, too, we have no logical argument; not every rascal is a thief, though every thief is a rascal.

(5) Another *topos* is from the accidental, [treated as if it were essential]. Thus Polycrates says in his eulogy of mice that 'they came to the rescue' by gnawing through the [enemy's] bowstrings. Or one might urge that an invitation to dine is a very great honor, for [in Sophocles' *Assembly of the Greeks*] it was the lack of an invitation [from Agamemnon] that enraged Achilles against the Greeks at Tenedos. What really enraged him, however, was the slight; it was quite accidental that this took the shape of his not being invited to dinner.

(6) Another *topos* is the fallacious argument from consequence. Thus in the *Apology for Paris* [of Polycrates] it is argued that Paris was high-minded, since he disdained the society of the crowd, and dwelt by himself on Mount Ida. Because men of lofty souls act thus, therefore we are to believe that Paris, too, was high-minded. Or, again, if a man goes smartly dressed, and roams about at night, he must be a rake, for such are the ways of rakes. A like argument is [the one on the happiness of beggars and exiles]: Beggars sing and dance in the temples; and exiles can live wherever they please; such liberties are enjoyed by those we account happy; and hence all who enjoy them may be regarded as happy. But there is a difference: How [under what circumstances do men enjoy them]? Accordingly, this *topos* also falls under the head of fallacies of omission.

(7) Another *topos* consists in treating as a cause what is not a cause; for example, in taking what happened along with or before a thing as the cause of it. People assume *post hoc* to be *propter hoc;* and this is especially true of men in public life. Thus Demades said that the policy of Demosthenes was the cause of all the mischief; 'for after it came the war.'

(8) Another *topos* consists in omitting any reference to time and manner [the time when, and the circumstances under which, a thing was done]. Thus, [Polycrates argues] that Paris had a right to take Helen, since her father left her free to choose [a husband]. [Here the element of time is neglected;] for she doubtless was not to be perpetually free—the permission concerned only her first choice, beyond which her father's authority did not extend. Or one might argue that to strike a free citizen is an act of wanton outrage; this is

not true, however, in all circumstances—it is true only when the act is unprovoked.

(9) Further, [in public speaking] as in 'eristical' combats, a spurious syllogism [enthymeme] may arise from a substitution of the absolute for what is not absolute but particular. Thus in Dialectic it may be argued that the nonexistent *is*, since the non-existent *is* non-existent, and that the unknowable can be known, since we can know that it is unknown. [Here the universal statement, 'the unknowable can be known,' is substituted for the particular statement, 'the only thing we can know about the unknowable is that it cannot be known.'] Similarly, then, in Rhetoric a spurious enthymeme may arise from the confusion of particular probability with probability absolute; but the probability of a thing is not something universal. As Agathon holds:

> And some perchance will say 'tis probable
> That many improbable things will happen to men.

Since what is against probability does occur, it follows that something improbable is likely to occur. If that is so, the improbable will be probable. [Here the fallacy lies in the fact that] probability is not something absolute. [The probability or improbability of an occurrence is not with regard to things in general, but with regard to specific antecedents.] As, in Eristic, it is the failure to add a limitation of relationship, of reference, or of manner, that does the trick, so here: the probability is not general, but specific. It is out of this *topos* [of the likely and unlikely] that the *Art of Rhetoric* of Corax is composed. For example, if the defendant is not open to the charge—if, say, a weakling is accused [by a strong man] of assault and battery—the defence will be: 'It is not probable.' But if the defendant—a strong man, say—is open to the charge, still the defence will be: 'It is not probable, for it was sure to be thought so.' [The strong man could be sure that people would think him likely to use violence.] And similarly with any other charge. [Whatever it be,] the defendant must either be open or not open to it; in either case, then, there is an apparent probability. In the first case, however, there *is* an actual probability; but in the second the probability is not absolute—it is, as we have said, particular. This [fallacious procedure of substituting the absolute] is what is meant by 'making the worse appear the better cause.' And therein lies the reason why people, rightly, could not abide the training advertised by Protagoras. The thing is a [logical] fraud; the probability concerned is not genuine but spurious, and has no place in any art except [mere] rhetoric and quibbling.

AIDS TO STUDY

A brief outline of the foregoing selections may help in the study of them:

Book I, Chapter 1

Both rhetoric and dialectic have in common that they deal with the realm of common knowledge; the art of rhetoric is the finding of ways by which we speak persuasively. (Paragraph 1.)

Books on rhetoric are defective because they confuse the proper functions of the orator and his audience and because they dwell on minor parts of rhetoric, such as how to 'butter up' the audience, and ignore the heart of the art, which is the finding of the best possible argument for one's position. Moreover, handbooks on rhetoric tend to ignore deliberative rhetoric and deal only with forensic rhetoric. (Paragraphs 2–7.)

Rhetoric has four values: it prevents the triumph of fraud and injustice; it gives us a more general means of instruction than any of the sciences; it makes us see both sides of any case; and it provides a man a means of defending himself or his position reasonably. (Paragraph 8.)

Book I, Chapter 2

Rhetoric, then, is the art of finding the available means of persuasion for any particular case. These means are of two sorts: (1) evidence of the specific case— 'facts'—which has but to be used; Aristotle calls such means 'non-artistic'; (2) seeing the relationship of general ideas to the specific case at hand; Aristotle calls such means 'artistic,' and they constitute the body of his system of rhetoric. (Paragraphs 11–12.)

Artistic means of persuasion are of three sorts: the establishment of the character of the speaker; the securing of emotional sympathy of the audience; and the finding of the logical grounds upon which a matter really rests. (Paragraphs 13–16.)

The rhetorician, then, must study human character and emotions, and he must know logic and ethics. Chiefly, he must know how to apply general principles to specific cases, or see which general principles are implicit in specific cases. For rhetoric deals with general classes and principles, not isolated facts or events. The rhetorician must distinguish between matters of probability and matters of certainty. (Paragraphs 17–26.)

Chiefly the rhetorician is involved with the application of the commonplaces of knowledge to cases at hand. Some general arguments apply to all kinds of events; others apply only to specific kinds of events. The rhetorician uses both sorts, but the general sort is more properly part of the study of persuasion. (Paragraphs 27–29.)

Book, I, Chapter 3

Rhetoric is of three sorts, depending on the relation to the audience. In deliberative rhetoric, the audience is to judge whether or not a future action is to be taken; in forensic or judicial rhetoric, the audience is to judge a matter that has already taken place; in epideictic or declamatory rhetoric, the audience is to observe critically whether something or somebody is to be praised or blamed. The deliberative rhetorician either encourages or discourages an act on the part of the listener; the forensic rhetorician either accuses or defends someone in connection with an action of the past; the epideictic rhetorician either praises or blames a person or situation of the present. The first deals with matters of advantage, the second with matters of justice, the last with matters of honor. (Paragraphs 30–32.)

Given these aims of his art, the rhetorician must find those general maxims which apply to matters of expediency, justice, and honor. (Paragraphs 33–36.)

Book II, Chapter 19

Four lines of argument common to any sort of problem are:
(1) Do the events in question fall in the realm of the possible or in the realm of the impossible? (The topic of the possible and the impossible.)
(2) Are there to be found unavoidable connections between causes and effects in the situation at hand? (The topic of past fact.)
(3) Are effects in the future from causes known in the present inevitable, likely, or unlikely? (The topic of future fact.)
(4) What is the comparative greatness or smallness of the fact or event in question? (The topic of size.)

Book II, Chapter 23

A list of topics, or lines of argument, which may apply in many cases. These are discussed in the notes which follow.

Plato's dialogue, which precedes these selections from Aristotle, was concerned with the ethics of rhetoric—with what is *proper* or *good* persuasion, as opposed to *false* or *bad* persuasion. Aristotle is concerned with questions of another sort: (1) if rhetoric is an art or science, how does it differ from other arts or sciences? (2) what is the relationship between rhetoric and logic, law, fact, etc.? (3) what sorts of things need men be persuaded about? and (4) what, after all, does persuade intelligent men? In short, Aristotle tries to set rhetoric in the scheme of human knowledge and analyzes its aims and scope and methods. Along with this, he gives a good bit of specific, practical advice to the young rhetorician.

Much of Aristotle's treatment of the subject has struck men through the ages as an elaboration of the obvious. And perhaps this is one reason the work has been considered a great work, for many great works point out what, after it is pointed out, we seem to have known all along. The rhetoric of Aristotle is a systematic treatment of good common sense.

Because it is common sense, the treatment is very concise: these selections may well strike the reader as an outline, and a not very greatly expanded one. It will not yield to a cursory reading: it must be read, as Coleridge liked to say, at all times with attention and oftentimes with thought. That is, we must pay close attention at every point, because Aristotle is everywhere summarizing; and very occasionally we must make some intellectual connections of our own: we find ourselves wondering, 'What is the connection between these two sentences?' and we must stop a moment to figure the connection out. We are called upon to study this selection in a way we were not called upon with Plato's dialogue.

Since every paragraph of this selection might prove a topic for extended thought or discussion, it is impossible to present a thoroughgoing note for it, without making the commentary book-length. But a few general remarks may help by suggesting the general drift of the selection.

Aristotle assumes that persuasion involves three things: (1) the character of the speaker, for unless we respect the speaker he is not likely to persuade us of anything; (2) the feelings of the listeners, for listeners must be disposed to consider our arguments seriously; and (3) the good sense of our argument, for we should assume that rational people will not, in the long run, agree with nonsense. Aristotle's criticism of the textbooks on rhetoric of his day is that they dwell on only a portion of this full view; and indeed, they give their attention primarily to means of establishing the character of the speaker and managing the emotions of the listeners. In short, they dwell on how to pull the wool over the eyes of people.

Aristotle insists that the real heart of rhetoric lies rather in the good sense of the argument itself: the best way to persuade people is to have a good case for our point of view, for one cannot fool all the people all the time—indeed, Aristotle had faith that one cannot fool most of the people any of the time.

Hence it is that he concerns himself primarily with how to make a good case. A convincing argument ('proof') stems from two sources: (1) various sorts of evidence, which have only to be used, and (2) arguments, which we have to find for ourselves. The first Aristotle calls 'non-artistic,' for they are not within the art of persuasion. The second he calls 'artistic,' for they are part of the art of persuasion. Let us pose a case and perhaps this will come clear. Suppose you return to your dormitory room and find your roommates, Bill and Joe, in a quarrel: Joe insists that Bill has cheated in a card game. Bill denies it. Now, both men are honor students; both are on the student tribunal; they have played cards together often all year long; today they were not playing for money. There are no witnesses; you have no evidence or 'non-artistic' proofs. You are thrown back on finding your own method of persuading yourself whether Bill or Joe is telling the truth (after all, if you are living with a liar, you want to know who he is; you cannot remain indifferent about the matter). What do you do?

Aristotle says there are a set of sources for persuasion available to you in any argument—he calls these *topoi* (or 'topics' or 'commonplaces'). For instance, you may reason that since these boys have played cards together for several months without cheating, the likelihood of cheating on this occasion is not great (*topos* 4: the argument from degree of more or less); or you may reason that since they have not cheated for money before, surely one would not cheat now for no stake (*topos* 5: the argument from time); or you might reason that, since Bill seems in most respects as honest as Joe, Joe's accusation may suggest some fault in his own character (*topos* 6: opponent's utterance turned against him); or you may reason that since there appears no motive for Bill's cheating, he very likely didn't do so (*topos* 9: logical division); or you may reason from what Aristotle calls 'induction,' but what we might call 'analogy' (*topos* 10): if through the months Bill has not taken our money or copied our lessons, surely he is not likely to cheat us in a card game; or you may argue from 'existing decisions' (*topos* 11) that since faculty and students generally have decided Bill is an honest man, his cheating his roommate is not likely; or you may argue from incentives and deterrents (*topos* 20) that since Bill has nothing to gain and much to lose by cheating, he was not likely to be motivated to cheat. I have given but some of the arguments you can frame in defense of Bill; surely many may also be found in justification of Joe (*topos* 21, 'incredible occurrences,' for instance).

The point is that in any such case, there are arguments which we can and do find for the position we take on any problem which confronts us. It is the mastering of these arguments which is essential for the good rhetorician, for common sense is often quite as persuasive as so-called 'facts.' And Aristotle's 'topics' are all matters of common sense; that is, they are instances of putting generally accepted logical procedures to work on a case at hand. The 'finding' of these 'artististic' proofs is not a matter of dreaming them up; it is rather a matter of recognizing which of the conventions of logic (Aristotle's 'dialectic') may apply sensibly to a matter at hand. This sort of 'finding' constitutes the most important part of rhetoric, traditionally called 'invention' or 'discovery'—the discovery of which sorts of intellectual appeals are applicable to the discussion of a disputed matter.

An Outline of Roman School Rhetoric

xxxi. 'And yet I think, Sulpicius,' continued Crassus, 'that after hearing them you will be less likely to wonder at my observations than to decide that, when you were longing to hear them, there was no ground for your longing. For I shall tell no mystery, nothing worthy of your waiting, nothing that you have not heard already, or that is new to anyone. For to begin with, in regard to what befits a free-born man of liberal education, I will not deny that I learned those commonplace and well-worn maxims of teachers in general: first, that the duty of an orator is to speak in a style fitted to convince; next that every speech has to do either with the investigation of a general question, wherein no persons or occasions are indicated, or with a problem that is concerned with specific individuals and times; moreover that in both cases, whatever the subject for debate, it is usual for inquiry to be made in respect thereof, either whether a deed was done or, if it was done, what is its character, or again by what name is it known or, as some add, whether it appears to have been done lawfully; further that contentions also arise out of the construction of a document, wherein there is some ambiguity or contradiction, or something is so expressed that the written word is at variance with the intention; and again that to all these kinds certain modes of proof are assigned as appropriate. Again I heard that, of such questions as are distinct from general issues, some have their place in courts of justice, others in deliberations; while there was yet a third kind, which had to do with the extolling or reviling of particular persons; and that there were prescribed commonplaces which we were to employ in the law-courts where equity was

Reprinted by permission of the publishers and The Loeb Classical Library from *Cicero, De Oratore,* trans. by E. W. Sutton and H. Rockham, Cambridge, Mass.: Harvard University Press, 1942.

84

our aim; others for use in deliberations, all of which were arranged for the benefit of those to whom we might be giving counsel; and others again in panegyric, wherein the sole consideration was the greatness of the individuals concerned. And, since all the activity and ability of an orator falls into five divisions, I learned that he must first hit upon what to say; then manage and marshal his discoveries, not merely in orderly fashion, but with a discriminating eye for the exact weight as it were of each argument; next go on to array them in the adornments of style; after that keep them guarded in his memory; and in the end deliver them with effect and charm: I had also been taught that, before speaking on the issue, we must first secure the goodwill of our audience; that next we must state our case; afterwards define the dispute; then establish our own allegations; subsequently disprove those of the other side; and in our peroration expand and reinforce all that was in our favour, while we weakened and demolished whatever went to support our opponents.

XXXII. 'I had listened also to the traditional precepts for the embellishment of discourse itself: that we must speak, in the first place, pure and correct Latin, secondly with simple lucidity, thirdly with elegance, lastly in a manner befitting the dignity of our topics and with a certain grace; and on these several points I had learnt particular maxims. Moreover I had seen art called in to aid even those qualities which are peculiarly the endowment of nature: for example, concerning delivery and the memory, I had taken a taste of certain rules which, though concise, involved much practice.

'For it is matters like these that employ nearly all the learning of your professors; and if I were to call this learning useless, I should be lying. For in fact it contains certain reminders, as it were, for the orator, as to the standard he must apply on each occasion, and must keep in mind, if he is not to wander from whatever course he has set himself. But to my thinking the virtue in all the rules is, not that orators by following them have won a reputation for eloquence, but that certain persons have noted and collected the doings of men who were naturally eloquent: thus eloquence is not the offspring of the art, but the art of eloquence: even so, as I said before, I do not reject art, for though perhaps hardly essential to right speaking, still it is no ignoble help towards right knowledge. There is also a certain practical training that you must undergo—though indeed you two are already in full career,—I mean it is for those who are at the start of their race, and can even thus early learn beforehand and practise, by a training like that for the games, what will have to be done in the fighting-line, so to speak, of the Courts.'

'This training,' said Sulpicius, 'is the very thing we wish to understand: and none the less we are longing to hear you on those precepts of the art over which you have briefly run, although those too are not unknown to us. But of them presently; for the moment we want your opinion on the training itself.'

XXXIII. 'I certainly approve,' replied Crassus, 'of what you yourselves are in the habit of doing, when you propound some case, closely resembling such as are brought into Court, and argue it in a fashion adapted as nearly as possible to real life. Most students however, in so doing, merely exercise their voices (and that in the wrong way), and their physical strength, and whip up their rate of utterance, and revel in a flood of verbiage. This mistake is due to their having heard it said that it is by speaking that men as a rule become speakers. But that other adage is just as true,—that by speaking badly men very easily succeed in becoming bad speakers. This is why, in those exercises of your own, though there is a value in plenty of extempore speaking, it is still more serviceable to take time for consideration, and to speak better prepared and more carefully. But the chief thing is what, to tell the truth, we do least (for it needs great pains which most of us shirk),—to write as much as possible. The pen is the best and most eminent author and teacher of eloquence, and rightly so. For if an extempore and casual speech is easily beaten by one prepared and thought-out, this latter in turn will assuredly be surpassed by what has been written with care and diligence. The truth is that all the commonplaces, whether furnished by art or by individual talent and wisdom, at any rate such as appertain to the subject of our writing, appear and rush forward as we are searching out and surveying the matter with all our natural acuteness; and all the thoughts and expressions, which are the most brilliant in their several kinds, must needs flow up in succession to the point of our pen; then too the actual marshalling and arrangement of words is made perfect in the course of writing, in a rhythm and measure proper to oratory as distinct from poetry.

'These are the things which in good orators produce applause and admiration; and no man will attain these except by long and large practice in writing, however ardently he may have trained himself in those off-hand declamations; he too who approaches oratory by way of long practice in writing, brings this advantage to his task, that even if he is extemporizing, whatever he may say bears a likeness to the written word; and moreover if ever, during a speech, he has introduced a written note, the rest of his discourse, when he turns away from the writing, will proceed in unchanging style. Just as when a boat is moving at high speed, if the crew rest upon their oars, the craft herself still keeps her way and her run, though the driving force of the oars has ceased, so in an unbroken discourse, when written notes are exhausted, the rest of the speech still maintains a like progress, under the impulse given by the similarity and energy of the written word.

XXXIV. 'For my part, in the daily exercises of youth, I used chiefly to set myself that task which I knew Gaius Carbo, my old enemy, was wont to practise: this was to set myself some poetry, the most impressive to be found, or to read as much of some speech as I could keep in my memory, and then to declaim upon the actual subject-matter of my reading, choosing as far as possible different words. But later I noticed this defect in my method, that those words which best befitted each subject, and were the most elegant and in fact the best, had been already seized upon by Ennius, if it was on his poetry that I was practising, or by Gracchus, if I chanced to have set myself a speech of his. Thus I saw that to employ the same expressions profited me nothing, while to employ others was a positive hindrance, in that I was forming the habit of using the less appropriate. Afterwards I resolved,—and this practice I followed when somewhat older,—to translate freely Greek speeches of the most eminent orators. The result of reading these was that, in rendering into Latin what I had read in Greek, I not only found myself using the best words—and yet quite familiar ones—but also coining by analogy certain words such as would be new to our people, provided only they were appropriate.

'To proceed, the control and training of voice, breathing, gestures and the tongue itself, call for exertion rather than art; and in these matters we must carefully consider whom we are to take as patterns, whom we should wish to be like. We have to study actors as well as orators, that bad practice may not lead us into some inelegant or ugly habit. The memory too must be trained by carefully learning by heart as many pieces as possible both from our Latin writers and the foreigner. Moreover in this work I do not altogether dislike the use as well, if you are accustomed to it, of that system of associating commonplaces with symbols which is taught in the profession. Then at last must our Oratory be conducted out of this sheltered training-ground at home, right into action, into the dust and uproar, into the camp and the fighting-line of public debate; she must face putting everything to the proof and test the strength of her talent, and her secluded preparation must be brought forth into the daylight of reality. We must also read the poets, acquaint ourselves with histories, study and peruse the masters and authors in every excellent art, and by way of practice praise, expound, emend, criticize and confute them; we must argue every question on both sides, and bring out on every topic whatever points can be deemed plausible; besides this we must become learned in the common law and familiar with the statutes, and must contemplate all the olden time, and investigate the ways of the senate, political philosophy, the rights of allies, the treaties and conventions, and the policy of empire; and lastly we have to cull, from all the forms of pleasantry, a certain charm of humour, with which to give a sprinkle of salt, as it were, to all of our discourse.

'Well, I have poured out for you all my ideas, and perhaps any chance patriarch, upon whom you had fastened at some party or other, would have given the same replies to your interrogatories.'

The Divisions of the Classical Oration

Then, after all these points about the case have been discovered, the separate divisions of the whole case must be considered. For it does not follow that everything which is to be said first must be studied first; for the reason that, if you wish the first part of the speech to have a close agreement and connexion with the main statement of the case, you must derive it from the matters which are to be discussed afterward. Therefore when the point for decision and the arguments which must be devised for the purpose of reaching a decision have been diligently discovered by the rules of art, and studied with careful thought, then, and not till then, the other parts of the oration are to be arranged in proper order. These seem to me to be just six in number: exordium, narrative, partition, confirmation, refutation, peroration.

Now since the exordium has to come first, we shall likewise give first the rule for a systematic treatment of the exordium. xv. An exordium is a passage which brings the mind of the auditor into a proper condition to receive the rest of the speech. This will be accomplished if he becomes well-disposed, attentive, and receptive. Therefore one who wishes his speech to have a good exordium must make a careful study beforehand of the kind of case which he has to present. There are five kinds of cases: honourable, difficult, mean, ambiguous, obscure. An honourable case is one which wins favour in the mind of the auditor at once without any speech of ours: the difficult is one which has alienated the sympathy of those who are about to listen to the speech. The mean is one which the auditor makes light of and thinks unworthy of serious attention; the ambiguous is one in which the point for decision is doubtful, or the case is partly honourable and partly discreditable so that it engenders both good-will and ill-will; the obscure case is one in which either the auditors are slow of wit, or the case involves matters which are rather difficult to grasp. Hence, since the kinds of cases are so diverse, it is necessary to construct the exordium on a different plan in each kind of case. The exordium is, then, divided into two species, *introduction* and *in-*

Reprinted by permission of the publishers and The Loeb Classical Library from *Cicero, De Inventione, etc.,* trans. by H. M. Hubbell, Cambridge, Mass.: Harvard University Press, 1949.

sinuation. An introduction is an address which directly and in plain language makes the auditor well-disposed, receptive, and attentive. Insinuation is an address which by dissimulation and indirection unobtrusively steals into the mind of the auditor.

In the difficult case, if the auditors are not completely hostile, it will be permissible to try to win their good-will by an introduction; if they are violently opposed it will be necessary to have recourse to the insinuation. For if amity and good-will are sought from auditors who are in a rage, not only is the desired result not obtained, but their hatred is increased and fanned into a flame. In the mean case, on the other hand, it is necessary to make the audience attentive in order to remove their disdain. If an ambiguous case has a doubtful point for the judge's decision, the exordium must begin with a discussion of this very point. But if the case is partly honourable and partly discreditable, it will be proper to try to win good-will so that the case may seem to be transferred to the honourable class. When, however, the case is really in the honourable class, it will be possible either to pass over the introduction or, if it is convenient, we shall begin with the narrative or with a law or some very strong argument which supports our plea: if, on the contrary, it is desirable to use the introduction, we must use the topics designed to produce good-will, that the advantage which already exists may be increased. xvi. In a case of the obscure kind the introduction must be used to make the audience receptive. . . .

The *exordium* ought to be sententious to a marked degree and of a high seriousness, and, to put it generally, should contain everything which contributes to dignity, because the best thing to do is that which especially commends the speaker to his audience. It should contain very little brilliance, vivacity, or finish of style, because these give rise to a suspicion of preparation and excessive ingenuity. As a result of this most of all the speech loses conviction and the speaker, authority.

The following are surely the most obvious faults of *exordia,* which are by all means to be avoided: it should not be general, common, interchangeable, tedious, unconnected, out of place, or contrary to the fundamental principles. A *general* exordium is one which can be tacked to many cases, so as to seem to suit them all. A *common* exordium is one equally applicable to both sides of the case. The *interchangeable* can with slight changes be used by the opponent in a speech on the other side. The *tedious* exordium is one which is spun out beyond all need with a superabundance of words or ideas. The *unconnected* is one which is not derived from the circumstances of the case nor closely knit with the rest of the speech, as a limb to a body. It is *out of place* if it produces a result different from what the nature of the case requires: for example, if it makes the audience receptive when the case calls for good-will, or uses an introduction when the situation demands an insinuation. It is contrary to fundamental principles when it achieves none of the purposes for which rules are given about exordia, that is, when it renders the audience neither well-disposed, nor attentive, nor receptive, or produces the opposite result; and nothing surely can be worse than that. This is enough to say about the exordium.

xix. The *narrative* is an exposition of events that have occurred or are supposed to have occurred. There are three kinds: one which contains just the case and the whole reason for the dispute; a second in which a digression is made beyond the strict limits of the case for the purpose of attacking somebody, or of making a comparison, or of amusing the audience in a way not incongruous with the business in hand, or for amplification. The third kind is wholly unconnected with public issues, which is recited or written solely for amusement but at the same time provides valuable training. It is subdivided into two classes: one concerned with events, the other principally with persons. That which consists of an exposition of events has three forms: *fabula, historia, argumentum. Fabula* is the term applied to a narrative in which the events are not true and have no verisimilitude, for example:

> Huge winged dragons yoked to a car.

Historia is an account of actual occurrences remote from the recollection of our own age, as:

> War on men of Carthage Appius decreed.

Argumentum is a fictitious narrative which nevertheless could have occurred. An example may be quoted from Terence:

> For after he had left the school of youth.

But the form of narrative which is concerned with persons is of such a sort that in it can be seen not only events but also the conversation and mental attitude of the characters. For example: 'He comes to me perpetually, crying, "What are you about, Micio? Why are you bringing the boy to ruin on our hands? Why this licence? Why these drinking parties? Why do you pile him up the guineas for such a life and let him spend so much at the tailor's? It's extremely silly of you." He himself is extremely hard, past right and sense.' This form of narrative should possess great vivacity, resulting from fluctuations of fortune, contrast of characters, severity, gentleness, hope, fear, suspicion, desire, dissimulation, delusion, pity, sudden change of fortune, unexpected disaster, sudden pleasure, a happy ending to the story. . . .

xxi. The narrative will be plausible if it seems to embody characteristics which are accustomed to appear in real life; if the proper qualities of the character are maintained, if reasons for their actions are plain, if there seems to have been ability to do the deed, if it can be shown that the time was opportune, the space sufficient and the place suitable for the events about to be narrated; if the story fits in with the nature of the actors in it, the habits of ordinary people and the beliefs of the audience. Verisimilitude can be secured by following these principles.

In addition to observing these precepts, one must also be on guard not to insert a narrative when it will be a hindrance or of no advantage, and also not to have it out of place or in a manner other than that which the case requires. A narrative can be a hindrance when a presentation of the events alone and by themselves gives great offence, which it will be necessary to mitigate in arguing and pleading the case. When this situation arises, it will be necessary to distribute the narrative piecemeal throughout the speech and to add an explanation directly after each section so that the remedy may heal the wound and the defence may immediately lessen the animosity. A narrative is of no advantage when the facts have been explained by the opponents and it is of no importance to us to tell the story again or in a different way. The narrative is also useless when the audience has grasped the facts so thoroughly that it is of no advantage to us to instruct them in a different fashion. In such a case one must dispense with narrative altogether. The narrative is out of place when it is not set in that part of the speech which the situation demands; this topic we shall take up when we discuss arrangement, for it affects the arrangement. The narrative is not presented in the manner required by the case when a point which helps the opponent is explained clearly and elegantly, or a point which helps the speaker is presented obscurely and carelessly. Therefore, to avoid this fault, the speaker must bend everything to the advantage of his case, by passing over all things that make against it which can be passed over, by touching lightly on what must be mentioned, and by telling his own side of the story carefully and clearly.

Sufficient has, I think, been said about narrative; let us now pass to the *partition*.

XXII. In an argument a partition correctly made renders the whole speech clear and perspicuous. It takes two forms, both of which greatly contribute to clarifying the case and determining the nature of the controversy. One form shows in what we agree with our opponents and what is left in dispute; as a result of this some definite problem is set for the auditor on which he ought to have his attention fixed. In the second form the matters which we intend to discuss are briefly set forth in a methodical way. This leads the auditor to hold definite points in his mind, and to understand that when these have been discussed the oration will be over.

Now I think I ought to present briefly the method of using each form of partition. A partition which shows what is agreed upon, and what is not, should turn the subject of agreement to the advantage of the speaker's case, in the following manner: 'I agree with my opponents that the mother was killed by her son.' In the same way on the other side of the case, 'It is agreed that Agamemnon was killed by Clytemnestra.' For here each speaker stated what was agreed upon, yet was mindful of the advantage of his own side of the case. Secondly, what is in controversy should be set forth in explaining the point for the judge's decision; how this is discovered has been stated above.

The form of partition which contains a methodical statement of topics to be discussed ought to have the following qualities: brevity, completeness, conciseness. Brevity is secured when no word is used unless necessary. It is useful in this place because the attention of the auditor should be attracted by the facts and topics of the case, and not by extraneous embellishments of style. Completeness is the quality by which we embrace in the partition all forms of argument which apply to the case, and about which we ought to speak, taking care that no useful argument be omitted or be introduced late as an addition to the plan of the speech, for this is faulty and unseemly in the highest degree. Conciseness in the partition is secured if only *genera* of things are given and they are not confused and mixed with their *species*. To explain: a *genus* is a class that embraces several *species*, as *animal*. A *species* is that which is a part of a *genus*, as *horse*. But often the same thing is a genus in relation to one thing and a species in relation to another. For example, man is a species of animal, but a genus of which Thebans or Trojans are species. xxiii. I have given this description with some care so that when the theory of classification is clearly understood, conciseness in dealing with classes may be secured in the partition. For one who divides his speech as follows: 'I shall show that through the covetousness, audacity and avarice of my opponents all disasters have come upon the state,' was not aware that in his partition he mentioned a genus and then combined it with a species of that genus. For covetousness or desire certainly is the genus of all appetites, and of this genus avarice is without doubt a species. You should therefore be on your guard lest after mentioning a genus you mention a species of it in the same partition, as if it were different and dissimilar. But if a genus has several species, after stating it straightforwardly in the first partition, the division into species may be most conveniently made when one comes to explain that particular point in the course of the speech after the partition. It also contributes to conciseness not to say that we shall prove more than is necessary, as is done in the following example: 'I shall show that my opponents were able to commit the crime with which we charge them, that they wished to, and that they did commit it;' for it would have been enough to prove that they did commit the crime; nor, when there is no partition in the case, because a single question is being debated (but this is a very rare occurrence), to use in spite of that fact a careful distribution.

There are other rules for the partition not so closely connected with oratorical practice; they are used in philosophy, and from them we have chosen the particular rules which seemed to apply and which we did not find in the other textbooks.

Now that the rules for partition have been stated, it is necessary to remind the orator that throughout the speech he should bear in mind to complete the sections in order one after another as they have been planned in the partition, and that after all have been dispatched he should bring the speech to a close so that nothing be introduced after the conclusion. The old man in the Andria of Terence makes a brief and neat partition of what he wishes his freedman to know: 'In this way you will learn my son's manner of life, my plan, and what I wish you to do in the matter.' And his narrative follows the plan laid down in the partition: first, his son's manner of life,

> For after he had left the school of youth . . .

then his plan:

> And now I am anxious . . .

then what he wishes Sosia to do, which was the last point in the partition, is stated last:

> Now your task is . . .

Just as he turned his attention first to each point as it arose, and after dispatching them all stopped speaking, so I favour turning our attention to each topic and when all have been dispatched, winding up the speech.

Now it seems desirable to give in turn the rules about *confirmation* as is demanded by the regular order of the speech. xxiv. Confirmation or proof is the part of the oration which by marshalling arguments lends credit, authority, and support to our case. For this section of the speech there are definite rules which will be divided among the different kinds of cases. But I think that it will not be inconvenient to set forth in the beginning, without any attempt at order or arrangement, a kind of raw material for general use from which all arguments are drawn, and then later to present the way in which each kind of case should be supported by all the forms of argumentation derived from this general store. . . .

xxxi. All argumentation, then, is to be carried on either by induction or by deduction.

Induction is a form of argument which leads the person with whom one is arguing to give assent to certain undisputed facts; through this assent it wins his approval of a doubtful proposition because this resembles the facts to which he has assented. For instance, in a dialogue by Aeschines Socraticus Socrates reveals that Aspasia reasoned thus with Xenophon's wife and with Xenophon himself: 'Please tell me, madam, if your neighbour had a better gold ornament than you have, would you prefer that one or your own?' 'That one,' she replied. 'Now, if she had dresses and other feminine finery more expensive than you have, would you prefer yours or hers?' 'Hers, of course,' she replied. 'Well now, if she had a better husband than you have, would you prefer your husband or hers?' At this the woman blushed. But Aspasia then began to speak to Xenophon. 'I wish you would tell me, Xenophon,' she said, 'if your neighbour had a better horse than yours, would you prefer your horse or his?' 'His,' was his answer. 'And if he had a better farm than you have, which farm would you prefer to have?' 'The better farm, naturally,' he said. 'Now, if he had a better wife than you have, would you prefer yours or his?' And at this Xenophon, too, himself was silent. Then Aspasia: 'Since both of you have failed to tell me the only thing I wished to hear, I myself will tell you what you both are thinking. That is, you, madam, wish to have the best husband, and you, Xenophon, desire above all things to have the finest wife. Therefore unless you can contrive that there be no better man or finer woman on earth you will certainly always be in dire want of what you consider best, namely, that you be the husband of the very best of wives, and that she be wedded to the very best of men.' In this instance, because assent has been given to undisputed statements, the result is that the point which would appear doubtful if asked by itself is through analogy conceded as certain, and this is due to the method employed in putting the question. Socrates used this conversational method a good deal, because he wished to present no arguments himself, but preferred to get a result from the material which the interlocutor had given him—a result which the interlocutor was bound to approve as following necessarily from what he had already granted.

xxxii. In argumentation of this kind I think the first rule to lay down is that the statement which we introduce as a basis for analogy ought to be of such a kind that its truth must be granted. For a statement on the strength of which we expect a doubtful point to be conceded, ought not itself to be doubtful. In the second place, one must make sure that the statement to be proved by the induction resembles those statements which we have presented previously as indisputable, for something granted to us previously will be no help if it is unlike the statement for the proof of which we wished the first point to be conceded. In the next place the interlocutor must not perceive what is the aim of those first examples or to what conclusion they will lead. For one who sees that if he gives the proper answer to the first question that he is asked, he will be compelled to grant also a proposition which is displeasing to him, will generally put a stop to further questioning by not answering or by answering incorrectly. Therefore by careful direction of the questions he must be led without his knowing it from the statement which he has granted to that which he does not wish to grant. Finally, he must either refuse to answer, or concede your point or deny it. If he denies it, you must show that it resembles the points which have previously been conceded, or use another induction. If he concedes the point, the argument must be brought to a close. If he refuses to answer, he must be lured into giving an answer, or since 'silence gives consent' you must finish the argument just as if he had conceded your point. Thus this style of argument is threefold: the first part consists of one or more similar cases, the second of the point which we wish to have conceded, for the sake of which the similar cases have been cited; the third is the conclusion which reinforces the concession or shows what results follow from it.

xxxiii. But because some may think the demonstration is not sufficiently clear unless we add an example from the field of public issues, it seems desirable to give an example of this sort also, not that the principle is different or that it is used differently in conversation and in a speech, but to satisfy the desire of those who after seeing something in one place cannot recognize it in another unless it is pointed out. Therefore let us take the case, well known among the Greeks, of Epaminondas the Theban general. He did not hand over the army to the officer who had legally succeeded him as commander, and keeping the army under his own command for a few days contrary to law, won a decisive victory over the Lacedaemonians. The prosecutor will be able to use the argument by analogy in defending the letter of the law against the intent, in the following way: 'If, gentlemen of the jury, Epaminondas should add to the law what he says the author of the law intended, and should subjoin this proviso, "except in the case that a commander shall for the common weal refuse to hand over his army," will you permit it? I think not. Or again, if you yourselves—though this is decidedly out of keeping with your wisdom and punctiliousness—if you yourselves without consulting the people should out of respect to him order this same proviso to be added to the law, will the people of Thebes permit this? Most assuredly not. Would it then seem right to you to follow a principle as if it were a part of the law, though it is wrong to make it a part of the law? I know your intelligence. It cannot seem right to you, gentlemen of the jury. Therefore if the intent of the law-maker cannot be amended in writing either by him or by you, beware lest it be much worse to alter in deed, *i.e.,* by your judicial act, what cannot be changed even in word.'

Enough has been said, I think, for the present about induction. In the next place let us consider the essence and nature of the syllogism.

xxxiv. *Deduction* or syllogistic reasoning is a form of argument which draws a probable conclusion from the fact under consideration itself; when this probable conclusion is set forth and recognized by itself it proves itself by its own import and reasoning. . . .

There are, then, five parts of an argument by deductive or syllogistic reasoning: *major premise* which sets forth briefly the principle from which springs the whole force and meaning of the syllogism; *proof* by which the brief statement of the major premise is supported by reasons and made plainer and more plausible; the *minor premise* in which is premised the point which on the basis of the major premise is pertinent to proving the case; the *proof* of the minor premise, by which what has been premised is established by reasons; the *conclusion* in which there is stated briefly what is proved by the whole deduction. The form of the syllogism that has the largest number of parts consists of these five; the second has four, the third three, the next two, but this is disputed; it is possible that some may think that it can have only one part. xxxviii. We shall give examples of those on which there is general agreement, and bring forward reasons for those which are in doubt.

The following is an example of a fivefold argument: 'It is right, gentlemen of the jury, to relate all laws to the advantage of the state and to interpret them with an eye to the public good and not according to their literal expression. For such was the uprightness and wisdom of our ancestors that in framing laws they had no object in view except the safety and welfare of the state. They did not themselves intend to write a law which would prove harmful, and they knew that if they did pass such a law, it would be repealed when the defect was recognized. For no one wishes laws to be upheld merely for their own sake, but for the sake of the state, because everyone believes that the state is best governed when administered according to law. All written laws ought, then, to be interpreted in relation to the object for which laws ought to be observed: that is, since we are servants of the community, let us interpret the laws with an eye to the advantage and profit of the community. For as it is right to think that the art of medicine produces nothing except what looks to the health of the body, since it is for this purpose that medicine was founded, so we should believe that nothing comes from the laws except what conduces to the welfare of the state, since the laws were made for this purpose. Therefore in this trial also, cease to search the letter of the law and rather, as is just, examine the law in relation to the public welfare. What was more useful to Thebes than the defeat of Sparta? What should Epaminondas, the Theban commander, have had in mind more than the victory of Thebes? What should he have regarded as dearer or more precious than such a glorious exploit of the Thebans, than a trophy so honourable, so magnificent? It is obvious that he was bound to forget the letter of the law and to consider the intent of the law-maker. But certainly this point has been examined and established beyond a doubt, that no law has been passed except for the good of the state. He thought it, therefore, stark madness not to interpret a law with an eye to the safety of the state when that law had been passed for the safety of the state. In view of this, if all laws ought to be related to the advantage of the state, and Epaminondas contributed to the safety of the state, surely he cannot by the same act have promoted the common interest and have failed to obey the laws.'

XXXIX. An argument consists of four parts when we state a premise, either major or minor, without giving the proof. This should be done either when the major premise is self-intelligible or when the minor premise is an obvious statement needing no proof. An argument in four parts with the proof of the major premise omitted is handled in this fashion: 'Gentlemen of the jury, you, who have sworn to decide according to the law, ought to obey the laws. But you cannot obey the laws unless you follow what is written in the law. What more certain proof of his intent could the author of the law have left than the statement which he wrote himself with great care and pains? Therefore, if there were no writtten documents we should be in sad need of them to learn from them the intent of the law-giver; neverthless we should not permit Epaminondas even if he were not under the jurisdiction of the court to interpret to us the meaning of the law; much less, since we have the law before us, should we suffer him to interpret the intent of the law-maker, not by what is quite plainly written, but by what suits his case. Hence, gentlemen of the jury, if you ought to obey the laws, and you cannot do this unless you follow what is written in the law, why not decide that he acted contrary to law?'

And an argument in four parts can be made as follows, with the proof of the minor premise omitted: 'We ought not to trust the statements of those who have often deceived us by false promises. For if we are harmed by their treachery, we shall have no right to blame anyone except ourselves. To be deceived once is annoying, it is foolish to be deceived twice; the third time it is a disgrace. Now the Carthaginians have deceived us many times in the past. It is therefore the height of folly to place confidence in the promises of those by whose treachery you have so often been deceived.'

If the proof of both premises is omitted, the argument becomes threefold; for example: 'We must either live in fear of the Carthaginians if we leave them with their power undiminished, or we must destroy their city. But we certainly should not live in fear. The alternative is, then, to destroy their city.' . . .

XLII. The *refutation* is that part of an oration in which arguments are used to impair, disprove, or weaken the confirmation or proof in our opponents' speech. It utilizes the same sources of invention that *confirmation* does, because any proposition can be attacked by the same methods of reasoning by which it can be supported. For nothing need be considered in all these quests for arguments except the attributes of persons or of actions. Therefore the rules for the invention and embellishment of arguments may properly be transferred from what has been said before to this part of the oration. In order, however, that some instructions may be given about this section too, we shall set forth the methods of refutation. Those who follow these rules will more easily be able to impair or disprove the arguments made against them.

Every argument is refuted in one of these ways: either one or more of its assumptions are not granted, or if the assumptions are granted it is denied that a conclusion follows from them, or the form of argument is shown to be fallacious, or a strong argument is met by one equally strong or stronger.

One of the assumptions of the opponents is not granted when either what they say is credible is denied to be such, or what they think is a parallel case is shown to be dissimilar, or a judicial decision is interpreted in a different sense, or decisions in general are denied validity, or what the adversaries regard as sound evidence is denied to be such, or one or both horns of a dilemma are shown to be unsound, or an enumeration is demonstrated to be incomplete, or a simple conclusion is shown to contain a fallacy. For everything which is used in argumentation, either as a probable or rigorous proof, must come under one of these heads, as we have shown above. . . .

Hermagoras puts the digression next, and then finally the peroration. In this digression he thinks a passage should be introduced unconnected with the case and the actual point to be decided; it might contain praise of oneself or abuse of the opponent, or lead to some other case which may supply confirmation or refutation not by argument but by adding emphasis by means of some amplification. If anyone thinks this is a proper division of a speech, he may follow Hermagoras' rule. For some of the rules for amplification and praise and vituperation have already been given, and the rest will be given in the proper place. But we do not think that this should be listed among the regular parts of the speech, because we disapprove of digressing from the main subject except in case of 'commonplaces'; and this topic is to be discussed later. Moreover, I am of the opinion that praise and vituperation should not be made a separate part, but should be closely interwoven with the argumentation itself. Now we shall discuss the peroration.

LII. The peroration is the end and conclusion of the whole speech; it has three parts, the summing-up, the *indignatio* or exciting of indignation or ill-will against the opponent, and the *conquestio* or the arousing of pity and sympathy.

The summing-up is a passage in which matters that have been discussed in different places here and there throughout the speech are brought together in one place and arranged so as to be seen at a glance in order to refresh the memory of the audience. If this is always treated in the same manner, it will be perfectly evident to everyone that it is being handled according to some rule or system. But if it is managed in different ways it will be possible to avoid both this suspicion and the boredom which comes from repetition. Therefore it will be proper at times to sum up in the manner which the majority of speakers employ, because it is easy, *i.e.* to touch on each single point and so to run briefly over all the arguments. At times, however, it is well to take the harder course and state the topics which you have set out in the partition and promised to discuss, and to recall to mind the lines of reasoning by which you have proved each point, in this fashion: 'We have demonstrated this, we have made this plain.' At times one may inquire of the audience what they might rightly wish to have proved to them. Thus the auditor will refresh his memory and think that there is nothing more that he ought to desire. . . .

LIII. The *indignatio* is a passage which results in arousing great hatred against some person, or violent offence at some action. In discussing this topic we wish it to be understood at the beginning that *indignatio* is used in connexion with all the topics which we laid out when giving rules for confirmation. In other words, all the attributes of persons and things can give occasion for any use of amplification that may be desired, or any method of arousing enmity; still we should consider what particular and separate rules can be given about *indignatio*. . . .

LV. *Conquestio* (lament or complaint) is a passage seeking to arouse the pity of the audience. In this the first necessity is to make the auditor's spirit gentle and merciful that he may be more easily moved by the *conquestio*. This ought to be done by the use of 'commonplaces' which set forth the power of fortune over all men and the weakness of the human race. When such a passage is delivered gravely and sententiously, the spirit of man is greatly abased and prepared for pity, for in viewing the misfortune of another he will contemplate his own weakness.

AIDS TO STUDY

In the selection from *De Oratore*, Cicero is outlining briefly the classical course in rhetoric:
1. The style of the speaker must depend upon the nature of the question being discussed.
2. There are three kinds of oratory, usually called the judicial, the deliberative, and the epidictic; and each kind entails methods of persuasion (commonplaces or *topoi*).
3. The preparation of a classical oration involves five divisions:
   a. Invention, or the 'discovery' of proper arguments for each case.
   b. Disposition, or the most effective ordering of the arguments.
   c. Elocution, or the proper diction and style for each argument.
   d. Memory or mnemonics, or the ways to remember what one has to say.
   e. Delivery or action, or what is now usually thought of as 'elocution' or 'platform style.'

4. There are six divisions of the oration as delivered:
   a. The exordium, or introduction, in which we prepare our listener or reader for what we have to say.
   b. The narrative, in which we state the facts of the case at hand.
   c. The partition, in which we clarify our view of the problem at issue and the points upon which any disagreement may rest.
   d. The confirmation, in which we offer our proofs for our side of the argument.
   e. The refutation, in which we weaken or disprove the contentions of our opponents.
   f. The peroration, in which we sum up, excite indignation against our opponents, or arouse sympathy for our view.

After this compact summary of the art of rhetoric, Cicero considers how important practice is to the rhetorician, and he gives especial attention to the sort of practice which is of greatest help to the student.

In the selections from *De Inventione,* the divisions of the oration are considered at greater length, and we are given practical advice about the problems which each part of an argument poses. What we should notice here is the constant emphasis upon *reasonableness:* we should assume that our listeners or readers are rational people, and we must appear to be rational in our attempts to persuade them of our view. Hence, we must constantly consider what the *basis* for our argument is; we must beware of wandering off the subject or discussing something that is not really at issue; we must analyze both our own and our opponents' arguments with some care; we must not blindly assume that we are right and virtuous and our opponents are wrong and wicked, if we mean to persuade sensible men of our views. Although both Aristotle and Cicero were concerned with 'winning' the argument, neither assumed that one should win at any cost; indeed, neither thought for a moment that one *could* win at any cost, for both assumed that the right argument would persuade rational men. The only way to win is to study the problem at issue in great depth and with great care, to be ever willing to analyze our own conclusions and to analyze with equal care the different conclusions of others.

The classical tradition of rhetoric was not simply a shoddy bag of tricks; it remained an important study for over a millennium because it was devoted to finding the truth about matters which concern us. And it remains today a powerful method for the discovery of truth. But like any powerful method for truth, it demands a careful observance of methods of procedure; and if we are to master the method, we must practice it as dutifully as the natural scientist practices his laboratory techniques or the surgeon practices his surgical methods.

Hence, these selections are not offered for your amusement, and they are not a sort of misty 'historical background' for your study. They outline the essence of modern, as well as ancient, rhetorical science. And the student who is not willing to learn the essence of this tradition and to put it into practice, in paper after paper or speech after speech, is not very likely to attain much mastery of his written or spoken language.

Practically speaking, what these selections come to is a series of questions we must ask ourselves and find answers to when we prepare either a paper or a speech:

1. What is it I am up to? What, exactly, is the subject of my remarks?
2. What kind of subject is it? Am I concerned with a matter of fact, or a matter of appropriate action, or a matter of proper attitude or opinion?
3. Upon what basis can a sensible answer to the problem at hand be found? What are the possible answers? Which seems most nearly true? Why?
4. Having settled upon my answer, what sorts of proof or persuasions are available to me? Which of these are most likely to persuade a rational hearer or reader?
5. Who is my reader or listener? Which of my proofs are most likely to persuade him?
6. In which order do I present the various proofs and persuasions I have found?
7. In what way do I best express each of the arguments I have to offer my reader or listener so that he will both understand them and sympathize with them?
8. If I am speaking, how do I manage to remember all that I have to say? And how do I behave most effectively in the saying of them?
9. How does my reader or listener expect me to proceed with what I have to say? Does not the order of the classical oration provide me a very sensible outline for any paper or speech I might have?

All of these questions have a way of adding up to a couple of more general ones: What makes me think that the preparing of good papers or speeches is an easy matter, one that requires only a few minutes and half-hearted attention? How can I expect to do easily and well so complicated a job as this without a very great deal of practice? Only an idiot would presume to play Beethoven's Emperor Concerto in a few minutes and with half-hearted attention; and only an idiot would prepare for such a performance by practicing any old way; wiser folks would follow some methodical system of practice, such as that of Carl Czerny. It is quite as idiotic to presume to present good writing or speech without practice; the wise student will avail himself of a methodical system of practice.

Plain, Grand, and Florid Styles

There is another threefold division, whereby, it is held, we may differentiate three styles of speaking, all of them correct. The first is termed the plain (or ἰσχνόν), the second grand and forcible (or ἁδρόν), and the third either intermediate or florid, the latter being a translation of ἀνθηρόν. The nature of these three styles is, broadly speaking, as follows. The first would seem best adapted for instructing, the second for moving, and the third (by whichever name we call it) for charming or, as others would have it, conciliating the audience; for instruction the quality most needed is acumen, for conciliation gentleness, and for stirring the emotions force. Consequently it is mainly in the plain style that we shall state our facts and advance our proofs, though it should be borne in mind that this style will often be sufficiently full in itself without any assistance whatever from the other two. The intermediate style will have more frequent recourse to metaphor and will make more attractive use of figures, while it will introduce alluring digressions, will be neat in rhythm and pleasing in its reflexions: its flow, however, will be gentle, like that of a river whose waters are clear, but overshadowed by the green banks on either side. But he whose eloquence is like to some great torrent that rolls down rocks and 'disdains a bridge' and carves out its own banks for itself, will sweep the judge from his feet, struggle as he may, and force him to go whither he bears him. This is the orator that will call the dead to life (as, for example, Cicero calls upon Appius Caecus); it is in his pages that his native land itself will cry aloud and at times address the orator himself, as it addresses Cicero in the speech delivered against Catiline in the senate. Such an orator will also

Reprinted by permission of the publishers and The Loeb Classical Library from *Quintilian, Institutio Oratoria,* trans. by H. E. Butler, Cambridge, Mass.: Harvard University Press, 1922.

exalt his style by amplification and rise even to *hyperbole,* as when Cicero cries, 'What Charybdis was ever so voracious!' or 'By the god of truth, even Ocean's self,' etc. (I choose these fine passages as being familiar to the student). It is such an one that will bring down the Gods to form part of his audience or even to speak with him, as in the following, 'For on you I call, ye hills and groves of Alba, on you, I say, ye fallen altars of the Albans, altars that were once the peers and equals of the holy places of Rome.' This is he that will inspire anger or pity, and while he speaks the judge will call upon the gods and weep, following him wherever he sweeps him from one emotion to another, and no longer asking merely for instruction. Wherefore if one of these three styles has to be selected to the exclusion of the others, who will hesitate to prefer this style to all others, since it is by far the strongest and the best adapted to the most important cases? For Homer himself assigns to Menelaus an eloquence, terse and pleasing, exact (for that is what is meant by 'making no errors in words') and devoid of all redundance, which qualities are virtues of the first type: and he says that from the lips of Nestor flowed speech sweeter than honey, than which assuredly we can conceive no greater delight: but when he seeks to express the supreme gift of eloquence possessed by Ulysses he gives a mighty voice and a vehemence of oratory equal to the snows of winter in the abundance and the vigour of its words. 'With him then,' he says, 'no mortal will contend, and men shall look upon him as on a god.' It is this force and impetuosity that Eupolis admires in Pericles, this that Aristophanes compares to the thunderbolt, this that is the power of true eloquence.

But eloquence cannot be confined even to these three forms of style. For just as the third style is intermediate between the grand and the plain style, so each of these three are separated by interspaces which are occupied by intermediate styles compounded of the two which lie on either side. For there are styles fuller or plainer than the plain, and gentler or more vehement than the vehement, while the gentler style itself may either rise to greater force or sink to milder tones. Thus we may discover almost countless species of styles, each differing from the other by some fine shade of difference. We may draw a parallel from the winds. It is generally accepted that there are four blowing from the four quarters of the globe, but we find there are also a large number of winds which lie between these, called by a variety of names, and in certain cases confined to certain districts and river valleys. The same thing may be noted in music. For after assigning five notes to the lyre, musicians fill up the intervals between the strings by a variety of notes, and between these again they interpose yet others, so that the original divisions admit of a number of gradations.

Eloquence has, therefore, a quantity of different aspects, but it is sheer folly to inquire which of these the orator should take as his model, since every species that is in itself correct has its use, and what is commonly called *style of speaking* does not depend on the orator. For he will use all styles, as circumstances may demand, and the choice will be determined not only by the case as a whole, but by the demands of the different portions of the case. For just as he will not speak in the same way when he is defending a client on a capital charge and when he is speaking in a lawsuit concerned with an inheritance, or discussing interdicts and suits taking the form of a wager, or claims in connexion with loans, so too he will preserve a due distinction between the speeches which he makes in the senate, before the people and in private consultations, while he will also introduce numerous modifications to suit the different persons and circumstances of time and place. Thus in one and the same speech he will use one style for stirring the emotions, and another to conciliate his hearers; it is from different sources that he will derive anger or pity, and the art which he employs in instructing the judge will be other than that which he employs to move him. He will not maintain the same tone throughout his *exordium, statement of fact, arguments, digression* and *peroration.* He will speak gravely, severely, sharply, with vehemence, energy, fullness, bitterness, or geniality, quietly, simply, flatteringly, gently, sweetly, briefly or wittily; he will not always be like himself, but he will never be unworthy of himself. Thus the purpose for which oratory was above all designed will be secured, that is to say, he will speak with profit and with power to effect his aim, while he will also win the praise not merely of the learned, but of the multitude as well.

They make the gravest mistake who consider that the style which is best adapted to win popularity and applause is a faulty and corrupt style of speaking which revels in license of diction or wantons in childish epigram or swells with stilted bombast or riots in empty commonplace or adorns itself with blossoms of eloquence which will fall to earth if but lightly shaken, or regards extravagance as sublime or raves wildly under the pretext of free speech. I am ready to admit that such qualities please many, and I feel no surprise that this should be the case. For any kind of eloquence is pleasing and attractive to the ear, and every effort of the voice inspires a natural pleasure in the soul of man; indeed this is the sole cause of those familiar gatherings in the Forum or on the Old Wall, so that there is small reason for wonder if any pleader is safe to draw a ring of listeners from the crowd. And when any unusually precious phrase strikes the ears of an uneducated audience, whatever its true merits, it wakens their admiration just for the very reason that they feel they could never have produced it themselves. And it deserves their admiration, since even such success is hard to attain. On the other hand, when such displays are compared with their betters, they sink into insignificance and fade out of sight, for they are like wool dyed red that pleases in the absence of purple, but, as Ovid says, if compared with a cloak of Tyrian dye, pales in the presence of the fairer hue. If, however, we test such corrupt eloquence by the touchstone of a critical taste, as, for example, we test inferior dyes with sulphur, it will lay aside the false brilliance that deceived the eye and fade to a pallor almost too repulsive to describe. Such passages shine only in the absence of the sunlight, just as certain tiny insects seem transformed in the darkness to little flames of fire. Finally, while many approve of things that are bad, no one disapproves of that which is good.

But the true orator will not merely be able to achieve all the feats of which I have spoken with supreme excellence, but with the utmost ease as well. For the sovereign power of eloquence and the voice that awakens well-deserved applause will be free from the perpetual distress of harassing anxiety which wastes and fevers the orator who painfully corrects himself and pines away over the laborious weighing and piecing together of his words. No, our orator, brilliant, sublime and opulent of speech, is lord and master of all the resources of eloquence, whose affluence surrounds him. For he that has reached the summit has no more weary hills to scale. At first the climber's toil is hard, but the higher he mounts the easier becomes the gradient and the richer the soil. And if by perseverance of study he pass even beyond these gentler slopes, fruits for which none have toiled thrust themselves upon him, and all things spring forth unbidden; and yet if they be not gathered daily, they will wither away. But even such wealth must observe the mean, without which nothing is either praiseworthy or beneficial, while brilliance must be attended by manliness, and imagination by soundness of taste. Thus the works of the orator will be great not extravagant, sublime not bombastic, bold not rash, severe but not gloomy, grave but not slow, rich but not luxuriant, pleasing but not effeminate, grand but not grandiose. It is the same with other qualities: the mean is safest, for the worst of all faults is to fly to extremes.

AIDS TO STUDY

While Quintilian distinguishes three general sorts of style—the plain, the intermediate, and the grand or forcible—and while he clearly considers the last of these the most exalted, it is well to notice that he is aware that no three-fold division is sufficient to describe all possible styles and that he is insistent that the style be fitting to the occasion if it is to be admired. Simple matters should be plainly put, imaginative matters imaginatively put, moving ideas movingly put, etc.

Study paragraph three with especial attention. The observant student will notice that when he considers the various styles, Quintilian uses those styles to illustrate: compare the way he describes the styles of Menelaus, Nestor, and Ulysses; and notice that Quintilian's descriptions of these three styles is written in the plain style—his intention is to make clear the distinction among them, after all. When he wishes to discredit the false flashy style, his own style becomes florid; when he describes the mastery of the true orator, his style verges toward the grand.

The fourth paragraph is also of great importance. What Quintilian is arguing is that, while a flashy style which makes use of current slang, of exaggerated figures of speech, and of unusual words and phrases may attract an uneducated audience, in the long run it fails. Of course, it fails immediately with an audience which is educated and sensible, for such an audience sees through it for the shoddy thing it is. The final sentence of the paragraph is a golden rule of composition, and perhaps of life: 'While many approve of things that are bad, no one disapproves of that which is good.' And the sentence which ends the selection is another of the rules that a serious student will take to heart.

Hugh Blair (1718–1800)

The Origin and Nature of Figurative Language

Having now finished what related to the construction of sentences, I proceed to other rules concerning style. My general division of the qualities of style, was into perspicuity and ornament. Perspicuity, both in single words and in sentences, I have considered. Ornament, as far as it arises from a graceful, strong, and melodious construction of words, has also been treated of. Another, and a great branch of the ornament of style, is, figurative language; which is now to be the subject of our consideration, and will require a full discussion.

Our first inquiry must be, what is meant by figures of speech?

In general, they always imply some departure from simplicity of expression; the idea which we intend to convey, not only enunciated to others, but enunciated, in a particular manner, and with some circumstance added, which is designed to render the impression more strong and vivid. When I say, for instance, 'That a good man enjoys comfort in the midst of adversity'; I just express my thought in the simplest manner possible. But when I say, 'To the upright there ariseth light in darkness'; the same sentiment is expressed in a figurative style; a new circumstance is introduced; light is put in the place of comfort, and darkness is used to suggest the idea of adversity. In the same manner, to say, 'It is impossible, by any search we can make, to explore the divine nature fully,' is to make a simple proposition. But when we say, 'Canst thou, by searching, find out God? Canst thou find out the Almighty to perfection? It is high as heaven, what canst thou do? deeper than hell, what canst thou know?' This introduces a figure into style; the proposition being not only expressed, but admiration and astonishment being expressed together with it.

From *Lectures on Rhetoric and Belles Lettres,* Lecture XIV, 'Figurative Language,' Philadelphia, 1833.

But, though figures imply a deviation from what may be reckoned the most simple form of speech, we are not thence to conclude, that they imply any thing uncommon, or unnatural. This is so far from being the case, that, on very many occasions, they are both the most natural, and the most common method of uttering our sentiments. It is impossible to compose any discourse without using them often; nay, there are few sentences of any length, in which some expression or other, that may be termed a figure, does not occur. From what causes this happens, shall be afterwards explained. The fact, in the mean time, shows, that they are to be accounted part of that language which nature dictates to men. They are not the inventions of the schools, nor the mere product of study: on the contrary, the most illiterate speak in figures, as often as the most learned. Whenever the imaginations of the vulgar are much awakened, or their passions inflamed against one another, they will pour forth a torrent of figurative language as forcible as could be employed by the most artificial declaimer.

What then is it, which has drawn the attention of critics and rhetoricians so much to these forms of speech? It is this: They remarked, that in them consists much of the beauty and the force of language; and found them always to bear some characters, or distinguishing marks, by the help of which they could reduce them under separate classes and heads. To this, perhaps, they owe their name of figures. As the figure, or shape of one body, distinguishes it from another, so these forms of speech have, each of them, a cast or turn peculiar to itself, which both distinguishes it from the rest, and distinguishes it from simple expression. Simple expression just makes our idea known to others; but figurative language, over and above, bestows a particular dress upon that idea; a dress, which both makes it to be remarked, and adorns it. Hence, this sort of language became early a capital object of attention to those who studied the powers of speech.

Figures, in general, may be described to be that language, which is prompted either by the imagination, or by the passions. The justness of this description will appear, from the more particular account I am afterwards to give of them. Rhetoricians commonly divide them into two great classes; figures of words, and figures of thought. The former, figures of words, are commonly called tropes, and consist in a word's being employed to signify something that is different from its original and primitive meaning; so that if you alter the word, you destroy the figure. Thus, in the instance I gave before; 'Light ariseth to the upright in darkness.' The trope consists in 'light and darkness' being not meant literally, but substituted for comfort and adversity, on account of some resemblance or analogy which they are supposed to bear to these conditions of life. The other class, termed figures of thought, supposes the words to be used in their proper and literal meaning, and the figure to consist in the turn of the thought; as is the case in exclamations, interrogations, apostrophes, and comparisons; where, though you vary the words that are used, or translate them from one language into another, you may, nevertheless, still preserve the same figure in the thought. This distinction, however, is of no great use, as nothing can be built upon it in practice; neither is it always very clear. It is of little importance, whether we give to some particular mode of expression the name of a trope, or of a figure; provided we remember, that figurative language always imports some colouring of the imagination, or from some emotion of passion, expressed in our style: and, perhaps, figures of imagination, and figures of passion, might be a more useful distribution of the subject. But without insisting on any artificial divisions, it will be more useful, that I inquire into the origin and the nature of figures. Only, before I proceed to this, there are two general observations which it may be proper to premise.

The first is, concerning the use of rules with respect to figurative language. I admit, that persons may both speak and write with propriety, who know not the names of any of the figures of speech, nor ever studied any rules relating to them. Nature, as was before observed, dictates the use of figures; and, like Mons. Jourdain, in Moliere, who had spoken for forty years in prose, without ever knowing it, many a one uses metaphorical expressions to good purpose, without any idea of what a metaphor is. It will not, however, follow thence, that rules are of no service. All science arises from observations on practice. Practice has always gone before method and rule; but method and rule have afterwards improved and perfected practice in every art. We every day meet with persons who sing agreeably without knowing one note of the gamut. Yet, it has been found of importance to reduce these notes to a scale, and to form an art of music; and it would be ridiculous to pretend, that the art is of no advantage, because the practice is founded in nature. Propriety and beauty of speech, are certainly as improveable as the ear or the voice; and to know the principles of this beauty, or the reasons which render one figure, or one manner of speech, preferable to another, cannot fail to assist and direct a proper choice.

But I must observe, in the next place, that although this part of style merits attention, and is a very proper object of science and rule; although much of the beauty of composition depends on figurative language; yet we must beware of imagining that it depends solely, or even chiefly, upon such language. It is not so. The great place which the doctrine of tropes and figures has occupied in systems of rhetoric; the over-anxious care which has been shown in giving names to a vast variety of them, and in ranging them under different classes, has often led persons to imagine, that if their composition was well bespangled with a number of these ornaments of speech, it wanted no other beauty: whence has arisen much stiffness and affectation. For it is, in truth, the sentiment or passion, which lies under the figured expression, that gives it any merit. The figure is only the dress; the sentiment is the body and the substance. No figures will render a cold or an empty composition interesting; whereas, if a sentiment be sublime or pathetic, it can support itself perfectly well, without any borrowed assistance. Hence, several of the most affecting and admired passages of the best authors, are expressed in the simplest language. The following sentiment from Virgil, for instance, makes its way at once to the heart, without the help of any figure whatever. He is describing an Argive, who falls in battle, in Italy, at a great distance from his native country:

> Sternitur, infelix, alieno vulnere, cœlumque
> Aspicit, et dulcis moriens reminiscitur Argos: [1]
> [*Æn.* x. 781.]

A single stroke of this kind, drawn as by the very pencil of nature, is worth a thousand figures. In the same manner, the simple style of scripture: 'He spoke, and it was done; he commanded, and it stood fast,' 'God said, let there be light; and there was light,' imparts a lofty conception, to much greater advantage, than if it had been decorated by the most pompous metaphors. The fact is, that the strong pathetic, and the pure sublime, not only have little dependence on figures of speech, but generally reject them. The proper region of these ornaments is, where a moderate degree of elevation and passion is predominant; and there they contribute to the embellishment of discourse, only when there is a basis of solid thought and natural sentiment; when they are inserted in their proper place; and when they rise, of themselves, from the subject without being sought after.

Having premised these observations, I proceed to give an account of the origin and nature of figures; principally of such as have their dependence on language; including that numerous tribe which the rhetoricians call tropes.

At the first rise of language, men would begin with giving names to the different objects which they discerned, or thought of. This nomenclature

---

[1] Anthares had from Argos travell'd far,
Alcides' friend, and brother of the war;
Now falling, by another's wound, his eyes
He casts to Heaven, on Argos thinks, and dies.

In this translation, much of the beauty of the original is lost. 'On Argos thinks, and dies,' is by no means equal to 'dulcis moriens reminiscitur Argos' 'As he dies, he remembers his beloged Argos.' It is indeed observable, that in most of those tender and pathetic passages, which do so much honour to Virgil, that great poet expresses himself with the utmost simplicity; as

Te, dulcis conjux, te solo in littore secum,
Te veniente die, te decedente canebat.
[*Georg.* IV]

would, at the beginning, be very narrow. According as men's ideas multiplied, and their acquaintance with objects increased, their stock of names and words would increase also. But to the infinite variety of objects and ideas, no language is adequate. No language is so copious, as to have a separate word for every separate idea. Men naturally sought to abridge this labour of multiplying words *in infinitum;* and, in order to lay less burden on their memories, made one word, which they had already appropriated to a certain idea or object, stand also for some other idea or object; between which and the primary one, they found, or fancied, some relation. Thus, the preposition, *in,* was originally invented to express the circumstance of place: 'The man was killed *in* the wood.' In progress of time, words were wanted to express men's being connected with certain conditions of fortune, or certain situations of mind; and some resemblance, or analogy, being fancied between these, and the place of bodies, the word *in,* was employed to express men's being so circumstanced; as, one's being *in* health, or *in* sickness, *in* prosperity or *in* adversity, *in* joy or *in* grief, *in* doubt, or *in* danger, or *in* safety. Here we see this preposition, *in,* plainly assuming a tropical signification, or carried off from its original meaning, to signify something else which relates to, or resembles it.

Tropes of this kind abound in all languages, and are plainly owing to the want of proper words. The operations of the mind and affections, in particular, are, in most languages, described by words taken from sensible objects. The reason is plain. The names of sensible objects were, in all languages, the words most early introduced; and were, by degrees, extended to those mental objects, of which men had more obscure conceptions, and to which they found it more difficult to assign distinct names. They borrowed, therefore, the name of some sensible idea, where their imagination found some affinity. Thus, we speak of a *piercing* judgment and a *clear* head; a *soft* or a *hard* heart; a *rough* or a *smooth* behaviour. We say, *inflamed* by anger, *warmed* by love, *swelled* with pride, *melted* into grief; and these are almost the only significant words which we have for such ideas.

But, although the barrenness of languages, and the want of words, be doubtless one cause of the invention of tropes; yet it is not the only, nor, perhaps, even the principal source of this form of speech. Tropes have arisen more frequently, and spread themselves wider, from the influence which imagination possesses over language. The train on which this has proceeded among all nations, I shall endeavour to explain.

Every object which makes any impression on the human mind, is constantly accompanied with certain circumstances and relations, that strike us at the same time. It never presents itself to our view *isolé,* as the French express it; that is, independent on, and separated from, every other thing:

but always occurs as somehow related to other objects; going before them, or following them; their effect or their cause; resembling them, or opposed to them; distinguished by certain qualities, or surrounded with certain circumstances. By this means, every idea or object carries in its train some other ideas, which may be considered as its accessories. These accessories often strike the imagination more than the principal idea itself. They are, perhaps, more agreeable ideas; or they are more familiar to our conceptions; or they recall to our memory a greater variety of important circumstances. The imagination is more disposed to rest upon some of them; and therefore, instead of using the proper name of the principal idea which it means to express, it employs in its place the name of the accessory or correspondent idea; although the principal have a proper and well known name of its own. Hence a vast variety of tropical or figurative words obtain currency in all languages, through choice, not necessity; and men of lively imaginations are every day adding to their number.

Thus, when we design to intimate the period at which a state enjoyed most reputation or glory, it were easy to employ the proper words for expressing this; but as this is readily connected, in our imagination, with the flourishing period of a plant or a tree, we lay hold of this correspondent idea, and say, 'The Roman empire flourished most under Augustus.' The leader of a faction is plain language: but because the head is the principal part of the human body, and is supposed to direct all the animal operations, resting upon this resemblance, we say, 'Catiline was the head of the party.' The word *voice,* was originally invented to signify the articulate sound, formed by the organs of the mouth; but, as by means of it men signify their ideas and their intentions to each other, *voice* soon assumed a great many other meanings, all derived from this primary effect. 'To give our voice' for any thing, signified, to give our sentiment in favour of it. Not only so; but *voice* was transferred to signify any intimation of will or judgment, though given without the least interposition of voice in its literal sense, or any sound uttered at all. Thus we speak of listening to the *voice* of conscience, the *voice* of nature, the *voice* of God. This usage takes place, not so much from barrenness of language, or want of a proper word, as from an allusion which we choose to make to *voice* in its primary sense, in order to convey our idea, connected with a circumstance which appears to the fancy to give it more sprightliness and force.

The account which I have now given, and which seems to be a full and fair one, of the introduction of tropes into all languages, coincides with what Cicero briefly hints, in his third book, De Oratore. 'Modus transferendi verba latè patet; quam necessitas primum genuit, coacta inopia et angustia; post autem delectatio, jucunditasque celebravit. Nam ut vestis, frigoris depellendi causâ reperta primo, post adhiberi capta est ad ornatum etiam corporis et dignitatem, sic verbi translatio instituta est inopiæ causâ, frequentata delectationis.'[2]

From what has been said, it clearly appears how that must come to pass, which I had occasion to mention in a former lecture, that all languages are most figurative in their early state. Both the causes to which I ascribed the origin of figures, concur in producing this effect at the beginnings of society. Language is then most barren: the stock of proper names which have been invented for things, is small; and, at the same time, imagination exerts great influence over the conceptions of men, and their method of uttering them; so that, both from necessity and from choice, their speech will, at that period, abound in tropes; for the savage tribes of men are always much given to wonder and astonishment. Every new object surprises, terrifies, and makes a strong impression on their mind; they are governed by imagination and passion, more than by reason; and of course, their speech must be deeply tinctured by their genius. In fact, we find, that this is the character of the American and Indian languages: bold, picturesque, and metaphorical; full of strong allusions to sensible qualities, and to such objects as struck them most in their wild and solitary life. An Indian chief makes a harangue to his tribe, in a style full of stronger metaphors than an European would use in an epic poem.

As language makes gradual progress towards refinement, almost every object comes to have a proper name given to it, and perspicuity and precision are more studied. But still, for the reasons before given, borrowed words, or as rhetoricians call them, tropes, must continue to occupy a considerable place. In every language, too, there are a multitude of words, which, though they were figurative in their first application to certain objects, yet, by long use, lose their figurative power wholly, and come to be considered as simple and literal expressions. In this case, are the terms which I remarked before, as transferred from sensible qualities to the operations or qualities of the mind, a *piercing* judgment, a *clear* head, a *hard* heart, and the like. There are other words which remain in a sort of middle state; which have neither lost wholly their figurative application, nor yet retain so much of it as to imprint any remarkable character of figured language on our style; such as these phrases, 'apprehend one's meaning': 'enter on a subject': 'follow out an argument': 'stir up strife': and a great many more, of which our language is full. In the use of such phrases, correct writers will always preserve a regard to the figure or allusion on which they are

[2] 'The figurative usage of words is very extensive; an usage to which necessity first gave rise, on account of the pausity of words, and barrenness of language; but which the pleasure that was found in it afterwards rendered frequent. For as garments were first contrived to defend our bodies from the cold, and afterwards were employed for the purpose of ornament and dignity, so figures of speech introduced by want, were cultivated for the sake of entertainment.'

founded, and will be careful not to apply them in any way that is inconsistent with it. One may be 'sheltered under the patronage of a great man': but it were wrong to say, 'sheltered under the mask of dissimulation,' as a mask conceals, but does not shelter. An object, in description, may be 'clothed,' if you will, 'with epithets'; but it is not so proper to speak of its being 'clothed with circumstances': as the word 'circumstances' alludes to standing round, not to clothing. Such attentions as these to the propriety of language are requisite in every composition.

What has been said on this subject, tends to throw light on the nature of language in general, and will lead to the reasons, why tropes or figures contribute to the beauty and grace of style.

First, They enrich language, and render it more copious. By their means, words and phrases are multiplied for expressing all sorts of ideas; for describing even the minutest differences; the nicest shades and colours of thought; which no language could possibly do by proper words alone, without assistance from tropes.

Secondly, They bestow dignity upon style. The familiarity of common words, to which our ears are much accustomed, tends to degrade style. When we want to adapt our language to the tone of an elevated subject, we should be greatly at a loss, if we could not borrow assistance from figures; which, properly employed, have a similar effect on language, with what is produced by the rich and splendid dress of a person of rank; to create respect, and to give an air of magnificence to him who wears it. Assistance of this kind, is often needed in prose compositions; but poetry could not subsist without it. Hence figures form the constant language of poetry. To say, that 'the sun rises,' is trite and common; but it becomes a magnificent image when expressed, as Mr. Thomson has done:

> But yonder comes the powerful king of day,
> Rejoicing in the east.—

To say that 'all men are subject alike to death,' presents only a vulgar idea; but it rises and fills the imagination, when painted thus by Horace:

> Pallida mors æquo pulsat pede, pauperum tabernas
> Regumque turres.[3]

In the third place, figures give us the pleasure of enjoying two objects presented together to our view, without confusion; the principal idea, which is the subject of the discourse, along with its accessory, which gives it the figurative dress. We see one thing in another, as Aristotle expresses it;

---

[3] With equal pace, impartial fate
Knocks at the palace, as the cottage gate.

which is always agreeable to the mind. For there is nothing with which the fancy is more delighted, than with comparisons, and resemblances of objects; and all tropes are founded upon some relation or analogy between one thing and another. When, for instance, in place of 'youth,' I say the 'morning of life'; the fancy is immediately entertained with all the resembling circumstances which presently occur between these two objects. At one moment, I have in my eye a certain period of human life, and a certain time of the day, so related to each other, that the imagination plays between them with pleasure, and contemplates two similar objects, in one view, without embarrassment or confusion. Not only so, but,

In the fourth place, figures are attended with this farther advantage, of giving us frequently a much clearer and more striking view of the principal object, than we could have of it were it expressed in simple terms, and divested of its accessory idea. This is, indeed their principal advantage, in virtue of which, they are very properly said to illustrate a subject, or to throw a light upon it. For they exhibit the object, on which they are employed, in a picturesque form; they can render an abstract conception, in some degree, an object of sense; they surround it with such circumstances, as enable the mind to lay hold of it steadily, and to contemplate it fully. 'Those persons,' says one, 'who gain the hearts of most people, who are chosen as the companions of their softer hours, and their reliefs from anxiety and care, are seldom persons of shining qualities, or strong virtues: it is rather the soft green of the soul, on which we rest our eyes, that are fatigued with beholding more glaring objects.' Here, by a happy allusion to a colour, the whole conception is conveyed clear and strong to the mind in one word. By a well chosen figure, even conviction is assisted, and the impression of a truth upon the mind made more lively and forcible than it would otherwise be. As in the following illustration of Dr. Young's: 'When we dip too deep in pleasure, we always stir a sediment that renders it impure and noxious'; or in this, 'A heart boiling with violent passions, will always send up infatuating fumes to the head.' An image that presents so much congruity between a moral and a sensible idea, serves like an argument from analogy, to enforce what the other asserts, and to induce belief.

Besides, whether we are endeavouring to raise sentiments of pleasure or aversion, we can always heighten the emotion by the figures which we introduce; leading the imagination to a train, either of agreeable or disagreeable, of exalting or debasing ideas, correspondent to the impression which we seek to make. When we want to render an object beautiful, or magnificent, we borrow images from all the most beautiful or splendid scenes of nature; we thereby naturally throw a lustre over our object; we enliven the reader's mind, and dispose him to go along with us, in the gay and pleasing impressions which we give him of the subject. This effect of figures is happily touched in the following lines of Dr. Akenside, and illustrated by a very sublime figure:

> ————Then th' inexpressive strain
> Diffuses its enchantment. Fancy dreams
> Of sacred fountains and Elysian groves,
> And vales of bliss; the intellectual power,
> Bends from his awful throne, a wond'ring ear,
> And smiles.————
> [*Pleas. of Imaginat.* I. 124.]

What I have now explained, concerning the use and effects of figures, naturally leads us to reflect on the wonderful power of language; and, indeed, we cannot reflect on it without the highest admiration. What a fine vehicle is it now become for all the conceptions of the human mind; even for the most subtile and delicate workings of the imagination! What a pliable and flexible instrument in the hand of one who can employ it skilfully; prepared to take every form which he chooses to give it! Not content with a simple communication of ideas and thoughts, it paints those ideas to the eye; it gives colouring and relievo, even to the most abstract conceptions. In the figures which it uses, it sets mirrors before us, where we may behold objects, a second time, in their likeness. It entertains us, as with a succession of the most splended pictures; disposes in the most artificial manner, of the light and shade, for viewing every thing to the best advantage: in fine, from being a rude and imperfect interpreter of men's wants and necessities, it has now passed into an instrument of the most delicate and refined luxury.

To make these effects of figurative language sensible, there are few authors in the English language to whom I can refer with more advantage than Mr. Addison, whose imagination is at once remarkably rich, and remarkably correct and chaste. When he is treating, for instance, of the effect which light and colours have to entertain the fancy, considered in Mr. Locke's view of them as secondary qualities, which have no real existence in matter, but are only ideas of the mind, with what beautiful painting has he adorned this philosophic speculation! 'Things,' says he, 'would make but a poor appearance to the eye, if we saw them only in their proper figures and motions. Now, we are every where entertained with pleasing shows and apparitions; we discover imaginary glories in the heavens, and in the earth, and see some of this visionary beauty poured out upon the whole creation. But what a rough unsightly sketch of nature should we be entertained with, did all her colouring disappear, and the several distinctions of light and shade vanish? In short, our souls are at present delightfully lost, and bewildered in a pleasing delusion: and we walk about like the enchanted hero of a romance, who sees beautiful castles, woods, and meadows: and at the same time hears the warbling of birds, and the purling of streams; but, upon the finishing of some secret spell, the fantastic scene breaks up, and the disconsolate knight finds himself on a barren heath, or in a solitary desert. It is not improbable, that something like this may be the state of the soul after its first separation, in respect of the images it will receive from matter.' No. 413, Spectator.

Having thus explained, at sufficient length, the origin, the nature, and the effects of tropes, I should proceed next to the several kinds and divisions of them. But, in treating of these, were I to follow the common tract of the scholastic writers on rhetoric, I should soon become tedious, and, I apprehend, useless at the same time. Their great business has been, with a most patient and frivolous industry, to branch them out under a vast number of divisions, according to all the several modes in which a word may be carried from its literal meaning, into one that is figurative, without doing any more; as if the mere knowledge of the names and classes of all the tropes that can be formed, could be of any advantage towards the proper, or graceful use of language. All that I purpose is, to give, in a few words, before finishing this lecture, a general view of the several sources whence the tropical meaning of words is derived: after which I shall, in subsequent lectures, descend to a more particular consideration of some of the most considerable figures of speech, and such as are in most frequent use; by treating of which, I shall give all the instruction I can, concerning the proper employment of figurative language, and point out the errors and abuses which are apt to be committed in this part of style.

All tropes, as I before observed, are founded on the relation which one object bears to another; in virtue of which, the name of the one can be substituted instead of the name of the other, and by such a substitution, the vivacity of the idea is commonly meant to be increased. These relations, some more, some less intimate, may all give rise to tropes. One of the first and most obvious relations, is that between a cause and its effect. Hence, in figurative language, the cause is sometimes put for the effect. Thus, Mr. Addison, writing of Italy:

> Blossoms, and fruits, and flowers, together rise,
> And the whole year in gay confusion lies.

Where the 'whole year' is plainly intended, to signify the effects or productions of all the seasons of the year. At other times, again, the effect is put for the cause; as, 'gray hairs' frequently for old age, which causes gray hairs; and 'shade,' for trees that produce the shade. The relation between the container and the thing contained, is also so intimate and obvious, as naturally to give rise to tropes:

—————Ille impiger hausit
Spumantem pateram et pleno se proluit auro.

Where every one sees, that the cup and the gold are put for the liquor that was contained in the golden cup. In the same manner, the name of any country is often used to denote the inhabitants of that country; and Heaven, very often employed to signify God, because he is conceived as dwelling in Heaven. To implore the assistance of Heaven, is the same as to implore the assistance of God. The relation betwixt any established sign and the thing signified, is a further source of tropes. Hence,

Cedant arma togæ; concedat laurea linguæ.

The 'toga,' being the badge of the civil professions, and the 'laurel' of military honours, the badge of each is put for the civil and military characters themselves. To 'assume the sceptre,' is a common phrase for entering on royal authority. To tropes, founded on these several relations, of cause and effect, container and contained, sign and thing signified, is given the name of Metonymy.

When the trope is founded on the relation between an antecedent and a consequent, or what goes before, and immediately follows, it is then called a Metalepsis; as in the Roman phrase of 'Fuit,' or 'Vixit,' to express that one was dead. 'Fuit Ilium et ingens gloria Dardanidum,' signifies, that the glory of Troy is now no more.

When the whole is put for a part, or a part for the whole; a genus for a species, or a species for a genus; the singular for the plural, or the plural for the singular number; in general, when any thing less, or any thing more, is put for the precise object meant; the figure is then called a Synecdoche. It is very common, for instance, to describe a whole object by some remarkable part of it; as when we say, 'a fleet of so many sail,' in the place of 'ships'; when we use the 'head' for the 'person,' the 'pole' for the 'earth,' the 'waves' for the 'sea.' In like manner, an attribute may be put for a subject; as, 'youth and beauty,' for 'the young and beautiful'; and sometimes a subject for its attribute. But it is needless to insist longer on this enumeration, which serves little purpose. I have said enough, to give an opening into that great variety of relations between objects, by means of which, the mind is assisted to pass easily from one to another; and understands, by the name of the one, the other to be meant. It is always some accessory idea, which recalls the principal to the imagination; and commonly recalls it with more force, than if the principal idea had been expressed.

The relation which is far the most fruitful of tropes I have not yet mentioned; that is, the relation of similitude and resemblance. On this is founded what is called the metaphor; when, in place of using the proper name of any object, we employ, in its place, the name of some other which is like it; which is a sort of picture of it, and which thereby awakens the conception of it with more force or grace. This figure is more frequent than all the rest put together; and the language, both of prose and verse, owes to it much of its elegance and grace. This, therefore, deserves very full and particular consideration; and shall be the subject of the next lecture.

AIDS TO STUDY

Most of us today are not willing to accept Blair's easy division of language into 'plain' and 'figurative.' And his example of a simple statement—'That a good man enjoys comfort in the midst of adversity'—does not strike us as so simple as he suggests; indeed, he himself later suggests that the use of *in* in such an expression as this is more or less figurative. Eighteenth-century rhetoricians took for granted that ideas could be separated from the words they were expressed in; today we are less sure of this, some people feeling that *all* language is figurative. You may find it interesting to read this selection in conjunction with the essays in this collection by C. S. Lewis and I. A. Richards.

It is not easy to get over this basic problem of definition of 'figurative language.' But if we can put off the problem, much of what Blair has to say is of considerable practical value for the writer. His reminder that figurative language is not a product of the school is a sobering one; his suggestions about the values of figures of speech may help encourage us to stretch our linguistic muscles; his examples are instructive, if we study them with care; and his division of 'tropes' or figures of speech is not so lengthy or complicated as to be frustrating or useless.

Of Wit, Humor, and Ridicule

SECTION I.—OF WIT

. . . [It] is the design of wit to excite in the mind an agreeable surprise, and that arising, not from any thing marvellous in the subject, but solely from the imagery she employs, or the strange assemblage of related ideas presented to the mind. This end is effected in one or other of these three ways: first, in debasing things pompous or seemingly grave; I say seemingly grave, because to vilify what is truly grave, has something shocking in it, which rarely fails to counteract the end; secondly, in aggrandizing things little and frivolous; thirdly, in setting ordinary objects, by means not only remote but apparently contrary, in a particular and uncommon point of view.[1] This will be better understood from the following observations and examples.

From *The Philosophy of Rhetoric,* Chapter II, 'Of Wit, Humor, and Ridicule,' London, Wm. Baylie, 1823.

[1] I know no language which affords a name for this species of imagery, but the English. The French *esprit* or *bel esprit,* though on some occasions rightly translated Wit, hath commonly a signification more extensive and generical. It must be owned, indeed, that in conformity to the style of French critics, the term Wit, in English writings, hath been sometimes used with equal latitude. But this is certainly a perversion of the word from its ordinary sense, through an excessive deference to the manner and idiom of our ingenious neighbours. Indeed, when an author varies the meaning in the same work, he not only occasions perplexity to his reader, but falls himself into an apparent inconsistency. An error of this kind in Mr. Pope has been lately pointed out by a very ingenious and judicious critic. 'In the essay on criticism it is said,
    "True wit is nature to advantage dressed":
'But immediately after this the poet adds,'
    "For works may have more wit than does 'em good."
'Now let us substitute the definition in the place of the thing, and it will stand thus: A work may have more of nature dressed to advantage, than will do it good. This is impossible; and it is evident, that the confusion arises from the poet's having annexed two different ideas to the same word.' Webb's Remarks on the Beauties of Poetry, Dialogue ii.

The materials employed by wit in the grotesque pieces she exhibits, are partly derived from those common fountains of whatever is directed to the imaginative powers, the ornaments of elocution, and the oratorical figures, simile, apostrophe, antithesis, metaphor; partly from those she in a manner appropriates to herself, irony, hyperbole, allusion, parody, and (if the reader will pardon my descending so low) paronomasia,[2] and pun. . . . This enchantress exults in reconciling contradictions, and in hitting on that special light and attitude wherein you can discover an unexpected similarity in objects, which, at first sight, appear the most dissimilar and heterogeneous. Thus high and low are coupled, humble and superb, momentous and trivial, common and extraordinary. Addison, indeed, observes,[3] that wit is often produced, not by the resemblance, but by the opposition of ideas. But this, of which, however, he hath not given us an instance, doth not constitute a different species, as the repugnancy in that case will always be found between objects in other respects resembling; for it is to the contrast of dissimilitude and likeness, remoteness and relation in the same objects, that its peculiar effect is imputable. Hence we hear of the flashes and the sallies of wit, phrases which imply suddenness, surprise, and contrariety. These are illustrated in the first by a term which implies an instantaneous emergence of light in darkness; in the second, by a word which denotes an abrupt transition to things distant. For we may remark in passing, that though language be older than criticism, those expressions adopted by the former to elucidate matters of taste, will be found to have a pretty close conformity to the purest discoveries of the latter.

Nay, of so much consequence here are surprise and novelty, that nothing is more tasteless, and sometimes disgusting, than a joke that has become stale by frequent repetition. For the same reason, even a pun or happy allusion will appear excellent when thrown out extempore in conversation, which would be deemed execrable in print. In like manner, a witty repartee is infinitely more pleasing than a witty attack. For though, in both cases, the thing may be equally new to the reader or hearer, the effect on him is greatly injured, when there is ground to suppose, that it may be the slow production of study and premeditation. This, however, holds most with regard to the inferior tribes of witticisms, of which their readiness is the best recommendation.

. . . Sublimity elevates, beauty charms, wit diverts. The first, as hath been already observed, enraptures, and as it were, dilates the soul; the second

---

[2] Paronomasia is properly that figure which the French call *jeu de mots*. Such as 'Inceptio est amentium, haud amantium.' Ter. Andr. 'Which tempted our attempt.' Milt. B. i. 'To begird the Almighty's throne, beseeching or besieging.' B. v.
[3] Spectator.

diffuseth over it a serene delight; the third tickles the fancy, and throws the spirits into an agreeable vibration.

To these reflections I shall subjoin examples in each of the three sorts of wit above explained.

It will, however, be proper to premise, that if the reader should not at first be sensible of the justness of the solutions and explications to be given, he ought not hastily to form an unfavorable conclusion. Wherever there is taste, the witty and the humorous make themselves perceived, and produce their effect instantaneously; but they are of so subtle a nature, that they will hardly endure to be touched, much less to undergo a strict analysis and scrutiny. They are like those volatile essences, which, being too delicate to bear the open air, evaporate almost as soon as they are exposed to it. Accordingly, the wittiest things will sometimes be made to appear insipid, and the most ingenious frigid, by scrutinizing them too narrowly. Besides, the very frame of spirit proper for being diverted with the laughable in objects, is so different from that which is necessary for philosophizing on them, that there is a risk, that when we are most disposed to inquire into the cause, we are least capable of feeling the effect; as it is certain, that when the effect hath its full influence on us, we have little inclination for investigating the cause. For these reasons, I have resolved to be brief in my illustrations, having often observed, that, in such nice and abstract inquiries, if a proper hint do not suggest the matter to the reader, he will be but more perplexed by long and elaborate discussions.

Of the first sort, which consists in the debasement of things great and eminent, Butler, amongst a thousand other instances, hath given us those which follow:

> And now had Phœbus in the lap
> Of Thetis, taken out his nap:
> And, like a lobster boiled, the morn
> From black to red began to turn.[4]

Here the low allegorical style of the first couplet, and the simile used in the second, afford us a just notion of this lowest species, which is distinguished by the name of the Ludicrous. Another specimen from the same author you have in these lines:

> Great on the bench, great in the saddle,
> That could as well bind o'er as swaddle,
> Mighty he was at both of these,
> And styled of war, as well as peace:

[4] Hudibras, Part ii. Canto 2.

> So some rats of amphibious nature,
> Are either for the land or water.[5]

In this coarse kind of drollery, those laughable translations or paraphrases of heroic and other serious poems, wherein the authors are said to be travestied, chiefly abound.

To the same class those instances must be referred, in which, though there is no direct comparison made, qualities of real dignity and importance are degraded, by being coupled with things mean and frivolous, as in some respect standing in the same predicament. An example of this I shall give from the same hand.

> For when the restless Greeks sat down
> So many years, before Troy town,
> And were renowned, as Homer writes,
> For well-soaled boots,[6] no less than fights.[7]

I shall only observe further, that this sort, whose aim is to debase, delights in the most homely expressions, provincial idioms, and cant phrases.

The second kind, consisting in the aggrandizement of little things, which is by far the most splendid, and displays a soaring imagination, these lines of Pope will serve to illustrate:

> As Berecynthia, while her offspring vie
> In homage to the mother of the sky,
> Surveys around her, in the blest abode,
> An hundred sons, and every son a god:
> Not with less glory mighty Dulness crowned,
> Shall take through Grub-street her triumphant round;
> And her Parnassus glancing o'er at once,
> Behold an hundred sons, and each a dunce.[8]

This whole similitude is spirited. The parent of the celestials is contrasted by the daughter of night and chaos; heaven by Grub-street; gods by dunces. Besides, the parody it contains on a beautiful passage in Virgil, adds a particular lustre to it.[9] This species we may term the Thrasonical, or the Mock-

---

[5] Ibid, Part i. Canto i.
[6] In allusion to the Ἐυχγήμιδες Ἀχαιοὶ, an expression which frequently occurs both in the Iliad and in the Odyssey.
[7] Hudibras, Part i. Canto 2.
[8] Dunciad, B. iii.
[9] The passage is this,—

> Felix prole virum, qualis Berecynthia mater
> Invehitur curru Phrygias turrita per urbes,
> Læta deum partu, centum complexa nepotes,
> Omnes cœlicolas, omnes supera alta tenentes.
>   [*Æneis*, vi.]

majestic. It affects the most pompous language, and sonorous phraseology, as much as the other affects the reverse, the vilest and most grovelling dialect.

I shall produce another example from the same writer, which is, indeed, inimitably fine. It represents a lady employed at her toilet, attended by her maid, under the allegory of the celebration of some solemn and religious ceremony. The passage is rather long for a quotation, but as the omission of any part would be a real mutilation, I shall give it entire.

> And now unveiled, the toilet stands displayed,
> Each silver vase in mystic order laid.
> First, robed in white, the nymph intent adores,
> With head uncovered, the cosmetic powers.
> A heavenly image in the glass appears,
> To that she bends, to that her eyes she rears;
> The inferior priestess, at her altar's side,
> Trembling begins the sacred rites of pride;
> Unnumbered treasures opes at once, and here
> The various offerings of the world appear;
> From each she nicely culls with curious toil,
> And decks the goddess with the glittering spoil.
> This casket India's glowing gems unlocks,
> And all Arabia breathes from yonder box.
> The tortoise here and elephant unite,
> Transformed to combs, the speckled, and the white.
> Here files of pins extend their shining rows,
> Puffs, powders, patches, bibles, billet doux.
> Now awful beauty puts on all its arms;
> The fair each moment rises in her charms,
> Repairs her smiles, awakens every grace,
> And calls forth all the wonders of her face;
> Sees by degrees a purer blush arise,
> And keener lightnings quicken in her eyes.[10]

To this class also we must refer the application of grave reflections to mere trifles. For that great and serious are naturally associated by the mind, and likewise little and trifling, is sufficiently evinced by the common modes of expression on these subjects used in every tongue. An apposite instance of such an application we have from Philips,

> My galligaskins, that have long withstood
> The winter's fury and encroaching frosts,
> By time subdued, (what will not time subdue!)
> An horrid chasm disclose.[11]

[10] Rape of the Lock, Canto 1.
[11] Splendid Shilling.

Like to this, but not equal, is that of Young,

> One day his wife, (for who can wives reclaim!)
> Levelled her barbarous needle at his fame.[12]

To both the preceding kinds the term Burlesque is applied, but especially to the first.

Of the third species of wit, which is by far the most multifarious, and which results from what I may call the queerness or singularity of the imagery, I shall give a few specimens that will serve to mark some of its principal varieties. To illustrate all would be impossible.

The first I shall exemplify, is where there is an apparent contrariety in the thing she exhibits as connected. This kind of contrast we have in these lines of Garth,

> Then Hydrops next appears amongst the throng;
> Bloated and big she slowly sails along:
> But like a miser in excess she's poor;
> And pines for thirst amidst her watery store.[13]

The wit in these lines doth not so much arise from the comparison they contain of the dropsy to a miser, (which falls under the description that immediately succeeds), as from the union of contraries they present to the imagination, poverty in the midst of opulence, and thirst in one who is already drenched in water.

A second sort, is where the things compared are what with dialecticians would come under the denomination of disparates, being such as can be ranked under no common genus. Of this I shall subjoin an example from Young,

> Health chiefly keeps an Atheist in the dark;
> A fever argues better than a Clarke:
> Let but the logic in his pulse decay,
> The Grecian he'll renounce, and learn to pray.[14]

Here, by implication, health is compared to a sophister, or darkener of the understanding, a fever to a metaphysical disputant, a regular pulse to false logic, for the word logic in the third line is used ironically. In other words, we have here modes and substances, the affections of body, and the exercise of reason strangely, but not insignificantly linked together; strangely, else the sentiment, however just, could not be denominated witty; significantly, because an unmeaning jumble of things incongruous would not be wit, but nonsense.

[12] Universal Passion.
[13] Dispensary.
[14] Universal Passion.

A third variety in this species springs from confounding artfully the proper and the metaphorical sense of an expression. In this way, one will assign as a motive, what is discovered to be perfectly absurd, when but ever so little attended to; and yet, from the ordinary meaning of the words, hath a specious appearance on a single glance. Of this kind you have an instance in the subsequent lines,

> While thus the lady talked, the knight
> Turned the outside of his eyes to white,
> As men of inward light are wont
> To turn their optics in upon 't.[15]

For whither can they turn their eyes more properly than to the light?

A fourth variety, much resembling the former, is when the argument or comparison (for all argument is a kind of comparison) is founded on the supposal of corporeal or personal attributes in what is strictly not susceptible of them, as in this,

> But Hudibras gave him a twitch
> As quick as lightning in the breech,
> Just in the place where honor's lodged
> As wise philosophers have judged;
> Because a kick in that place more
> Hurts honor than deep wounds before.[16]

Is demonstration itself more satisfactory? Can any thing be hurt but where it is? However, the mention of this as the sage deduction of philosophers, is no inconsiderable addition to the wit. Indeed, this particular circumstance belongs properly to the first species mentioned, in which high and low, great and little, are coupled. Another example not unlike the preceding you have in these words,

> What makes morality a crime,
> The most notorious of the time;
> Morality, which both the saints
> And wicked too cry out against?
> 'Cause grace and virtue are within
> Prohibited degrees of kin:
> And therefore no true saint allows
> They shall be suffered to espouse.[17]

When the two foregoing instances are compared together, we should say of the first, that it has more of simplicity and nature, and is therefore more

---

[15] Hudibras, Part iii. Canto 1.
[16] Hudibras, Part ii. Canto 3.
[17] Hudibras, Part iii. Canto 1.

pleasing; of the second, that it has more of ingenuity and conceit, and is consequently more surprising.

The fifth and only other variety I shall observe, is that which ariseth from a relation not in the things signified, but in the signs, of all relations, no doubt, the slightest. Identity here gives rise to puns and clinches. Resemblance to quibbles, cranks, and rhymes. Of these, I imagine, it is quite unnecessary to exhibit specimens. The wit here is so dependent on the sound, that it is commonly incapable of being transfused into another language, and as, among persons of taste and discernment, it is in less request than the other sorts above enumerated, those who abound in this, and never rise to any thing superior, are distinguished by the diminutive appellation of witlings.

Let it be remarked in general, that from one or more of the three last mentioned varieties, those plebeian tribes of witticism, the conundrums, the rebuses, the riddles, and some others, are lineally, though perhaps not all legitimately, descended. I shall only add, that I have not produced the fore-named varieties as an exact enumeration of all the subdivisions, of which the third species of wit is susceptible. It is capable, I acknowledge, of being almost infinitely diversified; and it is principally to its various exhibitions, that we apply the epithets sportive, spritely, ingenious, according as they recede more or less from those of the declaimer.

SECTION II.—OF HUMOR

As wit is the painting, humor is the pathetic, in this inferior sphere of eloquence. The nature and efficacy of humor may be thus unravelled. A just exhibition of any ardent or durable passion, excited by some adequate cause, instantly attacheth sympathy, the common tie of human souls, and thereby communicates the passion to the breast of the hearer. But when the emotion is either not violent or not durable, and the motive not any thing real, but imaginary, or at least quite disproportionate to the effect; or when the passion displays itself preposterously, so as rather to obstruct than to promote its aim; in these cases a natural representation, instead of fellow feeling, creates amusement, and universally awakens contempt. The portrait in the former case we call pathetic, in the latter humorous.[18] It was said, that the emotion

[18] It ought to be observed, that this term is also used to express any lively strictures of such specialties in temper and conduct, as have neither moment enough to interest sympathy, nor incongruity enough to excite contempt. In this case, humor not being addressed to passion, but to fancy, must be considered as a kind of moral painting, and differs from wit only in these two things: first, in that, character alone is the subject of the former, whereas all things whatever fall within the province of the latter; secondly, humor paints more simply by direct imitation, wit more variously by illustration and imagery. Of this kind of humor, merely graphical, Addison hath given us numberless

must be either not violent or not durable. This limitation is necessary, because a passion extreme in its degree, as well as lasting, cannot yield diversion to a well-disposed mind, but generally affects it with pity, not seldom with a mixture of horror and indignation. The sense of the ridiculous, though invariably the same, is in this case totally surmounted by a principle of our nature, much more powerful.

The passion which humor addresseth as its object, is, as hath been signified above, contempt. But it ought carefully to be noted, that every address, even every pertinent address to contempt, is not humorous. This passion is not less capable of being excited by the severe and tragic, than by the merry and comic manner.—The subject of humor is always character, but not every thing in character; its foibles generally, such as caprices, little extravagancies, weak anxieties, jealousies, childish fondness, pertness, vanity, and self-conceit. One finds the greatest scope for exercising this talent in telling familiar stories, or in acting any whimsical part in an assumed character. Such an one, we say, has the talent of humoring a tale, or any queer manner which he chooseth to exhibit. Thus we speak of the passions in tragedy, but of the humors in comedy; and even to express passion as appearing in the more trivial occurrences of life, we commonly use this term, as when we talk of good humor, ill humor, peevish or pleasant humor; hence it is that a capricious temper we call humorsome, the person possessed of it a humorist, and such facts or events as afford subject for the humorous, we denominate comical. . . .

The pathetic and the facetious differ not only in subject and effect, as will appear upon the most superficial review of what hath been said, but also in the manner of imitation. In this the man of humor descends to a minuteness which the orator disdains. The former will often successfully run into downright mimicry, and exhibit peculiarities in voice, gesture, and pronunciation, which in the other would be intolerable. The reason of the difference is this: That we may divert by exciting scorn and contempt, the individual must be exposed; that we may move by interesting the more generous principles of humanity, the language and sentiments, not so much of

---

examples in many of the characters he hath so finely drawn, and little incidents he hath so pleasantly related in his Tatlers and Spectators. I might remark of the word humor, as I did of the term wit, that we scarcely find in other languages a word exactly corresponding. The Latin *facetiae* seems to come the nearest. Thus Cicero, 'Huic generi orationis aspergentur etiam sales, qui in dicendo nimium quantum valent: quorum duo genera sunt, unum facetiarum, alterum dicacitatis: utetur utroque, sed altero in narrando aliquid venuste, altero in jaciendo mittendoque ridiculo; cujus genera plura sunt.' Orator, 26. Here one would think, that the philosopher must have had in his eye the different provinces of wit and humor, calling the former 'dicacitas,' the latter 'facetiae.' It is plain, however, that, both by him and other Latin authors, these two words are often confounded. There appears, indeed, to be more uniformity in the use that is made of the second term, than in the application of the first.

the individual, as of human nature, must be displayed. So very different, or rather opposite, are these two in this respect, that there could not be a more effectual expedient for undoing the charm of the most affecting representation, than an attempt in the speaker to mimic the personal singularities of the man for whom he desires to interest us.—On the other hand, in the humorous, where the end is diversion, even overacting, if moderate, is not improper.

It was observed already, that, though contempt be the only passion addressed by humor, yet this passion may with propriety and success be assailed by the severer eloquence, where there is not the smallest tincture of humor. This it will not be beside our purpose to specify, in order the more effectually to show the difference. Lord Bollingbroke, speaking of the state of these kingdoms from the time of the Restoration, has these words:—'The two brothers, Charles and James, when in exile, became infected with popery to such degrees as their different characters admitted of. Charles had parts; and his good understanding served as an antidote to repel the poison. James, the simplest man of his time, drank off the whole chalice. The poison met, in his composition, with all the fear, all the credulity, and all the obstinacy of temper proper to increase its virulence, and to strengthen its effect.—Drunk with superstitious, and even enthusiastic zeal, he ran headlong into his own ruin, whilst he endeavoured to precipitate ours. His parliament and his people did all they could to save themselves, by winning him. But all was vain. He had no principle on which they could take hold. Even his good qualities worked against them; and his love of his country went halves with his bigotry. How he succeeded we have heard from our fathers. The Revolution of one thousand six hundred and eighty-eight saved the nation, and ruined the king.' [19]—Nothing can be more contemptuous, and, at the same time, less derisive, than this representation. We should readily say of it, that it is strongly animated, and happily expressed; but no man who understands English would say it is humorous. I shall add one example from Dr. Swift: 'I should be exceedingly sorry to find the legislature make any new laws against the practice of duelling, because the methods are easy and many for a wise man to avoid a quarrel with honor, or engage in it with innocence. And I can discover no political evil in suffering bullies, sharpers, and rakes, to rid the world of each other by a method of their own, where the law hath not been able to find an expedient.' [20]

For a specimen of the humorous, take as a contrast to the two last examples, the following delineation of a fop:

> Sir Plume (of amber snuff-box justly vain,
> And the nice conduct of a clouded cane,)

[19] A Letter to Sir William Wyndham.
[20] Swift on Good Manners.

> With earnest eyes and round unthinking face,
> He first the snuff-box opened, then the case,
> And thus broke out, 'My lord, why,—what the devil?
> Z—ds!—damn the lock!—'fore Gad, you must be civil!
> Plague on't!—'tis past a jest,—nay prithee,—pox!
> Give her the hair,'—He spoke and rapped his box,
> 'It grieves me much,' replied the peer again,
> 'Who speaks so well, should ever speak in vain;
> But———' [21]

This, both in the descriptive and the dramatic part, particularly in the draught it contains of the baronet's mind, aspect, manner, and eloquence, (if we except the sarcastic term 'justly,' the double sense of the word 'opened,' and the fine irony couched in the reply), is purely facetious. An instance of wit and humor combined, where they reciprocally set off and enliven each other, Pope hath also furnished us with in another part of the same exquisite performance.

> Whether the nymph shall break Diana's law,
> Or some frail china jar receive a flaw;
> Or stain her honor, or her new brocade;
> Forget her prayers, or miss a masquerade;
> Or lose her heart, or necklace, at a ball;
> Or whether heaven has doomed that Shock must fall.[22]

This is humorous, in that it is a lively sketch of the female estimate of mischances, as our poet's commentator rightly terms it, marked out by a few striking lineaments. It is likewise witty, for, not to mention the play on words like that remarked in the former example, a trope familiar to this author, you have here a comparison of a woman's chastity to a piece of porcelain, her honor to a gaudy robe, her prayers to a fantastical disguise, her heart to a trinket; and all these together to her lap-dog, and that founded on one lucky circumstance (a malicious critic would perhaps discern or imagine more) by which these things, how unlike soever in other respects, may be compared, the impression they make on the mind of a fine lady. . . .

Wit and humor, as above explained, commonly concur in a tendency to provoke laughter, by exhibiting a curious and unexpected affinity; the first generally by comparison, either direct or implied; the second by connecting in some other relation, such as causality or vicinity, objects apparently the most dissimilar and heterogeneous; which incongruous affinity, we may remark by the way, gives the true meaning of the word Oddity, and is the proper object of laughter.

[21] Rape of the Lock, Canto 4.
[22] Rape of the Lock, Canto 2.

The difference between these and that grander kind of eloquence treated in the first part of this chapter, I shall, if possible, still farther illustrate, by a few similitudes borrowed from the optical science. The latter may be conceived as a plain mirror, which faithfully reflects the object, in color, figure, size, and posture. Wit, on the contrary, Proteus-like, transforms itself into a variety of shapes. It is now a convex speculum, which gives a just representation in form and color, but withal reduces the greatest objects to the most despicable littleness; now a concave speculum, which swells the smallest trifles to an enormous magnitude; now again a speculum of a cylindrical, a conical, or an irregular make, which, though in color, and even in attitude, it reflects a pretty strong resemblance, widely varies the proportions. Humor, when we consider the contrariety of its effects, contempt and laughter, (which constitute what in one word is termed Derision), to that sympathy and love often produced by the pathetic, may in respect of these be aptly compared to a concave mirror, when the object is placed beyond the focus; in which case it appears by reflection both diminished and inverted, circumstances which happily adumbrate the contemptible and the ridiculous.

SECTION III.—OF RIDICULE

The intention of raising a laugh is either merely to divert by that grateful titillation which it excites, or to influence the opinions and purposes of the hearers. In this also, the risible faculty, when suitably directed, hath often proved a very potent engine. When this is the view of the speaker, as there is always an air of reasoning conveyed under that species of imagery, narration or description, which stimulates laughter, these, thus blended, obtain the appellation of ridicule, the poignancy of which hath a similar effect in futile subjects to that produced by what is called the vehement in solemn and important matters.

Nor doth all the difference between these lie in the dignity of the subject. Ridicule is not only confined to questions of less moment, but is fitter for refuting error than for supporting truth, for restraining from wrong conduct, than for inciting to the practice of what is right. Nor are these the sole restrictions; it is not properly levelled at the false, but at the absurd in tenets; nor can the edge of ridicule strike with equal force every species of misconduct: it is not the criminal part which it attacks, but that which we denominate silly or foolish. With regard to doctrine, it is evident that it is not falsity or mistake, but palpable error or absurdity, (a thing hardly confutable by mere argument), which is the object of contempt; and consequently those dogmas are beyond the reach of cool reasoning which are within the rightful confines of ridicule. That they are generally conceived to be so, appears from the sense universally assigned to expressions like these, 'Such a position is ridiculous.—It doth not deserve a serious answer.' Every body knows that they import more than 'It is false,' being, in other words, 'This is such an extravagance as is not so much a subject of argument as of laughter.' . . . Those things which principally come under its lash are awkwardness, rusticity, ignorance, cowardice, levity, foppery, pedantry, and affectation of every kind. But against murder, cruelty, parricide, ingratitude, perfidy, to attempt to raise a laugh, would shew such an unnatural insensibility in the speaker, as would be excessively disgustful to any audience. To punish such enormities, the tragic poet must take a very different route. . . .

Another remarkable difference, the only one which remains to be observed, between the vehement or contentious and the derisive, consists in the manner of conducting them. As in each there is a mixture of argument, this in the former ought, in appearance at least, to have the ascendant, but not in the latter. The attack of the declaimer is direct and open; argument therefore is his avowed aim. On the contrary, the passions which he excites, ought never to appear to the auditors as the effects of his intention and address, but, both in him and them, as the native, the unavoidable consequences of the subject treated, and of that conviction which his reasoning produces in the understanding. Although, in fact, he intends to move his auditory, he only declares his purpose to convince them. To reverse this method, and profess an intention to work upon their passions, would be in effect to tell them that he meant to impose upon their understandings, and to bias them by his art, and consequently, would be to warn them to be on their guard against him. Nothing is better founded than the famous aphorism of rhetoricians, that the perfection of art consists in concealing art. On the other hand, the assault of him who ridicules is from its very nature covert and oblique. What we profess to contemn, we scorn to confute. It is on this account that the reasoning in ridicule, if at all delicate, is always conveyed under a species of disguise. Nay, sometimes, which is more astonishing, the contempt itself seems to be dissembled, and the rallier assumes an air of arguing gravely in defence of that which he actually exposeth as ridiculous. Hence, undoubtedly, it proceeds, that a serious manner commonly adds energy to a joke. The fact, however, is, that in this case the very dissimulation is dissembled. He would not have you think him in earnest, though he affects the appearance of it; knowing that otherwise his end would be frustrated. He wants that you should perceive that he is dissembling, which no real dissembler ever wanted. It is, indeed, this circumstance alone, which distinguishes an ironical expression from a lie. Accordingly, through the thinness of the veil employed, he takes care that the sneer shall be discovered. You are quickly made to perceive his aim, by means of the strange arguments he produces, the absurd consequences he draws, the odd embarrassments, which in his personated character he is involved in, and the still odder methods he takes to disentangle himself. . . . As the attack of ridicule, whatever form it adopts, is always indirect, that of irony may be said to be reverted. It resembles the manner of fighting ascribed to the ancient Parthians, who were ever more formidable in flight than in onset; who looked towards one quarter, and fought towards the opposite; whose bodies moved in one direction, and their arrows in the contrary. . . .

AIDS TO STUDY

This selection was not chosen for inclusion in this collection solely for its subject matter; it also illustrates, in part, why the grand tradition of rhetoric began to die out in the eighteenth century. For it is difficult to argue that Campbell was himself an exemplary writer; this is tough going—and one may well conclude, needlessly tough going. Campbell's approach to rhetoric was, in one of the unhappy senses of the term, philosophical: Campbell's writing is almost unbearably solemn; it is couched in the most abstract terminology; the diction is heavily Latinate, the sentence structure is complex and ponderous. Here is a man writing of wit and humor in almost the least witty and humorous fashion we can imagine. It is hard to escape the feeling that, in this selection, rhetoric, admittedly an important and serious study, is being considered too importantly and taken too seriously.

But to come to this conclusion after one quick reading is surely not fair; and no doubt this selection will require several readings, and very close attention. We may find ourselves like young Cicero, in effect translating a foreign language into our own. If we go to this trouble, we will find much in this selection of interest.

Wit, we will find, is a technique, a way of treating subject matter: it results from our treating seemingly important or grave matters as though they were unimportant or frivolous, or from treating any common matter in a manner that is different from or contrary to the way our audience expects it to be treated. That is, wit consists in an implied contradiction between the matter treated and the way it is treated.

Humor is an attitude, or a way of looking at things—or more specifically, a way at looking at people and what they do. If what people do is in keeping with their sentiments, we sympathize with them; but if it is not, we tend to laugh at them. And the basis for our laughter, Campbell holds, is contempt; and hence, humor is concerned with the foibles of people and the weaknesses of their character. It attaches to specific people and their specific acts. This is not to say that we never laugh at people we love; but what we laugh at is their actions which seem to us out of keeping with what seems to us sane and sensible. We can love the philosopher and yet laugh when, looking at the stars, he falls in a ditch; for we think people should watch where they are going and have a sort of contempt for those who do not, however much we may otherwise sympathize with them.

Ridicule is a matter of intention, Campbell says: if our purpose in making people laugh is to change their ways or opinions, our purpose is ridicule, or satire. One may, of course, directly argue that people should change their ways or notions—this is not satire or ridicule. The satirist puts on a false appearance (he 'dissembles'); he pretends he is not arguing, and indeed may pretend to be supporting that which he opposes. But, as Campbell remarks, he always leaves us a clue that we are not to take him seriously.

Finally, we should observe that wit, humor, and ridicule have limitations. Truly serious and important matters are not the subjects of ridicule or humor or wit: we do not ridicule proper honesty or bravery or humility; we do not find humor in catastrophe or moral rectitude or devotion to duty; we do not employ the manner of wit to deal with such matters.

Coleridge and After

The Science of Method

What is that which first strikes us, and strikes us at once, in a man of education? And which, among educated men, so instantly distinguishes the man of superior mind, that (as was observed with eminent propriety of the late Edmund Burke) 'we cannot stand under the same arch-way during a shower of rain, *without finding him out?*' Not the weight or novelty of his remarks; not any unusual interest of facts communicated by him; for we may suppose both the one and the other precluded by the shortness of our intercourse, and the triviality of the subjects. The difference will be impressed and felt, though the conversation should be confined to the state of the weather or the pavement. Still less will it arise from any peculiarity in his words and phrases. For if he be, as we now assume, a *well*-educated man as well as a man of superior powers, he will not fail to follow the golden rule of Julius Cæsar, *Insolens verbum, tanquam scopulum, evitare.* Unless where new things necessitate new terms, he will avoid an unusual word as a rock. It must have been among the earliest lessons of his youth, that the breach of this precept, at all times hazardous, becomes ridiculous in the topics of ordinary conversation. There remains but one other point of distinction possible; and this must be, and in fact is, the true cause of the impression made on us. It is the unpremeditated and evidently habitual *arrangement* of his words, grounded on the habit of foreseeing, in each integral part, or (more plainly) in every sentence, the whole that he then intends to communicate. However irregular and desultory his talk, there is *method* in the fragments.

Listen, on the other hand, to an ignorant man, though perhaps shrewd and able in his particular calling; whether he be describing or relating. We immediately perceive, that his memory alone is called into action; and that the objects and events recur in the narration in the same order, and with the

From *The Friend,* Second Section, Essay IV, 2nd ed., London, Rest Fenner, 1818.

same accompaniments, however accidental or impertinent, as they had first occurred to the narrator. The necessity of taking breath, the efforts of recollection, and the abrupt rectification of its failures, produce all his pauses; and with exception of the *'and then,'* the *'and there,'* and the still less significant, *'and so,'* they constitute likewise all his connections.

Our discussion, however, is confined to Method as employed in the formation of the understanding, and in the constructions of science and literature. It would indeed be superfluous to attempt a proof of its importance in the business and economy of active or domestic life. From the cotter's hearth or the workshop of the artisan, to the palace of the arsenal, the first merit, that which admits neither substitute nor equivalent, is, that *every thing is in its place.* Where this charm is wanting, every other merit either loses its name, or becomes an additional ground of accusation and regret. Of one, by whom it is eminently possessed, we say proverbially, he is like clock-work. The resemblance extends beyond the point of regularity, and yet falls short of the truth. Both do, indeed, at once divide and announce the silent and otherwise indistinguishable lapse of time. But the man of methodical industry and honorable pursuits, does more: he realizes its ideal divisions, and gives a character and individuality to its moments. If the idle are described as killing time, he may be justly said to call it into life and moral being, while he makes it the distinct object not only of the consciousness, but of the conscience. He organizes the hours, and gives them a soul: and that, the very essence of which is to fleet away, and evermore *to have been,* he takes up into his own permanence, and communicates to it the imperishableness of a spiritual nature. Of the good and faithful servant, whose energies, thus directed, are thus methodized, it is less truly affirmed, that He lives in time, than that Time lives in him. His days, months, and years, as the stops and punctual marks in the records of duties performed, will survive the wreck of worlds, and remain extant when time itself shall be no more.

But as the importance of Method in the duties of social life is incomparably greater, so are its practical elements proportionably obvious, and such as relate to the will far more than to the understanding. Henceforward, therefore, we contemplate its bearings on the latter.

The difference between the products of a well-disciplined and those of an uncultivated understanding, in relation to what we will now venture to call the *Science of Method,* is often and admirably exhibited by our great Dramatist. We scarcely need refer our readers to the Clown's evidence, in the first scene of the second act of 'Measure for Measure,' or the Nurse in 'Romeo and Juliet.' But not to leave the position, without an instance to illustrate it, we will take the 'easy-yielding' Mrs. Quickley's relation of the circumstances of Sir John Falstaff's debt to her.

FALSTAFF. What is the gross sum that I owe thee?

MRS. QUICKLEY. Marry, if thou wert an honest man, thyself and the money too. Thou didst swear to me upon a parcel-gilt goblet, sitting in my dolphin chamber, at the round table, by a sea-coal fire, on Wednesday in Whitsun week, when the prince broke thy head for likening his father to a singing-man in Windsor—thou didst swear to me then, as I was washing thy wound, to marry me and make me my lady thy wife. Canst thou deny it? Did not goodwife Keech, the butcher's wife, come in then and call me gossip Quickley?—coming into borrow a mess of vinegar: telling us she had a good dish of prawns—whereby thou didst desire to eat some—whereby I told thee they were ill for a green wound, &c. &c. &c.

[*Henry IV*. 1st. pt. act ii. sc. 1.]

And this, be it observed, is so far from being carried beyond the bounds of a fair imitation, that 'the poor soul's' thoughts and sentences are more closely interlinked than the truth of nature would have required, but that the connections and sequence, which the habit of Method can alone give, have in this instance a substitute in the fusion of passion. For the absence of Method, which characterizes the uneducated, is occasioned by an habitual submission of the understanding to mere events and images as such, and independent of any power in the mind to classify or appropriate them. The general accompaniments of time and place are the only relations which persons of this class appear to regard in their statements. As this constitutes *their* leading feature, the contrary excellence, as distinguishing the well-educated man, must be referred to the contrary habit. METHOD, therefore, becomes natural to the mind which has been accustomed to contemplate not *things* only, or for their own sake alone, but likewise and chiefly the *relations* of things, either their relations to each other, or to the observer, or to the state and apprehension of the hearers. To enumerate and analyze these relations, with the conditions under which alone they are discoverable, is to teach the science of Method.

The enviable results of this science, when knowledge has been ripened into those habits which at once secure and evince its possession, can scarcely be exhibited more forcibly as well as more pleasingly, than by contrasting with the former extract from Shakspeare the narration given by Hamlet to Horatio of the occurrences during his proposed transportation to England, and the events that interrupted his voyage.

HAM. Sir, in my heart there was a kind of fighting
That would not let me sleep: methought I lay
Worse than the mutines in the bilboes. Rashly,
And prais'd be rashness for it—*Let us know,*

> *Our indiscretion sometimes serves us well,*
> *When our deep plots do fail: and that should teach us,*
> *There's a divinity that shapes our ends,*
> *Rough-hew them how we will.*

HOR.   That is most certain.

HAM.   Up from my cabin,
My sea-gown scarf'd about me, in the dark
Grop'd I to find out them; had my desire;
Finger'd their pocket; and, in fine, withdrew
To my own room again: making so bold,
My fears forgetting manners, to unseal
Their grand commission; where *I* found, Horatio,
A royal knavery—an exact command,
Larded with many several sorts of reasons,
Importing Denmark's health, and England's too,
With, ho! such bugs and goblins in *my* life,
That on the supervize, no leisure bated,
No, not to stay the grinding of the axe,
My head should be struck off!

HOR.   Is't possible?

HAM.   Here's the commission.—Read it at more leisure.

[Act v. sc. 2.]

Here the events, with the circumstances of time and place, are all stated with equal compression and rapidity, not one introduced which could have been omitted without injury to the intelligibility of the whole process. If any tendency is discoverable, as far as the mere facts are in question, it is the tendency to omission: and, accordingly, the reader will observe, that the attention of the narrator is called back to one material circumstance, which he was hurrying by, by a direct question from the friend to whom the story is communicated, 'How WAS THIS SEALED?' But by a trait which is indeed peculiarly characteristic of Hamlet's mind, ever disposed to generalize, and meditative to excess (but which, with due abatement and reduction, is distinctive of every powerful and methodizing intellect), all the digressions and enlargements consist of reflections, truths, and principles of general and permanent interest, either directly expressed or disguised in playful satire.

> —————————I sat me down;
> Devis'd a new commission; wrote it fair.
> *I once did hold it, as our statists do,*
> *A baseness to write fair, and laboured much*
> *How to forget that learning;* but, sir, now
> It did me yeoman's service. Wilt thou know
> The effect of what I wrote?

HOR.   Aye, good my lord.

HAM.   An earnest conjuration from the king,
  As England was his faithful tributary;
  As love between them, like the palm, might flourish;
  As peace should still her wheaten garland wear,
  And many such like As's of great charge—
  That on the view and knowing of these contents
  He should the bearers put to sudden death,
  No shriving time allowed.
HOR.   How was this sealed?
HAM.   Why, even in that was heaven ordinant.
  I had my father's signet in my purse,
  Which was the model of that Danish seal:
  Folded the writ up in the form of the other;
  Subscribed it; gave't the impression; placed it safely,
  The changeling never known. Now, the next day
  Was our sea-fight; and what to this was sequent,
  Thou knowest already.
HOR.   So Guildenstern and Rosencrantz go to't?
HAM.   Why, man, they did make love to this employment.
  They are not near my conscience: their defeat
  Doth by their own insinuation grow.
  'Tis dangerous when the baser nature comes
  Between the pass and fell incensed points
  Of mighty opposites.

It would, perhaps, be sufficient to remark of the preceding passage, in connection with the humorous specimen of narration,

'Fermenting o'er with frothy circumstance,'

in Henry IV.; that if overlooking the different value of the *matter* in each, we considered the *form* alone, we should find both *immethodical;* Hamlet from the excess, Mrs. Quickley from the want, of reflection and generalization; and that Method, therefore, must result from the due mean or balance between our passive impressions and the mind's own re-action on the same. (Whether this re-action do not suppose or imply a primary act positively *originating* in the mind itself, and prior to the object in order of nature, though co-instantaneous in its manifestation, will be hereafter discussed.) But we had a further purpose in thus contrasting these extracts from our 'myriad-minded Bard,' (μυριόνους ἀνήρ.) We wished to bring forward, each for itself, these two elements of Method, or (to adopt an arithmetical term) its two main *factors*.

Instances of the want of generalization are of no rare occurrence in real life: and the narrations of Shakspeare's Hostess and the Tapster, differ from those of the ignorant and unthinking in general, by their superior humor, the poet's own gift and infusion, not by their want of Method, which is not greater than we often meet with in that class, of which they are the dramatic representatives. Instances of the opposite fault, arising from the excess of generalization and reflection in minds of the opposite class, will, like the minds themselves, occur less frequently in the course of our own personal experience. Yet they will not have been wanting to our readers, nor will they have passed unobserved, though the great poet himself (ὁ τὴν ἑαυτοῦ ψυχὴν ὥσει ὕλην τίνα ἀσώματον μορφαῖς ποικιλαῖς μορφώσας[1]) has more conveniently supplied the illustrations. To complete, therefore, the purpose aforementioned, that of presenting each of the two components as separately as possible, we chose an instance in which, by the surplus of its own activity, Hamlet's mind disturbs the arrangement, of which that very activity had been the cause and impulse.

Thus exuberance of mind, on the one hand, interferes with the *forms* of Method; but sterility of mind, on the other, wanting the spring and impulse to mental action, is wholly destructive of Method itself. For in attending too exclusively to the relations which the past or passing events and objects bear to general truth, and the moods of his own Thought, the most intelligent man is sometimes in danger of overlooking that other relation, in which they are likewise to be placed to the apprehension and sympathies of his hearers. His discourse appears like soliloquy intermixed with dialogue. But the uneducated and unreflecting talker overlooks *all* mental relations, both logical and psychological; and consequently precludes all Method, that is not purely accidental. Hence the nearer the things and incidents in time and place, the more distant, disjointed, and impertinent to each other, and to any common purpose, will they appear in his narration: and this from the want of a *staple,* or *starting-post,* in the narrator himself; from the absence of *the leading Thought,* which, borrowing a phrase from the nomenclature of legislation, we may not inaptly call the INITIATIVE. On the contrary, where the habit of Method is present and effective, things the most remote and diverse in time, place, and outward circumstance, are brought into mental contiguity and succession, the more striking as the less expected. But while we would impress the necessity of this habit, the illustrations adduced give proof that in undue preponderance, and when the prerogative of the mind is stretched into despotism, the discourse may degenerate into the grotesque or the fantastical.

With what a profound insight into the constitution of the human soul is this exhibited to us in the character of the Prince of Denmark, where flying from the sense of reality, and seeking a reprieve from the pressure of its

[1] *Translation.*—He that moulded his own soul, as some incorporeal material, into various forms.

[*Themistius.*]

duties, in that ideal activity, the overbalance of which, with the consequent indisposition to action, is his disease, he compels the reluctant good sense of the high yet healthful-minded Horatio, to follow him in his wayward meditation amid the graves? 'To what base uses we may return, Horatio! Why may not imagination trace the noble dust of Alexander, till he find it stopping a bung-hole? HOR. It were to consider too curiously to consider so. HAM. No, faith, not a jot; but to follow him thither with modesty enough and likelihood to lead it. As thus: Alexander died, Alexander was buried, Alexander returneth to dust—the dust is earth; of earth we make loam: and why of that loam, whereto he was converted, might they not stop a beer-barrel?

> Imperial Cæsar, dead and turn'd to clay,
> Might stop a hole to keep the wind away!'

But let it not escape our recollection, that when the objects thus connected are proportionate to the connecting energy, relatively to the real, or at least to the desirable sympathies of mankind; it is from the same character that we derive the genial method in the famous soliloquy, 'To be? or not to be?' which, admired as it is, and has been, has yet received only the first-fruits of the admiration due to it.

We have seen that from the confluence of innumerable impressions in each moment of time the mere passive memory must needs tend to confusion—a rule, the seeming exceptions to which (the thunder-bursts in Lear, for instance) are really confirmations of its truth. For, in many instances, the predominance of some mighty Passion takes the place of the guiding Thought, and the result presents the method of Nature, rather than the habit of the Individual. For Thought, Imagination (and we may add, Passion), are, in their very essence, the first, connective, the latter co-adunative: and it has been shown, that if the excess lead to Method misapplied, and to connections of the moment, the absence, or marked deficiency, either precludes Method altogether, both form and substance: or (as the following extract will exemplify) retains the outward form only.

> My liege and madam! to expostulate
> What majesty should be, what duty is,
> Why day is day, night night, and time is time,
> Were nothing but to waste night, day and time.
> Therefore—since brevity is the soul of wit,
> And tediousness the limbs and outward flourishes,
> I will be brief. Your noble son is mad:
> Mad call I it—for to define true madness,
> What is't, but to be nothing else but mad!
> But let that go.

QUEEN. *More matter with less art.*
POL.
> *Madam! I swear, I use no art at all.*
> *That he is mad, tis true: tis true, tis pity:*
> *And pity tis, tis true (a foolish figure!*
> *But farewell it, for I will use no art.)*
> *Mad let us grant him then: and now remains,*
> *That we find out the cause of this effect,*
> *Or rather say the cause of this defect:*
> *For this effect defective comes by cause.*
> *Thus it remains, and the remainder thus*
> *Perpend!*

[*Hamlet,* act ii. scene 2.]

Does not the irresistible sense of the ludicrous in this flourish of the soul-surviving body of old Polonius's intellect, not less than in the endless confirmations and most undeniable matters of fact, of Tapster Pompey or 'the hostess of the tavern' prove to our feelings, even before the word is found which presents the truth to our understandings, that confusion and formality are but the opposite poles of the same null-point?

It is Shakspeare's peculiar excellence, that throughout the whole of his splendid picture gallery (the reader will excuse the confest inadequacy of this metaphor), we find individuality every where, mere portrait no where. In all his various characters, we still feel ourselves communing with the same human nature, which is every where present as the vegetable sap in the branches, sprays, leaves, buds, blossoms, and fruits, their shapes, tastes, and odours. Speaking of the effect, i. e. his works themselves, we may define the excellence of *their* method as consisting in that just proportion, that union and interpenetration of the universal and the particular, which must ever pervade all works of decided genius and true science. For Method implies a *progressive transition,* and it is the meaning of the word in the original language. The Greek Μεθοδος, is literally *a way,* or *path of Transit.* Thus we extol the Elements of Euclid, or Socrates' discourse with the slave in the Menon, as *methodical,* a term which no one who holds himself bound to think or speak correctly, would apply to the alphabetical order or arrangement of a common dictionary. But as, without continuous transition, there can be no Method, so without a pre-conception there can be no transition with continuity. The term, Method, cannot therefore, otherwise than by abuse, be applied to a mere dead arrangement, containing in itself no principle of progression.

AIDS TO STUDY

Like Aristotle, Coleridge was interested in what he called 'method'—the conventions by which we make sense to one another. Not everything we may say makes sense; we used to sing:

> The horses go around; their feet are on the ground.
> Who's going to wind the clock while I'm away?
> Go get the Listerine; sister needs a beau.
> And a boy's best friend is his mother.

The individual bits of this song may be sensible, but they do not seem to make sense when put together. We can discover no *connection* between one item and the next. The items do not add up.

Coleridge assumed that two sorts of things were necessary for 'method': first, accurate observations of our experience; and second, understandable connections among those observations. A well-balanced mind manages both of these. Dame Quickly manages only the first: her memory is accurate; she observed accurately the various happenings of a given Wednesday, but her talk is only a listing of the various things that happened. And we find ourselves asking what Mrs. Keech's prawns have to do with the question at hand—namely, Falstaff's question, 'How much do I owe you?' Dame Quickly has not been able to see the connection between the question posed and the various events of a given day; she seems to think that everything is relevant.

Hamlet's mind suggests to Coleridge an imbalance in the other direction. Hamlet's talk consists of generalizations; he forgets the details of fact that well-balanced method requires. He is good at making connections, but at times we may wonder what it is that he is connecting. Polonius's speech, which is quoted later, is so meaninglessly general that it burlesques the notion of abstraction in speech. The old man seems to be making generalizations about nothing whatever; both the Queen and we are left to wonder what on earth he's talking about, and we both want less art and more matter.

Proper method, Coleridge implies, lies somewhere between Dame Quickly and Polonius: the balanced mind observes accurately and sees connections among its observations; and proper speech or writing demands both details and the drawing of conclusions from the details. To present one without the other is to fall short of the mark of good rhetoric.

The student who has read Hume and Kant will find little trouble with this essay, for Coleridge is working against the background of the problem of knowledge which these philosophers pondered. For the student who is unacquainted with this problem, a short and simplified account may be helpful. Hume was worried about how it is that the human mind managed to get from observations to conclusions about those observations. For instance, we observe one billiard ball strike another and we observe the second ball move. We conclude that the first ball caused the second to move. But we do not *observe* the causation. We see only ball A strike ball B and then we see ball B move. We see one event and then we see another event; but we do not see one event *cause* another event. We infer the causation from our observation of the two events. But, Hume concluded, we have no way of proving that one event causes another. All we know for certain is that there are events, one following another.

Kant replied to this dilemma by asserting that we must *assume* connections between events if the events of our experience are to have any meaning for us at all. The human mind is such as forces us to interpret relationships between the items of our observation. Hence the mind half observes and half creates its knowledge; it observes events and it creates connections between events. Human knowledge is possible only if the connections which the mind makes are the sorts of connections which really obtain in the world we live in. We must have faith that our mind's connections are real ones; most of us never question that faith; we take it for granted. And yet none of us assume that all the connections our minds make are real ones. I may connect peanut-butter sandwiches with hail storms, because of a peculiar experience of my own or a quirk of my mind. But I keep such a connection private and do not expect others to share it. The study of method, as Coleridge saw it, is the study of those connections which people do share. The good rhetorician must learn, as fully and carefully as he can, the logical conventions of his society—'the *relations* of things, either their relations to each other, or to the observer, or to the state and apprehension of the hearers. To enumerate and analyze these relations, with the conditions under which alone they are discoverable, is to teach the science of Method.'

The Philosophy of Style

Commenting on the seeming incongruity between his father's argumentative powers and his ignorance of formal logic, Tristram Shandy says:—'It was a matter of just wonder with my worthy tutor, and two or three fellows of that learned society, that a man who knew not so much as the names of his tools, should be able to work after that fashion with them.' Sterne's implied conclusion that a knowledge of the principles of reasoning neither makes, nor is essential to, a good reasoner, is doubtless true. Thus, too, is it with grammar. As Dr. Latham, condemning the usual school-drill in Lindley Murray, rightly remarks:—'Gross vulgarity is a fault to be prevented; but the proper prevention is to be got from habit—not rules.' Similarly, good composition is far less dependent on acquaintance with its laws, than on practice and natural aptitude. A clear head, a quick imagination, and a sensitive ear, will go far towards making all rhetorical precepts needless. And where there exists any mental flaw—where there is a deficient verbal memory, or an inadequate sense of logical dependence, or but little perception of order, or a lack of constructive ingenuity; no amount of instruction will insure good writing. Nevertheless, *some* result may be expected from a familiarity with the principles of style. The endeavour to conform to laws may tell, though slowly. And if in no other way, yet, as facilitating revision, a knowledge of the thing to be achieved—a clear idea of what constitutes a beauty, and what a blemish—cannot fail to be of service.

No general theory of expression seems yet to have been enunciated. The maxims contained in works on composition and rhetoric, are presented in an unorganized form. Standing as isolated dogmas—as empirical generalizations, they are neither so clearly apprehended, nor so much respected, as they would be were they deduced from some simple first principle. We are told

From *The Westminster Review*, October 1852.

that 'brevity is the soul of wit.' We hear styles condemned as verbose or involved. Blair says that every needless part of a sentence 'interrupts the description and clogs the image'; and again, that 'long sentences fatigue the reader's attention.' It is remarked by Lord Kaimes that, 'to give the utmost force to a period, it ought, if possible, to be closed with the word that makes the greatest figure.' Avoidance of parentheses, and the use of Saxon words in preference to those of Latin origin, are often insisted upon. But, however influential the precepts thus dogmatically expressed, they would be much more influential if reduced to something like scientific ordination. In this as in other cases, conviction is strengthened when we understand the *why*. And we may be sure that recognition of the general principle from which the rules of composition result, will not only bring them home to us with greater force, but will disclose other rules of like origin.

On seeking for some clue to the law underlying these current maxims, we may see implied in many of them, the importance of economizing the reader's or hearer's attention. To so present ideas that they may be apprehended with the least possible mental effort, is the desideratum towards which most of the rules above quoted point. When we condemn writing that is wordy, or confused, or intricate—when we praise this style as easy, and blame that as fatiguing, we consciously or unconsciously assume this desideratum as our standard of judgment. Regarding language as an apparatus of symbols for conveying thought, we may say that, as in a mechanical apparatus, the more simple and the better arranged its parts, the greater will be the effect produced. In either case, whatever force is absorbed by the machine is deducted from the result. A reader or listener has at each moment but a limited amount of mental power available. To recognize and interpret the symbols presented to him, requires part of this power; to arrange and combine the images suggested by them requires a further part; and only that part which remains can be used for framing the thought expressed. Hence, the more time and attention it takes to receive and understand each sentence, the less time and attention can be given to the contained idea; and the less vividly will that idea be conceived. How truly language must be regarded as a hindrance to thought, though the necessary instrument of it, we shall clearly perceive on remembering the comparative force with which simple ideas are communicated by signs. To say, 'Leave the room,' is less expressive than to point to the door. Placing a finger on the lips is more forcible than whispering, 'Do not speak.' A beck of the hand is better than, 'Come here.' No phrase can convey the idea of surprise so vividly as opening the eyes and raising the eyebrows. A shrug of the shoulders would lose much by translation into words. Again, it may be remarked that when oral language is employed, the strongest effects are produced by interjections, which condense entire sentences into syllables. And in other cases, where custom allows us to express thoughts by single words, as in *Beware, Heigho, Fudge,* much force would be lost by expanding them into specific propositions. Hence, carrying out the metaphor that language is the vehicle of thought, we may say that in all cases the friction and inertia of the vehicle deduct from its efficiency; and that in composition, the chief thing to be done, is, to reduce the friction and inertia to the smallest amounts. Let us then inquire whether economy of the recipient's attention is not the secret of effect, alike in the right choice and collocation of words, in the best arrangement of clauses in a sentence, in the proper order of its principal and subordinate propositions, in the judicious use of simile, metaphor, and other figures of speech, and even in the rhythmical sequence of syllables.

The greater forcibleness of Saxon English, or rather non-Latin English, first claims our attention. The several special reasons assignable for this may all be reduced to the general reason—economy. The most important of them is early association. A child's vocabulary is almost wholly Saxon. He says, *I have,* not *I possess—I wish,* not *I desire;* he does not *reflect,* he *thinks;* he does not beg for *amusement,* but for *play;* he calls things *nice* or *nasty,* not *pleasant* or *disagreeable.* The synonyms learned in after years, never become so closely, so organically, connected with the ideas signified, as do these original words used in childhood; the association remains less strong. But in what does a strong association between a word and an idea differ from a weak one? Essentially in the greater ease and rapidity of the suggestive action. Both of two words, if they be strictly synonymous, eventually call up the same image. The expression—It is *acid,* must in the end give rise to the same thought as—It is *sour;* but because the term *acid* was learnt later in life, and has not been so often followed by the ideal sensation symbolized, it does not so readily arouse that ideal sensation as the term *sour.* If we remember how slowly the meanings follow unfamiliar words in another language, and how increasing familiarity with them brings greater rapidity and ease of comprehension; and if we consider that the like effect must have resulted from using the words of our mother tongue from childhood upwards; we shall clearly see that the earliest learnt and oftenest used words, will, other things equal, call up images with less loss of time and energy than their later learnt equivalents.

The further superiority possessed by Saxon English in its comparative brevity, obviously comes under the same generalization. If it be an advantage to express an idea in the smallest number of words, then it must be an advantage to express it in the smallest number of syllables. If circuitous phrases and needless expletives distract the attention and diminish the strength of the impression produced, then so, too, must surplus articulations. A certain effort, though commonly an inappreciable one, is required to recognize every vowel and consonant. If, as all know, it is tiresome to listen to an indistinct speaker, or to read an ill-written manuscript; and if, as we cannot doubt, the fatigue is a cumulative result of the attention needed to catch successive syllables; it follows that attention is in such cases absorbed by each syllable. And this being so when the syllables are difficult of recognition, it will be so too, though in a less degree, when the recognition of them is easy. Hence, the shortness of Saxon words becomes a reason for their greater force. One qualification, however, must not be overlooked. A word which embodies the most important part of the idea to be conveyed, especially when emotion is to be produced, may often with advantage be a polysyllabic word. Thus it seems more forcible to say—'It is *magnificent,*' than—'It is *grand.*' The word *vast* is not so powerful a one as *stupendous.* Calling a thing *nasty* is not so effective as calling it *disgusting.* There seem to be several causes for this exceptional superiority of certain long words. We may ascribe it partly to the fact that a voluminous, mouth-filling epithet is, by its very size, suggestive of largeness or strength, as is shown by the pomposity of sesquipedalian verbiage; and when great power or intensity has to be suggested, this association of ideas aids the effect. A further cause may be that a word of several syllables admits of more emphatic articulation; and as emphatic articulation is a sign of emotion, the unusual impressiveness of the thing named is implied by it. Yet another cause is that a long word (of which the latter syllables are generally inferred as soon as the first are spoken) allows the hearer's consciousness more time to dwell on the quality predicated; and where, as in the above cases, it is to this predicated quality that the entire attention is called, an advantage results from keeping it before the mind for an appreciable interval. To make our generalization quite correct we must therefore say, that while in certain sentences expressing feeling, the word which more especially implies that feeling may often with advantage be a many-syllabled one; in the immense majority of cases, each word, serving but as a step to the idea embodied by the whole sentence, should, if possible, be a single syllable.

Once more, that frequent cause of strength in Saxon and other primitive words—their onomatopœia, may be similarly resolved into the more general cause. Both those directly imitative, as *splash, bang, whiz, roar,* &c., and those analogically imitative, as *rough, smooth, keen, blunt, thin, hard, crag,* &c., have a greater or less likeness to the things symbolized; and by making on the ears impressions allied to the ideas to be called up, they save part of the effort needed to call up such ideas, and leave more attention for the ideas themselves.

Economy of the recipient's mental energy may be assigned, too, as a manifest cause for the superiority of specific over generic words. That concrete terms produce more vivid impressions than abstract ones, and should, when possible, be used instead, is a current maxim of composition. As Dr. Campbell says, 'The more general the terms are, the picture is the fainter;

the more special they are, the brighter.' When aiming at effect we should avoid such a sentence as:

> When the manners, customs, and amusements of a nation are cruel and barbarous, the regulations of their penal code will be severe.

And in place of it we should write:

> When men delight in battles, bull-fights, and combats of gladiators, will they punish by hanging, burning, and the rack.

This superiority of specific expressions is clearly due to a saving of the effort required to translate words into thoughts. As we do not think in generals but in particulars—as, whenever any class of things is named, we represent it to ourselves by calling to mind individual members of the class; it follows that when a general word is used, the hearer or reader has to choose from his stock of images, one or more, by which he may figure to himself the whole group. In doing this, some delay must arise—some force be expended; and if, by employing a specific term, an appropriate image can be at once suggested, an economy is achieved, and a more vivid impression produced.

Turning now from the choice of words to their sequence, we find the same principle hold good. We have *a priori* reasons for believing that there is some one order of words by which every proposition may be more effectively expressed than by any other; and that this order is the one which presents the elements of the proposition in the succession in which they may be most readily put together. As in a narrative, the events should be stated in such sequence that the mind may not have to go backwards and forwards in order to rightly connect them; as in a group of sentences, the arrangement should be such that each of them may be understood as it comes, without waiting for subsequent ones; so in every sentence, the sequence of words should be that which suggests the constituents of the thought in the order most convenient for building it up. Duly to enforce this truth, and to prepare the way for applications of it, we must analyze the mental act by which the meaning of a series of words is apprehended.

We cannot more simply do this than by considering the proper collocation of substantive and adjective. Is it better to place the adjective before the substantive, or the substantive before the adjective? Ought we to say with the French—*un cheval noir;* or to say as we do—a black horse? Probably, most persons of culture will say that one order is as good as the other. Alive to the bias produced by habit, they will ascribe to that the preference they feel for our own form of expression. They will expect those educated in the use of the opposite form to have an equal preference for that. And thus they will conclude that neither of these instinctive judgments is of any worth. There is, however, a psychological ground for deciding in favour of the English custom. If 'a horse black' be the arrangement, then immediately on the utterance of the word 'horse,' there arises, or tends to arise, in the mind, an idea answering to that word; and as there has been nothing to indicate what *kind* of horse, any image of a horse suggests itself. Very likely, however, the image will be that of a brown horse: brown horses being the most familiar. The result is that when the word 'black' is added, a check is given to the process of thought. Either the picture of a brown horse already present to the imagination has to be suppressed, and the picture of a black one summoned in its place; or else, if the picture of a brown horse be yet unformed, the tendency to form it has to be stopped. Whichever is the case, some hindrance results. But if, on the other hand, 'a black horse' be the expression used, no mistake can be made. The word 'black,' indicating an abstract quality, arouses no definite idea. It simply prepares the mind for conceiving some object of that colour; and the attention is kept suspended until that object is known. If, then, by precedence of the adjective, the idea is always conveyed rightly, whereas precedence of the substantive is apt to produce a misconception; it follows that the one gives the mind less trouble than the other, and is therefore more forcible.

Possibly it will be objected that the adjective and substantive come so close together, that practically they may be considered as uttered at the same moment; and that on hearing the phrase, 'a horse black,' there is not time to imagine a wrongly coloured horse before the word 'black' follows to prevent it. It must be owned that it is not easy to decide by introspection whether this is so or not. But there are facts collaterally implying that it is not. Our ability to anticipate the words yet unspoken is one of them. If the ideas of the hearer lingered behind the expressions of the speaker, as the objection assumes, he could hardly foresee the end of a sentence by the time it was half delivered; yet this constantly happens. Were the supposition true, the mind, instead of anticipating, would fall more and more in arrear. If the meanings of words are not realized as fast as the words are uttered, then the loss of time over each word must entail an accumulation of delays and leave a hearer entirely behind. But whether the force of these replies be or be not admitted, it will scarcely be denied that the right formation of a picture must be facilitated by presenting its elements in the order in which they are wanted; even though the mind should do nothing until it has received them all.

What is here said respecting the succession of the adjective and substantive is applicable, by change of terms, to the adverb and verb. And without further explanation, it will be manifest, that in the use of prepositions and other particles, most languages spontaneously conform with more or less completeness to this law.

On similarly analyzing sentences considered as vehicles for entire propositions, we find not only that the same principle holds good, but that the advantage of respecting it becomes marked. In the arrangement of predicate and subject, for example, we are at once shown that as the predicate determines the aspect under which the subject is to be conceived, it should be placed first; and the striking effect produced by so placing it becomes comprehensible. Take the often-quoted contrast between—'Great is Diana of the Ephesians,' and—'Diana of the Ephesians is great.' When the fiirst arrangement is used, the utterance of the word 'great,' arousing vague associations of an imposing nature prepares the imagination to clothe with high attributes whatever follows; and when the words, 'Diana of the Ephesians' are heard, appropriate imagery already nascent in thought, is used in the formation of the picture: the mind being thus led directly, and without error, to the intended impression. But when the reverse order is followed, the idea, 'Diana of the Ephesians,' is formed with no special reference to greatness; and when the words, 'is great,' are added, it has to be formed afresh; whence arises a loss of mental energy, and a corresponding diminution of effect. The following verse from Coleridge's 'Ancient Mariner,' though incomplete as a sentence, well illustrates the same truth.

> *Alone, alone, all, all alone,*
> *Alone on a wide wide sea!*
> And never a saint took pity on
> My soul in agony.

Of course the principle equally applies when the predicate is a verb or a participle. And as effect is gained by placing first all words indicating the quality, conduct, or condition of the subject, it follows that the copula also should have precedence. It is true, that the general habit of our language resists this arrangement of predicate, copula, and subject; but we may readily find instances of the additional force gained by conforming to it. Thus in the line from 'Julius Cæsar'—

> Then *burst* his mighty heart,

priority is given to a word embodying both predicate and copula. In a passage contained in Sir W. Scott's 'Marmion,' the like order is systematically employed with great effect:

> The Border slogan rent the sky!
> *A Home! a Gordon! was* the cry;
> *Loud were* the clanging blows;
> *Advanced,—forced back,—now low, now high,*
>   The pennon sunk and rose;
> As *bends* the bark's mast in the gale
> When *rent are* rigging, shrouds, and sail,
>   It waver'd 'mid the foes.

Pursuing the principle further, it is obvious that for producing the greatest effect, not only should the main divisions of a sentence observe this sequence, but the subdivisions of these should have their parts similarly arranged. In nearly all cases, the predicate is accompanied by some limit or qualification called its complement. Commonly, also, the circumstances of the subject, which form its complement, have to be specified. And as these qualifications and circumstances must determine the mode in which the acts and things they belong to are conceived, precedence should be given to them. Lord Kaimes notices the fact that this order is preferable; though without giving the reason. He says:—'When a circumstance is placed at the beginning of the period, or near the beginning, the transition from it to the principal subject is agreeable: is like ascending or going upward.' A sentence arranged in illustration of this will be desirable. Here is one:

> Whatever it may be in theory, it is clear that in practice the French idea of liberty is—the right of every man to be master of the rest.

In this case, were the first two clauses, up to the word 'practice' inclusive, which qualify the subject, to be placed at the end instead of the beginning, much of the force would be lost; as thus:

> The French idea of liberty is—the right of every man to be master of the rest; in practice at least, if not in theory.

Similarly with respect to the conditions under which any fact is predicated. Observe in the following example the effect of putting them last:

> How immense would be the stimulus to progress, were the honour now given to wealth and title given exclusively to high achievements and intrinsic worth!

And then observe the superior effect of putting them first:

> Were the honour now given to wealth and title given exclusively to high achievements and intrinsic worth, how immense would be the stimulus to progress!

The effect of giving priority to the complement of the predicate, as well as the predicate itself, is finely displayed in the opening of 'Hyperion':

> *Deep in the shady sadness of a vale*
> *Far sunken from the healthy breath of morn,*
> *Far from the fiery noon, and eve's one star,*
> *Sat* grey-haired Saturn, quiet as a stone.

Here we see, not only that the predicate 'sat' precedes the subject 'Saturn,' and that the three lines in italics, constituting the complement of the predicate, come before it; but that in the structure of this complement also, the same order is followed: each line being so composed that the qualifying words are placed before the words suggesting concrete images.

The right succession of the principal and subordinate propositions in a sentence depends on the same law. Regard for economy of the recipient's attention, which, as we find, determines the best order for the subject, copula, predicate, and their complements, dictates that the subordinate proposition shall precede the principal one, when the sentence includes two. Containing, as the subordinate proposition does, some qualifying or explanatory idea, its priority prevents misconception of the principal one; and therefore saves the mental effort needed to correct such misconception. This will be seen in the annexed example.

> The secrecy once maintained in respect to the parliamentary debates, is still thought needful in diplomacy; and diplomacy being secret, England may any day be unawares betrayed by its ministers into a war costing a hundred thousand lives, and hundreds of millions of treasure: yet the English pique themselves on being a self-governed people.

The two subordinate propositions, ending with the semicolon and colon respectively, almost wholly determine the meaning of the principal proposition with which the sentence concludes; and the effect would be lost were they placed last instead of first.

From this general principle of right arrangement may also be inferred the proper order of those minor divisions into which the major divisions of sentences may be decomposed. In every sentence of any complexity the complement to the subject contains several clauses, and that to the predicate several others; and these may be arranged in greater or less conformity to the law of easy apprehension. Of course with these, as with the larger members, the succession should be from the less specific to the more specific—from the abstract to the concrete.

Now however we must notice a further condition to be fulfilled in the proper construction of a sentence; but still a condition dictated by the same general principle with the other: the condition, namely, that the words or the expressions which refer to the most nearly connected thoughts shall be brought the closest together. Evidently the single words, the minor clauses, and the leading divisions of every proposition, severally qualify each other. The longer the time that elapses between the mention of any qualifying member and the member qualified, the longer must the mind be exerted in carrying forward the qualifying member ready for use. And the more numerous the qualifications to be simultaneously remembered and rightly applied, the greater will be the mental power expended, and the smaller the effect produced. Hence, other things equal, force will be gained by so arranging the members of a sentence that these suspensions shall at any

moment be the fewest in number; and shall also be of the shortest duration.
The following is an instance of defective combination.

> A modern newspaper-statement, though probably true, would be
> laughed at, if quoted in a book as testimony; but the letter of a court
> gossip is thought good historical evidence, if written some centuries
> ago.

A re-arrangement of this, in accordance with the principle indicated above,
will be found to increase the effect. Thus:

> Though probably true, a modern newspaper-statement quoted in a
> book as testimony, would be laughed at; but the letter of a court
> gossip, if written some centuries ago, is thought good historical evi-
> dence.

By making this change, some of the suspensions are avoided and others
shortened; while there is less liability to produce premature conceptions. The
passage quoted below from 'Paradise Lost' affords a fine instance of a sentence well arranged; alike in the priority of the subordinate members, in the
avoidance of long and numerous suspensions, and in the correspondence
between the sequence of the clauses and the sequence of the phenomena
described, which, by the way, is a further prerequisite to easy apprehension,
and therefore to effect.

> As when a prowling wolf,
> Whom hunger drives to seek new haunt for prey,
> Watching where shepherds pen their flocks at eve,
> In hurdled cotes amid the field secure,
> Leaps o'er the fence with ease into the fold:
> Or as a thief, bent to unhoard the cash
> Of some rich burgher, whose substantial doors,
> Cross-barr'd and bolted fast, fear no assault,
> In at the window climbs, or o'er the tiles:
> So clomb the first grand Thief into God's fold;
> So since into his Church lewd hirelings climb.

The habitual use of sentences in which all or most of the descriptive and
limiting elements precede those described and limited, gives rise to what is
called the inverted style: a title which is, however, by no means confined to
this structure, but is often used where the order of the words is simply unusual. A more appropriate title would be the *direct style,* as contrasted with
the other, or *indirect style:* the peculiarity of the one being, that it conveys
each thought step by step with little liability to error; and of the other, that
it conveys each thought by a series of approximations, which successively
correct the erroneous preconceptions that have been raised.

The superiority of the direct over the indirect form of sentence, implied by the several conclusions above drawn, must not, however, be affirmed without reservation. Though, up to a certain point, it is well for the qualifying clauses of a proposition to precede those qualified; yet, as carrying forward each qualifying clause costs some mental effort, it follows that when the number of them and the time they are carried become great, we reach a limit beyond which more is lost than is gained. Other things equal, the arrangement should be such that no concrete image shall be suggested until the materials out of which it is to be framed have been presented. And yet, as lately pointed out, other things equal, the fewer the materials to be held at once, and the shorter the distance they have to be borne, the better. Hence in some cases it becomes a question whether most mental effort will be entailed by the many and long suspensions, or by the correction of successive misconceptions.

This question may sometimes be decided by considering the capacity of the persons addressed. A greater grasp of mind is required for the ready apprehension of thoughts expressed in the direct manner, where the sentences are anywise intricate. To recollect a number of preliminaries stated in elucidation of a coming idea, and to apply them all to the formation of it when suggested, demands a good memory and considerable power of concentration. To one possessing these, the direct method will mostly seem the best; while to one deficient in them it will seem the worst. Just as it may cost a strong man less effort to carry a hundred-weight from place to place at once, than by a stone at a time; so, to an active mind it may be easier to bear along all the qualifications of an idea and at once rightly form it when named, than to first imperfectly conceive such idea, and then carry back to it, one by one, the details and limitations afterwards mentioned. While conversely, as for a boy the only possible mode of transferring a hundred-weight, is that of taking it in portions; so, for a weak mind, the only possible mode of forming a compound conception may be that of building it up by carrying separately its several parts.

That the indirect method—the method of conveying the meaning by a series of approximations—is best fitted for the uncultivated, may indeed be inferred from their habitual use of it. The form of expression adopted by the savage, as in—'Water, give me,' is the simplest type of this arrangement. In pleonasms, which are comparatively prevalent among the uneducated, the same essential structure is seen; as, for instance in—'The men, they were there.' Again, the old possessive case—'The king, his crown,' conforms to the like order of thought. Moreover, the fact that the indirect mode is called the natural one, implies that it is the one spontaneously employed by the common people; that is—the one easiest for undisciplined minds.

There are many cases, however, in which neither the direct nor the indirect mode is the best; but in which an intermediate mode is preferable to both. When the number of circumstances and qualifications to be included in the sentence is great, the judicious course is neither to enumerate them all before introducing the idea to which they belong, nor to put this idea first and let it be remodelled to agree with the particulars afterwards mentioned; but to do a little of each. It is desirable to avoid so extremely indirect an arrangement as the following:—

> We came to our journey's end, at last, with no small difficulty, after much fatigue, through deep roads, and bad weather.

Yet to transform this into an entirely direct sentence would be unadvisable; as witness:—

> At last, with no small difficulty, after much fatigue, through deep roads, and bad weather, we came to our journey's end.

Dr. Whately, from whom we quote the first of these two arrangements, proposes this construction:—

> At last, after much fatigue, through deep roads and bad weather, we came, with no small difficulty, to our journey's end.

Here by introducing the words 'we came' a little earlier in the sentence, the labour of carrying forward so many particulars is diminished, and the subsequent qualification 'with no small difficulty' entails an addition to the thought that is easily made. But a further improvement may be effected by putting the words 'we came' still earlier; especially if at the same time the qualifications be rearranged in conformity with the principle already explained, that the more abstract elements of the thought should come before the more concrete. Observe the result of making these two changes:

> At last, with no small difficulty, and after much fatigue, we came, through deep roads and bad weather, to our journey's end.

This reads with comparative smoothness; that is—with less hindrance from suspensions and reconstructions of thought.

It should be further remarked, that even when addressing vigorous intellects, the direct mode is unfit for communicating ideas of a complex or abstract character. So long as the mind has not much to do, it may be well able to grasp all the preparatory clauses of a sentence, and to use them effectively; but if some subtlety in the argument absorb the attention it may happen that the mind, doubly strained, will break down, and allow the elements of the thought to lapse into confusion.

Let us pass now to figures of speech. In them we may equally discern the same general law of effect. Implied in rules given for the choice and right use of them, we shall find the same fundamental requirement—economy of attention. It is indeed chiefly because they so well subserve this requirement, that figures of speech are employed.

Let us begin with the figure called Synecdoche. The advantage sometimes gained by putting a part for the whole, is due to the more convenient, or more vivid, presentation of the idea. If, instead of writing 'a fleet of ten ships,' we write 'a fleet of ten *sail*,' the picture of a group of vessels at sea is more readily suggested; and is so because the sails constitute the most conspicuous parts of vessels so circumstanced. To say, 'All *hands* to the pumps,' is better than to say, 'All *men* to the pumps'; as it calls up a picture of the men in the special attitude intended, and so saves effort. Bringing '*grey hairs* with sorrow to the grave,' is another expression, the effect of which has the same cause.

The effectiveness of Metonymy may be similarly accounted for. 'The low morality of *the bar*,' is a phrase both more brief and significant than the literal one it stands for. A belief in the ultimate supremacy of intelligence over brute force, is conveyed in a more concrete form, and therefore more representable form, if we substitute *the pen* and *the sword* for the two abstract terms. To say, 'Beware of drinking!' is less effective than to say, 'Beware of *the bottle!*' and is so, clearly because it calls up a less specific image.

The Simile is in many cases used chiefly with a view to ornament; but whenever it increases the *force* of a passage, it does so by being an economy. Here is an instance.

> The illusion that great men and great events came oftener in early times than they come now, is due partly to historical perspective. As in a range of equidistant columns, the furthest off seem the closest; so, the conspicuous objects of the past seem more thickly clustered the more remote they are.

To express literally the thought thus conveyed, would take many sentences; and the first elements of the picture would become faint while the imagination was busy in adding the others. But by the help of a comparison much of the effort otherwise required is saved.

Concerning the position of the Simile,[1] it needs only to remark, that what has been said about the order of the adjective and substantive, predicate and subject, principal and subordinate propositions, &c., is applicable here. As whatever qualifies should precede whatever is qualified, force will generally be gained by placing the simile before the object or act to which it is applied.

[1] Properly the term 'simile' is applicable only to the entire figure, including the two things compared and the comparison drawn between them. But as there exists no name for the illustrative member of the figure, there seems no alternative but to employ 'simile' to express this also. The context will in each case show in which sense the word is used.

That this arrangement is the best, may be seen in the following passage from the 'Lady of the Lake':—

> As wreath of snow, on mountain breast,
> Slides from the rock that gave it rest,
> Poor Ellen glided from her stay,
> And at the monarch's feet she lay.

Inverting these couplets will be found to diminish the effect considerably. There are cases, however, even where the simile is a simple one, in which it may with advantage be placed last; as in these lines from Alexander Smith's 'Life Drama':—

> I see the future stretch
> All dark and barren as a rainy sea.

The reason for this seems to be, that so abstract an idea as that attaching to the word 'future,' does not present itself to the mind in any definite form; and hence the subsequent arrival at the simile entails no reconstruction of the thought.

Such however are not the only cases in which this order is the more forcible. As putting the simile first is advantageous only when it is carried forward in the mind to assist in forming an image of the object or act; it must happen that if, from length or complexity, it cannot be so carried forward, the advantage is not gained. The annexed sonnet, by Coleridge, is defective from this cause.

> As when a child, on some long winter's night,
> Affrighted, clinging to its grandam's knees,
> With eager wond'ring and perturb'd delight
> Listens strange tales of fearful dark decrees,
> Mutter'd to wretch by necromantic spell;
> Or of those hags who at the witching time
> Of murky midnight, ride the air sublime,
> And mingle foul embrace with fiends of hell;
> Cold horror drinks its blood! Anon the tear
> More gentle starts, to hear the beldame tell
> Of pretty babes, that lov'd each other dear,
> Murder'd by cruel uncle's mandate fell:
> Ev'n such the shiv'ring joys thy tones impart,
> Ev'n so, thou, Siddons, meltest my sad heart.

Here, from the lapse of time and accumulation of circumstances, the first member of the comparison is forgotten before the second is reached; and requires re-reading. Had the main idea been first mentioned, less effort would have been required to retain it, and to modify the conception of it into harmony with the illustrative ideas, than to remember the illustrative ideas, and refer back to them for help in forming the final image.

The superiority of the Metaphor to the Simile is ascribed by Dr. Whately to the fact that 'all men are more gratified at catching the resemblance for themselves, than in having it pointed out to them.' But after what has been said, the great economy it achieves will seem the more probable cause. Lear's exclamation—

> Ingratitude! thou marble-hearted fiend,

would lose part of its effect were it changed into—

> Ingratitude! thou fiend with heart like marble;

and the loss would result partly from the position of the simile and partly from the extra number of words required. When the comparison is an involved one, the greater force of the metaphor, due to its relative brevity, becomes much more conspicuous. If, drawing an analogy between mental and physical phenomena, we say,

> As, in passing through a crystal, beams of white light are decomposed into the colours of the rainbow; so, in traversing the soul of the poet, the colourless rays of truth are transformed into brightly-tinted poetry;——

it is clear that in receiving the two sets of words expressing the two halves of the comparison, and in carrying the meaning of the one to help in interpreting the other, considerable attention is absorbed. Most of this is saved by putting the comparison in a metaphorical form, thus:—

> The white light of truth, in traversing the many-sided transparent soul of the poet, is refracted into iris-hued poetry.

How much is conveyed in a few words by using Metaphor, and how vivid the effect consequently produced, is everywhere shown. From 'A Life Drama' may be quoted the phrase,

> I spear'd him with a jest,

as a fine instance among the many which that poem contains. A passage in the 'Prometheus Unbound,' of Shelley, displays the power of the metaphor to great advantage.

> Methought among the lawns together
> We wandered, underneath the young gray dawn,
> And multitudes of dense white fleecy clouds
> Were wandering in thick flocks along the mountains
> *Shepherded* by the slow unwilling wind.

This last expression is remarkable for the distinctness with which it calls up the features of the scene; bringing the mind by a bound to the desired conception.

But a limit is put to the advantageous use of Metaphor, by the condition that it must be simple enough to be understood from a hint. Evidently, if there be any obscurity in the meaning or application of it, no economy of attention will be achieved; but rather the reverse. Hence, when the comparison is complex, it is better to put it in the form of a Simile. There is, however, a species of figure, sometimes classed under Allegory, but which might well be called Compound Metaphor, that enables us to retain the brevity of the metaphorical form even where the analogy is intricate. This is done by indicating the application of the figure at the outset, and then leaving the reader or hearer to continue the parallel. Emerson has employed it with great effect in the first of his *Lectures on the Times*.

> The main interest which any aspects of the Times can have for us, is the great spirit which gazes through them, the light which they can shed on the wonderful questions, What are we? and Whither do we tend? We do not wish to be deceived. Here we drift, like white sail across the wild ocean, now bright on the wave, now darkling in the trough of the sea; but from what port did we sail? Who knows? Or to what port are we bound? Who knows? There is no one to tell us but such poor weather-tossed mariners as ourselves, whom we speak as we pass, or who have hoisted some signal, or floated to us some letter in a bottle from afar. But what know they more than we? They also found themselves on this wondrous sea. No; from the older sailors nothing. Over all their speaking-trumpets the gray sea and the loud winds answer—Not in us; not in Time.

The division of Simile from Metaphor is by no means definite. Between the one extreme in which the two elements of the comparison are detailed at full length and the analogy pointed out, and the other extreme in which the comparison is implied instead of stated, come intermediate forms, in which the comparison is partly stated and partly implied. For instance:—

> Astonished at the performances of the English plough, the Hindoos paint it, set it up, and worship it; thus turning a tool into an idol. Linguists do the same with language.

Here there is an evident advantage in leaving the reader or hearer to complete the figure. And generally these intermediate forms are good in proportion as they do this; provided the mode of completion be obvious.

Passing over much that may be said of like purport on Hyperbole, Personification, Apostrophe, &c., let us close our remarks on construction by a typical example of effective expression. The general principle which has been

enunciated is that, other things equal, the force of a verbal form or arrangement is great, in proportion as the mental effort demanded from the recipient
is small. The corollaries from this general principle have been severally
illustrated. But though conformity now to this and now to that requirement
has been exemplified, no case of entire conformity has yet been quoted. It is
indeed difficult to find one; for the English idiom does not commonly permit
the order which theory dictates. A few, however, occur in Ossian. Here is
one :—

> Like autumn's dark storms pouring from two echoing hills, towards
> each other approached the heroes. Like two deep streams from high
> rocks meeting, mixing, roaring on the plain: loud, rough, and dark
> in battle meet Lochlin and Inisfail. * * * As the noise of the troubled
> ocean when roll the waves on high; as the last peal of the thunder of
> heaven; such is the din of war.

Except in the position of the verb in the first two similes, the theoretically
best arrangement is fully carried out in each of these sentences. The simile
comes before the qualified image, the adjectives before the substantives, the
predicate and copula before the subject, and their respective complements
before them. That the passage is bombastic proves nothing; or rather, proves
our case. For what is bombast but a force of expression too great for the magnitude of the ideas embodied? All that may rightly be inferred is, that only
in rare cases should *all* the conditions to effective expression be fulfilled.

A more complex application of the theory may now be made. Not only in
the structures of sentences, and the uses of figures of speech, may we trace
economy of the recipient's mental energy as the cause of force; but we may
trace this same cause in the successful choice and arrangement of the minor
images out of which some large thought is to be built. To select from a scene
or event described, those elements which carry many others with them; and
so, by saying a few things but suggesting many, to abridge the description;
is the secret of producing a vivid impression. An extract from Tennyson's
'Mariana' will well illustrate this.

> All day within the dreamy house,
> The doors upon their hinges creaked,
> The blue fly sung in the pane; the mouse
> Behind the mouldering wainscot shriek'd,
> Or from the crevice peer'd about.

The several circumstances here specified bring with them many appropriate
associations. When alone the creaking of a distant door is much more ob-
trusive than when talking to friends. Our attention is rarely drawn by the
buzzing of a fly in the window, save when everything is still. While the
inmates are moving about the house, mice usually keep silence; and it is

only when extreme quietness reigns that they peep from their retreats. Hence each of the facts mentioned, presupposing various others, calls up these with more or less distinctness; and revives the feeling of dull solitude with which they are connected in our experience. Were all of them detailed instead of suggested, the mental energies would be so frittered away in attending that little impression of dreariness would be produced. Similarly in other cases. In the choice of component ideas, as in the choice of expressions, the aim must be to convey the greatest quantity of thoughts with the smallest quantity of words.

The same principle may sometimes be advantageously carried yet further, by indirectly suggesting some entirely distinct thought in addition to the one expressed. Thus if we say,

> The head of a good classic is as full of ancient myths, as that of a servant-girl of ghost stories;

it is manifest that besides the fact asserted, there is an implied opinion respecting the small value of much that passes as classical learning; and as this implied opinion is recognized much sooner than it can be put into words, there is gain in omitting it. In other cases, again, great effect is produced by an overt omission; provided the nature of the idea left out is obvious. A good instance occurs in *Heroes and Hero-worship*. After describing the way in which Burns was sacrificed to the idle curiosity of lion-hunters—people who sought to amuse themselves, and who got their amusement while 'the Hero's life went for it!' Carlyle suggests a parallel thus:—

> Richter says, in the Island of Sumatra there is a kind of 'Light-chafers,' large Fire-flies, which people stick upon spits, and illuminate the ways with at night. Persons of condition can thus travel with a pleasant radiance, which they much admire. Great honour to the Fire-flies! But—!—

Before inquiring whether the law of effect thus far traced, explains the impressiveness of poetry as compared with prose, it will be needful to notice some causes of force in expression which had not yet been mentioned. These are not, properly speaking, additional causes; but rather secondary ones, originating from those already specified. One is that mental excitement spontaneously prompts those forms of speech which have been pointed out as the most effective. 'Out with him!' 'Away with him!' are the cries of angry citizens at a disturbed meeting. A voyager, describing a terrible storm he had witnessed, would rise to some such climax as—'Crack went the ropes, and down came the mast.' Astonishment may be heard expressed in the phrase—'Never was there such a sight!' All of which sentences are contracted after the direct type. Again, there is the fact that excited persons are given to figures of speech. The vituperation of the vulgar abounds with them. 'Beast,' 'brute,' 'gallows rogue,' 'cut-throat villain,' these, and like metaphors or metaphorical epithets, call to mind a street quarrel. Further, it may be noticed that extreme brevity is a trait of passionate language. The sentences are generally incomplete; and frequently important words are left to be gathered from the context. Great admiration does not vent itself in a precise proposition, as—'It is beautiful'; but in the simple exclamation,—'Beautiful!' He who, when reading a lawyer's letter, should say, 'Vile rascal!' would be thought angry; while, 'He is a vile rascal,' would imply comparative coolness. Thus alike in the order of the words, in the frequent use of figures, and in extreme conciseness, the natural utterances of excitement conform to the theoretical conditions to forcible expression.

Hence such forms of speech acquire a secondary strength from association. Having, in daily intercourse, heard them in connection with vivid mental impressions; and having been accustomed to meet with them in writing of unusual power; they come to have in themselves a species of force. The emotions that have from time to time been produced by the strong thoughts wrapped up in these forms, are partially aroused by the forms themselves. These create a preparatory sympathy; and when the striking ideas looked for are reached, they are the more vividly pictured.

The continuous use of words and forms that are alike forcible in themselves and forcible from their associations, produces the impressive species of composition which we call poetry. The poet habitually adopts those symbols of thought, and those methods of using them, which instinct and analysis agree in choosing as most effective. On turning back to the various specimens which have been quoted, it will be seen that the direct or inverted form of sentence predominates in them; and that to a degree inadmissible in prose. Not only in the frequency, but in what is termed the violence of the inversions, may this distinction be remarked. The abundant use of figures, again, exhibits the same truth. Metaphors, similes, hyperboles, and personifications, are the poet's colours, which he has liberty to employ almost without limit. We characterize as 'poetical' the prose which uses these appliances of language with frequency; and condemn it as 'over florid' or 'affected' long before they occur with the profusion allowed in verse. Once more, in brevity—the other requisite of forcible expression which theory points out and emotion spontaneously fulfils—poetical phraseology differs from ordinary phraseology. Imperfect periods are frequent; elisions are perpetual; and many minor words which would be deemed essential in prose, are dispensed with.

Thus poetry is especially impressive partly because it conforms to all the laws of effective speech, and partly because in so doing it imitates the natural utterances of excitement. While the matter embodied is idealized emotion, the vehicle is the idealized language of emotion. As the musical composer catches the cadences in which our feelings of joy and sympathy, grief and despair, vent themselves, and out of these germs evolves melodies suggesting higher phases of these feelings; so, the poet develops from the typical expressions in which men utter passion and sentiment, those choice forms of verbal combination in which concentrated passion and sentiment may be fitly presented.

There is one peculiarity of poetry conducing much to its effect—the peculiarity which is indeed usually thought its characteristic one—still remaining to be considered: we mean its rhythmical structure. This, improbable though it seems, will be found to come under the same generalization with the others. Like each of them, it is an idealization of the natural language of emotion, which is not uncommonly more or less metrical if the emotion be not too violent; and like each of them it economizes the reader's or hearer's attention. In the peculiar tone and manner we adopt in uttering versified language, may be discerned its relationship to the feelings; and the pleasure which its measured movement gives, is ascribable to the comparative ease with which words metrically arranged can be recognized. This last position will not be at once admitted; but explanation will justify it. If, as we have seen, there is an expenditure of mental energy in so listening to verbal articulations as to identify the words, or in that silent repetition of them which goes on in reading, then, any mode of so combining words as to present a regular recurrence of certain traits which can be anticipated, will diminish that strain on the attention entailed by the total irregularity of prose. Just as the body, when receiving a series of varying concussions, must keep its muscles ready to meet the most violent of them, as not knowing when such may come; so, the mind when receiving unarranged articulations, must keep its perceptive faculties active enough to recognize the least easily caught sounds. And as, if the concussions recur in a definite order, the body may husband its forces by adjusting the resistance needful for each concussion; so, if the syllables be rhythmically arranged, the mind may economize its energies by anticipating the attention required for each syllable. Far-fetched though this idea will be thought, introspection countenances it. That we *do* take advantage of metrical language to adjust our perceptive faculties to the expected articulations, is clear from the fact that we are balked by halting versification. Much as at the bottom of a flight of stairs, a step more or less than we counted upon gives us a shock; so, too, does a misplaced accent or a supernumerary syllable. In the one case, we *know* that there is an erroneous pre-adjustment; and we can scarcely doubt that there is one in the other. But if we habitually pre-adjust our perceptions to the measured movement of verse, the physical analogy above given renders it probable that by so doing we economize attention; and hence that metrical language is more effective than prose, because it enables us to do this.

Were there space, it might be worth while to inquire whether the pleasure we take in rhyme, and also that which we take in euphony, are not partly ascribable to the same general cause.

A few paragraphs only, can be devoted to a second division of our subject. To pursue in detail the laws of effect, as applying to the larger features of composition, would carry us beyond our limits. But we may briefly indicate a further aspect of the general principle hitherto traced, and hint a few of its wider applications.

Thus far, we have considered only those causes of force in language which depend on economy of the mental *energies*. We have now to glance at those which depend on economy of the mental *sensibilities*. Questionable though this division may be as a psychological one, it will serve roughly to indicate the remaining field of investigation. It will suggest that besides considering the extent to which any faculty or group of faculties is tasked in receiving a form of words and constructing its contained idea, we have to consider the state in which this faculty or group of faculties is left; and how the reception of subsequent sentences and images will be influenced by that state. Without going fully into so wide a topic as the action of faculties and its reactive effects, it will suffice to recall the fact that every faculty is exhausted by exercise. This generalization, which our bodily experiences force upon us, and which in daily speech is recognized as true of the mind as a whole, is true of each mental power, from the simplest of the senses to the most complex of the sentiments. If we hold a flower to the nose for long, we become insensible to its scent. We say of a brilliant flash of lightning that it blinds us; which means that our eyes have for a time lost their ability to appreciate light. After eating honey, we are apt to think our tea is without sugar. The phrase 'a deafening roar,' implies that men find a very loud sound temporarily incapacitates them for hearing faint sounds. To a hand which has for some time carried a heavy body, small bodies afterwards lifted seem to have lost their weight. Now, the truth thus exemplified, may be traced throughout. Alike of the reflective faculties, the imagination, the perceptions of the beautiful, the ludicrous, the sublime, it may be shown that action exhausts; and that in proportion as the action is violent the subsequent prostration is great.

Equally throughout the whole nature, may be traced the law that exercised faculties are ever tending to resume their original states. Not only after continued rest, do they regain their full powers—not only are brief cessations in the demands on them followed by partial re-invigoration; but even while they are in action, the resulting exhaustion is ever being neutralized. The processes of waste and repair go on together. Hence with faculties habitually exercised—as the senses of all persons, or the muscles of any one who is strong—it happens that, during moderate activity, the repair is so nearly equal to the waste, that the diminution of power is scarcely appreciable. It is only when effort has been long continued, or has been violent, that repair becomes so far in arrear of waste as to cause a perceptible enfeeblement. In all cases, however, when, by the action of a faculty, waste has been incurred, *some* lapse of time must take place before full efficiency can be reacquired; and this time must be long in proportion as the waste has been great.

Keeping in mind these general truths, we shall be in a condition to understand certain causes of effect in composition now to be considered. Every perception received, and every conception framed, entailing some amount of waste in the nervous system, and the efficiency of the faculties employed being for a time, though often but momentarily, diminished; the resulting partial inability affects the acts of perception and conception that immediately succeed. Hence the vividness with which images are pictured must, in many cases, depend on the order of their presentation; even when one order is as convenient to the understanding as the other. Sundry facts illustrate this truth, and are explained by it: instance climax and anticlimax. The marked effect obtained by placing last the most striking of any series of ideas, and the weakness—often the ludicrous weakness—produced by reversing this arrangement, depends on the general law indicated. As immediately after looking at the sun we cannot perceive the light of a fire, while by looking at the fire first and the sun afterwards we can perceive both; so, after receiving a brilliant, or weighty, or terrible thought, we cannot properly appreciate a less brilliant, less weighty, or less terrible one, though by reversing the order, we can appreciate each. In Antithesis, again, the like truth is exemplified. The opposition of two thoughts which are the reverse of each other in some prominent trait, insures an impressive effect; and does this by giving a momentary relaxation to the faculties addressed. If, after a series of ordinary images exciting in a moderate degree to the emotion of reverence, or approbation, or beauty, the mind has presented to it an insignificant, or unworthy, or ugly image: the structure which yields the emotion of reverence, or approbation, or beauty, having for the time nothing to do, tends to resume its full power; and will immediately afterwards appreciate anything vast, admirable, or beautiful better than it would otherwise do. Conversely, where the idea of absurdity due to extreme insignificance is to be produced, it may be intensified by placing it after something impressive; especially if the form of phrase implies that something still more impressive is coming. A good illustration of the effect gained by thus presenting a petty idea to a consciousness which has not yet recovered from the shock of an exciting one, occurs in a sketch by Balzac. His hero writes to a mistress who has cooled towards him, the following letter:—

> Madame,—Votre conduite m'étonne autant qu'elle m'afflige. Non contente de me déchirer le cœur par vos dédains, vous avez l'indéli-

catesse de me retenir une brosse à dents, que mes moyens ne me permettent pas de remplacer, mes propriétés étant grevées d'hypothèques au delà de leur valeur.

Adieu, trop belle et trop ingrate amie! Puissions-nous nous revoir dans un monde meilleur!

CHARLES-EDOUARD.

Thus the phenomena of Climax, Antithesis, and Anti-climax, alike result from this general principle. Improbable as these momentary variations in susceptibility may seem, we cannot doubt their occurrence when we contemplate the analogous variations in the susceptibility of the senses. Every one knows that a patch of black on a white ground looks blacker, and a patch of white on a black ground looks whiter, than elsewhere. As the blackness and the whiteness are really the same, the only assignable cause, is a difference in their actions upon us, dependent on the different states of our faculties. The effect is due to a visual antithesis.

But this extension of the general principle of economy—this further condition to effective composition, that the sensitiveness of the faculties must be husbanded—includes much more than has been yet hinted. Not only does it follow that certain arrangements and certain juxtapositions of connected ideas are best; but also that some modes of dividing and presenting a subject will be more striking than others, irrespective of logical cohesion. We are shown why we must progress from the less interesting to the more interesting; alike in the composition as a whole, and in each successive portion. At the same time, the indicated requirement negatives long continuity of the same kind of thought, or repeated production of like effects. It warns us against the error committed by Pope in his poems and by Bacon in his essays—the error of constantly employing forcible forms of expression. As the easiest posture by and by becomes fatiguing, and is with pleasure exchanged for one less easy; so, the most perfectly-constructed sentences unceasingly used must cause weariness, and relief will be given by using those of inferior kinds. Further, we may infer not only that we ought to avoid generally combining our words in one manner, however good, or working out our figures and illustrations in one way, however telling; but that we ought to avoid anything like uniform adherence to the wider conditions of effect. We should not make every division of our subject progress in interest; we should not always rise to a climax. As we saw that in single sentences it is but rarely allowable to fulfil all the conditions to strength; so, in the larger sections of a composition we must not often conform entirely to the principles indicated. We must subordinate the component effects to the total effect.

The species of composition which the law we have traced out indicates as the perfect one, is the one which genius tends naturally to produce. As we found that the kinds of sentence which are theoretically best, are those commonly employed by superior minds, and by inferior minds when temporarily exalted; so, we shall find that the ideal form for a poem, essay, or fiction, is that which the ideal writer would evolve spontaneously. One in whom the powers of expression fully responded to the state of feeling, would unconsciously use that variety in the mode of presenting his thoughts, which Art demands. Constant employment of one species of phraseology implies an undeveloped linguistic faculty. To have a specific style is to be poor in speech. If we remember that in the far past, men had only nouns and verbs to convey their ideas with, and that from then to now the progress has been towards more numerous implements of thought, and towards greater complexity and variety in their combinations; we may infer that, in the use of sentences, we are at present much what the primitive man was in the use of words; and that a continuance of the process which has hitherto gone on, must produce increasing heterogeneity in our modes of expression. As now, in a fine nature, the play of the features, the tones of the voice and its cadences, vary in harmony with every thought uttered; so, in one possessed of fully-developed powers of language, the mould in which each combination of words is cast will vary with, and be appropriate to, the mental state. That a perfectly-endowed man must unconsciously write in all styles, we may infer from considering how styles originate. Why is Johnson pompous, Goldsmith simple? Why is one author abrupt, another involved, another concise? Evidently in each case the habitual mode of utterance depends on the habitual balance of the nature. The dominant feelings have by use trained the intellect to represent them. But while long habit has made it do this efficiently, it remains, from lack of practice, unable to do the like for the less active feelings; and when these are excited, the usual verbal forms undergo but slight modifications. But let the ability of the intellect to represent the mental state be complete, and this fixity of style will disappear. The perfect writer will be now rhythmical and now irregular; here his language will be plain and there ornate; sometimes his sentences will be balanced and at other times unsymmetrical; for a while there will be considerable sameness, and then again great variety. His mode of expression naturally responding to his thought and emotion, there will flow from his pen a composition changing as the aspects of his subject change. He will thus without effort conform to what we have seen to be the laws of effect. And while his work presents to the reader that variety needful to prevent continuous exertion of the same faculties, it will also answer to the description of all highly-organized products both of man and nature. It will be, not a series of like parts simply placed in juxtaposition, but one whole made up of unlike parts that are mutually dependent.

POSTSCRIPT.—The conclusion that because of their comparative brevity and because of those stronger associations formed by more frequent use, words of Old-English origin are preferable to words derived from Latin or Greek, should be taken with two qualifications, which it seems needful to add here.

In some cases the word furnished by our original tongue, and the corresponding word directly or indirectly derived from Latin, though nominally equivalents, are not actually such; and the word of Latin origin, by certain extra connotations it has acquired, may be the more expressive. For instance, we have no word of native origin which can be advantageously substituted for the word 'grand.' No such words as 'big' or 'great,' which connote little more than superiority in size or quantity, can be used instead: they do not imply that qualitative superiority which is associated with the idea of grandeur. As adopted into our own language, the word 'grand' has been differentiated from 'great' by habitual use in those cases where the greatness has an æsthetic superiority. In this case, then, a word of Latin origin is better than its nearest equivalent of native origin, because by use it has acquired an additional meaning. And here, too, we may conveniently note the fact that the greater brevity of a word does not invariably conduce to greater force. Where the word, instead of being one conveying a subordinate component of the idea the sentence expresses, is one conveying the central element of the idea, on which the attention may with advantage rest a moment, a longer word is sometimes better than a shorter word. Thus it may be held that the sentence—'It is grand' is not so effective as the sentence—'It is magnificent.' Besides the fact that here greater length of the word favours a longer dwelling on the essential part of the thought, there is the fact that its greater length, aided by its division into syllables, gives opportunity for a cadence appropriate to the feeling produced by the thing characterized. By an ascent of the voice on the syllable 'nif,' and an utterance of this syllable, not only in a higher note, but with greater emphasis than the preceding or succeeding syllables, there is implied that emotion which contemplation of the object produces; and the emotion thus implied is, by sympathy, communicated. One may say that in the case of these two words, if the imposingness is alone to be considered, the word 'magnificent' may with advantage be employed; but if the sentence expresses a proposition in which, not the imposingness itself, but something *about* the imposingness, is to be expressed, then the word 'grand' is preferable.

The second qualification above referred to, concerns the superiority of words derived from Latin or Greek, in cases where more or less abstract ideas have to be expressed. In such cases it is undesirable to use words having concrete associations: for such words, by the very vividness with which they call up thoughts of particular objects or particular actions, impede the formation of conceptions which refer, not to particular objects and actions, but to general truths concerning objects or actions of kinds that are more or less various. Thus, such an expression as 'the colligation of facts' is better for philosophical purposes than such an expression as 'the tying together of facts.' This last expression cannot be used without suggesting the thought of a bundle of material things bound up by a string or cord—a thought which, in so far as the materiality of its components is concerned, conflicts with the conception to be suggested. Though it is true that when its derivation is remembered, 'colligation' raises the same thought, yet, as the thought is not so promptly or irresistibly raised, it stands less in the way of the abstract conception with which attention should be exclusively occupied.

AIDS TO STUDY

Spencer is trying to bring the various rules of handbooks of writing under one general law or principle—that of economy or efficiency: the best communication conveys its message with least expenditure of mental energy and sensibility on the part of the hearer or reader. In view of this general rule, he examines the problems of the choice of words, the order of sentence elements, the nature of figures of speech, and the selection of details in composition, and the comparative power of poetry and prose, the function of rhythm in language, and the uses of variation in rhetoric.

Spencer's ideas about composition are provocative at least: each of his considerations will bear discussion, if the student will trouble himself to understand each point and search his reading and listening for examples which either bear out or seem to contradict the points being made. For example, Spencer argues that the placement of the adjective before the noun usually is sensible, for the adjective is often more general in its implication than the noun which follows. Hence in 'a big dog,' one's concept of 'bigness' is less exact than his concept of 'dog'; and the concept of 'bigness,' being rather vague, is sharpened when the word *dog* appears. If the order were reversed, our more specific concept of *dog* would have to be changed when the word *big* appeared. For the phrase 'a big dog,' this seems to work very well; but one wonders about such phrases as 'a Pomeranian dog,' 'a muzzled dog,' or 'a mad dog.' If you can gather such examples for each of Spencer's points, you can find lively discussions of this essay.

In general, Spencer seems to argue that English sentences ought to run rather differently from the usual patterns of our speech and writing. It might be interesting to test his ideas against the style of *Time* magazine: one waggish critic, speaking of *Time*-style, commented, 'Backward ran sentences till reeled the mind.' What would Spencer's attitude toward such a sentence be?

Of the Four Methods of Experimental Inquiry

I. METHOD OF AGREEMENT

The simplest and most obvious modes of singling out from among the circumstances which precede or follow a phenomenon those with which it is really connected by an invariable law are two in number. One is by comparing together different instances in which the phenomenon occurs. The other is by comparing instances in which the phenomenon does occur with instances in other respects similar in which it does not. These two methods may be respectively denominated the method of agreement and the method of difference.

In illustrating these methods, it will be necessary to bear in mind the twofold character of inquiries into the laws of phenomena, which may be either inquiries into the cause of a given effect or into the effects or properties of a given cause. We shall consider the methods in their application to either order of investigation and shall draw our examples equally from both.

We shall denote antecedents by the large letters of the alphabet and the consequents corresponding to them by the small. Let A, then, be an agent or cause, and let the object of our inquiry be to ascertain what are the effects of this cause. If we can either find or produce the agent A in such varieties of circumstances that the different cases have no circumstance in common except A, then whatever effect we find to be produced in all our trials is indicated as the effect of A. Suppose, for example, that A is tried along with B and C and that the effect is *a b c;* and suppose that A is next tried with D and E, but without B and C, and that the effect is *a d e.* Then we may reason thus: *b* and *c* are not effects of A, for they were not produced by it in the second experiment; nor are *d* and *e,* for they

From *System of Logic,* Chapter VIII, 8th ed., New York, 1881.

were not produced in the first. Whatever is really the effect of A must have been produced in both instances; now this condition is fulfilled by no circumstance except *a*. The phenomenon *a* cannot have been the effect of B or C, since it was produced where they were not; nor of D or E, since it was produced where they were not. Therefore, it is the effect of A.

For example, let the antecedent A be the contact of an alkaline substance and an oil. This combination being tried under several varieties of circumstances, resembling each other in nothing else, the results agree in the production of a greasy and detersive or saponaceous substance; it is, therefore, concluded that the combination of an oil and an alkali causes the production of a soap. It is thus we inquire by the method of agreement into the effect of a given cause.

In a similar manner we may inquire into the cause of a given effect. Let *a* be the effect. Here, as shown in the last chapter, we have only the resource of observation without experiment: we cannot take a phenomenon of which we know not the origin and try to find its mode of production by producing it: if we succeeded in such a random trial, it could only be by accident. But if we can observe *a* in two different combinations, *a b c* and *a d e;* and if we know or can discover that the antecedent circumstances in these cases respectively were A B C and A D E, we may conclude, by a reasoning similar to that in the preceding example, that A is the antecedent connected with the consequent *a* by a law of causation. B and C, we may say, cannot be causes of *a,* since on its second occurrence they were not present; nor are D and E, for they were not present on its first occurrence. A, alone of the five circumstances, was found among the antecedents of *a* in both instances.

For example, let the effect *a* be crystallization. We compare instances in which bodies are known to assume crystalline structure but which have no other point of agreement, and we find them to have one and, as far as we can observe, only one, antecedent in common: the deposition of a solid matter from a liquid state, either a state of fusion or of solution. We conclude, therefore, that the solidification of a substance from a liquid state is an invariable antecedent of its crystallization.

In this example we may go farther and say it is not only the invariable antecedent but the cause, or, at least, the proximate event which completes the cause. For in this case we are able, after detecting the antecedent A, to produce it artificially and, by finding that *a* follows it, verify the result of our induction. The importance of thus reversing the proof was strikingly manifested when, by keeping a phial of water charged with siliceous particles undisturbed for years, a chemist (I believe Dr. Wollaston) succeeded in obtaining crystals of quartz, and in the equally interesting experiment in which Sir James Hall produced artificial marble by the cooling of its materials from fusion under immense pressure; two admirable examples of the light which may be thrown upon the most secret processes of Nature by well-contrived interrogation of her.

But if we cannot artificially produce the phenomenon A, the conclusion that it is the cause of *a* remains subject to very considerable doubt. Though an invariable, it may not be the unconditional antecedent of *a,* but may precede it as day precedes night or night day. This uncertainty arises from the impossibility of assuring ourselves that A is the *only* immediate antecedent common to both the instances. If we could be certain of having ascertained all the invariable antecedents, we might be sure that the unconditional invariable antecedent, or cause, must be found somewhere among them. Unfortunately it is hardly ever possible to ascertain all the antecedents, unless the phenomenon is one which we can produce artificially. Even then, the difficulty is merely lightened, not removed: men knew how to raise water in pumps long before they adverted to what was really the operating circumstance in the means they employed, namely, the pressure of the atmosphere on the open surface of the water. It is, however, much easier to analyze completely a set of arrangements made by ourselves than the whole complex mass of the agencies which nature happens to be exerting at the moment of the production of a given phenomenon. We may overlook some of the material circumstances in an experiment with an electrical machine; but we shall, at the worst, be better acquainted with them than with those of a thunderstorm.

The mode of discovering and proving laws of nature which we have now examined proceeds on the following axiom: whatever circumstances can be excluded without prejudice to the phenomenon, or can be absent notwithstanding its presence, is not connected with it in the way of causation. The casual circumstances being thus eliminated, if only one remains, that one is the cause which we are in search of; if more than one, they either are, or contain among them, the cause; and so, *mutatis mutandis,* of the effect. As this method proceeds by comparing different instances to ascertain in what they agree, I have termed it the method of agreement, and we may adopt as its regulating principle the following canon:

FIRST CANON

If two or more instances of the phenomenon under investigation have only one circumstance in common, the circumstance in which alone all the instances agree is the cause (or effect) of the given phenomenon.

Quitting for the present the method of agreement, to which we shall almost immediately return, we proceed to a still more potent instrument of the investigation of nature, the method of difference.

2. METHOD OF DIFFERENCE

In the method of agreement, we endeavored to obtain instances which agreed in the given circumstance but differed in every other; in the present method we require, on the contrary, two instances resembling one another in every other respect, but differing in the presence or absence of the phenomenon we wish to study. If our object be to discover the effects of an agent A, we must procure A in some set of ascertained circumstances, as A B C, and having noted the effects produced, compare then with the effect of the remaining circumstances B C, when A is absent. If the effect of A B C is *a b c,* and the effect of B C *b c,* it is evident that the effect of A is *a.* So again, if we begin at the other end and desire to investigate the cause of an effect *a,* we must select an instance, as *a b c,* in which the effect occurs, and in which the antecedents were A B C, and we must look out for another instance in which the remaining circumstances, *b c,* occur without *a.* If the antecedents, in that instance, are B C, we know that the cause of *a* must be A—either A alone, or A in conjunction with some of the other circumstances present.

It is scarcely necessary to give examples of a logical process to which we owe almost all the inductive conclusions we draw in daily life. When a man is shot through the heart, it is by this method we know that it was the gunshot which killed him, for he was in the fullness of life immediately before, all circumstances being the same except the wound.

The axioms implied in this method are evidently the following: whatever antecedent cannot be excluded without preventing the phenomenon is the cause, or a condition, of that phenomenon; whatever consequent can be excluded, with no other difference in the antecedents than the absence of a particular one, is the effect of that one. Instead of comparing different instances of a phenomenon to discover in what they agree, this method compares an instance of its occurrence with an instance of its non-occurrence to discover in what they differ. The canon which is the regulating principle of the method of difference may be expressed as follows:

SECOND CANON

If an instance in which the phenomenon under investigation occurs and an instance in which it does not occur have every circumstance in common save one, that one occurring only in the former, the circumstance in which alone the two instances differ is the effect, or the cause, or an indispensable part of the cause, of the phenomenon.

3. MUTUAL RELATION OF THESE TWO METHODS

The two methods which we have now stated have many features of resemblance, but there are also many distinctions between them. Both are methods of *elimination*. This term (employed in the theory of equations to denote the process by which one after another of the elements of a question is excluded, and the solution made to depend on the relation between the remaining elements only) is well suited to express the operation, analogous to this, which has been understood since the time of Bacon to be the foundation of experimental inquiry, namely, the successive exclusion of the various circumstances which are found to accompany a phenomenon in a given instance, in order to ascertain what are those among them which can be absent consistently with the existence of the phenomenon. The method of agreement stands on the ground that whatever can be eliminated is not connected with the phenomenon by any law. The method of difference has for its foundation that whatever cannot be eliminated is connected with the phenomenon by a law.

Of these methods, that of difference is more particularly a method of artificial experiment, while that of agreement is more especially the resource employed where experimentation is impossible. A few reflections will prove the fact and point out the reason of it.

It is inherent in the peculiar character of the method of difference that the nature of the combinations which it requires is much more strictly defined than in the method of agreement. The two instances which are to be compared with one another must be exactly similar in all circumstances except the one which we are attempting to investigate: they must be in the relation of A B C and B C, or of *a b c* and *b c*. It is true that this similarity of circumstances needs not extend to such as are already known to be immaterial to the result. And in the case of most phenomena we learn at once, from the commonest experience, that most of the coexistent phenomena of the universe may be either present or absent without affecting the given phenomenon, or, if present, are present indifferently when the phenomenon does not happen and when it does. Still, even limiting the identity which is required between the two instances, A B C and B C, to such circumstances as are not already known to be indifferent, it is very seldom that nature affords two instances, of which we can be assured that they stand in this precise relation to one another. In the spontaneous operations of nature there is generally such complication and such obscurity, they are mostly either on so overwhelmingly large or on so inaccessibly minute a scale, we are so ignorant of a great part of the facts which really take place, and even those of which we are not ignorant are so multitudinous, and therefore so seldom exactly alike in any two cases, that a spontaneous experiment of the kind required by the method of difference is commonly not to be found. When, on the contrary, we obtain a phenomenon by an artificial experiment, a pair of instances such as the method requires is obtained almost as a matter of course, provided the process does not last a long time. A certain state of surrounding circumstances existed before we commenced the experiment; this is B C. We then introduce A, say, for instance, by merely bringing an object from another part of the room before there has been time for any change in the other elements. It is, in short (as M. Comte observes), the very nature of an experiment to introduce into the pre-existing state of circumstances a change perfectly definite. We choose a previous state of things with which we are well acquainted, so that no unforeseen alteration in that state is likely to pass unobserved; and into this we introduce, as rapidly as possible, the phenomenon which we wish to study; so that, in general, we are entitled to feel complete assurance that the pre-existing state and the state which we have produced differ in nothing except the presence or absence of that phenomenon. If a bird is taken from a cage and instantly plunged into carbonic acid gas, the experimentalist may be fully assured (at all events after one or two repetitions) that no circumstance capable of causing suffocation had supervened in the interim except the change from immersion in the atmosphere to immersion in carbonic acid gas. There is one doubt, indeed, which may remain in some cases of this description; the effect may have been produced not by the change, but by the means employed to produce the change. The possibility, however, of this last supposition generally admits of being conclusively tested by other experiments. It thus appears that in the study of the various kinds of phenomena which we can, by our voluntary agency, modify or control, we can, in general, satisfy the requisitions of the method of difference, but that by the spontaneous operations of nature those requisitions are seldom fulfilled.

The reverse of this is the case with the method of agreement. We do not here require instances of so special and determinate a kind. Any instances whatever in which nature presents us with a phenomenon may be examined for the purposes of this method; and, if all such instances agree in anything, a conclusion of considerable value is already attained. We can seldom, indeed, be sure that the one point of agreement is the only one; but this ignorance does not, as in the method of difference, vitiate the conclusion; the certainty of the result, as far as it goes, is not affected. We have ascertained one invariable antecedent or consequent, however many other invariable antecedents or consequents may still remain unascertained. If A B C,

A D E, A F G, are all equally followed by *a,* then *a* is an invariable consequent of A. If *a b c, a d e, a f g,* all number A among their antecedents, then A is connected as an antecedent, by some invariable law, with *a.* But to determine whether this invariable antecedent is a cause or this invariable consequent an effect, we must be able, in addition, to produce the one by means of the other, or, at least, to obtain that which alone constitutes our assurance of having produced anything, namely, an instance in which the effect, *a,* has come into existence with no other change in the pre-existing circumstances than the addition of A. And this, if we can do it, is an application of the method of difference, not of the method of agreement.

It thus appears to be by the method of difference alone that we can ever, in the way of direct experience, arrive with certainty at causes. The method of agreement leads only to laws of phenomena (as some writers call them, but improperly, since laws of causation are also laws of phenomena), that is, to uniformities which either are not laws of causation or in which the question of causation must for the present remain undecided. The method of agreement is chiefly to be resorted to as a means of suggesting applications of the method of difference (as in the last example the comparison of A B C, A D E, A F G, suggested that A was the antecedent on which to try the experiment whether it could produce *a*), or as an inferior resource, in case the method of difference is impracticable; which, as we before showed, generally arises from the impossibility of artificially producing the phenomena. And hence it is that the method of agreement, though applicable in principle to either case, is more emphatically the method of investigation on those subjects where artificial experimentation is impossible, because on those it is, generally, our only resource of a directly inductive nature, while, in the phenomena which we can produce at pleasure, the method of difference generally affords a more efficacious process which will ascertain causes as well as mere laws.

4. JOINT METHOD OF AGREEMENT AND DIFFERENCE

There are, however, many cases in which, though our power of producing the phenomenon is complete, the method of difference either cannot be made available at all, or not without a previous employment of the method of agreement. This occurs when the agency by which we can produce the phenomenon is not that of one single antecedent, but a combination of antecedents, which we have no power of separating from each other and exhibiting apart. For instance, suppose the subject of inquiry to be the cause of the double refraction of light. We can produce this phenomenon at pleasure by employing any one of the many substances which are known to refract light in that peculiar manner. But if, taking one of those substances, as Iceland spar, for example, we wish to determine on which of the properties of Iceland spar this remarkable phenomenon depends, we can make no use, for that purpose, of the method of difference; for we cannot find another substance precisely resembling Iceland spar except in some one property. The only mode, therefore, of prosecuting this inquiry is that afforded by the method of agreement, by which, in fact, through a comparison of all the known substances which have the property of doubly refracting light, it was ascertained that they agree in the circumstance of being crystalline substances; and though the converse does not hold, though all crystalline substances have not the property of double refraction, it was concluded, with reason, that there is a real connection between these two properties, that either crystalline structure or the cause which gives rise to that structure is one of the conditions of double refraction.

Out of this employment of the method of agreement arises a peculiar modification of that method which is sometimes of great avail in the investigation of nature. In cases similar to the above, in which it is not possible to obtain the precise pair of instances which our second canon requires —instances agreeing in every antecedent except A or in every consequent except a—we may yet be able, by a double employment of the method of agreement, to discover in what the instances which contain A or a differ from those which do not.

If we compare various instances in which a occurs and find that they all have in common the circumstance A, and (as far as can be observed) no other cirucumstance, the method of agreement, so far, bears testimony to a connection between A and a. In order to convert this evidence of connection into proof of causation by the direct method of difference, we ought to be able, in some one of these instances, as for example, A B C, to leave out A, and observe whether by doing so, a is prevented. Now supposing (what is often the case) that we are not able to try this decisive experiment, yet, provided we can by any means discover what would be its result if we could try it, the advantage will be the same. Suppose, then, that as we previously examined a variety of instances in which a occurred and found them to agree in containing A, so we now observe a variety of instances in which a does not occur and find them agree in not containing A, which establishes, by the method of agreement, the same connection between the absence of A and the absence of a which was before established between their presence. As, then, it had been shown that whenever A is present a is present, so, it being now shown that when A is taken away a is removed along with it, we have by the one proposition A B C, *a b c,* by the other B C, *b c,* the positive and negative instances which the method of difference requires.

This method may be called the indirect method of difference, or the joint method of agreement and difference, and consists in a double employment of the method of agreement, each proof being independent of the other and corroborating it. But it is not equivalent to a proof by the direct method of difference. For the requisitions of the method of difference are not satisfied unless we can be quite sure either that the instances affirmative of *a* agree in no antecedent whatever but A, or that the instances negative of *a* agree in nothing but the negation of A. Now, if it were possible, which it never is, to have this assurance, we should not need the joint method; for either of the two sets of instances separately would then be sufficient to prove causation. This indirect method, therefore, can only be regarded as a great extension and improvement of the method of agreement, but not as participating in the more cogent nature of the method of difference. The following may be stated as its canon:

THIRD CANON

If two or more instances in which the phenomenon occurs have only one circumstance in common, while two or more instances in which it does not occur have nothing in common save the absence of that circumstance, the circumstance in which alone the two sets of instances differ is the effect, or the cause, or an indispensable part of the cause, of the phenomenon.

We shall presently see that the joint method of agreement and difference constitutes, in another respect not yet adverted to, an improvement upon the common method of agreement, namely, in being unaffected by a characteristic imperfection of that method, the nature of which still remains to be pointed out. But as we cannot enter into this exposition without introducing a new element of complexity into this long and intricate discussion, I shall postpone it to a subsequent chapter and shall at once proceed to a statement of two other methods, which will complete the enumeration of the means which mankind possess for exploring the laws of nature by specific observation and experience.

5. METHOD OF RESIDUES

The first of these has been aptly denominated the method of residues. Its principle is very simple. Subducting from any given phenomenon all the portions which, by virtue of preceding inductions, can be assigned to known causes, the remainder will be the effect of the antecedents which had been overlooked or of which the effect was as yet an unknown quantity.

Suppose, as before, that we have the antecedents A B C, followed by the consequents *a b c,* and that by previous inductions (founded, we will suppose, on the method of difference) we have ascertained the causes of some of these effects or the effects of some of these causes, and are thence apprised that the effect of A is *a,* and that the effect of B is *b.* Subtracting the sum of these effects from the total phenomenon, there remains *c,* which now, without any fresh experiments, we may know to be the effect of C. This method of residues is in truth a peculiar modification of the method of difference. If the instance A B C, *a b c,* could have been compared with a single instance A B, *a b,* we should have proved C to be the cause of *c* by the common process of the method of difference. In the present case, however, instead of a single instance A B, we have had to study separately the causes A and B, and to infer from the effects which they produce separately what effect they must produce in the case A B C, where they act together. Of the two instances, therefore, which the method of difference requires—the one positive, the other negative—the negative one, or that in which the given phenomenon is absent, is not the direct result of observation and experiment, but has been arrived at by deduction. As one of the forms of the method of difference, the method of residues partakes of its rigorous certainty, provided the previous inductions, those which gave the effects of A and B, were obtained by the same infallible method, and provided we are certain that C is the *only* antecedent to which the residual phenomenon *c* can be referred, the only agent of which we had not already calculated and subducted the effect. But, as we can never be quite certain of this, the evidence derived from the method of residues is not complete unless we can obtain C artificially and try it separately, or unless its agency, when once suggested, can be accounted for and proved deductively from known laws.

Even with these reservations, the method of residues is one of the most important among our instruments of discovery. Of all the methods of investigating laws of nature, this is the most fertile in unexpected results, often informing us of sequences in which neither the cause nor the effect were sufficiently conspicuous to attract of themselves the attention of observers. The agent C may be an obscure circumstance, not likely to have been perceived unless sought for, nor likely to have been sought for until attention had been awakened by the insufficiency of the obvious causes to account for the whole of the effect. And *c* may be so disguised by its intermixture with *a* and *b,* that it would scarcely have presented itself spontaneously as a subject of separate study. Of these uses of the method, we shall presently cite some remarkable examples. The canon of the method of residues is as follows:

FOURTH CANON

Subduct from any phenomenon such part as is known by previous inductions to be the effect of certain antecedents, and the residue of the phenomenon is the effect of the remaining antecedents.

6. METHOD OF CONCOMITANT VARIATIONS

There remains a class of laws which it is impracticable to ascertain by any of the three methods which I have attempted to characterize, namely, the laws of those permanent causes, or indestructible natural agents which it is impossible either to exclude or to isolate, which we can neither hinder from being present, nor contrive that they shall be present alone. It would appear at first sight that we could by no means separate the effects of these agents from the effects of those other phenomena with which they cannot be prevented from co-existing. In respect, indeed, to most of the permanent causes, no such difficulty exists, since, thought we cannot eliminate them as co-existing facts, we can eliminate them as influencing agents by simply trying our experiment in a local situation beyond the limits of their influence. The pendulum, for example, has its oscillations disturbed by the vicinity of a mountain: we remove the pendulum to a sufficient distance from the mountain, and the disturbance ceases: from these data we can determine by the method of difference the amount of effect due to the mountain, and beyond a certain distance everything goes on precisely as it would do if the mountain exercised no influence whatever, which, accordingly, we, with sufficient reason, conclude to be the fact.

The difficulty, therefore, in applying the methods already treated of to determine the effects of permanent causes is confined to the cases in which it is impossible for us to get out of the local limits of their influence. The pendulum can be removed from the influence of the mountain, but it cannot be removed from the influence of the earth: we cannot take away the earth from the pendulum nor the pendulum from the earth, to ascertain whether it would continue to vibrate if the action which the earth exerts upon it were withdrawn. On what evidence, then, do we ascribe its vibrations to the earth's influence? Not on any sanctioned by the method of difference; for one of the two instances, the negative instance, is wanting. Nor by the method of agreement; for, though all pendulums agree in this, that during their oscillations the earth is always present, why may we not as well ascribe the phenomenon to the sun, which is equally a co-existent fact in all the experiments? It is evident that to establish even so simple a fact of causation as this, there was required some method over and above those which we have yet examined.

As another example, let us take the phenomenon heat. Independently of all hypothesis as to the real nature of the agency so called, this fact is certain, that we are unable to exhaust any body of the whole of its heat. It is equally certain that no one ever perceived heat not emanating from a body. Being unable, then, to separate body and heat, we cannot effect such a variation of circumstances as the foregoing three methods require; we cannot ascertain by those methods what portion of the phenomena exhibited by any body is due to the heat contained in it. If we could observe a body with its heat and the same body entirely divested of heat, the method of difference would show the effect due to the heat, apart from that due to the body. If we could observe heat under circumstances agreeing in nothing but heat and, therefore, not characterized also by the presence of a body, we could ascertain the effects of heat, from an instance of heat with a body and an instance of heat without a body, by the method of agreement; or we could determine by the method of difference what effect was due to the body, when the remainder which was due to the heat would be given by the method of residues. But we can do none of these things; and without them the application of any of the three methods to the solution of this problem would be illusory. It would be idle, for instance, to attempt to ascertain the effect of heat by subtracting from the phenomena exhibited by a body all that is due to its other properties; for, as we have never been able to observe any bodies without a portion of heat in them, effects due to that heat might form a part of the very results which we were affecting to subtract in order that the effect of heat might be shown by the residue.

If, therefore, there were no other methods of experimental investigation than these three, we should be unable to determine the effects due to heat as a cause. But we have still a resource. Though we cannot exclude an antecedent altogether, we may be able to produce, or nature may produce for us, some modification in it. By a modification is here meant a change in it not amounting to its total removal. If some modification in the antecedent A is always followed by a change in the consequent a, the other consequents b and c remaining the same, or *vice versa*, if every change in a is found to have been preceded by some modification in A, none being observable in any of the other antecedents, we may safely conclude that a is, wholly or in part, an effect traceable to A, or at least in some way connected with it through causation. For example, in the case of heat, though we cannot expel it altogether from any body, we can modify it in quantity, we can increase or diminish it; and, doing so, we find by the various methods of experimentation or observation already treated of that such increase or diminution of heat is followed by expansion or contraction of the body. In this manner we arrive at the conclusion, otherwise unattainable by us, that one of the effects of heat is to enlarge the dimensions of bodies, or, what is the same thing in other words, to widen the distances between their particles.

A change in a thing not amounting to its total removal, that is, a change which leaves it still the same thing it was, must be a change either in its quantity or in some of its variable relations to other things, of which variable relations the principal is its position in space. In the previous example, the modification which was produced in the antecedent was an alteration in its quantity. Let us now suppose the question to be, what influence the moon exerts on the surface of the earth. We cannot try an experiment in the absence of the moon, so as to observe what terrestrial phenomena her annihilation would put an end to; but, when we find that all the variations in the *position* of the moon are followed by corresponding variations in the time and place of high water, the place being always either the part of the earth which is nearest to, or that which is most remote from, the moon, we have ample evidence that the moon is, wholly or partially, the cause which determines the tides. It very commonly happens, as it does in this instance, that the variations of an effect are correspondent or analogous to those of its cause; as the moon moves farther toward the east, the high-water point does the same; but this is not an indispensable condition, as may be seen in the same example; for along with that high-water point there is at the same instant another high-water point diametrically opposite to it, and which, therefore, of necessity, moves toward the west, as the moon, followed by the nearer of the tide waves, advances toward the east, and yet both these motions are equally effects of the moon's motion.

That the oscillations of the pendulum are caused by the earth is proved by similar evidence. Those oscillations take place between equidistant points on the two sides of a line, which, being perpendicular to the earth, varies with every variation in the earth's position, either in space or relatively to the object. Speaking accurately, we only know by the method now characterized, that all terrestrial bodies tend to the earth, and not to some unknown fixed point lying in the same direction. In every twenty-four hours, by the earth's rotation, the line drawn from the body at right angles to the earth coincides successively with all the radii of a circle, and in the course of six months the place of that circle varies by nearly two hundred millions of miles; yet, in all these changes of the earth's position, the line in which bodies tend to fall continues to be directed toward it: which proves that terrestrial gravity is directed to the earth and not, as was once fancied by some, to a fixed point of space.

The method by which these results were obtained may be termed the method of concomitant variations; it is regulated by the following canon:

FIFTH CANON
Whatever phenomenon varies in any manner whenever another phenomenon varies in some particular manner is either a cause or an effect of that phenomenon, or is connected with it through some fact of causation.

The last clause is subjoined because it by no means follows, when two phenomena accompany each other in their variations, that the one is cause and the other effect. The same thing may and indeed must happen supposing them to be two different effects of a common cause; and by this method alone it would never be possible to ascertain which of the suppositions is the true one. The only way to solve the doubt would be that which we have so often adverted to, viz., by endeavoring to ascertain whether we can produce the one set of variations by means of the other. In the case of heat, for example, by increasing the temperature of a body we increase its bulk, but by increasing its bulk we do not increase its temperature; on the contrary (as in the rarefaction of air under the receiver of an air-pump), we generally diminish it; therefore heat is not an effect, but a cause, of increase of bulk. If we cannot ourselves produce the variations, we must endeavor, though it is an attempt which is seldom successful, to find them produced by nature in some case in which the pre-existing circumstances are perfectly known to us.

It is scarcely necessary to say that, in order to ascertain the uniform concomitance of variations in the effect with variations in the cause, the same precautions must be used as in any other case of the determination of an invariable sequence. We must endeavor to retain all the other antecedents unchanged, while that particular one is subjected to the requisite series of variations; or, in other words, that we may be warranted in inferring causation from concomitance of variations, the concomitance itself must be proved by the method of difference.

It might at first appear that the method of concomitant variations assumes a new axiom, or law of causation in general, namely, that every modification of the cause is followed by a change in the effect. And it does usually happen that when a phenomenon A causes a phenomenon *a,* any variation in the quantity or in the various relations of A is uniformly followed by a variation in the quantity or relations of *a.* To take a familiar instance, that of gravitation. The sun causes a certain tendency to motion in the earth; here we have cause and effect; but that tendency is *toward* the sun and, therefore, varies in direction as the sun varies in the relation of position; and, moreover, the tendency varies in intensity in a certain numerical correspondence to the sun's distance from the earth, that is, according to another relation of the sun. Thus we see that there is not only an invariable connection between the sun and the earth's gravitation, but that two of the relations of the sun, its position with respect to the earth and its distance from the earth, are invariably connected as antecedents with the quantity and direction of the earth's gravitation. The cause of the earth's gravitating at all is simply the sun; but the cause of its gravitating with a given intensity and in a given direction is the existence of the sun in a given direction and at a given distance. It is not strange that a modified cause, which is in truth a different cause, should produce a different effect.

Although it is for the most part true that a modification of the cause is followed by a modification of the effect, the method of concomitant variations does not, however, presuppose this as an axiom. It only requires the converse proposition, that anything on whose modifications modifications of an effect are invariably consequent must be the cause (or connected with the cause) of that effect; a proposition the truth of which is evident; for if the thing itself had no influence on the effect, neither could the modifications of the thing have any influence. If the stars have no power over the fortunes of mankind, it is implied in the very terms that the conjunctions or oppositions of different stars can have no such power.

Although the most striking applications of the method of concomitant variations take place in the cases in which the method of difference, strictly so called, is impossible, its use is not confined to those cases; it may often usefully follow after the method of difference, to give additional precision to a solution which that has found. When by the method of difference it has first been ascertained that a certain object produces a certain effect, the method of concomitant variations may be usefully called in to determine according to what law the quantity or the different relations of the effect follow those of the cause.

7. LIMITATIONS OF THIS LAST METHOD

The case in which this method admits of the most extensive employment is that in which the variations of the cause are variations of quantity. Of such variations we may in general affirm with safety that they will be attended not only with variations but with similar variations of the effect: the proposition that more of the cause is followed by more of the effect being a corollary from the principle of the composition of causes, which, as we have seen, is the general rule of causation; cases of the opposite description, in which causes change their properties on being conjoined with one another, being, on the contrary, special and exceptional. Suppose, then, that when A changes in quantity, a also changes in quantity, and in such a manner that we can trace the numerical relation which the changes of the one bear to such changes of the other as take place within our limits of observation. We may then, with certain precautions, safely conclude that the same numerical relation will hold beyond those limits. If, for instance, we find that when A is double, a is double, that when A is treble or quadruple, a is treble or quadruple, we may conclude that if A were a half or a third, a would be a half or a third, and, finally, that if A were annihiliated, a would be annihilated, and that a is wholly the effect of A, or wholly the effect of the same cause with A. And so with any other numerical relation according to which A and a would vanish simultaneously, as, for instance, if a were proportional to the square of A. If, on the other hand, a is not wholly the effect of A, but yet varies when A varies, it is probably a mathematical function not of A alone but of A and something else; its changes, for example, may be such as would occur if part of it remained constant or varied on some other principle, and the remainder varied in some numerical relations to the variations of A. In that case, when A diminishes, a will be seen to approach not toward zero, but toward some other limit; and when the series of variations is such as to indicate what the limit is, if constant, or the law of its variation, if variable, the limit will exactly measure how much of a is the effect of some other and independent cause, and the remainder will be the effect of A (or of the cause of A).

These conclusions, however, must not be drawn without certain precautions. In the first place, the possibility of drawing them at all manifestly supposes that we are acquainted not only with the variations but with the absolute quantities both of A and a. If we do not know the total quantities, we cannot, of course, determine the real numerical relation according to which those quantities vary. It is, therefore, an error to conclude, as some have concluded, that because increase of heat expands bodies, that is, increases the distance between their particles, therefore the distance is wholly the effect of heat, and that if we could entirely exhaust the body of its heat, the particles would be in complete contact. This is no more than a guess, and of the most hazardous sort, not a legitimate induction; for, since we neither know how much heat there is in any body nor what is the real distance between any two of its particles, we cannot judge whether the contraction of the distance does or does not follow the diminution of the quantity of heat according to such a numerical relation that the two quantities would vanish simultaneously.

In contrast with this, let us consider a case in which the absolute quantities are known, the case contemplated in the first law of motion, viz., that all bodies in motion continue to move in a straight line with uniform velocity until acted upon by some new force. This assertion is in open opposition to first appearances; all terrestrial objects, when in motion, gradually abate their velocity and at last stop, which, accordingly, the ancients, with their *inductio per enumerationem simplicem,* imagined to be the law. Every moving body, however, encounters various obstacles, as friction, the resistance of the atmosphere, etc., which we know by daily experience to be causes capable of destroying motion. It was suggested that the whole of the retardation might be owing to these causes. How was this inquired into? If the obstacles could have been entirely removed, the case would have been amenable to the method of difference. They could not be removed; they could only be diminished; and the case, therefore, admitted only of the method of concomitant variations. This, accordingly, being employed, it was found that every diminution of the obstacles diminished the retardation of the motion; and, inasmuch as in this case (unlike the case of heat) the total quantities both of the antecedent and of the consequent were known, it was practicable to estimate, with an approach to accuracy, both the amount of the retardation and the amount of the retarding causes, or resistances, and to judge how near they both were to being exhausted; and it appeared that the effect dwindled as rapidly and at each step was as far on the road toward annihilation as the cause was. The simple oscillation of a weight suspended from a fixed point and moved a little out of the perpendicular, which in ordinary circumstances lasts but a few minutes, was prolonged in Borda's experiments to more than thirty hours by diminishing as much as possible the friction at the point of suspension and by making the body oscillate in a space exhausted as nearly as possible of its air. There could, therefore, be no hesitation in assigning the whole of the retardation of motion to the influence of the obstacles; and since, after subducting this retardation from the total phenomenon, the remainder was a uniform velocity, the result was the proposition known as the first law of motion.

There is also another characteristic uncertainty affecting the inference that the law of variation which the quantities observe within our limits of observation will hold beyond those limits. There is, of course, in the first instance, the possibility that beyond the limits, and in circumstances, therefore, of which we have no direct experience, some counteracting cause might develop itself; either a new agent, or a new property of the agents concerned, which lies dormant in the circumstances we are able to observe. This is an element of uncertainty which enters largely into all our predictions of effects; but it is not peculiarly applicable to the method of concomitant variations. The uncertainty, however, of which I am about to speak is characteristic of that method, especially in the cases in which the extreme limits of our observation are very narrow in comparison with the possible variations in the quantities of the phenomena. Anyone who has the slightest acquaintance with mathematics is aware that very different laws of variation may produce numerical results which differ but slightly from one another within narrow limits; and it is often only when the absolute amounts of variation are considerable that the difference between the results given by one law and by another becomes appreciable. When, therefore, such variations in the quantity of the antecedents as we have the means of observing are small in comparison with the total quantities, there is much danger lest we should mistake the numerical law and be led to miscalculate the variations which would take place beyond the limits, a miscalculation which would vitiate any conclusion respecting the dependence of the effect upon the cause that could be founded on those variations. Examples are not wanting of such mistakes. 'The formulae,' says Sir John Herschel,[1] 'which have been empirically deduced for the elasticity of steam (till very recently), and those for the resistance of fluids, and other similar subjects,' when relied on beyond the limits of the observations from which they were deduced, 'have almost invariably failed to support the theoretical structures which have been erected on them.'

In this uncertainty, the conclusion we may draw from the concomitant variations of a and A to the existence of an invariable and exclusive connection between them, or to the permanency of the same numerical relation between their variations when the quantities are much greater or smaller than those which we have had the means of observing, cannot be considered to rest on a complete induction. All that in such a case can be regarded as proved on the subject of causation is that there is some connection between the two phenomena; that A, or something which can influence A, must be *one* of the causes which collectively determine a. We may, however, feel assured that the relation which we have observed to exist between the variations of A and a will hold true in all cases which fall between the same extreme limits; that is, wherever the utmost increase or diminution in which the result has been found by observation to coincide with the law is not exceeded.

The four methods which it has now been attempted to describe are the only possible modes of experimental inquiry—of direct induction *a posteriori,* as distinguished from deduction; at least, I know not, nor am able to imagine any others. And even of these, the method of residues, as we have seen, is not independent of deduction, though, as it also requires specific experience, it may, without impropriety, be included among methods of direct observation and experiment.

These, then, with such assistance as can be obtained from deduction, com-

[1] *Discourse on the Study of Natural Philosophy,* p. 179.

pose the available resources of the human mind for ascertaining the laws of the succession of phenomena. Before proceeding to point out certain circumstances by which the employment of these methods is subjected to an immense increase of complication and of difficulty, it is expedient to illustrate the use of the methods by suitable examples drawn from actual physical investigations. These, accordingly, will form the subject of the succeeding chapter.

AIDS TO STUDY

This chapter from John Stuart Mill's study of induction deals with the problem of causation—how do we know what causes what? One doesn't have to live long in the world to discover that all notions of causation are not equally persuasive. As a child he encounters assertions that toads cause warts, that candy and gum cause cavities, that fire causes smoke, that cigarettes cause lung cancer, that reading and study cause stunted growth, that faulty electrical wiring causes fires, that green apples cause stomach-ache, and innumerable others. A good part of achieving intellectual maturity is involved in winnowing the wheat from the chaff in these assertions; and one must have some method by which to separate sensible notions from foolish ones. If 'common sense' would suffice for this purpose, it is difficult to see how foolish notions could remain in the world; clearly, common sense will not suffice. We must learn methods by which we can satisfy ourselves and others that our views of causation are not merely guesswork—or merely what we want to believe because it makes us comfortable. And we must learn to apply these methods with care to each problem that confronts us. Mill's canons give us methods to apply to problems of cause and effect—ways of measuring the persuasiveness of the notions we and others have. Perhaps no other essay in this collection is of more importance in the modern world, if we want to make sure that what we say and write is to be taken seriously by educated people; for in a scientific age, conclusions about causes and effects are taken with especial seriousness by the educated community, and a person whose notions of causation are 'superstitious' is quickly dismissed as a knave or a fool.

A number of problems arise in connection with this essay, perhaps the first of which is connected with its title: Mill heads this chapter with 'four methods,' but gives us *five* canons. The four methods, of course, are those of agreement, of difference, of residue, and of concomitant variation; the 'joint method of agreement and difference' is not logically a fifth method, but rather a combination of the first two methods he discusses.

The canons themselves will probably not cause difficulty. As Mill states them, they are easy enough to understand in the abstract. But we should observe two things in connection with them. First, Mill is concerned with physical causation—causes and effects in the physical universe. He does not undertake in this chapter to consider moral, ethical, or intellectual causation, and there is no hint that he means his canons to extend beyond what we may think of as the world of things. We are not warranted, therefore, to extend his 'laws' to matters of political policy or moral rectitude.

Second, since Mill restricts himself to matters of physical science, we may need some help from our classmates in this field of study. The examples Mill gives may profitably be discussed in class or dormitory by those who know something about them—that alkaline substances and oil produce greasy or soapy substances; that crystallization always proceeds from a liquid state; that a water pump depends upon air pressure on the surface of the water; that carbon dioxide suffocates birds; that Iceland spar produces birefringence; that oscillations of a pendulum are related to the earth; that heat and expansion of materials are closely related; that the moon affects the tides. If knowledgeable classmates cannot be found, introductory textbooks and encyclopedia articles can be; and we should make use of them.

A final word should be said of the abuses of the methods Mill here outlines. Throughout his discussion, we should notice that Mill is insisting that we employ his canons with caution. An alleged cause must *regularly* precede or accompany an event and must regularly be absent in the absence of the event; we must be reasonably sure that we have taken into account all possible causes and effects; we must remain content to believe that what we take to be a cause may be but an associated effect of a cause we have not discovered. In short, we should not be hasty or arrogant in our conclusions about the causes of things.

A serious error we can make, in the assessment of cause and effect, is the error known by the Latin phrase *post hoc ergo propter hoc* (after this, therefore because of this)—after walking under a ladder, I was hit by a truck; therefore walking under the ladder caused the accident; after I washed the car it rained; therefore my washing the car caused the rainstorm; after Mr. Jones visited his doctor the doctor was found slain; therefore Mr. Jones killed him—the list is endless, alas, for, as was suggested at the beginning of this note, the common sense of humanity does not seem sufficient to eliminate remarkably thoughtless notions of cause and effect.

The Interinanimation of Words

I turn now to that other sense of 'context'—the literary context—which I distinguished last time from the technical sense of 'context,' as a recurrent group of events, that is convenient for the theorem of meaning. Let us consider some of the effects on words of their combination in sentences, and how their meaning depends upon the other words before and after them in the sentence. What happens when we try with a sentence to decide what single words in it mean?

The sentence, of course, as Aristotle taught, is the unit of discourse. We can hardly give too much importance here to the influence of our modern way of separating words in writing. In conversation we do not ordinarily separate them so—unless we are asking questions about words. With languages which have not been used in writing and thus subjected to a special kind of grammatical analysis—it is worth recalling that grammar takes its name from writing—there is often very great uncertainty as to where one word ends and another begins. The written form gives words far more independence than they possess as units of sound in speech and we derive thence a habit of supposing that they have far more independence as regards their meanings than they usually have in either written or spoken discourse.

The mutual dependence of words varies evidently with the type of discourse. At one end of the scale, in the strict exposition of some highly criticized and settled science through technicalized and rigid speech, a large proportion of them are independent. They mean the same whatever other words they are put with; or if a word fluctuates, it moves only into a small number of stable positions, which can be recorded and are anchored to defintions. That is the ideal limit towards which we aim in exposition. Unfortunately we tend—increasingly since the seventeenth century—to take rigid discourse as the norm, and impose its standards upon the rest of speech. This is much as if we thought that water, for all its virtues, in canals, baths and turbines, were really a weak form of ice. The other end of the scale is in poetry—in some forms of poetry rather. We know very much less about the behavior of words in these cases—when their virtue is to have no fixed and settled meaning separable from those of the other words they occur with. There are many more possibilities here than the theory of language has yet tried to think out. Often the whole utterance in which the co-operating meanings of the component words hang on one another is not itself stable in meaning. It utters not one meaning but a *movement* among meanings. Of course, even in the strictest prose we always have one thing that may be described as a movement of meaning. We have change as the sentence develops. In 'The cat is on the mat' we begin with the cat and end with the mat. There is a progression of some sort in every explicit sentence. But in the strictest prose the meanings of the separate words theoretically stay put and thought passes from one to another of them. At the other end of the scale the whole meaning of the sentence shifts, and with it any meanings we may try to ascribe to the individual words. In the extreme case it will go on moving as long as we bring fresh wits to study it. When Octavius Cæsar is gazing down at Cleopatra dead, he says,

> She looks like sleep,
> As she would catch another Antony
> In her strong toil of grace.

'Her strong toil of grace.' Where, in terms of what entries in what possible dictionary, do the meanings here of *toil* and *grace* come to rest?

But my subject is Rhetoric rather than Poetics and I want to keep to prose which is not too far from the strict scientific or 'rigid' end of this scale of dependent variabilities. In the kind of prose I am talking now, you have usually to wait till I have gone on a bit before you can decide how you will understand the opening parts of the sentences. If, instead, I were reading you the first few theorems of Euclid, that would not be so. You would understand, as soon as I said 'a triangle,' what the word meant, and though what I went on to say might qualify the meaning ('having two sides equal'), it would not destroy or completely change the meaning that you had so far given to the word. But in most prose, and more than we ordinarily suppose, the opening words have to wait for those that follow to settle what they shall mean—if indeed that ever gets settled.

All this holds good not only as to the *sense* of the waiting words but as regards all the other functions of language which we can distinguish and set over against the mere sense. It holds for the *feeling* if any towards what I am talking about, for *the relation towards my audience* I want to establish or maintain with the remark, and for the *confidence* I have in the soundness of the remark—to mention three main sorts of these other language functions. In speech, of course, I have the aid of intonation for these purposes. But, as with the meanings of words, so with the intonation structure. The intonation of the opening words is likely to be ambiguous; it waits till the utterance is completed for its full interpretation.

In writing we have to replace intonation as far as we can. Most of the more recondite virtues of prose style come from the skill with which the rival claims of these various language functions are reconciled and combined. And many of the rather mysterious terms that are usually employed in discussing these matters, *harmony, rhythm, grace, texture, smoothness, suppleness, impressiveness,* and so on are best taken up for analysis from this point of view. Or rather the passages which seem to exemplify these qualities (or fail to) are best examined with the multiplicity of the language functions in mind. For we can obviously do nothing with such words as these by themselves, in the blue. They may mean all sorts of different things in different literary contexts.

I have been leading up—or down, if you like—to an extremely simple and obvious but fundamental remark: that no word can be judged as to whether it is good or bad, correct or incorrect, beautiful or ugly, or anything else that matters to a writer, in isolation. That seems so evident that I am almost ashamed to say it, and yet it flies straight in the face of the only doctrine that for two hundred years has been officially inculcated—when any doctrine is inculcated in these matters. I mean the doctrine of Usage. The doctrine that there is a right or a good use for every word and that literary virtue consists in making that good use of it.

There are several bones that can be picked with that doctrine—as it has been expounded in many epochs and, in particular for us, from the middle of the eighteenth century onwards. It is the worst legacy we have from that, in other ways, happy century. At its best it can be found in George Campbell's *Philosophy of Rhetoric*—otherwise an excellent book in many respects. At its worst, or nearly its worst, the doctrine can be found in most of the Manuals of Rhetoric and Composition which have afflicted the schools—American schools especially. It asserts that 'Good use is the general, present-day practice of the best writers.' One bone we could pick would be with that 'best.' How are they the best writers except by using the words in the best ways? We settle that they *are* the best writers because we find them using their words successfully. We do not settle that theirs is the right, the 'good usage' of the words because *they* use them so. Never was there a crazier case of putting the cart before the horse. It is as though we were to maintain that apples are healthy because [1] wise people eat them, instead of recognizing that it is the other way about—that it is what the food will do for us which makes us eat it, not the fact that we eat it which makes it good food.

But that is not the main bone I have to pick with the doctrine, which is that it blanks out and hides the interinanimation between words. I had better cite you a sentence or two in evidence, or you may think I am inventing a ghost to exorcize. I will take them from a *Manual of Rhetoric* which carries the names of three authors: Messrs. Gardiner, Kittredge and Arnold. And I choose this book because the regard which I have for Mr. Kittredge's name makes a doctrine which has that sanction seem the better worth refuting. The authors write: 'Usage governs language. There is no other standard. By usage, however, is meant the practice of the best writers and speakers.' (I have already asked what standard is supposed to settle which are the best.) They go on to consider 'four great general principles of choice: *correctness, precision, appropriateness* and *expressiveness*,' which, they say, 'within the limits of good usage and in every case controlled by it . . . should guide us in the choice of words.' And this is what they say of correctness: 'Correctness is the most elementary of all requirements. The meanings of words are settled by usage. If we us a word incorrectly—that is in a sense which does not customarily belong to it—our readers will miss our thought, or, at best, they must arrive at it by inference and guesswork.'

Inference and guesswork! What else is interpretation? How, apart from inference and skilled guesswork, can we be supposed ever to understand a writer or speaker's thought? This is, I think, a fine case of poking the fire from the top. But I have still my main bit of evidence to give you. My authors say: 'In studying the four great principles of choice, we observe that only the first (correctness) involves the question of right and wrong. The others deal with questions of discrimination between better and worse—that is with the closer adaptation of words to the thoughts and feelings which we undertake to express. Further, it is only in dealing with the first principle (correctness) that we can keep our attention entirely on the single word.'

There! that is the view I wished to illustrate. Let us not boggle about the oddities of its expression: 'right and wrong,' 'better and worse'; or worry as to how by keeping 'our attention entirely on a single word' we could settle anything at all about it—except perhaps about its spelling! The important point is that words are here supposed just sheerly to possess their sense, as men have their names in the reverse case, and to carry this meaning with them into sentences regardless of the neighbour words. That is the assumption I am attacking, because, if we follow up its practical consequences in

---

[1] 'Because' is offering to play one of its most troublesome tricks here, of course in the shift from 'cause' to 'reason.'

writing and reading and trace its effects upon interpretation, we shall find among them no small proportion of the total of our verbal misunderstandings.

I am anxious not to seem to be illustrating this sort of misunderstanding myself here, unwittingly, in my interpretation of this passage. I know well enough that the authors probably had in mind such incorrectness as occurs when people say 'ingenious' when they mean 'ingenuous'; and I know that the Usage Doctrine can be interpreted in several ways which make it true and innocuous.

It can say and truly, for example, that we learn how to use words from responding to them and noting how other people use them. Just how we do so learn is a deep but explorable question. It can say equally truly, that a general conformity between users is a condition of communication. *That* no one would dream of disputing. But if we consider conformity we see that there are two kinds of conformity. Conformity in the general process of interpretation, and conformity in the specific products. We all know how the duller critics of the eighteenth century (the century that gave us the current Doctrine of Usage) the people Wordsworth was thinking of when he wrote his Preface, confused the poetic product with the poetic process and thought a poem good because it used poetic diction—the words that former good poets had used—and used them in the same ways. The Usage Doctrine, in the noxious interpretation of it, is just that blunder in a more pervasive and more dangerous incidence. The noxious interpretation is the common one. Its evil is that it takes the senses of an author's words to be things we know before we read him, fixed factors with which he has to build up the meaning of his sentences as a mosaic is put together of discrete independent tesserae. Instead, they are resultants which we arrive at only through the interplay of the interpretative possibilities of the whole utterance. In brief, we have to guess them and we guess much better when we realize we are guessing, and watch out for indications, than when we think we know.[2]

There are as many morals for the writer as for the reader in all this, but I will keep to interpretation. A word or phrase when isolated momentarily from its controlling neighbours is free to develop irrelevant senses which may then beguile half the other words to follow it. And this is at least equally true with the language functions *other than sense,* with *feeling,* say. I will give you one example of an erratic interpretation of feeling, and if I take it from the same *Manual of Rhetoric* that is because it illustrates one of the things to which the mosaic view or habit of interpretation, as opposed to the organic, often leads.

The Authors give the following from Bacon's *Advancement of Learning.* And in re-reading it I will ask you to note how cunningly Bacon, in describ-

[2] See the Note at the end of this Lecture.

ing some misuses of learning, takes back with one hand what he seems to be offering with the other, indicating both why men do prefer misuses and why they should not do so.

> But the greatest error of all the rest is the mistaking or misplacing of the last or furthest end of knowledge. For men have entered into a desire of learning and knowledge, sometimes upon a natural curiosity and inquisitive appetite; sometimes to entertain their minds with variety and delight; sometimes for ornament and reputation; and sometimes to enable them to victory of wit and contradiction; and most times for lucre and profession; and seldom sincerely to give a true account of their gift of reason, to the benefit and use of men: as if there were sought in knowledge a couch, whereupon to rest a searching or restless spirit; or a terrace, for a wandering and variable mind to walk up and down with a fair prospect; or a tower of state, for a proud mind to raise itself upon; or a fort or commanding ground, for strife and contention; or a shop, for profit or sale; and not a rich storehouse, for the glory of the Creator and the relief of man's estate.

There is much to take to heart here—especially as to the couch aspect of the Usage Doctrine, and, I must admit, the tower and the fort—but what the authors say about it is this:

> Here the splendor of the imagery is no mere embellishment. Without it, Bacon could not have given adequate expression to his enthusiastic appreciation of learning and his fine scorn for the unworthy uses to which it is sometimes put. At the same time, the figures elevate the passage from the ordinary levels of prose to a noble eloquence. (p. 372)

What splendor is there in the imagery? These images have no splendor as Bacon uses them, but are severely efficient, a compact means for saying what he has to say. His 'enthusiastic appreciation' (a poor phrase, I suggest, to smudge over him!) of the use of knowledge and his 'fine scorn' of unworthy uses are given only if we refuse to be beguiled by the possibilities of splendor in the isolated images. Loose them even a little from their service, let their 'splendor' act independently, and they begin at once to fight against his intention. For the terrace, the tower and the fort, if they were allowed to 'elevate,' would make the misplacings of the last and furthest end of knowledge seem much grander than 'a true account of their gift of reason, to the benefit and use of men'—as a terrace or tower of state or a fort will seem grander than a mere rich storehouse.

Let me go on to some further types of the mutual control and interanimation between words. So far I have considered only the influence of words actually present in the passage, but we have to include words which are not actually being uttered and are only in the background. Take the case of what are variously called expressive, symbolic, or simulative words—words which 'somehow illustrate the meaning more immediately than do ordinary speech forms,' to quote Leonard Bloomfield. Examples are *flip, flap, flop, flitter, flimmer, flicker, flutter, flash, flush, flare, glare, glitter, glow, gloat, glimmer, bang, bump, lump, thump, thwack, whack, sniff, sniffle, snuff*. . . Why should these seem so peculiarly appropriate, or fitting, to the meanings we use them for? The popular view is that these words just simply imitate, are copies of, what they mean. But that is a short-cut theory which often does not work, and we can, I think, go further and do better. As Bloomfield, in his excellent book, *Language,* says, 'the explanation is a matter of grammatical structure, to the speaker it seems as if the sounds were especially suited to the meaning.' The speaker usually thinks moreover that the word seems suited because in some way it resembles the meaning, or, if this seems un-plausible, that there must be *some* direct connection between them. If it is not the sound of the word which resembles the meaning then perhaps the tongue and lip movements instead imitate something to do with the meaning and so on. Sir Richard Paget's theories of imitative gestures are likely to be appealed to nowadays.

The most that the modern linguist—who compares the very different words which are used in different languages for their meanings—is prepared to allow towards this resemblance of sound and sense is that 'we can distinguish, with various degrees of clearness and with doubtful cases on the border line, a system of initial and final root-forming morphemes of vague signification.' Note how guarded Bloomfield is over such a point.

I must explain what a morpheme is. Two or more words are said to share a morpheme when they have, at the same time, something in common in their meaning and something in common in their sound. The joint semantic-phonetic unit which distinguishes them is what is called a morpheme. It is the togetherness of a peculiar sound and a peculiar meaning for a number of words.

Thus *flash, flare, flame, flicker, flimmer* have in common the sound (fl-) and a suggestion of a 'moving light'—and this joint possession is the mor-pheme. Similarly *blare, flare, glare, stare* have the sound (-ɛə) in common and also the meaning 'big light or noise' shall we say, and this couple—sound and meaning is the morpheme. So with 'smoothly wet' and (sl-) in *slime, slip, slush, slobber, slide, slither*. But *pare, pear, pair*, though they have a sound in common, have no meaning in common, so have no common mor-pheme.

Of course, the existence of a group of words with a common morpheme has an influence on the formation of other words, and on the pronunciation of other words—assimilating them to the group. Thus, given *skid* and *skate,* that is a strong additional reason, against an English convention, for saying *skee* rather than *shee.*

This pedantic looking term, *morpheme,* is useful because with its help we manage to avoid saying that the sound (sl-) somehow itself means something like 'smoothly wet or slippery' and gain a way of saying no more than that a group of words which share that sound also share a peculiar meaning. And that is all we are entitled to say. To go further and say that the words share the meaning *because* they contain this sound and because this sound has that meaning is to bring in more than we know—an explanation or theory to account for what we do know. And actually it is a bad explanation. For this sound, by itself, means nothing. It is not the shared sound but each of the words which has the meaning. The sound by itself either means nothing at all—as with (fl) in *flame, flare, flash, flicker*—or as with (-ɛə) in *blare, flare, glare, stare* it has by itself only an irrelevant meaning, namely, that of *air,* 'what we breathe.'

The theoretical position here is worth close study because it is typical of a very large group of positions in which we tend, too boldly and too innocently, to go beyond our evidence and to assume, as the obvious explanation, as almost a datum, what is really the conclusion of a vague and quick and unchecked inductive argument, often a bad and unwarrantable argument. Why should a group of words with a sound in common have similar meanings unless there was a correspondence of some kind between the sound and the meaning? That seems plausible. But state the argument more explicitly, look over the evidence carefully, and it becomes unplausible, for then we have to notice the other words which share the sound but do not share the meaning and the other words which share the meaning without the sound. Then we see that we have been applying to words the sort of argument which would represent a fashion as a spontaneous expression of original taste on the part of all who follow it. We find in fact that we have been looking at the problem upside down. That so far from a perceived correspondence between sound and meaning being the explanation of the sharing, the existence of a group of words with a common sound and meaning is the explanation of our belief in a correspondence.

This situation, I said a moment ago, is typical. We can hardly, I think, exaggerate in an estimate of the number of literary and rhetorical problems which, as usually formulated, are upside down in this fashion. For example, our common assumption that when a word such as *beautiful* or *art* or *religion* or *good,* is used in a great variety of ways, there will be found something in common to all the uses, something which is the fundamental or essential meaning of the word and the explanation of its use. So we spend our wits trying to discover this common essential meaning, without considering that we are looking for it, most often, only as a result of a weak and hasty inductive argument. This assumption that the same word ought to have or must have the same meaning, in an important respect, is one of those bullying assumptions that the context theorem of meanings would defend us from—in the way I discussed in my lecture last week.

But to come back to this parallel assumption that some words, apart from other words, and in their own right in virtue of their sound must mean certain things. It was Aristotle who said that there can be no natural connection between the sound of any language and the things signified, and, if we set the problem right side up and remember the other words before examining it, we shall have to agree with him. Indeed, if we ask the question fairly it becomes—when we get it clear—nearly senseless. What resemblance or natural connection can there be between the semantic and phonetic elements in the morpheme? One is a sound, the other a reference. 'Is (fl-) really like "moving light" in any way in which (sl-) or (gl-) is not?' Is that not like asking whether the taste of turkey is like growing in some way that the taste of mint is not?

I conclude then that these expressive or symbolic words get their feeling of being peculiarly fitting from the other words sharing the morpheme which support them in the background of the mind. If that is so, all sorts of consequences are at once evident. In translation, for example, the expressive word in another language will not necessarily sound at all like the original word. It will be a word that is backed up by other words in a somewhat analogous fashion. Evidently again, a proper appreciation of the expressiveness of a word in a foreign language will be no matter of merely knowing its meaning and relishing its sound. It is a matter of having, in the background of the mind, the other words in the language which share morphemes with it. Thus no one can appreciate these expressive features of foreign words justly without a really wide familiarity with the language. Without that our estimates are merely whimsical.

We can, and I think should, extend this notion of a word as being backed up by other words that are not uttered or thought of. A first extension is to words that sound alike but do not share a morpheme, do not have a common meaning but only some relevant meaning. Thus *blare, scare* and *dare* do not share a morpheme, but on occasion the peculiar force of *blare* may well come to it in part from the others. This, of course, is only recognizing on a larger, wider scale the principle that Lewis Carroll was using in Jabberwocky. Its relevance to the theory of rhymes and assonances is obvious.

Another and a wider extension would include not only influences from words which in part sound alike, but from other words which in part overlap in meaning. Words, for example, which we might have used instead, and, together with these, the reasons why we did not use them. Another such extension looks to the other uses, in other contexts, of what we, too simply, call 'the same word.' The meaning of a word on some occasions is quite as much in what it keeps out, or at a distance, as in what it brings in. And, on other occasions, the meaning comes from other partly parallel uses whose relevance we can feel, without necessarily being able to state it explicitly. But with these last leaps I may seem in danger of making the force of a word, the feeling that no other word could possibly do so well or take its place, a matter whose explanation will drag in the whole of the rest of the language. I am not sure, though, that we need be shy of something very like this as a conclusion. A really masterly use of a language—in free or fluid, not technical discourse—Shakespeare's use of English for example, goes a long way towards using the language as a whole.

Cleopatra, taking up the asp, says to it:

> Come, thou mortal wretch,
> With thy sharp teeth this knot intrinsicate
> Of life at once untie; poor venomous fool,
> Be angry, and despatch!

Consider how many senses of *mortal*, besides 'death-dealing' come in; compare: 'I have immortal longings in me.' Consider *knot:* 'This knot intrinsicate of life': 'Something to be undone,' 'Something that troubles us until it is undone,' 'Something by which all holding-together hangs,' 'The nexus of all meaning.' Whether the homophone *not* enters in here may be thought a doubtful matter. I feel it does. But consider *intrinsicate* along with *knot.* Edward Dowden, following the fashion of his time in making Shakespeare as simple as possible, gives 'intricate' as the meaning here of *intrinsicate.* And the Oxford Dictionary, sad to say, does likewise. But Shakespeare is bringing together half a dozen meanings from *intrinsic* and *intrinse:* 'Familiar,' 'intimate,' 'secret,' 'private,' 'innermost,' 'essential,' 'that which constitutes the very nature and being of a thing'—all the medical and philosophic meanings of his time as well as 'intricate' and 'involved.' What the word does is exhausted by no one of these meanings and its force comes from all of them and more. As the movement of my hand uses nearly the whole skeletal system of the muscles and is supported by them, so a phrase may take its powers from an immense system of supporting uses of other words in other contexts.

NOTE

The word *usage* itself well illustrates some of the more troublesome shifts of meaning. An improved Rhetoric has among its aims an improved control over these. Here perhaps a list of some of the senses of *usage* may help us in avoiding misunderstanding.

(1) The most inclusive sense is 'the entire range of the powers which the word can exert as an instrument of communication in all situations and in co-operation with any other words.'

(In this sense 'Usage, and usage alone, undoubtedly controls language.')

(2) 'Some specific power which, in a limited range of situations and with a limited type of verbal context the word normally exerts.'

(This is often called a *use* or *sense* and is what the Dictionary attempts to record in its definitions, by giving other words, phrases and sentences with the same specific power.)

(3) An instance of 2, at a certain place in Shakespeare, say, which may be appealed to to show that the word can have that power.

(4) A supposed fixed 'proper' meaning that the word must be kept to (has in its own right, etc.) This notion is derived from 1, 2, and 3 by over-simplification and a misconception of the working of language which, typically, takes the meaning of a sentence to be something built up from separate meanings of its words—instead of recognizing that it is the other way about and that the meanings of words are derived from the meanings of sentences in which they occur. This misconception assimilates the process by which words have their meanings determined with that by which they have their spelling determined and is the origin of a large part of misinterpretation.

Bluspels and Flalansferes

Philologists often tell us that our language is full of dead metaphors. In this sentence, the word 'dead' and the word 'metaphors' may turn out to be ambiguous; but the fact, or group of facts, referred to, is one about which there is no great disagreement. We all know in a rough and ready way, and all admit, these things which are being called 'dead metaphors,' and for the moment I do not propose to debate the propriety of the name. But while their existence is not disputed, their nature, and their relation to thought, gives rise to a great deal of controversy. For the benefit of any who happen to have avoided this controversy hitherto, I had better make plain what it is, by a concrete example. Bréal in his *Semantics* often spoke in metaphorical, that is consciously, rhetorically, metaphorical language, of language itself. Messrs. Ogden and Richards in *The Meaning of Meaning* took Bréal to task on the ground that 'it is impossible thus to handle a scientific subject in metaphorical terms.' Barfield in his *Poetic Diction* retorted that Ogden and Richards were, as a matter of fact, just as metaphorical as Bréal. They had forgotten, he complained, that all language has a figurative origin and that the 'scientific' terms on which they piqued themselves—words like *organism, stimulus, reference*—were not miraculously exempt. On the contrary, he maintained, 'these authors who professed to eschew figurative expressions were really confining themselves to one very old kind of figure; they were rigid under the spell of those verbal ghosts of the physical sciences which to-day make up practically the whole meaning-system of so many European minds.' [1] Whether Ogden and Richards will see fit, or have seen fit, to reply

From *Rehabilitations and Other Essays,* London, Oxford University Press, 1939. Copyright 1939 by C. S. Lewis. Reprinted by permission of Curtis, Brown Ltd. and the Estate of C. S. Lewis.
[1] A. O. Barfield, *Poetic Diction,* 1928, pp. 139, 140.

to this, I do not know; but the lines on which any reply would run are already traditional. In fact the whole debate may be represented by a very simple dialogue.

A. You are being metaphorical.

B. You are just as metaphorical as I am, but you don't know it.

A. No, I'm not. Of course I know all about *attending* once having meant *stretching,* and the rest of it. But that is not what it means now. It may have been a metaphor to Adam—but I am not using it metaphorically. What I *mean* is a pure concept with no metaphor about it at all. The fact that it *was* a metaphor is no more relevant than the fact that my pen is made of wood. You are simply confusing derivation with meaning.

There is clearly a great deal to be said for both sides. On the one hand it seems odd to suppose that what we *mean* is conditioned by a dead metaphor of which we may be quite ignorant. On the other hand, we see from day to day, that when a man uses a current and admitted metaphor without knowing it, he usually gets led into nonsense; and when, we are tempted to ask, does a metaphor become so old that we can ignore it with impunity? It seems harsh to rule that a man must know the whole semantic history of every word he uses—a history usually undiscoverable—or else talk without thinking. And yet, on the other hand, an obstinate suspicion creeps in that we cannot entirely jump off our own shadows, and that we deceive ourselves if we suppose that a new and purely conceptual notion of *attention* has replaced and superseded the old metaphor of stretching. Here, then, is the problem which I want to consider. How far, if at all, is thinking limited by these dead metaphors? Is Anatole France in any sense right when he reduces 'The soul possesses God' to 'the breath sits on the bright sky'? Or is the other party right when it urges 'Derivations are one thing. Meanings are another'? Or is the truth somewhere between them?

The first and easiest case to study is that in which we ourselves invent a new metaphor. This may happen in one of two ways. It may be that when we are trying to express clearly to ourselves or to others a conception which we have never perfectly understood, a new metaphor simply starts forth, under the pressure of composition or argument. When this happens, the result is often as surprising and illuminating to us as to our audience; and I am inclined to think that this is what happens with the great, new metaphors of the poets. And when it does happen, it is plain that our new understanding is bound up with the new metaphor. In fact, the situation is for our purpose indistinguishable from that which arises when we hear a new metaphor from others; and for that reason, it need not be separately discussed. One of the ways, then, in which we invent a new metaphor, is by *finding* it, as unexpectedly as we might find it in the pages of a book; and whatever is true of the new metaphors that we find in books will also be true of those which we reach by a kind of lucky chance, or inspiration. But, of course, there is another way in which we invent new metaphors. When we are trying to explain, to some one younger or less instructed than ourselves, a matter which is already perfectly clear in our own minds, we may deliberately, and even painfully, pitch about for the metaphor that is likely to help him. Now when this happens, it is quite plain that our thought, our power of meaning, is not much helped or hindered by the metaphor that we use. On the contrary, we are often acutely aware of the discrepancy between our meaning and our image. We know that our metaphor is in some respects misleading; and probably, if we have acquired the tutorial shuffle, we warn our audience that it is 'not to be pressed.' It is apparently possible, in this case at least, to use metaphor and yet to keep our thinking independent of it. But we must observe that it is possible, only because we have other methods of expressing the same idea. We have already our own way of expressing the thing: we could say it, or we suppose that we could say it, literally instead. This clear conception we owe to other sources—to our previous studies. We can adopt the new metaphor as a temporary tool which we dominate and by which we are not dominated ourselves, only because we have other tools in our box.

Let us now take the opposite situation—that in which it is we ourselves who are being instructed. I am no mathematician; and some one is trying to explain to me the theory that space is finite. Stated thus, the new doctrine is, to me, meaningless. But suppose he proceeds as follows.

'You,' he may say, 'can intuit only three dimensions; you therefore cannot conceive how space should be limited. But I think I can show you how that which must appear infinite in three dimensions, might nevertheless be finite in four. Look at it this way. Imagine a race of people who knew only two dimensions—like the Flatlanders. And suppose they were living on a globe. They would have no conception, of course, that the globe was curved—for it is curved round in that third dimension of which they have no inkling. They will therefore imagine that they are living on a plane; but they will soon find out that it is a plane which nowhere comes to an end; there are no edges to it. Nor would they be able even to imagine an edge. For an edge would mean that, after a certain point, there would be nothing to walk on; nothing below their feet. But that *below* and *above* dimension is just what their minds have not got; they have only backwards and forwards, and left and right. They would thus be forced to assert that their globe, which they could not see as a globe, was infinite. You can see perfectly well that it is finite. And now, can you not conceive that as these Flatlanders are to you, so you might be to a creature that intuited four dimensions? Can you not conceive how that which seems necessarily infinite to your three-dimensional consciousness might none the less be really finite?' The result of such a metaphor on my mind would be—in fact, has been—that something which before was sheerly meaningless acquires at least a faint hint of meaning. And if the particular example does not appeal to every one, yet every one has had experiences of the same sort. For all of us there are things which we cannot fully understand at all, but of which we can get a faint inkling by means of metaphor. And in such cases the relation between the thought and the metaphor is precisely the opposite of the relation which arises when it is we ourselves who understand and then invent the metaphors to help others. We are here entirely at the mercy of the metaphor. If our instructor has chosen it badly, we shall be thinking nonsense. If we have not got the imagery clearly before us, we shall be thinking nonsense. If we have it before us without knowing that it is metaphor—if we forget that our Flatlanders on their globe are a copy of the thing and mistake them for the thing itself—then again we shall be thinking nonsense. What truth we can attain in such a situation depends rigidly on three conditions. First, that the imagery should be originally well chosen; secondly, that we should apprehend the exact imagery; and thirdly that we should know that the metaphor is a metaphor. (That metaphors, misread as statements of fact, are the source of monstrous errors, need hardly be pointed out.)

I have now attempted to show two different kinds of metaphorical situation as they are at their birth. They are the two extremes, and furnish the limits within which our inquiry must work. On the one hand, there is the metaphor which we invent to teach by; on the other, the metaphor from which we learn. They might be called the Master's metaphor, and the Pupil's metaphor. The first is freely chosen; it is one among many possible modes of expression; it does not at all hinder, and only very slightly helps, the thought of its maker. The second is not chosen at all; it is the unique expression of a meaning that we cannot have on any other terms; it dominates completely the thought of the recipient; his truth cannot rise above the truth of the original metaphor. And between the Master's metaphor and the Pupil's there comes, of course, an endless number of types, dotted about in every kind of intermediate position. Indeed, these Pupil-Teachers' metaphors are the ordinary stuff of our conversation. To divide them into a series of classes and sub-classes and to attempt to discuss these separately would be very laborious, and, I trust, unnecessary. If we can find a true doctrine about the two extremes, we shall not be at a loss to give an account of what falls between them. To find the truth about any given metaphorical situation will merely be to plot its position. In so far as it inclines to the 'magistral' extreme, so far our thought will be independent of it; in so far as it has a 'pupillary' element, so far it will be the unique expression, and therefore the iron limit of our thinking. To fill in this framework would be, as Aristotle used to say, 'anybody's business.'

Our problem, it will be remembered, was the problem of 'dead' or 'forgotten' metaphors. We have now gained some light on the relation between thought and metaphor as it is at the outset, when the metaphor is first made; and we have seen that this relation varies greatly according to what I have called the 'metaphorical situation.' There is, in fact, one relation in the case of the Master's metaphor, and an almost opposite relation in that of the Pupil's metaphor. The next step must clearly be to see what becomes of these two relations as the metaphors in question progress to the state of death or fossilization.

The question of the Master's Metaphor need not detain us long. I may attempt to explain the Kantian philosophy to a pupil by the following metaphor. 'Kant answered the question "How do I know that whatever comes round the corner will be blue?" by the supposition "I am wearing blue spectacles." ' In time I may come to use 'the blue spectacles' as a kind of shorthand for the whole Kantian machinery of the categories and forms of perception. And let us suppose, for the sake of analogy with the real history of language, that I continue to use this expression long after I have forgotten the metaphor which originally gave rise to it. And perhaps by this time the form of the word will have changed. Instead of the 'blue spectacles' I may now talk of the *bloospel* or even the *bluspel*. If I live long enough to reach my dotage I may even enter on a philological period in which I attempt to find the derivation of this mysterious word. I may suppose that the second element is derived from the word *spell* and look back with interest on the supposed period when Kant appeared to me to be magical; or else, arguing that the whole word is clearly formed on the analogy of *gospel,* may indulge in unhistorical reminiscences of the days when the *Critique* seemed to me irrefragably true. But how far, if at all, will my thinking about Kant be affected by all this linguistic process? In practice, no doubt, there will be some subtle influence; the mere continued use of the word *bluspel* may have led me to attribute to it a unity and substantiality which I should have hesitated to attribute to 'the whole Kantian machinery of the categories and forms of perception.' But that is a result rather of the noun-making than of the death of the metaphor. It is an interesting fact, but hardly relevant to our present inquiry. For the rest, the mere forgetting of the metaphor does not seem to alter my thinking about Kant, just as the original metaphor did not limit my thinking about Kant; provided always—and this is of the last importance—that it was, to begin with, a genuine Master's metaphor. I had my conception of Kant's philosophy before I ever thought of the blue spectacles. If I have continued philosophical studies I have it still. The 'blue spectacles' phrase was from the first a temporary dress assumed by my thought for a special purpose, and ready to be laid aside at my pleasure; it did not penetrate the thinking itself, and its subsequent history is irrelevant.

To any one who attempts to refute my later views on Kant by telling me that I don't know the real meaning of *bluspel,* I may confidently retort 'Derivations aren't meanings.' To be sure, if there was any *pupillary* element in its original use, if I received, as well as gave, new understanding when I used it, then the whole situation will be different. And it is fair to admit that in practice very few metaphors can be purely magistral; only that which to some degree enlightens ourselves is likely to enlighten others. It is hardly possible that when I first used the metaphor of the blue spectacles I did not gain some new awareness of the Kantian philosophy; and, so far, it was not purely magistral. But I am deliberately idealizing for the sake of clarity. Purely magistral metaphor may never occur. What is important for us is to grasp that *just in so far* as any metaphor began by being magistral, so far I can continue to use it long after I have forgotten its metaphorical nature, and my thinking will be neither helped nor hindered by the fact that it was originally a metaphor, nor yet by my forgetfulness of that fact. It is a mere accident. Here, derivations are irrelevant to meanings.

Let us now turn to the opposite situation, that of the Pupil's Metaphor. And let us continue to use our old example of the unmathematical man who has had the finitude of space suggested to him (we can hardly say 'explained') by the metaphor of the Flatlanders on their sphere. The question here is rather more complicated. In the case of the Master's metaphor, by hypothesis, the master knew, and would continue to know, what he meant, independently of the metaphor. In the present instance, however, the fossilization of the metaphor may take place in two different ways. The pupil may himself become a mathematician, or he may remain as ignorant of mathematics as he was before; and in either case, he may continue to use the metaphor of the Flatlanders while forgetting its real content and its metaphorical nature.

I will take the second possibility first. From the imagery of the Flatlanders' sphere I have got my first inkling of the new meaning. My thought is entirely conditioned by this imagery. I do not apprehend the thing at all, except by seeing 'it could be something like this.' Let us suppose that in my anxiety to docket this new experience, I label the inkling or vague notion, 'the Flatlanders' sphere.' When I next hear the fourth dimension spoken of, I shall say, 'Ah yes—the Flatlanders' sphere and all that.' In a few years (to continue our artificial parallel) I may be talking glibly of the *Flalansfere* and may even have forgotten the whole of the imagery which this word once represented. And I am still, according to the hypothesis, profoundly ignorant of mathematics. My situation will then surely be most ridiculous. The meaning of *Flalansfere* I never knew except through the imagery. I could get beyond the imagery, to that whereof the imagery was a copy, only by learning mathematics; but this I have neglected to do. Yet I have lost the imagery.

Nothing remains, then, but the conclusion that the word *Flalansfere* is now really meaningless. My thinking, which could never get beyond the imagery, at once its boundary and its support, has now lost that support. I mean strictly nothing when I speak of the *Flalansfere*. I am only talking, not thinking, when I use the word. But this fact will be long concealed from me, because *Flalansfere,* being a noun, can be endlessly fitted into various contexts, so as to conform to syntactical usage and to give an appearance of meaning. It will even conform to the logical rules; and I can make many judgements about the *Flalansfere;* such as *it is what it is,* and has *attributes* (for otherwise of course it wouldn't be a thing, and if it wasn't a thing, how could I be talking about it?), and is a *substance* (for it can be the subject of a sentence). And what *affective* overtones the word may have taken on by that time, it is dangerous to predict. It had an air of mystery from the first: before the end I shall probably be building temples to it, and exhorting my countrymen to fight and die for the *Flalansfere*. But the *Flalansfere,* when once we have forgotten the metaphor, is only a noise.

But how if I proceed, after once having grasped the metaphor of the Flatlanders, to become a mathematician? In this case, too, I may well continue to use the metaphor, and may corrupt it in form till it becomes a single noun, the *Flalansfere*. But I shall have advanced, by other means, from the original symbolism; and I shall be able to study the thing symbolized without reference to the metaphor that first introduced me to it. It will then be no harm though I should forget that *Flalansfere* had ever been metaphorical. As the metaphor, even if it survived, would no longer limit my thoughts, so its fossilization cannot confuse them.

The results which emerge may now be summarized as follows. Our thought is independent of the metaphors we employ, in so far as these metaphors are optional: that is, in so far as we are able to have the same idea without them. For that is the real characteristic both of the magistral metaphors and of those which become optional, as the Flatlanders would become, if the pupil learned mathematics. On the other hand, where the metaphor is our only method of reaching a given idea at all, there our thinking is limited by the metaphor so long as we retain the metaphor; and when the metaphor becomes fossilized, our 'thinking' is not thinking at all, but mere sound or mere incipient movements in the larynx. We are now in a position to reply to the statement that 'Derivations are not meanings,' and to the claim that 'we know what we mean by words without knowing the fossilized metaphors they contain.' We can see that such a statement, as it stands, is neither wholly true nor wholly false. The truth will vary from word to word, and from speaker to speaker. No rule of thumb is possible, we must take every case on its merits. A word can bear a meaning in the mouth of a speaker who has forgotten its hidden metaphor, and a meaning independent of that metaphor, but only on certain conditions. Either the metaphor must have been optional from the beginning, and have remained optional through all the generations of its use, so that the conception has always used and still uses the imagery as a mere tool; or else, at some period subsequent to its creation, we must have gone on to acquire, independently of the metaphor, such new knowledge of the object indicated by it as enables us now, at least, to dispense with it. To put the same thing in another way, meaning is independent of derivation, only if the metaphor was originally 'magistral'; or if, in the case of an originally pupillary metaphor, some quite new kind of apprehension has arisen to replace the metaphorical apprehension which has been lost. The two conditions may be best illustrated by a concrete example. Let us take the word for *soul* as it exists in the Romance language. How far is a man entitled to say that what he means by the word *âme* or *anima* is quite independent of the image of *breathing,* and that he means just the same (and just as much) whether he happens to know that 'derivation' or not? We can only answer that it depends on a variety of things. I will enumerate all the formal possibilities for the sake of clearness: one of them, of course, is too grotestque to appear for any other purpose.

1. The metaphor may originally have been magistral. Primitive men, we are to suppose, were clearly aware, on the one hand, of an entity called *soul;* and, on the other, of a process or object called *breath*. And they used the second figuratively to suggest the first—presumably when revealing their wisdom to primitive women and primitive children. And we may suppose, further, that this magistral relation to the metaphor has never been lost: that all generations, from the probably arboreal to the man saying 'Blast your soul' in a pub this evening, have kept clearly before them these two separate entities, and used the one metaphorically to denote the other, while at the same time being well able to conceive the soul unmetaphorically, and using the metaphor merely as a colour or trope which adorned but did not influence their thought. Now if all this were true, it would unquestionably follow that when a man says *anima* his meaning is not affected by the old image of breath; and also, it does not matter in the least whether he knows that the word once suggested that image or not. But of course all this is not true.

2. The metaphor may originally have been pupillary. So far from being a voluntary ornament or paedagogic device, the ideas of *breath* or *something like breath* may have been the only possible inkling that our parents could gain of the soul. But if this was so, how does the modern user of the word stand? Clearly, if he has ceased to be aware of the metaphorical element in *anima,* without replacing the metaphorical apprehension by some new knowledge of the soul, borrowed from other sources, then he will mean nothing by it; we must not, on that account, suppose that he will cease to use it, or even to use it (as we say) intelligibly—i.e. to use it in sentences

constructed according to the laws of grammar, and to insert these sentences into those conversational and literary contexts where usage demands their insertion. If, on the other hand, he has some independent knowledge of the entity which our ancestors indicated by their metaphor of breath, then indeed he may mean something.

I take it that it is this last situation in which we commonly suppose ourselves to be. It doesn't matter, we would claim, what the majestic root GNA really stood for: we have learned a great deal about *knowing* since those days, and it is these more recent acquisitions that we use in our thinking. The first name for a thing may easily be determined by some inconsiderable accident. As we learn more, we mean more; the radical meaning of the old syllables does not bind us; what we have learned since has set us free. Assuredly, the accident which led the Romans to call all Hellenes *Graeci* did not continue to limit their power of apprehending Greece. And as long as we are dealing with sensible objects this view is hardly to be disputed. The difficulty begins with objects of thought. It may be stated as follows.

Our claim to independence of the metaphor is, as we have seen, a claim to know the object otherwise than through that metaphor. If we can throw the Flatlanders overboard and still think the fourth dimension, then, and not otherwise, we can forget what *Flalansfere* once meant and still think coherently. That was what happened, you will remember, to the man who went on and learned mathematics. He came to apprehend that of which the Flatlanders' sphere was only the image, and consequently was free to think beyond the metaphor and to forget the metaphor altogether. In our previous account of him, however, we carefully omitted to draw attention to one very remarkable fact: namely, that when he deserted metaphor for mathematics, he did not really pass from symbol to symbolized, but only from one set of symbols to another. The equations and what-nots are as unreal, as metaphorical, if you like, as the Flatlanders' sphere. The mathematical problem I need not pursue further; we see at once that it casts a disquieting light on our linguistic problem. We have hitherto been speaking as if we had two methods of thought open to us: the metaphorical, and the literal. We talked as if the creator of a magistral metaphor had it always in his power to think the same concept *literally* if he chose. We talked as if the present-day user of the word *anima* could prove his right to neglect that word's buried metaphor by turning round and giving us an account of the soul which was not metaphorical at all. That he has power to dispense with the particular metaphor of *breath,* is of course agreed. But we have not yet inquired what he can substitute for it. If we turn to those who are most anxious to tell us about the soul—I mean the psychologists—we shall find that the word *anima* has simply been replaced by complexes, repressions, censors, engrams, and the like. In other words the *breath* has been exchanged for *tyings-up, shovings-*

back, Roman magistrates, and *scratchings.* If we inquire what has replaced
the metaphorical *bright sky* of primitive theology, we shall only get a *perfect
substance,* that is, a *completely made lying-under,* or—which is very much
better, but equally metaphorical—a universal Father, or perhaps (in English) a *loaf-carver,* in Latin a *householder,* in Romance *a person older than.*
The point need not be laboured. It is abundantly clear that the freedom from
a given metaphor which we admittedly enjoy in some cases is often only a
freedom to choose between the metaphor and others.

Certain reassurances may, indeed, be held out. In the first place, our distinction between the different kinds of metaphorical situation can stand;
though it is hardly so important as we had hoped. To have a choice of metaphors (as we have in some cases) is to know more than we know when we
are the slaves of a unique metaphor. And, in the second place, all description
or identification, all direction of our own thought or another's, is not so
metaphorical as definition. If, when challenged on the word *anima,* we proceed to define, we shall only reshuffle the buried metaphors; but if we
simply say (or think) 'what I am,' or 'what is going on in here,' we shall
have at least something before us which we do not know by metaphor. We
shall at least be no worse off than the arboreal psychologists. At the same
time, this method will not really carry us far. 'What's going on here' is really
the content of *haec anima:* for *anima* we want *'The sort of thing* that is
going on here,' and once we are committed to *sorts* and *kinds* we are adrift
among metaphors.

We have already said that when a man claims to think independently of
the buried metaphor in one of his words, his claim may sometimes be
allowed. But it was allowed only in so far as he could really supply the place
of that buried metaphor with new and independent apprehension of his own.
We now see that this new apprehension will usually turn out to be itself
metaphorical; or else, what is very much worse, instead of new apprehension
we shall have simply words—each word enshrining one more ignored metaphor. For if he does not know the history of *anima,* how should he know the
history of the equally metaphorical words in which he defines it, if challenged? And if he does not know their history and therefore their metaphors, and if he cannot define *them* without yet further metaphors, what
can his discourse be but an endless ringing of the changes on such *bluspels*
and *Flalansferes* as seem to mean, indeed, but do not mean? In reality, the
man has played us a very elementary trick. He claimed that he could think
without metaphor, and in ignorance of the metaphors fossilized in his words.
He made good the claim by pointing to the knowledge of his object which
he possessed independently of the metaphor; and the proof of this knowledge
was the definition or description which he could produce. We did not at first
observe that where we were promised a freedom from metaphor we were

given only a power of changing the metaphors in rapid succession. The things he speaks of he has never apprehended *literally*. Yet only such genuinely literal apprehension could enable him to forget the metaphors which he was actually using and yet to have a meaning. Either literalness, or else metaphor understood: one or other of these we must have; the third alternative is nonsense. But literalness we cannot have. The man who does not consciously use metaphors talks without meaning. We might even formulate a rule: the meaning in any given composition is in inverse ratio to the author's belief in his own literalness.

If a man has seen ships and the sea, he may abandon the metaphor of a *sea-stallion* and call a boat a boat. But suppose a man who has never seen the sea, or ships, yet who knows of them just as much as he can glean, say from the following list of *Kenningar*—sea-stallions, winged logs, wave riders, ocean trains. If he keeps all these together in his mind, and knows them for the metaphors they are, he will be able to think of ships, very imperfectly indeed, and under strict limits, but not wholly in vain. But if instead of this he pins his faith on the particular *kenning ocean-trains,* because that *kenning,* with its comfortable air of machinery, seems to him somehow more safely prosaic, less flighty and dangerous than its fellows, and if, contracting that to the form *oshtrans,* he proceeds to forget that it was a metaphor, then, while he talks grammatically, he has ceased to think of anything. It will not avail him to stamp his feet and swear that he is literal; to say 'An *oshtran* is an *oshtran,* and there's an end. I mean what I mean. What I mean is what I say.'

The remedy lies, indeed, in the opposite direction. When we pass beyond pointing to individual sensible objects, when we begin to think of causes, relations, of mental states or acts, we become incurably metaphorical. We apprehend none of these things except through metaphor: we know of the ships only what the *Kenningar* will tell us. Our only choice is to use the metaphors and thus to think something, though less than we could wish; or else to be driven by unrecognized metaphors and so think nothing at all. I myself would prefer to embrace the former choice, as far as my ignorance and laziness allow me.

To speak more plainly, he who would increase the meaning and decrease the meaningless verbiage in his own speech and writing, must do two things. He must become conscious of the fossilized metaphors in his words; and he must freely use new metaphors, which he creates for himself. The first depends upon knowledge, and therefore on leisure; the second on a certain degree of imaginative ability. The second is perhaps the more important of the two: we are never less the slaves of metaphor than when we are making metaphor, or hearing it new made. When we are thinking hard of the Flatlanders, and at the same time fully aware that they *are* a metaphor, we are in a situation almost infinitely superior to that of the man who talks of the *Flalansfere* and thinks that he is being literal and straightforward.

If our argument has been sound, it leads us to certain rather remarkable conclusions. In the first place it would seem that we must be content with a very modest quantity of thinking as the core of all our talking. I do not wish to exaggerate our poverty. Not all our words are equally metaphorical, not all our metaphors are equally forgotten. And even where the old metaphor is lost there is often a hope that we may still restore meaning by pointing to some sensible object, some sensation, or some concrete memory. But no man can or will confine his cognitive efforts to this narrow field. At the very humblest we must speak of things in the plural, we must point not only to isolated sensations, but to groups and classes of sensations; and the universal latent in every group and every plural inflection cannot be thought without metaphor. Thus far beyond the security of literal meaning all of us, we may be sure, are going to be driven by our daily needs; indeed, not to go thus far would be to abandon reason itself. In practice we all really intend to go much farther. Why should we not? We have in our hands the key of metaphor, and it would be pusillanimous to abandon its significant use, because we have come to realize that its meaningless use is necessarily prevalent. We must indeed learn to use it more cautiously; and one of the chief benefits to be derived from our inquiry is the new standard of criticism which we must henceforward apply both to our own apparent thought and to that of others. We shall find, too, that real meaning, judged by this standard, does not come always where we have learned to expect. *Flalansferes* and *bluspels* will clearly be most prevalent in certain types of writers. The percentage of of mere syntax masquerading as meaning may vary from something like 100 per cent. in political writers, journalists, psychologists, and economists, to something like forty per cent. in the writers of children's stories. Some scientists will fare better than others: the historian, the geographer, and sometimes the biologist will speak significantly more often than their colleagues; the mathematician, who seldom forgets that his symbols are symbolic, may often rise for short stretches to ninety per cent. of meaning and ten of verbiage. The philosophers will differ as widely from one another as any of the other groups differ among themselves: for a good metaphysical library contains at once some of the most verbal, and some of the most significant literature in the world. Those who have prided themselves on being literal, and who have endeavoured to speak plainly, with no mystical tomfoolery, about the highest abstractions, will be found to be among the least significant of writers: I doubt if we shall find more than a beggarly five per cent. of meaning in the pages of some celebrated 'tough minded' thinkers, and how the account of Kant or Spinoza stands, none knows but heaven. But open your Plato, and you will find yourself among the great creators of metaphor, and therefore among the masters of meaning. If we turn to Theology—or rather to the literature of religion—the result will be more surprising still; for unless our whole argument is wrong, we shall have to admit that a man who says *heaven* and thinks of the visible sky is pretty sure to mean more than a man who tells us that heaven is a state of mind. It may indeed be otherwise; the second man may be a mystic who is remembering and pointing to an actual and concrete experience of his own. But it is long, long odds. Bunyan and Dante stand where they did; the scale of Bishop Butler, and of better men than he, flies up and kicks the beam.

It will have escaped no one that in such a scale of writers the poets will take the highest place; and among the poets those who have at once the tenderest care for old words and the surest instinct for the creation of new metaphors. But it must not be supposed that I am in any sense putting forward the imagination as the organ of truth. We are not talking of truth, but of meaning: meaning which is the antecedent condition both of truth and falsehood, whose antithesis is not error but nonsense. I am a rationalist. For me, reason is the natural organ of truth; but imagination is the organ of meaning. Imagination, producing new metaphors or revivifying old, is not the cause of truth, but its condition. It is, I confess, undeniable that such a view indirectly implies a kind of truth or rightness in the imagination itself. I said at the outset that the truth we won by metaphor could not be greater than the truth of the metaphor itself; and we have seen since that all our truth, or all but a few fragments, is won by metaphor. And thence, I confess, it does follow that if our thinking is ever true, then the metaphors by which we think must have been good metaphors. It does follow that if those original equations, between good and light, or evil and dark, between breath and soul and all the others, were from the beginning arbitrary and fanciful—if there is not, in fact, a kind of psycho-physical parallelism (or more) in the universe—then all our thinking is nonsensical. But we cannot, without contradiction, believe it to be nonsensical. And so, admittedly, the view I have taken has metaphysical implications. But so has every view.

Lexical Definition

§ 1. *The Nature of Lexical Definition.* Lexical definition is that sort of word-thing definition in which we are explaining the actual way in which some actual word has been used by some actual persons.

It is obvious that lexical definition is something that really happens. Parents, teachers of foreign languages, and probably all persons at some time or other, engage deliberately in the business of telling a person the meaning of a sign. Whatever supposed sorts of definition may turn out to be mare's nests, this sort is real. The child asks what 'magenta' means and the parent tells him. The pupil asks what 'soif' means and the teacher tells him.

Lexical definition is a form of history. It refers to the real past. It tells what certain persons meant by a certain word at a certain less or more specified time and place. In a 'modern' dictionary the time meant is the most recent period down to the instant of writing, and there is a strong expectation that the same persons will continue to use this word in the same way for a considerable future time after the publication of the dictionary. This expectation will very probably be verified for most of the words and falsified for a few. The dictionary is much less reliable as prediction than as history. The future of languages never perfectly resembles their past.

There are altogether three persons involved in lexical definition, first the definer who is explaining the meaning of the word, second the hearer to whom the meaning is being explained, and third the people whose usage of the word gives it whatever meaning it has. Thus Dr. Johnson (person 1) in his dictionary attempted to tell his readers (person 2) what English-

From *Definition,* by Richard Robinson, Oxford, The Clarendon Press, 1950. Reprinted by permission of The Clarendon Press, Oxford.

men of the eighteenth century (person 3) meant by the word 'pastern.'[1] Always this third person must be there, if the sign is to be a sign and the lexical definition of it a reasonable enterprise. The question 'What does this word mean?' is more accurately: 'What do (or did) certain persons use this word to mean?' All meaning is meaning by or for some living thing. The meaning of a word is what it means to some person or persons. It may mean nothing to anybody now, like a lost language; but it must have meant something to somebody once, or it is not and never was a sign. To talk of a sign that means nothing to anybody is either to contradict oneself or to say that the thing is not really a sign. The relation to a person who uses it or understands it is essential to the occurrence of a sign. The less clear the definer makes it who precisely is the third person he is talking about, the less useful his definition. We want to know whether this is what the word meant to the majority of Englishmen or only to a few, and whether in other centuries also or only in this one, and so on.

This essential third person is, however, unconsciously ignored by most of the people who use dictionaries. They look upon a dictionary not as they look upon a book of history but rather as they look upon a book of mathematical tables. A table of square roots is not history. It is a table of eternal facts that were not made by men and cannot be unmade by them, but must be followed and respected if men are to succeed in their purposes. When we wish to infer the diameter of a circular floor from its area, we must either obey the table of square roots or get a false answer. As the square root of 1,369, is and always must be, 37, no matter what any human may have thought or said or done, and this fact is pretty sure to be accurately stated in one's book of mathematical tables, so, men think, the meaning of a word is and always must be such and such, no matter how men have actually spoken and written, and this eternal and independent meaning is pretty sure to be accurately stated in one's dictionary. As the engineer who goes against the mathematical tables comes to grief, they think, the writer or speaker who goes against the dictionary comes to grief. They do not, however, clearly represent to themselves what sort of grief he comes to. In particular, they do not think that he becomes unintelligible, but rather that he becomes improper, or vulgar, or uneducated, or in some other way liable to contempt.

Such are the ideas of the majority about dictionaries, and they have probably been shared by the majority of the dictionary-writers themselves.

Yet it is perfectly clear, when we reflect on the matter, that the meanings

---

[1] [Boswell reports this incident about Samuel Johnson: 'A lady once asked him how he came to define *Pastern* the *knee* of a horse: instead of making an elaborate defence, as she expected, he at once answered, "Ignorance, Madam, pure ignorance." *Life of Johnson* (Oxford Standard Authors Edition), p. 211. ED.]

of words cannot possibly be independent of man as square roots are. A word is a man-made contrivance, and its meaning can only be what some man means by it. The third person must be there.

From which it seems to follow that a good dictionary would be only history. Why is it then that most of the users and most of the makers of dictionaries regard them not as histories but as authorities like a table of square roots?

It is because we have strong and ineradicable feelings of approval and disapproval about the various ways of using words. There are men who cannot help feeling a stab of contempt for one whom they hear splitting an infinitive, or pronouncing 'garage' to rhyme with 'carriage,' or using 'transpired' to mean 'occurred.' At every time in every language there are variations in usage or dialect that make no difference to intelligibility. Some of these variations are seized upon as indicators and carriers of differences in human excellence. If one class of the community is more admired or envied or respected than another, and this class has some peculiarities of dialect, those peculiarities become indicators and carriers of excellence. At least, this always happens in communities where there is a formal education in the study of written documents. Then the desire to be excellent and to be considered excellent will always be at work pushing people to discover and adopt the dialect of the preferred class. To assist them in this, books will be written recording the dialect of the preferred class. Among such books are most dictionaries.

Dictionaries, then, tend to be histories not of all the usages prevailing at a given time and place but of those of the preferred group of persons. The average small one-language dictionary is designed largely to enable people to talk and write without arousing contempt in the preferred class. Certain undesirable usages are recorded but characterized as '(vulg.).' Desirable usages are given no special description, for it is understood that the general purpose of the book is precisely to give the desirable meanings.

The bigger and more scientific the dictionary, the more this purpose of teaching socially correct vocabulary yields to the purpose of recording actual vocabulary. But even the huge *Oxford English Dictionary* teaches as well as records. For example, it urges us to write '-ize' and not '-ise' in all cases descended from the Greek '-ιζειν.'

Dictionaries, therefore, usually do not give us very pure cases of lexical definition. At the best, they mostly tend only to give us true lexical definitions of the vocabulary of a respected class. At the worst they go beyond this to some ideal dialect invented by grammarians. Their aim is to get us accepted by the educated rather than to describe how men have actually spoken and written.

The authoritative character, therefore, which we feel to belong to the dictionary as much as to the table of square roots is the authority of the laws not of number or of inanimate nature, but of human nature driving us to seek excellence and the reputation of excellence, and of human customs and taboos placing goodness and badness now in one set of usages and later in another.

A large dictionary commonly makes various other kinds of assertion about a word besides the fundamental lexical one that certain persons use the word to mean a certain thing; and one of these other kinds had better be noticed here. If the lexicographer disbelieves in the existence of the thing meant by the word, he often expresses his disbelief. Thus he will define 'phlogiston' as 'the supposed cause of fire.' Those who used the word 'phlogiston,' however, did not mean by it the supposed cause of fire; they meant the real cause of fire. If we take the word 'supposed' as part of the meaning of 'pholgiston' it makes the definition false. It is really the lexicographer's way of adding his opinion that there is no such thing. He does this because all of us, as soon as we learn the meaning of a word, always wish to have an opinion whether such a thing really occurs. When he omits the word 'supposed,' when he defines 'soul' simply as 'the immortal part of man,' he by contrast implies that he believes there is such a thing. . . .

§ 4. *Lexical Definition can never be Perfect.* Another of the disputed points about definitions is whether they should be brief or not. Should lexical definitions be brief?

Lexical definitions are historical statements. They are scientific statements in the broad sense in which utterance is either scientific or poetic. Brevity always has both advantages and disadvantages in scientific discourse. It tends to give speed and to increase one's grasp, but also to lose detail and accuracy and richness of insight. The more an activity is pursued for its own sake, the less desirable, as a rule, is brevity. The nearer an activity comes to being merely a means, the better it is that it should be brief, for a mere means is an unsatisfying activity from which we wish to escape. Most lexical definitions, whose purpose is to make somebody know the meaning of some word, are merely means to the ulterior purpose of using that word; the quicker this further purpose can be achieved the better; therefore the shorter the definition the better.

On the other hand, every brief lexical definition of a word in common use is grossly inaccurate or at best grossly partial, because all words that have been used by many people have many sorts and nuances and dimensions of meaning. That is why there is room for colossal dictionaries. Hence a lexical definition even when regarded as a mere tool must often contain far more than a dozen words; and when the lover of language undertakes to state the meaning of a word for its own sake he may well expand his definition to far more than a dozen pages. Let us bring these facts home to ourselves by calling to mind for a time the complexities of the actual meanings of words, and the consequent complexities of accurate lexicography.

Living language is always in flux. All words in common speech are liable to change their meanings from time to time. Many of them change their meanings as we pass from place to place across the earth, notably the common words for living kinds, such as 'robin' and "sycamore.' Many more of them change their meanings as we pass from class to class in the same place, especially from the common man to the learned. Most of all they change their meanings as we pass from age to age. 'Enthusiasm' no longer means what it meant in the eighteenth century. Copious examples and long discussions of this perpetual changing are set out in many philological works, e.g. Hermann Paul's *Prinzipien der Sprachgeschichte*. Even the scientist, consciously aiming at fixity of reference, often finds his words changing in his hands, or deliberately changes their meanings to meet a new situation or avoid a greater inconvenience. Any volume of the periodical *Science* will show instances of this in biology. For example, as biologists have come to learn more of the multiplicity of chemical reactions occurring in living beings, they have had difficulty in keeping the word 'respiration' to a definite meaning. The mathematician, dealing with things that do not change or grow in his hands, or with ideas that do not have to fit the eddies of time and space, is the least likely to find his words changing their meanings; but he, too, finds them doing so. The spread of education on the whole slows down the rate of change; but it never obliterates it, and in one way it increases it, namely, by encouraging research, which brings novelties that upset old nomenclatures.

The flux of language has obvious inconveniences. We see the man from one country failing to indicate which specific grain he means to the man from another. We see a pair of words that were usefully distinct in meaning coming to be synonymous, as 'paradox' and 'contradiction.' We see slang making a word so ambiguous that we hesitate to use it in its ancient sense without adding explanations; this has recently happened, for example, to the word 'dumb' in U.S.A. A word, we feel, should be like a pair of forceps which could pass the same specimen from hand to hand without fear of losing it; but in fact it is often a prestidigitator who secretly switches the specimen as he conveys it from one man to the next, and we are deceived as to what the other man is talking about. We see thousands of words taking on new meanings, through dozens of different sorts of cause, without losing their old ones, so that they come to be multivocal. We have seen, though perhaps we never shall again, languages that were one throughout an area dividing into dialects more and more estranged from each other until intercommunication ceases.

Hence men have tried to arrest the flux, especially in those ages before the nineteenth century when the conviction had not prevailed that all things are always changing, and not in a cycle but towards something new and unknown. Now it is believed that the universe is on an irresistible process in the evolution of living individuals, in the degradation of energy towards the heat-death, and in many other aspects, and that thought, conditioned by its social circumstances, can never be quite the same as at any previous time. All this represses most enterprises for the fixing of language; but in the eighteenth century Swift issued a serious proposal for such an undertaking. Samuel Johnson tells us in the introduction to his dictionary that he, too, felt the 'wish that the instrument might be less apt to decay, and that signs might be permanent, like the things they denote.' He started, he says, with Swift's hope of fixing the language, but saw it to be impossible. He never ceased, however, to hope to delay the rate of change; and he definitely regarded himself as not merely an historian of what the English language had done, but also in part a legislator of what it should do.

The flux of word-meanings cannot be stopped because its causes cannot be removed. We are told that in illiterate cultures there is sometimes a very rapid change of vocabulary because words easily acquire unfortunate associations and become taboo; probably this cause will always continue to operate to some extent, even in the most literate and emancipated culture man ever achieves. Changes in things must effect changes in the meanings of words. 'Car' cannot mean the same now as it did before steam and petroleum engines. No man has time to study carefully the past meaning of all the words he uses; the major part of his vocabulary has been acquired without the aid of the dictionary or any other intentional teaching, by unconscious inference from examples of its use; and inevitably his inference is often slightly wrong. Inevitably a degradation, by which a word of peculiar meaning comes to be only a synonym for an existing word, is occasionally given prominence and weight by a great man's use, as when Dickens called a book *Our Mutual Friend*. To achieve the urgent end of the moment, we use whatever words occur to us as most efficient then and there for that purpose; and it is rare that our sole purpose is to please some academy by preserving the ancient meanings of words.

Men will never forgo the beauties and delights and conveniences of metaphor; and metaphors will always tend to decay into literal senses, thus changing or adding to the meaning of the word. Men will always be finding themselves with a new thing to express and no word for it, and usually they will meet the problem by applying whichever old word seems nearest, and thus the old word will acquire another meaning or a stretched meaning. Very rarely will they do what A. E. Housman bade them do, invent a new noise to mean the new thing. For they like to feel that they are not creating language but using an established and approved language; the closeness of the old sense of the word to the new sense helps to make the new sense intelligible, and indeed often conceals from everybody the fact that a new sense has arisen. Such are a few of the causes that have ensured and will ensure the mutability of language. Owing to them the meanings of almost every common word are different at different times and multiple at all times.

And the flux has many advantages too. Its primary advantage is its primary cause: the ability to meet the urgent needs of the present moment with the vocabulary one has in store. But this momentary advantage does not always cost a general drawback. On the contrary, the changeability of vocabulary gives it its power to meet the new circumstances, and to express the new ideas, that are always arising.

No brief lexical definition of a word, then, is likely to embrace the multiplicity of uses the word has had at different times or even at one time. A lexical definition could nearly always be truer by being longer. In practice even the largest dictionaries and the fullest definitions are obliged to make a selection, just as any sort of history is a selection, even a thousand-page history of a single day in the life of a single man. The most momentous and unfortunate kind of selection commonly made is that the lexicographer excludes all spoken language and confines himself to the written form. Within the written language he usually further confines himself to the vocabulary of the writers he to some extent approves; and, as he is usually a literary man, this usually means that there is no record of those writings that are completely outside the literary interest, such as notices in barber-shops or factories. Selection being inevitable, it is rational to select for record the vocabularies of the writers we value and of the societies whose approval we need or value. The necessity for selection enforces the lexicographer's tendency to become an arbiter instead of an historian.

Even if by a miracle a lexicographer succeeded in giving a complete list of the meanings of a word, he would still not have given a complete account of the word, for the following reasons.

People use two or more senses of a word at the same time, not merely in puns but also for the most serious science and the most profound poetry. Often they would be unable to separate the meanings which the lexicographer analyses. What to him is ambiguity is to them the livingness of language. The dictionary hides the way in which the different meanings of the word are yet one meaning.

A word has other dimensions besides its indicativeness, and a complete account of it would have to give its nature in these other dimensions too. Besides indicating it expresses. A word for x indicates x and expresses the idea of x. When a man says 'grey,' he indicates grey and expresses his idea of grey.

Every word carries with it, in each speaker's mind in which it lives, certain associations other than its main association to what it indicates, associations to other things or associated emotions and attitudes. No dictionary can record these associations when they are peculiar to one or a few persons, nor needs to. But often the same association holds for nearly all speakers of the language. Often a word arouses nearly the same emotion or attitude in all its users. Then it is very desirable that this emotional or pragmatic dimension should be recorded as well as the indicative dimension. No dictionaries, however, attempt to do this in any thorough or systematic way. They give the emotional dimensions only for certain special cases. Thus a dictionary may say of the word 'nigger': 'negro (now usually contemptuous),' giving first the indicative and then the emotional force of the word. The *Oxford English Dictionary* defines 'good' as 'the most general adj. of commendation, implying the existence in a high, or at least satisfactory, degree of characteristic qualities which are either admirable in themselves or useful for some purpose'; it thus assigns to the word a very definite emotional dimension and almost no indicative dimension. If there are words that have no indicative dimension, but merely express, they are, of course, the words for which the dictionary is most likely to define the emotional dimension.

In most languages each word has specific ways of combining with other words, and may be used in a sentence only in those ways. This may be called the syntactical dimension of the word. Thus 'heavy,' heaviness,' 'heavily,' are three words that have exactly the same indicative force, and nearly the same emotional force, but distinct syntactic forces. This dimension, too, must be specified in any complete account of the word. Many dictionaries specify it systematically for all words. That is easy to do in some languages because along this dimension all the words of the language fall into one and only one of a few well-marked classes that have been determined and can be indicated by a brief symbol.

Besides the syntactical relations of a word to the other words in a sentence, there are the relations of the word to the other elements in the context of its occurrence, such as the speaker, his sex, the hearer, his sex, the time, and the place. There are words whose occurrence or non-occurrence is determined in part neither by what is to be indicated nor by what is to be expressed, nor by the other words in the sentence, but by something else in the context. Thus in the Koasati language *ó.t* and *ó.c* both indicate the same thing, namely, 'he is building a fire,' and both, so far as I know, express the same emotion and demand the same syntactical function in the sentence; but the former is to be uttered only by a woman and the latter only by a man.[2] There are also, apparently, languages in which one's speech

[2] Mary Haas in *Language*, XX 144.

must vary with the sex of one's hearer, even in sentences whose indicative meaning is nothing to do with the hearer.[3]

This contextual dimension is very obvious in words like 'I,' 'you,' 'he,' 'this,' 'to-day,' 'here'; for in them it controls the indicative reference. What they indicate varies from occasion to occasion because it is determined by the occasion. 'To-day' is to mean on each occasion the day on which the word is uttered.

The contextual dimension appears to be absent from most words in Indo-European languages. But where it is present a complete lexical definition of the word would include it.

Thus a complete lexical definition of a word might have to define it along four dimensions at least, the contextual, the syntactic, the expressive, and the indicative; and the indicative definition would nearly always be very complex.

So much by way of calling to mind that lexical definition cannot be at once brief and accurate, and that it is a very difficult matter to do well.

Stipulative Definition

§ 1. *The Nature of Stipulative Definition.* We have examined word-thing definition in general, and also the lexical species of it. Let us now examine its other species, the stipulative.

'Whatsoever Adam called every living creature, that was the name thereof.'

Humpty Dumpty insisted that words were to mean what he chose that they should mean. He did not concern himself with any lexical inquires, that is, with finding out what some set of people actually had meant by some word. He laid down what the word was to mean when he used it. That was stipulative definition.

The maker of dictionaries sometimes regards himself as a legislator rather than as an historian, as saying how words ought to be used rather than how they are used. So far as he does this, he regards himself as giving stipulative definitions, not lexical ones.

Above all, the mathematicians, ever since Euclid at latest, have been making their own meanings for words. 'By a *denumerable* series,' they say, for example, 'we shall mean a series which you can put into one-one correspondence with the positive integers without changing its order.' This

[3] See the same article, pp. 148–9.

is not an historical description of what has been meant by 'denumerable' in the past or is commonly meant by it now. It is an announcement of what is going to be meant by it in the present work, or a request to the reader to take it in that sense.

By 'stipulative' word-thing definition, then, I mean the explicit and self-conscious setting up of the meaning-relation between some word and some object, the act of assigning an object to a name (or a name to an object), not the act of recording an already existing assignment. This is the kind of definition that Whitehead and Russell had in mind when they wrote that 'a definition is a declaration that a certain newly introduced symbol . . . *is to mean,*' &c.[1]

When we stipulate that a certain thing is to be the meaning of a certain word, the word may or may not have previously existed as a name for something else. Before the mathematicians began to use 'denumerable' as the name of a species of series, perhaps the word existed as the name of something else, and perhaps it did not exist at all but was invented for this very purpose. Which of these is the fact makes no difference to the nature of stipulative definition; but, in case the word did previously exist as the name of something else, then, as Pascal points out, that previous meaning is entirely annulled by the new stipulation. A stipulative definition stipulates that, whatever the word may mean in other communications or even in earlier parts of this communication, it is for the rest of this communication to be taken as having *no meaning whatever* except the one now stipulated. Any previous meanings are thereby abolished for the remainder of this communication.

The element of deliberate, arbitrary, selfconscious choice of a name for a certain thing, or of a thing for a certain name, is the essential and constant element in what I am calling 'stipulative definition,' the element which I believe it important to realize and distinguish. Whether this individual choice agrees with or differs from the common usage of the word defined, and whether there *is* any common usage of it or not, is irrelevant to the essence of stipulation. A stipulative definition may vary, in this respect, all the way from stipulating an entirely novel noise as the name of an entirely novel thing, to merely confirming and adopting common usage. Often it consists merely in adopting one of the many common meanings of a common word and discarding the rest, that is, in announcing which of the established meanings you are going to use. The essence is that stipulative definition is the adoption of elementary sign-uses, while lexical definition is the reporting of them.

A defining sentence, taken out of context, may or may not indicate clearly what kind of definition it means. The following is obviously stipulative:

[1] *Principia Mathematica,* 2nd ed., I, p. 11.

1. Let us mean by a 'pencil' a right cylinder whose cross-section is a regular polygon.

The following is obviously lexical:

2. By 'pencil' some geometers have meant a right cylinder whose cross-section is a regular polygon.

But the following might be either, if considered by itself:

3. A pencil is a right cylinder whose cross-section is a regular polygon.

The third type of formula for expressing a definition is very common; and many persons have a feeling that it is the only correct type, the other two not really expressing definitions at all, but, at nearest, larger thoughts in which a definition is an element. They are therefore inclined to say that the present distinction between lexical and stipulative definition is merely a distinction between the various circumstances that may accompany a definition, and fails to show any differentiation of definition itself. Yet surely no one, after reflection, wishes to regard definition merely as a string of words, but rather as a thought or other human activity or else as the object of that thought. If we take it as a human activity, the activity of thinking or communicating that certain persons used a certain word to mean a certain thing is specifically distinct from the activity of choosing a certain word to mean a certain thing.

This type of nominal definition was called 'stipulation' by James Mackaye in his *The Logic of Language*. In Latin the word *stipulatio* was a legal term meaning a promise given on demand, an engagement, agreement, bargain, or contract. This kind of definition has also been called 'imposition,' because it is the act of imposing a name upon an object; and 'original definition,' because it originates a usage; and 'institution,' for the same reason; and 'legislative definition,' because it does not report a fact but rather enacts a law. It might also be called 'propositive,' or 'invitatory,' or 'imperative.' A large part of it, but not the whole, is covered by the notion of 'redefinition.' [2] A smaller part of it is covered by Professor Dubs's 'scientific definition'; [3] for he means by this phrase the type of definition most commonly found in works of science, if we exclude works devoted to the scientific study of languages, in which, of course, there are many lexical definitions. In the course of this book I have called it mainly 'stipulative' but sometimes 'legislative' definition. 'Legislative' has the advantage of being more immediately intelligible; but when a verb is required 'legislate' gives a seriously inaccurate impression.

[2] e.g. Mr. John Wisdom in *Mind*, 1941, p. 410.
[3] *Philosophical Review*, 1943, pp. 566–7.

The following division of stipulation into two species is worth noticing. One may give a name to a thing or one may give a thing to a name. Here is an example of giving a name to a thing: 'Some people, when they see another person enjoying goods which they lack, experience bitterness and hate of the enjoyer; in what follows this type of reaction will be referred to as "envy." ' And here is an example of giving a thing to a name: 'Is envy really a bad thing?—It depends what you mean by "envy." If you mean feeling bitterness and hate towards a man because he has some good which you lack, then,' &c. Each of these is a species of definition because in each we arrive at a rule by which a certain word means a certain thing. They differ in that in one we start from the thing and connect it to a word, while in the other we start from the word and connect it to a thing. They might be called the thing-word and the word-thing forms of definition. The distinction between the thing-word and the word-thing mode of arriving at a nominal definition applies both to stipulative and to lexical definition.

A lexical definition cannot be at the same time brief and perfect, because words in common usage have many meanings. But a stipulative definition is not under this limitation, because it is not an attempt to report the infinite varieties of actual usage but rather an attempt to replace them by a single unambiguous usage. We rarely have a good reason for stipulating that a word is to have more than one meaning.

§ 2. *The Truthvalue of Stipulative Definitions.* The distinction between lexical and stipulative definition explains the disagreement over the question whether definitions have a truthvalue. Lexical definitions have a truthvalue but stipulative definitions have not. A lexical definition is an assertion that certain people use a certain word in a certain way, and is therefore either true or false. A stipulative definition, however, is not an assertion at all. Therefore, since assertions are the only sentences that have a truthvalue, it has no truthvalue. It is more like a *request* to the reader that he will understand the word in a certain way, or a *command;* and these, though significant utterances, have no truthvalue. It is a proposal rather than a proposition. It looks to the future not the past. This is the fundamental reason why it can be brief and yet satisfactory. It does not have, as every true statement has, the task of following the sinuosities of reality. It is an arbitrary choice. If it succeeds in establishing a usage, the subsequent lexical definition of that usage will not be an arbitrary choice. As W. E. Johnson wrote, there is an absolutely first introduction and naming, as at christening a child, and there is an introduction and naming that is relative to a particular person, as in social introductions. The former is arbitrary in a way in which the others are not (I 94–5).

The arbitrariness and the lack of truthvalue that are proper to stipulative definition are often asserted of definition as such. Thus Galileo said that all definitions are arbitrary.[4]

Those who generalize the truth that stipulative definition is neither true nor false into the falsehood that definition as such is neither true nor false are often led into contradiction thereby. Thus James Mackaye in *The Logic of Language* maintains that definition is neither true nor false, but speaks of Plato's dialogue *Euthyphro* as 'verifying' a proposed definition.

But though stipulation *as such* cannot be true or false, it usually *implies* an element of assertion, and consequently of truth or falsehood, in the following way. Every word-thing definition professes to connect a word with a thing, and therefore assumes that the word and the thing both exist in some way. The assumption that the word exists cannot be false in stipulative definition; for in uttering the definition we utter the word and thus make it exist. But it can be false in lexical definition, for the existence there implied is utterance by other persons. The assumption that the thing exists can be false in both kinds of word-thing definition. Thus the geometers who defined 'horned angles' as those made by the intersection of curves as opposed to straight lines were implying and believing in the possibility of such a thing, whereas the angle between any two curves can only be the angle between the two straight lines that are tangent to the curves at the point of intersection. John Stuart Mill remarked that a definition is usually accompanied by a tacit existence-proposition, because he wished to separate the two and maintain that the pure definition has no truthvalue. He did not remark that it is practically impossible to make or receive a word-thing definition without having an opinion about the existence of the object assigned to the word by the definition, whether occurrent or merely imaginary, whether selfconsistent or selfcontradictory. He did not remark that one very common reason for stipulating a new meaning for a word is the discovery of the existence or non-existence of something. Einstein stipulated a new meaning for the word 'simultaneous' because he realized that the only way of determining which distant events are simultaneous with events here is by using electromagnetic waves and that the speed of such waves is the same whatever the speed of their source.

There is still another way in which truth or falsehood enters into stipulative definition. In stipulating a meaning for a word, a writer demands that his reader shall understand the word in that sense whenever it occurs in that work. The writer thereby lays upon himself the duty of using the word only in that sense, and tacitly promises to do so, and tacitly prophesies that he will do so. But sometimes a writer does not use the word only in the sense he has stipulated. Then his stipulation implied a false promise and a false prediction. When he does use the word only in the sense he

[4] *Two New Sciences,* tr. Crew and De Salvio, New York, 1914, p. 162.

stipulated, his stipulation implies a true promise and a true prediction. The Port Royal Logic said: 'The definition of names cannot be contested . . . for we cannot deny that a man has given to a sound the signification which he says he has given to it.'[5] This is a complete mistake. We often find a writer evidently using a word in a sense other than the sense he stipulated earlier in the work; and I shall give one or two examples of this on another occasion. It is not necessarily a case of dishonesty. Or at any rate the dishonesty may be in the words themselves rather than in the writer; for words often deceive their own utterers about what they mean as they are uttered!

Words, wrote Virginia Woolf in *The Death of the Moth* (p. 131):

> Words . . . are the wildest, freest, most irresponsible, most un-teachable of all things. Of course, you can catch them and sort them and place them in alphabetical order in dictionaries. But words do not live in dictionaries; they live in the mind. . . . Thus to lay down any laws for such irreclaimable vagabonds is worse than useless. A few trifling rules of grammar and spelling are all the constraint we can put on them. All we can say about them, as we peer at them over the edge of that deep, dark and only fitfully illuminated cavern in which they live—the mind—all we can say about them is that they seem to like people to think and to feel before they use them, but to think and to feel not about them, but about something different. They are highly sensitive, easily made self-conscious. They do not like to have their purity or their impurity discussed. . . . Nor do they like being lifted out on the point of a pen and examined separately. They hang together, in sentences, in paragraphs, sometimes for whole pages at a time. They hate being useful; they hate making money; they hate being lectured about in public. In short, they hate anything that stamps them with one meaning or confines them to one attitude, for it is their nature to change.

That stipulative definitions lack truthvalue does not prevent words stipulatively defined from being used to make true or false statements. If you stipulate that 'nacks' is to mean roses and 'braze' is to mean smell sweet, it is false that nacks never braze. That there is nothing necessary about the relation between any elementary sign and its meaning does not prevent there being something necessary about some sentences. One plus one is necessarily two although it is not necessary that we should use the word 'one' to name one. The false belief that the arbitrariness of all nominal definitions involves the arbitrariness of all statements was held by Thomas Hobbes according to Leibniz;[6] but I have not yet found it in Hobbes's work.

[5] Trans. Baynes, p. 81.
[6] *Opera Philosophica,* ed. J. E. Erdmann, 1840, p. 80.

Stipulative definitions are arbitrary in a way that lexical definitions are not; but in a loose sense they are both arbitrary. In stipulation we freely make any word mean anything we choose, whereas in lexical definition we try to report truly what actual persons have actually meant by the word. That is the strict sense in which stipulation is arbitrary and lexical definition is not. But they are both arbitrary, and all word-thing definition is arbitrary, in this loose sense that there is no connexion between a word and the thing it means except that some human beings use that word to mean that thing. There is no connexion between the word 'cock-a-doodle-doo' and the cry of a cock except that some people use the one sound to mean the other sound, and mistakenly think that the two sounds resemble each other. . . .

§ 4. *Rules for Stipulative Definition.* The above discussion of the advantages and disadvantages of stipulation suggests certain rules of stipulation that we may usefully lay upon ourselves.

In the first place, certain rules emerge from the previous discussion without need of much further argument.

1. The supreme rule of stipulation is surely to *stipulate as little as possible.* Do not change received definitions when you have nothing to complain of in them, says the Port Royal Logic. And the reason for it is that stipulation as such is sure to do some harm and is not sure to do any good. It is sure to do some harm because it is a destruction of custom or at least a going outside custom, and this always makes for awkwardness and ugliness and failures of communication. It sometimes does good which outweighs the harm; but whether it does so is always a matter for careful reflection in the particular case. Dozens of would-be scientific writers are unreadable and unread to-day merely because of unrestrained stipulation. We should scrutinize our stipulations after we have made them to see whether they have really been useful, whether they have really done more good than harm. The next four rules, nos. 2–5, are mostly applications of this supreme rule.

2. Everything can already be referred to by phrases or at any rate by sentences, but not everything can already be referred to by a single word; that is, not everything has a name. The question whether to stipulate is therefore often the question whether we must have a name for a certain thing, or can get along well enough with the phrase that already exists for it. This indicates the rule: *Let us not stipulate until we have good reason to believe that the phrase which already covers our designation is too cumbrous for our purposes.*

Humpty Dumpty stipulates a new meaning and uses it once only. He is like a man who, wishing to say that the sky is overcast, says instead: 'By "soda" I shall mean that the sky is overcast. Soda.' He uses eleven words to say what four would say better, and these four are included in his eleven.

We cannot, however, lay down the principle that it is always bad to stipulate a usage that is to be used once only. It often happens that a complicated statement can be better understood if one phrase in it is replaced by a single symbol, and this symbol is stipulatively defined, for this occasion only, in the next sentence. We often find it easier to grasp a shorter sentence plus the special definition of one of its symbols, than to grasp a longer sentence with everything written out and no attached definition. Even for a single use, therefore, it may be good to stipulate a name. But the weaker principle remains, that we should not stipulate unless we have good reason to believe that the phrase already covering our designatum is too cumbrous for our purpose.

3. *Let us not stipulate until we have good reason to believe that there is no name for the thing we wish to name.* Stipulation has become so common and attractive nowadays that many writers tend to invent a name if they cannot dig one out of their own memories by a day's reflection. But it is not sufficient to consult one's memory. It is required to consult also the experts, including the experts in those fields of study which the accidents of contemporary departmentalization separate from one's own. It often happens that, say, a philosopher invents a new term to name something for which, say, the lawyers have long had an agreed term. Professor Dubs illustrates the violation of this rule by the definition of 'evolution' as 'a directional change with a transition to novelty'; for that, he points out, is just what the word 'change' already means.[7]

4. *Let us not stipulate two different symbols to mean the same thing,* since evidently this doubles the bad results without increasing the good results. If the reader is inclined to disbelieve that any writer ever does this, he will find on p. 438 of *Purposive Behavior in Animals and Men* that one of Professor E. C. Tolman's new formations, 'behavior-feint,' is explicitly defined to mean the same as another of his new formations, 'behavior-adjustment.'

5. *Let us not stipulate one symbol for two different things.* This rule is given by Pascal.[8] It is obviously correct, and easy to violate through overlooking an ambiguity in one's method of stipulating, or through overlooking another sense which the word already has. Thus Cohen and Nagel's *Logic* has two senses of 'independent': (1) propositions are independent of each other if neither implies the truth of the other; (2) propositions are independent of each other if neither the truth nor the falsity of one implies either the truth or the falsity of the other. They use the first sense in dis-

---

[7] *Philosophical Review,* 1943, pp. 576–7.
[8] *L'Esprit de la Géometrie,* p. 281, in Vol. II of Havet's edition of the *Pensées.* He has other rules for stipulation, pp. 301–2.

cussing postulates, and the second in discussing the various possibilities of implication among any pair of propositions.

6. *Let us not attempt to change the emotional force of a word by stipulation.* The result, as we have seen in Veblen's 'waste,' is almost bound to be a failure, and is likely to be a deception as well. The emotional powers of language are open to man's manipulation only partially and indirectly, much like a living plant. There is no question of changing a potato into a tomato at will. This is why literary as opposed to scientific writers are against stipulation. They deal largely in the emotional powers of language, and they know that these cannot be controlled by stipulation. They know the falsity of their own words: 'What's in a name? That which we call a rose by any other name would smell as sweet." The most that stipulation can do here is to direct the emotional force of a word upon a new object by redefining the descriptive force of the word.

7. In general, we should *make sure that our stipulation is not a deception and will not deceive,* or at least that the likelihood of its deceiving someone is strongly outweighed by the good it will do. . . .

Richard M. Weaver (1910–1963)

Ultimate Terms in Contemporary Rhetoric

We have shown that rhetorical force must be conceived as a power transmitted through the links of a chain that extends upward toward some
ultimate source. The higher links of that chain must always be of unique
interest to the student of rhetoric, pointing, as they do, to some prime mover
of human impulse. Here I propose to turn away from general considerations and to make an empirical study of the terms on these higher levels
of force which are seen to be operating in our age.

We shall define term simply here as a name capable of entering into a
proposition. In our treatment of rhetorical sources, we have regarded the
full predication consisting of a proposition as the true validator. But a single
term is an incipient proposition, awaiting only the necessary coupling with
another term; and it cannot be denied that single names set up expectancies
of propositional embodiment. This causes everyone to realize the critical
nature of the process of naming. Given the name 'patriot,' for example,
we might expect to see coupled with it 'Brutus,' or 'Washington,' or 'Parnell';
given the term 'hot,' we might expect to see 'sun,' 'stove,' and so on. In
sum, single terms have their potencies, this being part of the phenomenon of
names, and we shall here present a few of the most noteworthy in our
time, with some remarks upon their etiology.

Naturally this survey will include the 'bad' terms as well as the 'good'
terms, since we are interested to record historically those expressions to
which the populace, in its actual usage and response, appears to attribute
the greatest sanction. A prescriptive rhetoric may specify those terms which,
in all seasons, ought to carry the greatest potency, but since the affections

of one age are frequently a source of wonder to another, the most we can do under the caption 'contemporary rhetoric' is to give a descriptive account and withhold the moral until the end. For despite the variations of fashion, an age which is not simply distraught manages to achieve some system of relationship among the attractive and among the repulsive terms, so that we can work out an order of weight and precedence in the prevailing rhetoric once we have discerned the 'rhetorical absolutes'—the terms to which the very highest respect is paid.

It is best to begin boldly by asking ourselves, what is the 'god term' of the present age? By 'god term' we mean that expression about which all other expressions are ranked as subordinate and serving dominations and powers. Its force imparts to the others their lesser degree of force, and fixes the scale by which degrees of comparison are understood. In the absence of a strong and evenly diffused religion, there may be several terms competing for this primacy, so that the question is not always capable of definite answer. Yet if one has to select the one term which in our day carries the greatest blessing, and—to apply a useful test—whose antonym carries the greatest rebuke, one will not go far wrong in naming 'progress.' This seems to be the ultimate generator of force flowing down through many links of ancillary terms. If one can 'make it stick,' it will validate almost anything. It would be difficult to think of any type of person or of any institution which could not be recommended to the public through the enhancing power of this word. A politician is urged upon the voters as a 'progressive leader'; a community is proud to style itself 'progressive'; technologies and methodologies claim to the 'progressive'; a peculiar kind of emphasis in modern education calls itself 'progressive,' and so on without limit. There is no word whose power to move is more implicitly trusted than 'progressive.' But unlike some other words we shall examine in the course of this chapter, its rise to supreme position is not obscure, and it possesses some intelligible referents.

Before going into the story of its elevation, we must prepare ground by noting that it is the nature of the conscious life of man to revolve around some concept of value. So true is this that when the concept is withdrawn, or when it is forced into competition with another concept, the human being suffers an almost intolerable sense of being lost. He has to know where he is in the ideological cosmos in order to coordinate his activities. Probably the greatest cruelty which can be inflicted upon the psychic man is this deprivation of a sense of tendency. Accordingly every age, including those of rudest cultivation, sets up some kind of sign post. In highly cultivated ages, with individuals of exceptional intellectual strength, this may take the form of a metaphysic. But with the ordinary man, even in such advanced ages, it is likely to be some idea abstracted from religion or historical speculation, and made to inhere in a few sensible and immediate examples.

Since the sixteenth century we have tended to accept as inevitable an historical development that takes the form of a changing relationship between ourselves and nature, in which we pass increasingly into the role of master of nature. When I say that this seems inevitable to us, I mean that it seems something so close to what our more religious forebears considered the working of providence that we regard as impiety any disposition to challenge or even suspect it. By a transposition of terms, 'progress' becomes the salvation man is placed on earth to work out; and just as there can be no achievement more important than salvation, so there can be no activity more justified in enlisting our sympathy and support than 'progress.' As our historical sketch would imply, the term began to be used in the sixteenth century in the sense of continuous development or improvement; it reached an apogee in the nineteenth century, amid noisy demonstrations of man's mastery of nature, and now in the twentieth century it keeps its place as one of the least assailable of the 'uncontested terms,' despite critical doubts in certain philosophic quarters. It is probably the only term which gives to the average American or West European of today a concept of something bigger than himself, which he is socially impelled to accept and even to sacrifice for. This capacity to demand sacrifice is probably the surest indicator of the 'god term,' for when a term is so sacrosanct that the material goods of this life must be mysteriously rendered up for it, then we feel justified in saying that it is in some sense ultimate. Today no one is startled to hear of a man's sacrificing health or wealth for the 'progress' of the community, whereas such sacrifices for other ends may be regarded as self-indulgent or even treasonable. And this is just because 'progress' is the coordinator of all socially respectable effort.

Perhaps these observations will help the speaker who would speak against the stream of 'progress,' or who, on the other hand, would parry some blow aimed at him through the potency of the word, to realize what a momentum he is opposing.

Another word of great rhetorical force which owes its origin to the same historical transformation is 'fact.' Today's speaker says 'It is a fact' with all the gravity and air of finality with which his less secular-minded ancestor would have said 'It is the truth.' [1] 'These are facts'; 'Facts tend to show'; and "He knows the facts" will be recognized as common locutions drawing upon the rhetorical resource of this word. The word 'fact' went into the ascendent when our system of verification changed during the Renaissance. Prior to that time, the type of conclusion that men felt obligated to accept came either through divine revelation, or through dialectic, which obeys

---

[1] It is surely worth observing that nowhere in the King James Version of the Bible does the word 'fact' occur.

logical law. But these were displaced by the system of verification through correspondence with physical reality. Since then things have been true only when measurably true, or when susceptible to some kind of quantification. Quite simply, 'fact' came to be the touchstone after the truth of speculative inquiry had been replaced by the truth of empirical investigation. Today when the average citizen says 'It is a fact' or says that he 'knows the facts in the case,' he means that he has the kind of knowledge to which all other knowledges must defer. Possibly it should be pointed out that his 'facts' are frequently not facts at all in the etymological sense; often they will be deductions several steps removed from simply factual data. Yet the 'facts' of his case carry with them this aura of scientific irrefragability, and he will likely regard any questioning of them as sophistry. In his vocabulary a fact is a fact, and all evidence so denominated has the prestige of science.

These last remarks will remind us at once of the strongly rhetorical character of the word 'science' itself. If there is good reason for placing 'progress' rather than 'science' at the top of our series, it is only that the former has more scope, 'science' being the methodological tool of 'progress.' It seems clear, moreover, that 'science' owes its present status to an hypostatization. The hypostatized term is one which treats as a substance or a concrete reality that which has only conceptual existence; and every reader will be able to supply numberless illustrations of how 'science' is used without any specific referent. Any utterance beginning 'Science says' provides one: 'Science says there is no difference in brain capacity between the races'; 'Science now knows the cause of encephalitis'; 'Science says that smoking does not harm the throat.' Science is not, as here it would seem to be, a single concrete entity speaking with one authoritative voice. Behind these large abstractions (and this is not an argument against abstractions as such) there are many scientists holding many different theories and employing many different methods of investigation. The whole force of the word nevertheless depends upon a bland assumption that all scientists meet periodically in synod and there decide and publish what science believes. Yet anyone with the slightest scientific training knows that this is very far from a possibility. Let us consider therefore the changed quality of the utterance when it is amended to read 'A majority of scientists say'; or 'Many scientists believe'; or 'Some scientific experiments have indicated.' The change will not do. There has to be a creature called 'science'; and its creation has as a matter of practice been easy, because modern man has been conditioned to believe that the powers and processes which have transformed his material world represent a very sure form of knowledge, and that there must be a way of identifying that knowledge. Obviously the rhetorical aggrandizement of 'science' here parallels that of 'fact,' the one representing generally and the other specifically the whole subject matter of trustworthy perception.

Furthermore, the term 'science' like 'progress' seems to satisfy a primal need. Man feels lost without a touchstone of knowledge just as he feels lost without the direction-finder provided by progress. It is curious to note that actually the word is only another name for knowledge (L. *scientia*), so that if we should go by strict etymology, we should insist that the expression 'science knows' (*i.e.,* 'knowledge knows') is pure tautology. But our rhetoric seems to get around this by implying that science is *the* knowledge. Other knowledges may contain elements of quackery, and may reflect the selfish aims of the knower; but 'science,' once we have given the word its incorporation, is the undiluted essence of knowledge. The word as it comes to us then is a little pathetic in its appeal, inasmuch as it reflects the deeply human feeling that somewhere somehow there must be people who know things 'as they are.' Once God or his ministry was the depository of such knowledge, but now, with the general decay of religious faith, it is the scientists who must speak *ex cathedra,* whether they wish to or not.

The term 'modern' shares in the rhetorical forces of the others thus far discussed, and stands not far below the top. Its place in the general ordering is intelligible through the same history. Where progress is real, there is a natural presumption that the latest will be the best. Hence it is generally thought that to describe anything as 'modern' is to credit it with all the improvemens which have been made up to now. Then by a transference the term is applied to realms where valuation is, or ought to be, of a different source. In consequence, we have 'modern living' urged upon us as an ideal; 'the modern mind' is mentioned as something superior to previous minds; sometimes the modifier stands alone as an epithet of approval: 'to become modern' or 'to sound modern' are expressions that carry valuation. It is of course idle not to expect an age to feel that some of its ways and habits of mind are the best; but the extensive transformations of the past hundred years seem to have given 'modern' a much more decisive meaning. It is as if a difference of degree had changed into a difference of kind. But the very fact that a word is not used very analytically may increase its rhetorical potency, as we shall see later in connection with a special group of terms.

Another word definitely high up in the hierarchy we have outlined is 'efficient.' It seems to have acquired its force through a kind of no-nonsense connotation. If a thing is efficient, it is a good adaptation of means to ends, with small loss through friction. Thus as a word expressing a good understanding and management of cause and effect, it may have a fairly definite referent; but when it is lifted above this and made to serve as a term of general endorsement, we have to be on our guard against the stratagems of evil rhetoric. When we find, to cite a familiar example, the phrase 'efficiency apartments' used to give an attractive aspect to inadequate dwellings, we may suspect the motive behind such juxtaposition. In many similar cases, 'efficient,' which is a term above reproach in engineering and physics, is made to hold our attention where ethical and aesthetic considerations are entitled to priority. Certain notorious forms of government and certain brutal forms of warfare are undeniably efficient; but here the featuring of efficiency unfairly narrows the question.

Another term which might seem to have a different provenance but which participates in the impulse we have been studying is 'American.' One must first recognize the element of national egotism which makes this a word of approval with us, but there are reasons for saying that the force of 'American' is much more broadly based than this. 'This is the American way' or 'It is the American thing to do' are expressions whose intent will not seem at all curious to the average American. Now the peculiar effect that is intended here comes from the circumstance that 'American' and 'progressive' have an area of synonymity. The Western World has long stood as a symbol for the future; and accordingly there has been a very wide tendency in this country, and also I believe among many people in Europe, to identify that which is American with that which is destined to be. And this is much the same as identifying it with the achievements of 'progress.' The typical American is quite fatuous in this regard: to him America is the goal toward which all creation moves; and he judges a country's civilization by its resemblance to the American model. The matter of changing nationalities brings out this point very well. For a citizen of a European country to become a citizen of the United States is considered natural and right, and I have known those so transferring their nationality to be congratulated upon their good sense and their anticipated good fortune. On the contrary, when an American takes out British citizenship (French or German would be worse), this transference is felt to be a little scandalous. It is regarded as somehow perverse, or as going against the stream of things. Even some of our intellectuals grow uneasy over the action of Henry James and T. S. Eliot, and the masses cannot comprehend it at all. Their adoption of British citizenship is not mere defection from a country; it is treason to history. If Americans wish to become Europeans, what has happened to the hope of the world? is, I imagine, the question at the back of their minds. The tremendous spread of American fashions in behavior and entertainment must add something to the impetus, but I believe the original source to be this prior idea that America, typifying 'progress,' is what the remainder of the world is trying to be like.

It follows naturally that in the popular consciousness of this country, 'un-American' is the ultimate in negation. An anecdote will serve to illustrate this. Several years ago a leading cigarette manufacturer in this country had reason to believe that very damaging reports were being circulated about his product. The reports were such that had they not been stopped, the sale of this brand of cigarettes might have been reduced. The company thereupon inaugurated an extensive advertising campaign, the object of which was to halt these rumors in the most effective way possible. The concocters of the advertising copy evidently concluded after due deliberation that the strongest term of condemnation which could be conceived was 'un-American,' for this was the term employed in the campaign. Soon the newspapers were filled with advertising rebuking this 'un-American' type of depreciation which had injured their sales. From examples such as this we may infer that 'American' stands not only for what is forward in history, but also for what is ethically superior, or at least for a standard of fairness not matched by other nations.

And as long as the popular mind carries this impression, it will be futile to protest against such titles as 'The Committee on un-American activities.' While 'American' and 'un-American' continue to stand for these polar distinctions, the average citizen is not going to find much wrong with a group set up to investigate what is 'un-American' and therefore reprehensible. At the same time, however, it would strike him as most droll if the British were to set up a 'Committee on un-British Activities' or the French a 'Committee on un-French Activities.' The American, like other nationals, is not apt to be much better than he has been taught, and he has been taught systematically that his country is a special creation. That is why some of his ultimate terms seem to the general view provincial, and why he may be moved to polarities which represent only local poles.

If we look within the area covered by 'American,' however, we find significant changes in the position of terms which are reflections of cultural and ideological changes. Among the once powerful but now waning terms are those expressive of the pioneer ideal of ruggedness and self-sufficiency. In the space of fifty years or less we have seen the phrase 'two-fisted American' pass from the category of highly effective images to that of comic anachronisms. Generally, whoever talks the older language of strenuosity is regarded as a reactionary, it being assumed by social democrats that a socially organized world is one in which cooperation removes the necessity for struggle. Even the rhetorical trump cards of the 1920's, which Sinclair Lewis treated with such satire, are comparatively impotent today, as the new social consciousness causes terms of centrally planned living to move toward the head of the series.

Other terms not necessarily connected with the American story have passed a zenith of influence and are in decline; of these perhaps the once effective 'history' is the most interesting example. It is still to be met in such expressions as 'History proves' and 'History teaches'; yet one feels that it has lost the force it possessed in the previous century. Then it was easy for Byron—'the orator in poetry'—to write, 'History with all her volumes vast has but one page'; or for the commemorative speaker to deduce profound lessons from history. But people today seem not to find history so eloquent. A likely explanation is that history, taken as whole, is conceptual rather than factual, and therefore a skepticism has developed as to what it teaches. Moreover, since the teachings of history are principally moral, ethical, or religious, they must encounter today that threshold resentment of anything which savors of the prescriptive. Since 'history' is inseparable from judgment of historical fact, there has to be a considerable community of mind before history can be allowed to have a voice. Did the overthrow of Napoleon represent 'progress' in history or the reverse? I should say that the most common rhetorical uses of 'history' at the present are by intellectuals, whose personal philosophy can provide it with some kind of definition, and by journalists, who seem to use it unreflectively. For the contemporary masses it is substantially true that 'history is bunk.'

An instructive example of how a coveted term can be monopolized may be seen in 'allies.' Three times within the memory of those still young, 'allies' (often capitalized) has been used to distinguish those fighting on our side from the enemy. During the First World War it was a supreme term; during the Second World War it was again used with effect; and at the time of the present writing it is being used to designate that nondescript combination fighting in the name of the United Nations in Korea. The curious fact about the use of this term is that in each case the enemy also has been constituted of 'allies.' In the First World War Germany, Austria-Hungary, and Turkey were 'allies'; in the Second, Germany and Italy; and in the present conflict the North Koreans and the Chinese and perhaps the Russians are 'allies.' But in the rhetorical situation it is not possible to refer to them as 'allies,' since we reserve that term for the alliance representing our side. The reason for such restriction is that when men or nations are 'allied,' it is implied that they are united on some sound principle or for some good cause. Lying at the source of this feeling is the principle discussed by Plato, that friendship can exist only among the good, since good is an integrating force and evil a disintegrating one. We do not, for example, refer to a band of thieves as 'the allies' because that term would impute laudable motives. By confining the term to our side we make an evaluation in our favor. We thus style ourselves the group joined for purposes of good. If we should allow it to be felt for a moment that the opposed combination is also made up of allies, we should concede that they are united by a principle, which in war is never done. So as the usage goes, we are always allies in war and the enemy is just the enemy, regardless of how many nations he has been able to confederate. Here is clearly another instance of how tendencies may exist in even the most innocent-seeming language.

Now let us turn to the terms of repulsion. Some terms of repulsion are also ultimate in the sense of standing at the end of the series, and no survey of the vocabulary can ignore these prime repellants. The counterpart of the 'god term' is the 'devil term,' and it has already been suggested that with us 'un-American' comes nearest to filling that role. Sometimes, however, currents of politics and popular feeling cause something more specific to be placed in that position. There seems indeed to be some obscure psychic law which compels every nation to have in its national imagination an enemy. Perhaps this is but a version of the tribal need for a scapegoat, or for something which will personify 'the adversary.' If a nation did not have an enemy, an enemy would have to be invented to take care of those expressions of scorn and hatred to which peoples must give vent. When another political state is not available to receive the discharge of such emotions, then a class will be chosen, or a race, or a type, or a political faction, and this will be held up to a practically standardized form of repudiation. Perhaps the truth is that we need the enemy in order to define ourselves, but I will not here venture further into psychological complexities. In this type of study it will be enough to recall that during the first half century of our nation's existence, 'Tory' was such a devil term. In the period following our Civil War, 'rebel' took its place in the Northern section and 'Yankee' in the Southern, although in the previous epoch both of these had been terms of esteem. Most readers will remember that during the First World War 'pro-German' was a term of destructive force. During the Second World War 'Nazi' and 'Fascist' carried about equal power to condemn, and then, following the breach with Russia, 'Communist' displaced them both. Now 'Communist' is beyond any rival the devil term, and as such it is employed even by the American president when he feels the need of a strong rhetorical point.

A singular truth about these terms is that, unlike several which were examined in our favorable list, they defy any real analysis. That is to say, one cannot explain how they generate their peculiar force of repudiation. One only recognizes them as publicly-agreed-upon devil terms. It is the same with all. 'Tory' persists in use, though it has long lost any connection with redcoats and British domination. Analysis of 'rebel' and 'Yankee' only turns up embarrassing contradictions of position. Similarly we have all seen 'Nazi' and 'Fascist' used without rational perception; and we see this now, in even greater degree, with 'Communist.' However one might like to reject such usage as mere ignorance, to do so would only evade a very important problem. Most likely these are instances of the 'charismatic term,' which will be discussed in detail presently.

No student of contemporary usage can be unmindful of the curious reprobative force which has been acquired by the term 'prejudice.' Etymologically it signifies nothing more than a prejudgment, or a judgment before all the facts are in; and since all of us have to proceed to a great extent on judgments of that kind, the word should not be any more exciting than 'hypothesis.' But in its rhetorical applications 'prejudice' presumes far beyond that. It is used, as a matter of fact, to characterize unfavorably any value judgment whatever. If 'blue' is said to be a better color than 'red,' that is prejudice. If people of outstanding cultural achievement are praised through contrast with another people, that is prejudice. If one mode of life is presented as superior to another, that is prejudice. And behind all is the implication, if not the declaration, that it is un-American to be prejudiced.

I suspect that what the users of this term are attempting, whether consciously or not, is to sneak 'prejudiced' forward as an uncontested term, and in this way to disarm the opposition by making all positional judgments reprehensible. It must be observed in passing that no people are so prejudiced in the sense of being committed to valuations as those who are engaged in castigating others for prejudice. What they expect is that they can nullify the prejudices of those who oppose them, and then get their own installed in the guise of the *sensus communis*. Mark Twain's statement, 'I know that I am prejudiced in this matter, but I would be ashamed of myself if I weren't' is a therapeutic insight into the process; but it will take more than a witticism to make headway against the repulsive force gathered behind 'prejudice.'

If the rhetorical use of the term has any rational content, this probably comes through a chain of deductions from the nature of democracy; and we know that in controversies centered about the meaning of democracy, the air is usually filled with cries of 'prejudice.' If democracy is taken crudely to mean equality, as it very frequently is, it is then a contradiction of democracy to assign inferiority and superiority on whatever grounds. But since the whole process of evaluation is a process of such assignment, the various inequalities which are left when it has done its work are contradictions of this root notion and hence are 'prejudice'—the assumption of course being that when all the facts are in, these inequalities will be found illusory. The man who dislikes a certain class or race or style has merely not taken pains to learn that it is just as good as any other. If all inequality is deception, then superiorities must be accounted the products of immature judgment. This affords plausible ground, as we have suggested, for the coupling of 'prejudice' and 'ignorance.'

Before leaving the subject of the ordered series of good and bad terms, one feels obliged to say something about the way in which hierarchies can be inverted. Under the impulse of strong frustration there is a natural tendency to institute a pretense that the best is the worst and the worst is the best—an inversion sometimes encountered in literature and in social deportment. The best illustration for purpose of study here comes from a department of speech which I shall call 'GI rhetoric.' The average American youth, put into uniform, translated to a new and usually barren environment, and imbued from many sources with a mission of killing, has undergone a pretty severe dislocation. All of this runs counter to the benevolent platitudes on which he was brought up, and there is little ground for wonder if he adopts the inverted pose. This is made doubly likely by the facts that he is at a passionate age and that he is thrust into an atmosphere of superinduced excitement. It would be unnatural for him not to acquire a rhetoric of strong impulse and of contumacious tendency.

What he does is to make an almost complete inversion. In this special world of his he recoils from those terms used by politicians and other civilians and by the 'top brass' when they are enunciating public sentiments. Dropping the conventional terms of attraction, this uprooted and specially focussed young man puts in their place terms of repulsion. To be more specific, where the others use terms reflecting love, hope, and charity, he uses almost exclusively terms connected with the excretory and reproductive functions. Such terms comprise what Kenneth Burke has ingeniously called 'the imagery of killing.' By an apparently universal psychological law, faeces and the act of defecation are linked with the idea of killing, of destruction, of total repudiation—perhaps the word 'elimination' would comprise the whole body of notions. The reproductive act is associated especially with the idea of aggressive exploitation. Consequently when the GI feels that he must give his speech a proper show of spirit, he places the symbols for these things in places which would normally be filled by prestige terms from the 'regular' list. For specimens of such language presented in literature, the reader is referred to the fiction of Ernest Hemingway and Norman Mailer.

Anyone who has been compelled to listen to such rhetoric will recall the monotony of the vocabulary and the vehemence of the delivery. From these two characteristics we may infer a great need and a narrow means of satisfaction, together with the tension which must result from maintaining so arduous an inversion. Whereas previously the aim had been to love (in the broad sense) it is now to kill; whereas it had been freedom and individuality, it is now restriction and brutalization. In taking revenge for a change which so contradicts his upbringing he is quite capable, as the evidence has already proved, of defiantly placing the lower level above the higher. Sometimes a clever GI will invent combinations and will effect metaphorical departures, but the ordinary ones are limited to a reiteration of the stock terms—to a reiteration, with emphasis of intonation, upon 'the imagery of killing.'[2] Taken as a whole, this rhetoric is a clear if limited example of how the

---

[2] Compare Sherwood Anderson's analysis of the same phenomenon in *A Story Teller's Story* (New York, 1928), p. 198: 'There was in the factories where I worked and where the efficient Ford type of man was just beginning his dull reign this strange and futile outpouring of men's lives in vileness through their lips. Ennui was at work. The talk of the men about me was not Rabelaisian. In old Rabelais there was the salt of infinite wit and I have no doubt that the Rabelaisian flashes that came from our own Lincoln, Washington, and others had point and a flare to them.

But in the factories and in army camps!'

machine may be put in reverse—of how, consequently, a sort of devil worship may get into language.

A similar inversion of hierarchy is to be seen in the world of competitive sports, although to a lesser extent. The great majority of us in the Western world have been brought up under the influence, direct or indirect, of Christianity, which is a religion of extreme altruism. Its terms of value all derive from a law of self-effacement and of consideration for others, and these terms tend to appear whenever we try to rationalize or vindicate our conduct. But in the world of competitive sports, the direction is opposite: there one is applauded for egotistic display and for success at the expense of others—should one mention in particular American professional baseball? Thus the terms with which an athlete is commended will generally point away from the direction of Christian passivity, although when an athlete's character is described for the benefit of the general public, some way is usually found to place him in the other ethos, as by calling attention to his natural kindness, his interest in children, or his readiness to share his money.

Certainly many of the contradictions of our conduct may be explained through the presence of these small inverted hierarchies. When, to cite one further familiar example, the acquisitive, hard-driving local capitalist is made the chief lay official of a Christian church, one knows that in a definite area there has been a transvaluation of values.

Earlier in the chapter we referred to terms of considerable potency whose referents it is virtually impossible to discover or to construct through imagination. I shall approach this group by calling them 'charismatic terms.' It is the nature of the charismatic term to have a power which is not derived, but which is in some mysterious way given. By this I mean to say that we cannot explain their compulsiveness through referents of objectively known character and tendency. We normally 'understand' a rhetorical term's appeal through its connection with something we apprehend, even when we object morally to the source of the impulse. Now 'progress' is an understandable term in this sense, since it rests upon certain observable if not always commendable aspects of our world. Likewise the referential support of 'fact' needs no demonstrating. These derive their force from a reading of palpable circumstance. But in charismatic terms we are confronted with a different creation: these terms seem to have broken loose somehow and to operate independently of referential connections (although in some instances an earlier history of referential connection may be made out). Their meaning seems inexplicable unless we accept the hypothesis that their content proceeds out of a popular will that they *shall* mean something. In effect, they are rhetorical by common consent, or by 'charisma.' As is the case with charismatic authority, where the populace gives the leader a power which can by no means be explained through his personal attributes, and permits him to use it effectively and even arrogantly. the charismatic term is given its load of impulsion without reference, and it functions by convention. The number of such terms is small in any one period, but they are perhaps the most efficacious terms of all.

Such rhetorical sensibility as I have leads me to believe that one of the principal charismatic terms of our age is 'freedom.' The greatest sacrifices that contemporary man is called upon to make are demanded in the name of 'freedom'; yet the referent which the average man attaches to this word is most obscure. Burke's dictum that 'freedom inheres in something sensible' has not prevented its breaking loose from all anchorages. And the evident truth that the average man, given a choice between exemption from responsibility and responsibility, will choose the latter, makes no impression against its power. The fact, moreover, that the most extensive use of the term is made by modern politicians and statesmen in an effort to get men to assume more responsibility (in the form of military service, increased taxes, abridgement of rights, etc.) seems to carry no weight either.[3] The fact that what the American pioneer considered freedom has become wholly impossible to the modern apartment-dwelling metropolitan seems not to have damaged its potency. Unless we accept some philosophical interpretation, such as the proposition that freedom consists only in the discharge of responsibility, there seems no possibility of a correlation between the use of the word and circumstantial reality. Yet 'freedom' remains an ultimate term, for which people are asked to yield up their first-born.

There is plenty of evidence that 'democracy' is becoming the same kind of term. The variety of things it is used to symbolize is too weird and too contradictory for one to find even a core meaning in present-day usages. More important than this for us is the fact, noted by George Orwell, that people resist any attempt to define democracy, as if to connect it with a clear and fixed referent were to vitiate it. It may well be that such resistance to definition of democracy arises from a subconscious fear that a term defined in the usual manner has its charisma taken away. The situation then is that 'democracy' means 'be democratic,' and that means exhibit a certain attitude which you can learn by imitating your fellows.

If rationality is measured by correlations and by analyzable content, then these terms are irrational; and there is one further modern development in the creation of such terms which is strongly suggestive of irrational impulse. This is the increasing tendency to employ in the place of the term itself an abbreviated or telescoped form—which form is nearly always used with even more reckless assumption of authority. I seldom read the abbreviation 'U S' in the newspapers without wincing at the complete arrogance of its rhetorical

[3] One is inevitably reminded of the slogan of Oceania in Orwell's *Nineteen Eighty-four:* 'Freedom is Slavery.'

tone. Daily we see 'U S Cracks Down on Communists'; 'U S Gives OK to Atomic Weapons'; 'U S Shocked by Death of Official.' Who or what is this 'U S'? It is clear that 'U S' does not suggest a union of forty-eight states having republican forms of government and held together by a constitution of expressly delimited authority. It suggests rather an abstract force out of a new world of forces, whose will is law and whom the individual citizen has no way to placate. Consider the individual citizen confronted by 'U S' or 'FBI.' As long as terms stand for identifiable organs of government, the citizen feels that he knows the world he moves around in, but when the forces of government are referred to by these bloodless abstractions, he cannot avoid feeling that they are one thing and he another. Let us note while dealing with this subject the enormous proliferation of such forms during the past twenty years or so. If 'U S' is the most powerful and prepossessing of the group, it drags behind it in train the previously mentioned 'FBI,' and 'NPA,' 'ERP,' 'FDIC,' 'WPA,' 'HOLC,' and 'OSS,' to take a few at random. It is a fact of ominous significance that this use of foreshortened forms is preferred by totalitarians, both the professed and the disguised. Americans were hearing the terms 'OGPU,' 'AMTORG' and 'NEP' before their own government turned to large-scale state planning. Since then we have spawned them ourselves, and, it is to be feared, out of similar impulse. George Orwell, one of the truest humanists of our age, has described the phenomenon thus: 'Even in the early decades of the twentieth century, telescoped words and phrases had been one of the characteristic features of political language; and it had been noticed that the tendency to use abbreviations of this kind was most marked in totalitarian countries and totalitarian organizations. Examples were such words as Nazi, Gestapo, Comintern, Inprecor, Agitprop.'[4]

I venture to suggest that what this whole trend indicates is an attempt by the government, as distinguished from the people, to confer charismatic authority. In the earlier specimens of charismatic terms we were examining, we beheld something like the creation of a spontaneous general will. But these later ones of truncated form are handed down from above, and their potency is by fiat of whatever group is administering in the name of democracy. Actually the process is no more anomalous than the issuing of pamphlets to soldiers telling them whom they shall hate and whom they shall like (or try to like), but the whole business of switching impulse on and off from a central headquarters has very much the meaning of *Gleichschaltung* as that word has been interpreted for me by a native German. Yet it is a disturbing fact that such process should increase in times of peace, because the persistent use of such abbreviations can only mean a serious divorce between rhetorical impulse and rational thought. When the ultimate terms become a series of

---

[4] 'Principles of Newspeak,' *Nineteen Eighty-four* (New York, 1949), p. 310.

bare abstractions, the understanding of power is supplanted by a worship of power, and in our condition this can mean only state worship.

It is easy to see, however, that a group determined upon control will have as one of its first objectives the appropriation of sources of charismatic authority. Probably the surest way to detect the fabricated charismatic term is to identify those terms ordinarily of limited power which are being moved up to the front line. That is to say, we may suspect the act of fabrication when terms of secondary or even tertiary rhetorical rank are pushed forward by unnatural pressure into ultimate positions. This process can nearly always be observed in times of crisis. During the last war, for example, 'defense' and 'war effort' were certainly regarded as culminative terms. We may say this because almost no one thinks of these terms as the natural sanctions of his mode of life. He may think thus of 'progress' or 'happiness' or even 'freedom'; but 'defense' and 'war effort' are ultimate sanctions only when measured against an emergency situation. When the United States was preparing for entry into that conflict, every departure from our normal way of life could be justified as a 'defense' measure. Plants making bombs to be dropped on other continents were called 'defense' plants. Correspondingly, once the conflict had been entered, everything that was done in military or civilian areas was judged by its contribution to the 'war effort.' This last became for a period of years the supreme term: not God or Heaven or happiness, but successful effort in the war. It was a term to end all other terms or a rhetoric to silence all other rhetoric. No one was able to make his claim heard against 'the war effort.'

It is most important to realize, therefore, that under the stress of feeling or preoccupation, quite secondary terms can be moved up to the position of ultimate terms, where they will remain until reflection is allowed to resume sway. There are many signs to show that the term 'aggressor' is now undergoing such manipulation. Despite the fact that almost no term is more difficult to correlate with objective phenomena, it is being rapidly promoted to ultimate 'bad' term. The likelihood is that 'aggressor' will soon become a depository for all the resentments and fears which naturally arise in a people. As such, it will function as did 'infidel' in the mediaeval period and as 'reactionary' has functioned in the recent past. Manifestly it is of great advantage to a nation bent upon organizing its power to be able to stigmatize some neighbor as 'aggressor,' so that the term's capacity for irrational assumption is a great temptation for those who are not moral in their use of rhetoric. This passage from natural or popular to state-engendered charisma produces one of the most dangerous lesions of modern society.

An ethics of rhetoric requires that ultimate terms be ultimate in some rational sense. The only way to achieve that objective is through an ordering of our own minds and our own passions. Every one of psychological sophistication knows that there is a pleasure in willed perversity, and the setting up of perverse shibboleths is a fairly common source of that pleasure. War cries, school slogans, coterie passwords, and all similar expressions are examples of such creation. There may be areas of play in which these are nothing more than a diversion; but there are other areas in which such expressions lure us down the roads of hatred and tragedy. That is the tendency of all words of false or 'engineered' charisma. They often sound like the very gospel of one's society, but in fact they betray us; they get us to do what the adversary of the human being wants us to do. It is worth considering whether the real civil disobedience must not begin with our language.

Lastly, the student of rhetoric must realize that in the contemporary world he is confronted not only by evil practitioners, but also, and probably to an unprecedented degree, by men who are conditioned by the evil created by others. The machinery of propagation and inculcation is today so immense that no one avoids entirely the assimilation and use of some terms which have a downward tendency. It is especially easy to pick up a tone without realizing its trend. Perhaps the best that any of us can do is to hold a dialectic with himself to see what the wider circumferences of his terms of persuasion are. This process will not only improve the consistency of one's thinking but it will also, if the foregoing analysis is sound, prevent his becoming a creature of evil public forces and a victim of his own thoughtless rhetoric.

Formal and Informal Logic

So far the philosophical thickets in which I have rummaged have been thickets that have grown up because of boundary disputes between theories or views which were not themselves philosophers' theories or views. The litigations between the disputants were, necessarily, philosophical troubles, but the original disputants were, for example, mathematicians and men in the street, physiologists and landscape painters, or psychologists and moral instructors.

But now I want to discuss a domestic issue which has fairly recently broken out between certain philosophers and certain philosophically-minded logicians. I shall not do more than give an outline sketch of the situation, since I want to conclude by characterizing against this outline some pervasive features of the variegated thickets in which I have been rummaging.

Since Aristotle, there has existed a branch of inquiries, often entitled 'Formal Logic,' which has always adhered more or less closely to general philosophical inquiries. It is not easy to describe this liaison between Formal Logic and philosophy. The systematic presentation of the rules of syllogistic inference is a very different sort of activity from, say, the elucidation of the concept of pleasure. The Aristotle who inaugurated the former is the same thinker as the Aristotle who considerably developed the latter, yet the kinds of thinking in which he was involved are very widely different. The technical problems in the theory of the syllogism have a strong resemblance to the problems of Euclidean geometry; the ideals of systematization and rigorous proof are at work, questions of switches and shades of significance are barred, false moves are demonstrable fallacies. The problems in, say, the theory of pleasure or perception or moral responsibility are not like this. Aristotle debates with Plato and Socrates, and the issues become better defined as the debate progresses, but the debate does not take the shape of a chain of theorems, nor do the arguments used in that debate admit of notational codification. Whether a given philosophical argument is valid or fallacious is, in general, itself a debatable question. Simple inspection cannot decide. More often it is a question of whether the argument has much, little or no force. Yet different though Formal Logic is from philosophy, the operations characteristic of Formal Logic exercise a detectable, if minor, control over the operations characteristic of philosophy. For good or for ill, the ways in which Aristotle debates the notion of *pleasure,* the *soul* or the *continuum* reflect lessons which he had taught himself in his logical inquiries. Nor is Aristotle peculiar in this. With a negligible number of exceptions, every philosopher of genius and nearly every philosopher of even high talent from Aristotle to the present day has given himself some schooling in some parts of Formal Logic, and his subsequent philosophical reasonings have exhibited the effects upon him of this self-schooling, including sometimes his revolts against it.

In some respects the following analogy holds. Fighting in battles is markedly unlike parade-ground drill. The best conducted drill-evolutions would be the worst possible battle-movements, and the most favourable terrain for a rearguard action would entirely forbid what the barrack-square is made for. None the less the efficient and resourceful fighter is also the well-drilled soldier. The ways in which he takes advantage of the irregularities of the ground show the marks of the schooling he had received on the asphalt. He can improvise operations in the dark and at the risk of his life now, partly because he had learned before to do highly stereotyped and formalized things in broad daylight and in conditions of unmitigated tedium. It is not the stereotyped motions of drill, but its standards of perfection of control which are transmitted from the parade-ground to the battlefield.

Aristotelian Formal Logic gave weapon-drill in only a limited variety of rather short-range inference-weapons. The supplementations given by the Megarian and Stoic logicians were, unfortunately, only slightly and belatedly influential. It was left to the nineteenth and twentieth centuries to generalize and systematize the discipline. In particular, the discipline was then in considerable measure mathematicized, and mathematicized in two separate ways. First, the new builders of Formal Logic, being themselves mathematicians, knew how to give mathematical shape, mathematical rigour and mathematical notations to this branch of abstract theory. Secondly, since their interest in Formal Logic derived from dissatisfaction with the logical foundations of mathematics itself, Formal Logic came to be not only mathematical in style but also mathematical in subject-matter; to be employed, that is, primarily in order to fix the logical powers of the terms or concepts on which hinged the proofs of propositions in pure mathematics.

Formal or Symbolic Logic has grown up into a science or discipline of such scope, such rigour and such fertility that it is now out of all danger of surviving only as the nursery-governess of philosophy. Indeed, philosophers are now complacent if they and their pupils are capable of doing their school-room sums in the subject, and gratified and flattered if original logicians are willing to join them, from time to time, in their own expeditions over the moors.

Now, perhaps, I can indicate in a very provisional way the nature of the dispute which has already begun between Formal Logic and general philosophy. Some properly zealous, if sometimes gratuitously jealous Formal Logicians are now beginning to say to the philosopher 'It is time that you stopped trying to solve your problems by your old-fashioned exercises in improvisation and trial-and-error. Your problems are, as you say yourself, logical problems, and we have now got the procedures for solving logical problems. Where you grope, we calculate. Where you haggle, we employ the cash-register. Where you ponder imponderable pros and cons, we work out the correct logical change.'

The natural response of the offended and also jealous philosopher is this. 'Yes, you have invented or hit upon a private game, with fewer pieces but more squares than are provided by chess. You have converted the words "logic" and "logical" to your private ends, and now you invite us to cease exploring the moors in order to become conductors on your trams. And for what? For nothing, apparently, but the proliferation of truistic formulae. No philosophical problem of any interest to anyone has yet been solved by reducing it to the shape or size that suits some slot in your slot-machine. Your cash-register is indeed quite impeccable and totally neutral, and for that reason it cannot be appealed to for aid in the settlement of any bargaining-disputes. There was the notion, once projected by Leibniz and later championed by Russell, that philosophers would soon be so equipped and drilled that they would be able to decide their issues by calculation. But now we have learned, what we should have foreseen, that questions which can be decided by calculation are different, *toto caelo* different, from the problems that perplex. There is one person to whom it is impertinence to give the advice that he should keep one foot on the kerb—and that is the pathfinder. Kerbs cannot exist where the road is unmade, and roads cannot be made where the route has not been found.'

You can guess for yourselves the abusive nouns which are now liable to be interchanged. 'Muddler-through,' 'romantic,' 'anti-scientist,' 'hunch-rider,' 'litterateur' and of course 'Platonist' come from the one side; from the other side there come 'Formalist,' 'computer,' 'reductionist,' 'pseudo-scientist' and, of course, 'Platonist.'

As might be anticipated, neither party is right, though both are more nearly right than the appeasers who try to blend the operations of the one party with the operations of the other. The drill-sergeant is wrong who thinks that soldiering consists in going through the motions tabulated in the drill-book. The *franc-tireur* is wrong who thinks that soldiering consists in out-bursts of amateur gunmanship. But neither is so wrong as the scenario-writer who represents fighting soldiers as heroes going berserk in close column of platoons.

Let us examine, rather more closely, the actual work, as distinct from the intermittent promises of Formal Logicians. Aristotle, it is nearly enough correct to say, examined certain ranges of inferences, namely those which pivot on the notions of *all, some,* and *not*. He saw that from two premisses like 'some men are blue-eyed' and 'some men are red-haired' it does not follow that any men are both blue-eyed and red-haired, or, of course, that none are. On the other hand from 'all men are mortal' and 'all philosophers are men' it does follow that all philosophers are mortal. There are rules governing the employment of *all, some* and *not* such that all inferences pivoting on two or all three of these concepts, arranged in certain ways, are valid, while all inferences pivoting on them arranged in certain other ways are invalid. These rules are perfectly general, anyhow in this sense, that differences of concrete subject-matter make no difference to the validity or fallaciousness of the inferences. The quantifier-words 'all' and 'some' can be followed indifferently by 'men,' 'cows,' 'gods' or what you will, without affecting our decision that the inference holds or does not hold. What determines whether a proposed syllogism is valid or fallacious is the work given to 'all,' 'some' and 'not,' irrespective of the concrete topics of its premisses and conclusion. So, for brevity, we can say that Aristotle was investigating the logical powers of certain topic-neutral concepts, namely those of *all, some* and *not*. These are sometimes listed among what are nowadays called the 'logical constants.'

In a similar way the Megarian and Stoic logicians began the investigation of the logical powers of the equally topic-neutral concepts of *and, or,* and *if;* they concentrated on certain propositional conjunctions or connectives, where Aristotle had concentrated on certain quantifiers. They were studying the legitimacy and illegitimacy of possible arguments in so far as they hinged on these particular topic-neutral conjunctions.

These studies yielded a modest degree of codification of the inference-patterns that were examined, and even a semi-Euclideanization of the rules of these inferences. Certain crucial fallacy-patterns were classified. So it was natural, though, as we now know, quite mistaken to suppose that any piece of valid reasoning whatsoever was, by some device or other of rewording,

reducible to one of the already scheduled patterns, and every piece of fallacious reasoning reducible to one of the already registered howlers. Some
terms like 'all,' 'some' and 'not,' and perhaps also 'and,' 'or' and 'if' do carry
inferences; the rest, it was mistakenly supposed, do not.

Part of what characterizes the terms which do, on this view, carry inferences is that these terms or 'logical constants' are indifferent to subject-matter
or are topic-neutral; so part of what characterizes all the other terms which
were supposed not to carry inferences is that they are not topic-neutral. Inferences are valid or invalid in virtue of their forms, and to say this, it was
supposed, was to say that they were valid or invalid because of the ways in
which certain topic-neutral or purely formal expressions occurred in certain
positions and arrangements in their premisses and conclusions. This tempt-
ingly crisp doctrine, whose obituary notice has yet to be written, might easily
suggest the following demarcation of Formal Logic from philosophy. Formal
Logic, it might be said, maps the inference-powers of the topic-neutral
expressions or logical constants on which our arguments pivot; philosophy
has to do with the topical or subject-matter concepts which provide the fat
and the lean, but not the joints or the tendons of discourse. The philosopher
examines such notions as *pleasure, colour, the future,* and *responsibility,* while
the Formal Logician examines such notions as *all, some, not, if* and *or.*

But this way of making the division quickly breaks down. To begin with,
topic-neutrality is not enough to qualify an expression as a logical constant.
European languages, ancient and modern, and especially the largely unin-
flected languages, are rich in topic-neutral expressions, most of which have,
for very good reasons, received no attention at all from Formal Logicians.
We may call English expressions 'topic-neutral' if a foreigner who understood them, but only them, could get no clue at all from an English paragraph
containing them what that paragraph was about. Such expressions can or
must occur in any paragraph about any topic, abstract or concrete, biograph-
ical or legal, philosophical or scientific. They are not dedicated to this topic
as distinct from that. They are like coins which enable one to bargain for any
commodity or services whatsoever. You cannot tell from the coins in the cus-
tomer's hand what he is going to buy. In this way 'not,' 'and,' 'all,' 'some,'
'a,' 'the,' 'is,' 'is a member of,' etc., certainly are topic-neutral, but so are
'several,' 'most,' 'few,' 'three,' 'half,' 'although,' 'because,' 'perhaps,' 'may,'
as well as hosts of other conjunctions, particles, prepositions, pronouns, ad-
verbs, etc. Some expressions seem to be nearly but not quite topic-neutral.
The temporal conjunctions 'while,' 'after' and 'before,' and the spatial conjunction 'where' could be used not in all, but only in nearly all sorts of discourse. Our foreigner could tell from the occurrence of temporal conjunctions
in the paragraph that no purely geometrical matter was being discussed.

But not only do Formal Logicians very properly ignore the great majority of topic-neutral expressions, as not being in their beat; they also, very properly, bestow their professional attentions upon the logical powers of certain classes of expressions which are by no means topic-neutral. Relational expressions like 'north of,' 'taller than' and 'encompasses' are pivots of strict inferences, and it has proved necessary and feasible to divide such expressions up into families according to the sorts of inferences which they do and do not carry. 'Taller-than,' for example, is transitive, in the sense that if A is taller than B, and B than C, then A is taller than C. But 'next to' and 'mother of' are not transitive. A can be next to B and B to C without A being next to C; and Sarah cannot be the mother of the child of her own daughter. This does not prevent us from discovering rigorous parities of reasoning between, for example, inferences hinging on 'north of' and inferences hinging on 'encompasses.' But the feature of parity cannot always be detached for separate examination by publication of some elided topic-neutral expression. Sometimes it can. 'Fatter than' works, in some directions, like 'hotter than,' and what is common to the two can be brought out by the rewording 'more fat than' and 'more hot than,' where the expression 'more so and so than' is a detachable topic-neutral expression.

So we should say, perhaps, with considerable loss of crispness and misleadingness, that Formal Logic is a certain sort of study of parities of reasoning or certain special kinds of parities of reasoning; and that it is convenient, when possible, to exhibit these parities by operations with topic-neutral expressions detached from any particular topical contexts; but that this is not essential and is not always possible. Not all strict inferences pivot on the recognized logical constants, and not all topic-neutral expressions qualify for treatment as logical constants.

A further amendment is required. I have spoken as if our ordinary 'and,' 'or,' 'if,' 'all,' 'some' and so on are identical with the logical constants with which the Formal Logician operates. But this is not true. The logician's 'and,' 'not,' 'all,' 'some' and the rest are not our familiar civilian terms; they are conscript terms, in uniform and under military discipline, with memories, indeed, of their previous more free and easy civilian lives, though they are not living those lives now. Two instances are enough. If you hear on good authority that she took arsenic and fell ill you will reject the rumour that she fell ill and took arsenic. This familiar use of 'and' carries with it the temporal notion expressed by 'and subsequently' and even the causal notion expressed by 'and in consequence.' The logicians' conscript 'and' does only its appointed duty—a duty in which 'she took arsenic and fell ill' is an absolute paraphrase of 'she fell ill and took arsenic.' This might be called the minimal force of 'and.' In some cases the overlap between the military duties and the civilian work and play of an expression is even slighter. What corresponds in the glossary of Formal Logic to the civilian word 'if' is an expression which plays only a very small, though certainly cardinal part of the role or roles of that civilian word.

This point that Formal Logic operates (1) only with some, and not with all topic-neutral expressions, and (2) only with artificial extracts from the selected few topic-neutral expressions of ordinary discourse is sometimes used by philosophers as a criticism of the programme of Formal Logic. Where the philosopher concerns himself with full-blooded concepts like that of *pleasure* or *memory,* the Formal Logician concerns himself only with meatless concepts like those of *not* and *some;* and even these have to be filed down to reduced size and unnatural shape before the Formal Logician will deign to inspect them. Moreover, the philosopher investigates concepts which, in one way or another, generate genuine perplexities. He investigates the concept, say, of *seeing* and not that of, say, *perspiring,* since the former is charged with paradoxes where the latter is not. But, the criticism goes, the Formal Logician investigates the inference-carrying labours of concepts which engender no paradoxes whatsoever; what he finds out about *and* and *not* are only elaborations of what every child has completely mastered in his early talking years.

I mention this allegation here because it makes the right opening for me. It is quite false that doing Formal Logic is doing gratuitous and profitless philosophy upon philosophically transparent concepts. It is quite false, equally, that the philosopher is doing makeshift and amateurish Formal Logic upon wrongly chosen because non-logical concepts. The battlefield is not a makeshift parade-ground; and the parade-ground is not a sham battlefield.

None the less, there remains a very important way in which the adjective 'logical' is properly used to characterize both the inquiries which belong to Formal Logic and the inquiries which belong to philosophy. The Formal Logician really is working out the logic of *and, not, all, some,* etc., and the philosopher really is exploring the logic of the concepts of *pleasure, seeing, chance,* etc., even though the work of the one is greatly unlike the work of the other in procedure and in objectives. Neither is doing what the other is doing, much less is either doing improperly what the other is doing properly. Yet we are not punning when we say, for example, that the considerations which are decisive for both are 'logical' considerations, any more than we are punning if we say that the choice of drill-evolutions and the choice of battle-evolutions are both decided by 'military' considerations. How can this be?

I find the following partial parallel of some assistance. Trading begins with barter of goods for goods, and, by means of fixed places and times for markets, such barter-dealings can reach a fairly high degree of systematization. Though the relative exchange-values of different sorts of goods vary with times and places, some measure of stabilization can be achieved by tacit or explicit convention. There is, however, even at this stage, a strong pressure upon traders to use just a few kinds of consumable goods not only for consumption, but also, at least for a short time, as a sort of informal currency. Dried fishes, cigarettes or iron bars, though wanted for use, come also to be wanted because any other trader can be relied on to accept them, whether he himself wants to use them or not, because they will always be exchangeable anywhere for consumable goods. So long as they are reasonably imperishable, easy to store and handle, easy to count or weigh, and certain to be wanted some day by someone for consumption purposes, they are negotiable as exchange-tokens. From this stage to the stage of operating with a conventional currency or legal tender is a relatively short step. Though no one, perhaps, can be expected to want to use metal discs for any consumption purpose, everyone can be expected to want to use them for exchange-purposes. They might be described as auxiliary goods, goods which are of little or no utility in themselves, but of great utility for getting and disposing of other goods which are wanted for themselves.

For future purposes we should notice another kind of auxiliary goods. Baskets, pitchers, sacks, brown paper and string are, to exaggerate a little, of no use in themselves, but only for the collection and housing of goods which we do want for themselves. But clearly the way in which baskets and string are auxiliary to marketing and storing is different from the way in which coins are auxiliary. A basket or keg is only being actually useful to us when we are in possession of goods for it to contain. A coin is useful to us in another way. While we possess the coin, we do not possess what we shall buy with it. But still there is a certain similarity between them. A coin is commodity-neutral, for I can buy any sort of commodity with it. A sack or a piece of string is, in lower degree, commodity-neutral. You cannot tell from the fact that I go to market with a sack or some string precisely what kinds of goods I shall bring back with its aid. It would be useful for any of a fairly wide range of goods, though not, of course, for all kinds of goods.

Linguistic dealings between men have some of the features of market-dealings between men. There is a comparable pressure upon language to evolve idioms, which may or may not be separate words, to subserve in stabilized ways different kinds of constantly recurring linguistic negotiations. We need and therefore we get a variety of topic-neutral words, inflections, constructions, etc., some of which function rather like baskets, pitchers, string and wrapping-paper, while others function rather like the dried fishes, cigarettes or iron bars and, later on, rather like the coins and currency notes, part or the whole of whose utility is to serve as instruments of exchange.

There arises, I suppose, a special pressure upon language to provide idioms of this latter kind, when a society reaches the stage where many matters of interest and importance to everyone have to be settled or decided by special kinds of talk. I mean, for example, when offenders have to be tried and convicted or acquitted; when treaties and contracts have to be entered into and observed or enforced; when witnesses have to be cross-examined; when legislators have to draft practicable measures and defend them against critics; when private rights and public duties have to be precisely fixed; when complicated commercial arrangements have to be made; when teachers have to set tests to their pupils; and, by no means earliest, when theorists have to consider in detail the strengths and weaknesses of their own and one another's theories.

Those topic-neutral words of natural languages which are nearest to the officially recognized logical constants roughly coincide, perhaps, with the best consolidated exchange-auxiliaries that our native tongues have provided. They exist to be negotiating instruments. The conscript expressions actually used by Formal Logicians, together with the methodically designed expressions of mathematics, correspond in many respects with a legal tender. A sentence with one or more 'logical words' in it, is a sentence with one or more price-tickets on it. Other topic-neutral words, inflections, etc., correspond more closely with the paper, string, sacks and pitchers with which we go to and return from the market.

Now perhaps we are in a position to see more clearly some of the ways in which the Formal Logician's interests are unlike those of the philosopher and yet not entirely separate. The ordinary person is much concerned both with the domestic or consumption-utility of different goods and also, as a marketer, with their exchange-values, i.e. what they can be got for or what they would fetch; and these considerations vary with every different kind and quantity of goods. No such problems exist for the bank clerk about the coins that he takes in and gives out. A sixpenny-bit buys whatever costs sixpence, and its purchasing power stands to the purchasing power of a penny or a half-crown in known and fixed relations. Its value is stamped on its face.

Somewhat similarly there is and can be no incertitude about the exchange-values of the numerals of simple arithmetic or the conscript logical constants of the Formal Logician, since they have been designed or chartered to do just what they do. Nor can there be much incertitude about the inference-carrying powers of such vernacular words as 'not,' 'some,' 'and' and 'or,' since their prime business is to make negotiations decidable.

Where the philosopher has to investigate both the special content of, say, the concepts of *enjoying* and *remembering* and their kinds of logical behaviour, the logician does not have to investigate his semi-technical concepts of *and* and *not*. Their work is what they are chartered to do, and he drew up their charters or at least has read them. On the other hand, a special theoretical task does remain for him to do. Much as arithmetic and algebra have problems of their own, which begin when the elementary use of numbers in counting is mastered, so the Formal Logician has his analogous problems, which begin long after the elementary mastery is achieved of his chartered *all, some* and *not; and, or, if* and the rest. His occupational problems are not how to determine the exchange-equivalents of his logical constants, but how to derive some from others, to establish, that is, the principles of the calculation of them. His task is to incorporate them in a sort of Euclidean deductive system. The experienced but uneducated bus-conductor could write down the beginning of an endless list of the correct change that can be given for different coins and handfuls of coins, but to do this would not be to do arithmetic. The accountant, unlike our bus-conductor, must know how to calculate, and some other experts must have developed the science which the accountant applies.

The topic-neutral expressions of our natural language which are the civilian counterparts to the conscript logical constants do not behave quite as their conscript counterparts behave, though the differences are sometimes slight and sometimes not troublesomely gross. For obvious reasons, logicians have conscripted only the soldierly-looking civilians and, as we have seen, there are good reasons why the languages of highly organized societies provide a certain number of decision-facilitating expressions.

But most of the terms of everyday and technical discourse are not like coins or even like cowrie-shells. They are like consumption-goods, which can, indeed, be traded for and traded with. But their barter-values are not stamped upon their faces. They can, for the most part, be the hinges of legitimate and illegitimate inferences; there are parities of reasoning between inferences pivoting on one of them and inferences pivoting on some others of them; but there is, ordinarily, no way of extracting from them some implicit logical constant or web of logical constants to be credited with the carriage of those inferences—any more than there is really an invisible half-crown lurking inside a bag of potatoes which renders these potatoes the barter-equivalent of a basket of fruit or a couple of lobsters.

They have their logical powers or barter-values, but they are not to be read off the terms of their official charters, since they have no charters. The philosopher's problem is to extract their logical powers from the dealings which we transact with them, somewhat as the phonetician has to extract the principles of phonetics from the ways in which we have learned to pronounce our words—though the method and purposes of the extraction are hugely different.

How then, it remains to be asked, is the philosopher a client of the Formal Logician? Part of the answer I have already suggested. To know how to go through completely stereotyped movements in artificial parade-ground conditions with perfect correctness is to have learned not indeed how to conduct oneself in battle but how rigorously to apply standards of soldierly efficiency even to unrehearsed actions and decisions in novel and nasty situations and in irregular and unfamiliar country.

Or, which is not quite the same thing, it is rather like what geometry is to the cartographer. He finds no Euclidean straight hedgerows or Euclidean plane meadows. Yet he could not map the sinuous hedgerows that he finds or the undulating meadows save against the ideally regular boundaries and levels in terms of which alone can he calculate out the relative positions and heights of the natural objects which he is to record from the visual observations that he makes. The cartographer is one of the clients of geometry. The possibility of his map being approximately correct or precise is the gift of Euclid. So is the possibility of his reading off his map distances, areas and bearings which he did not measure when constructing his map.

Or, lastly, it is what accountancy is to the merchant, who, though his problems are not arithmetical problems, still, in his handling of them, needs the constant back-room check of the properly balanced ledger. The trader is a client of the accountant.

But patently fighting cannot be reduced to drill, cartography cannot be reduced to geometry, trading cannot be reduced to balancing accounts. Nor can the handling of philosophical problems be reduced to either the derivation or the application of theorems about logical constants. The philosopher is perforce doing what might be called 'Informal Logic,' and the suggestion that his problems, his results or his procedures should or could be formalized is as wildly astray as would be the corresponding suggestions about the soldier, the cartographer and the trader. We could go further and say that the whole point of drill, of geometry, of accountancy and of Formal Logic would be gone if they could be completely dissociated from their clients. It would be like reserving the roads for the sole use of steam-rollers, or like forbidding all trade save money-changing.

What I have been trying to think out during the course of these lectures is the ways in which live problems in Informal Logic are forced upon us, willy-nilly by the interferences which are unwittingly committed between different teams of ideas. The thinker, who is also Everyman, learns, *ambulando*, how to impose some measure of internal order and logical discipline upon the players in his different conceptual teams. What he does not learn *ambulando* is how to contrast and co-ordinate team with team; how, for example, to contrast and co-ordinate what he knows about seeing and hearing with what he finds out in the course of developing his optical, acoustic, and neurophysiological theories; or how to contrast and co-ordinate what he knows about our daily control of things and happenings in the world with what he knows about the implications of truths in the future tense; or how to contrast and co-ordinate what he knows about the everyday furniture of the mundane globe with the conclusions of his theories about the ultimate constitution of matter.

Let me bring together some specific points which I have tried to illustrate. I think that they hang together.

First, we are under no pressure to examine the logical behaviour of isolated concepts, selected at random, perhaps, from a dictionary. We have no special puzzles about the notions of *perspiration, off-side* or *taxation.* The pressure comes when we find (for instance) that the things which we know well are the right sorts of things to say with verbs like 'see' and 'hear' and all the others of that not very well defined family seem to be put out of court by, or else to put out of court, the things which we also know well are the right sorts of things to say with expressions like 'optic nerve,' 'neural impulse,' 'light-waves' and all the rest of their not very well-defined families. Our characteristic questions are not questions in the logical statics of insulated and single concepts, but questions in the logical dynamics of apparently interfering systems of concepts.

Consequently to understand the work of an original philosopher it is necessary to see—and not merely to see but to feel—the logical *impasse* by which he was held up. We should always be asking the question Just what was the conceptual fix that he was in? What dilemma was pinching him? Nor is it always easy to identify or describe this *impasse,* since he himself would seldom, if ever, be able to diagnose his trouble. To be able to diagnose it would be to be half way out of it. To him, while in the trouble, the situation feels like that of a man in a fog whose left foot feels securely planted on the solid bank, and whose right foot feels securely planted on a reliable boat—and yet the bank and the boat seem to move independently. He cannot lift either foot from its foothold and yet he cannot, it seems, keep his feet together.

Kant, to take a particular example, wholeheartedly believed in Newtonian physics; he also wholeheartedly believed in the autonomy of morals. Yet the Laws of Motion seemed to leave no room for the Moral Law, and the absolute obligation for men to act in certain ways, and therewith the possibility of their doing so seemed to leave no room for the physical necessity of the motions of all, including human, bodies. Neither the truths of science nor the truths of morals could be abandoned, yet each seemed to disqualify the other.

Parallel with this *impasse* or rather, as I think, subterranean to it was another deeper and wider crevasse. Mechanical principles contain the explanations of all bodily states and processes. But plants, insects, animals and men are bodily organisations. So all their states and processes can be mechanically explained. Yet living things are not merely complex mechanisms; the biological sciences are not mere off-shoots of mechanics. Where there is life there is purposiveness, and where there is sentient, mobile and, especially, conscious and intellectual life there are progressively higher and higher levels or types of purposiveness. The biologist, the zoologist and the psychologist must conduct their inquiries as if they were vitalists, even though they feel intellectual obligations to pay lip-service to mechanism. So Kant, and not Kant alone, had one foot securely planted on the solid bank of Newtonian mechanics, and the other foot securely planted on the boat of a semi-Aristotelian vitalism.

It is sometimes suggested that Kant set himself the tasks of analysing a heap of concepts, such as *space, time, causation, duty, life,* and *purpose.* But this would be misleading in at least two important ways. First, he did not set himself these tasks; they set themselves to him. Secondly, they did not attack him in a random sequence of local raids; they were the spearheads of a concerted offensive from two flanks. His tactics against these several units had and had to have a strategy behind them.

Next, I hope to have shown that the settlement or even partial settlement of a piece of litigation between theories cannot be achieved by any one stereotyped manœuvre. There is no one regulation move or sequence of moves as a result of which the correct logical bearings between the disputing positions can be fixed. This is not to say that we may not often discern or seem to discern some fairly broad similarities of pattern between one dilemma and another; and these may sometimes suggest ways of tackling the one issue on the analogy of ways which have been effective in tackling the other. But such broad analogies may be hindrances as well as helps. A darling model may in a new application work like a Procrustean bed.

To say this is to say, in another way, that the hope that philosophical problems can be, by some stereotyped operations, reduced to standard problems in Formal Logic is a baseless dream. Formal Logic may provide the exploratory Informal Logician with a compass by which to steer, but not with a course on which to steer and certainly not with rails to obviate steering. Where there is virgin forest, there can be no rails; where rails exist the jungle has long since been cleared.

None the less, the debating operations by which alone the Informal Logician can move are controlled by logical considerations, even though not, save pretty indirectly, by considerations of Formal Logic. There is, for example, at least some force in the argument that to enjoy doing something cannot be a case of a sensation of some sort being set up in the agent by his action, since acute sensations distract the attention from everything else than those sensations, whereas great enjoyment goes with complete absorption in the activity enjoyed; and such force as there is in this argument works directly towards some grasp of the cross-bearings between the concepts of *pleasure, activity, attention* and *feeling*.

A little while ago I distinguished between everyday civilian concepts and the conscript concepts with which the Formal Logician and the mathematician operate. I said that the functions of the latter were to be read off their charters, where the conduct in inference of the former could not be read off their charters, since they were under no charters. But a reservation, has to be made for the technical terms of specialisms like games, sciences and professions. The rules for the employment of these terms are, in some degree, explicit. A person who has mastered the apparatus to which they belong knows enough to be able to state, sometimes with great precision, what the job of one of them is with relation to the jobs of the rest of them. Their team-roles are more or less well inter-defined.

It follows, what seems to be true in fact, that the employer of such officially incorporated terms, is ordinarily embarrassed by few, if any, perplexities in the course of his regular, technical use of them. But there are two kinds of situation in which even he, and especially he can be embarrassed. The first is when the theory, business or other activity which the apparatus subserves is itself in process of major development or change—when, that is, the roles of all or most of the members of the apparatus are being enlarged or twisted. If the property-laws of a state are being stretched to cover countless different kinds of Crown property, State property, and the property of nationalized industries and of chartered public companies, then the lawyer himself will, for a time, find himself divided between the old and the new forces of his own technical dictions. When Auction Bridge was giving place to Contract Bridge, or when Association Football was breeding Rugby Football, or when geometry was absorbing non-Euclidean geometries or when 1953 physical theory is growing away, in some directions, from 1943 physical theory, the regular or habitual functions of many of the technical terms employed fall short of their new functions; and their employer feels doubts, for the time being, whether he is not playing fast and loose with their *real* meanings, namely those that he learned long ago. Yesterday's impossibilities are today's possibilities, yet are not these prohibited by the well-known rules? Surely it is still *really* a foul to pick up the football with the hands?

The second situation in which the employer of a technical apparatus of internally well-disciplined terms may be perplexed about their employment is, in general, the more important. This is the situation in which he is required to discuss inter-theory questions, questions, that is, whose answers are not contributions to the body of his theory, but are, instead, contributions to the understanding of the gist and drift of his theory by outsiders, whether they be thoughtful citizens at large, or themselves the sponsors of other special theories. This is the situation of the lawyer debating with the ordinary citizen, or with the psychologist or with the political reformer; or it is the situation of the theologian debating with the astro-physicist or the geneticist or with the ordinary citizen. In such situations perfect internal control of the concepts of his theory is compatible with the greatest embarrassment in marrying his occupational dictions with the occupational or public dictions of his interlocutor. Indeed, to strike a pessimistic note, the more at home he is with his specialized conceptual apparatus, the less capable will he be apt to be of operating outside of it. What work so well during his daily employment must, he will feel, be the proper implements to employ elsewhere. Of course diplomatic negotiations can best be conducted in the well-tried idioms of the Stock Exchange, the Trade Union, the regiment or the chapel.

The point here is that, odd though it sounds, an intelligent man may both know perfectly how to put a concept to its regular work within its appropriate field of employment, and thus have complete mastery of its domestic logical duties and immunities, and yet be quite at a loss to determine its external or public logic. He can, perhaps, think lucidly as a geometrician and still be perplexed about the relations between geometrical points and pencilled dots on paper or molecules or atoms; or he can, perhaps, think lucidly as an economist and still be perplexed about the identity or non-identity of his marginal farmer, with this or that unprosperous smallholder. Ability to use the private lingo of a theory does not necessarily carry with it the ability to render this lingo into public dictions which are neutral between theories. It is often the very powerfulness of the domestic logic of a well-organized theory or discipline which engenders the litigations between it and other theories or, perhaps more often, between it and common knowledge. For it is just to this well-known drill that the thinker who has been trained in it feels obliged to try to subjugate the members of these other conceptual teams.

So what I hope to have done is to have brought out for examination some features of what I have dubbed the 'informal logic' of our ordinary and our technical concepts; and shown how questions about this informal logic are forced upon us by the unanticipated and unpreventable quarrels which break out from time to time between one team of ideas and another. What is often, though not very helpfully, described as 'the analysis of concepts,' is rather an operation—if you like a 'synoptic' operation—of working out the parities and the disparities of reasoning between arguments hinging on the concepts of one conceptual apparatus and arguments hinging on those of another. The need to undertake such operations first makes itself felt only when some dilemma shows its horns.

AIDS TO STUDY

This essay is difficult only in the sense that you must keep your mind on it; if your attention strays, you will soon be lost, for the argument is a close one. Moreover, the basic analogies used are to be kept in mind as you go along; they are not employed and then dropped, but retained throughout the discussion. If you managed to keep your attention fixed on the essay throughout the first reading, I do not have to tell you that it is a fascinating discussion. If you were bewildered or bored, you were not paying attention; read it again, and this time shut out distractions and disruptions.

A note on what is referred to as Aristotelian Formal Logic may prove of help in your understanding of this discussion. As Mr. Ryle makes clear, this logic was a highly formalized set of rules about certain sorts of inferences. The basic form for this method of inference is the proposition, which consists of two terms and a copula:

$$\text{TERM} \left\{ \begin{array}{c} \text{is} \\ \text{are} \end{array} \right\} \text{TERM}$$

Examples:

> *Apples* are *fruits*
> *Boys* are *males*
> *People who fail to watch their step* are *fools*

As used in the Aristotelian system, the proposition took one of four forms—and the forms were dependent upon the 'logical constants' or 'topic-neutral' words Ryle refers to:

1. The proposition might affirm that every member of the first term is also a member of the second term: *all* apples are fruits; *all* boys are males.
2. The proposition might affirm that one or more members, but not necessarily all, of the first term are also members of the second: *some* boys are students; *some* people are fools.
3. The proposition might deny that any member of either term is a member of the other: *no* boys are girls; *no* birds are mammals.
4. The proposition might deny that any member of the second term is a member of a portion of the first term: *some* girls are *not* mothers; *some* students are *not* sophomores.

I have put the descriptions of these four forms of the proposition in what may strike you as an odd fashion. But this method was designed to chart a way we could be sure that certain inferences must always follow from our statements in these forms. What the logicians call 'distribution' is an all-important observation. And a term is said to be 'distributed' when the proposition implies something about every member of the term. Clearly enough, when I affirm that 'all goolies are troglies,' I imply that every member of the gooly class is also a member of the trogly class; when I say that 'no moompers are dibbers,' I imply that every member of the moomper class is excluded from the dibber class and likewise that every member of the dibber class is excluded from the moomper class. Just as clearly, when I assert that 'some lottles are tromps,' I do not necessarily imply anything about every lottle or every tromp. Perhaps less clearly, but just as important to the system, when I say that 'some driggers are not pippers,' though I do not imply anything about every drigger, I do imply that every pipper is excluded from the partial class indicated by 'some driggers.' In short, the capitalized terms are distributed in the four forms of the proposition:

> All *TERM* is *term*
> No *TERM* is *TERM*
> Some *term* is *term*
> Some *term* is not *TERM*

Now, certain inferences—called immediate inferences—may be made from these propositions. For instance, if it is true that 'all X is Y,' it is true that 'some X is Y' (for 'some is' in this system does not imply 'some is not'); and it is also true that 'some Y is X.' It is not necessarily true that 'all Y is X,' for all freshmen may be students, but it does not follow that all students are freshmen. And inferences may be drawn from each of the other four forms, as well as some other inferences from 'all X is Y.'

But the chief weapon of this system of thinking is the syllogism. The syllogism is a series of three propositions operating on three terms. The first two propositions are called 'premises,' the last is called the 'conclusion.' Here is an example:

> All X is Y (All philosophers are men)
> All Y is Z (All men are mortals)
> Therefore All X is Z (Therefore all philosophers are mortals)

One term (here Y or men) is common to the two premises, but absent from the conclusion; the other terms (X and Z, philosophers and mortals) are found in one of the premises and in the conclusion. The term common to the premises is known as the 'middle term'; the others are called 'end terms.'

The rules for valid syllogisms may be simply drawn. First, the syllogism must follow the general form outlined above: three propositions operating on three terms, one of which is common to the premises and the others of which are to be found in one premise and in the conclusion. Second, if both premises affirm, the conclusion must affirm; if one premise denies, the conclusion must deny; if both premises deny, no valid conclusion may be drawn. Third, if one premise is limited in quantity to 'some,' the conclusion must be limited to 'some'; if both premises are limited to 'some,' no conclusion may be drawn. Fourth, the common or 'middle' term must be distributed in at least one premise. And fifth, an 'end' term which is distributed in the conclusion must have been distributed in its premise. If all these rules are kept, the conclusion is an unavoidable one; if any of the rules is breached, the conclusion does not necessarily follow—it is 'invalid.'

If my premises are true ones and my syllogism is valid, my conclusion must be true—it is inescapable. If, on the other hand, one or both of my premises are false, the conclusion may be false, however 'valid' my reasoning with the syllogism. So, if it is true that all philosophers are men and all men are mortal, it is necessarily true that all philosophers are mortal. On the other hand, if it is false that all women are mothers, it may be false that all coeds are mothers, even though it is true that all coeds are women—my conclusion is logically 'valid,' but nonetheless false. In short, this system of logic is a system for making certain that one's conclusions are unavoidable ones—unavoidably true ones if the assumptions or premises with which it starts are true. It is like arithmetic in this respect: if it is true that I have two dollars and get two more dollars, it is true that I have four dollars. If, of course, I did not really have the two dollars to start with, it is not true that I now have four; but the error is not one in arithmetic, but rather one in my arithmetical assumption or premise.

The syllogism has undergone attacks through the centuries as an elaboration of the obvious or a very cumbersome version of 'common sense,' and hence an unnecessary logical instrument. Truly, anybody can see that if all football players are students and all coeds are students, it does not follow that some football players are coeds. But not everyone seems able to see that the following conclusion, from the same syllogistic form, is equally illogical: All communists read Marx; all students in Political Science 105 read Marx; therefore some of the college students are communists. (The fallacy in both cases is the 'fallacy of the undistributed middle term.') And a good deal of the nonsense in contemporary thought results from a lack of training in this valuable logical discipline.

A Puzzling Element in the Notion of Thinking

Usually when we philosophers discuss questions about thinking, we concentrate, for very good reasons, upon what people do or might think; that is, on the opinions that they form, the beliefs that they have, the theories that they construct, the conclusions that they reach and the premisses from which they reach them. In a word, our usual questions are questions about the truths or falsehoods that people do or might accept. Their thoughts, of which we discuss the structures, the implications and the evidential backings, are the results in which their former ponderings and calculations have terminated. For when a person knows or believes that something is the case, his knowledge or belief is something that he now has or possesses, and the pondering which got him there is now over. While he is still wondering and pondering, he is still short of his destination. When he has settled his problem, his task of trying to settle it is finished.

It should not be forgotten that some of the problems that we have to try to settle are not theoretical problems but practical problems. We have to try to decide what to do, as well as try to decide what is the case. The solution of a problem is not always a truth or a falsehood.

We should not assume, either, that all thinking is trying to settle problems, whether theoretical or practical. This would be too restrictive. A person is certainly thinking when he is going over a poem that he knows perfectly, or dwelling on the incidents of yesterday's football match. He has, or need have no problems to solve or results to aim at. Not all of our walks are journeys.

Lastly, we should not assume that all or even most of the truths or false-

From *Proceedings of The British Academy*, Vol. XLIV, 1958, pp. 129–44. Copyright © 1959 by The British Academy. Reprinted by permission of the British Academy and the author.

hoods that are ours are the fruits of our own ponderings. Fortunately and unfortunately, a great part of what we believe and know we have taken over from other people. Most of the things that we know we have not discovered for ourselves, but have been taught. Most of the things that we believe we believe simply because we have been told them. As with worldly goods, so with truths and falsehoods, much of what we possess is inherited or donated.

It is a vexatious fact about the English language that we use the verb 'to think' both for the beliefs or opinions that a man has, and for the pondering and reflecting that a man does; and that we use the noun 'thought' both for the truth or falsehood that he accepts, and for the activity of reflecting which, perhaps, preceded his acceptance of it. To think, in the sense of 'believe,' is not to think, in the sense of 'ponder.' There is only the verbal appearance of a contradiction in saying that while a person is still thinking, he does not yet know what to think; and that when he does know what to think, he has no more thinking to do.

The problems which I wish to discuss are questions not about the propositions that a person does or might believe, but about his activities of pondering, perpending, musing, reflecting, calculating, meditating, and so on. I shall be talking about the thinking which is the travelling and not the being at one's destination; the winnowing and not the grain; the bargaining and not the goods; the work and not the repose.

A person does not have to be advanced in age or highly schooled in order to be able to give satisfactory answers to ordinary interrogations about his thinking. A child who has never heard a word of psychological or philosophical discourse is not in the least embarrassed at being asked what he had been thinking about while sitting in the swing. Indeed, if asked not very long afterwards, he is likely to be quite ready to give a moderately detailed account of the thoughts that he had had, and even perhaps of the rough sequence in which he had had them. The task does not feel to him hugely different from the task of recounting what he had been doing so quietly or so noisily in the nursery or what he had seen and whom he had met during his afternoon walk.

Nonetheless, familiar though we are with the task of recounting our thoughts, we are embarrassed by a quite different task, set to us by the psychologist or the philosopher, the task, namely, of saying what the having of these thoughts had consisted in. I mean this. If during a certain period I had been, say, singing or mending a gate or writing a testimonial, then when recounting afterwards what I had been doing, I could, if required, mention the concrete ingredients of my activity, namely the noises that I had uttered, the hammer-blows that I had struck, and the ink-marks that I had made on the paper. Of course, a mere catalogue of these concrete happenings would not yet amount to an account of what I had been doing. Singing a song is not just uttering one noise after another; the sequence of noises must be a directed sequence. Still, if no noises are made, no song is sung; and if no ink-marks are produced, no testimonial is written. If I recollect singing or writing a testimonial, then I recollect that I made some noises or some ink-marks.

But when I recollect, however clearly, a stretch, however recent, of my musing or pondering, I do not seem to be, in the same way, automatically primed with answers to questions about the concrete ingredients of the thoughts the having of which I have no difficulty in recounting. I tell you, for example, '. . . and then the idea occurred to me that, since it was Sunday, I might not be able to get petrol at the next village.' If now you ask me to say what concrete shape the occurring of this slightly complex idea had taken, I may well be stumped for an answer, so stumped, even, as half to resent the putting of the question.

You might press your irksome question in this way. You say, 'Well, you have just recounted to us in a dozen or more English words the idea that had occurred to you. Did the idea itself occur to you in English words? Does your recollection of the idea occurring to you incorporate the recollection of your saying something to yourself in a dozen or more English words, whether in your head or *sotto voce?* Or, having recently returned from France, did you perhaps say something to the same effect to yourself in a dozen or more French words?' To this very specific question my answer might be, 'Yes; I do now recall saying something to myself in my head, in English words, to the effect that as it was Sunday there might be no petrol available in the next village.' But my answer might be, 'No; I don't recall saying anything to myself at all.' Or my answer might be, 'Well, I'm not absolutely sure that I did not just say "Sunday" in my head, but I'm sure that I did not say anything more.'

Your pertinacity is irritating, since I want to say that it does not really matter whether I said anything to myself or not. Having the idea in question did not require my saying anything to myself, in the way in which singing does require uttering noises and repairing a gate does require *either* hammering *or* wire-tying *or* bolt-tightening *or* something of the same concrete sort.

Ignoring my irritation you now press me with another batch of specific queries. You say, 'If when you had that idea you did not say anything to yourself in your head or *sotto voce,* then was it that instead you saw some things in your mind's eye? Was it that you had mental pictures blurred or sharp, well coloured or ill coloured, maybe of villagers entering a village church, and of a garage with its doors closed; so that it was in this concrete shape, or something like it, that the idea came to you that since it was Sunday you might not be able to get petrol?' Again I might answer, 'Yes, I did visualize scenes like this.' But I might answer, 'No, I am sure that I did not visualize anything.' Or I might answer, 'Well, I do remember seeing in my mind's eye the duck-pond of the village in question: I usually do when I think of that village. But this had nothing to do with the special idea that the garage there might be closed for Sunday.' Once again I might be irked at the question being pressed at all. Why should my thinking the thought have gone with either the saying of something to myself or with the seeing of something in my mind's eye or with any other proprietary happenings?

There are, however, certain special thinking-activities which certainly do seem to require our saying things in our heads or *sotto voce* or aloud, and we need to examine what there is about these special activities which requires the inward or outward production of words and phrases.

(*a*) If I have been trying to compose a poem or an after-dinner speech, then I must indeed have been producing to myself words and phrases, examining them, cancelling or improving them, assembling them and rehearsing assemblages of them. That is, if my thinking happens to be a piece of thinking what to say and how to say it, then it must incorporate the tentative, exploratory, and critical saying of things to myself; and then, if asked to recount in retrospect whether I had been saying things to myself in English or in French, I should answer without hesitation. There is here no question of my first thinking out my poem or my speech, and only then, in reply to posthumous interrogations, putting my composition into words. The thinking was itself a piece of word-hunting, phrase-concocting, and sentence-mending. It was thinking *up* words, phrases and sentences.

(*b*) If I have been doing a slightly complex piece of computation, whether in my head or on paper, like multiplying £13 12*s*. 4*d*. by 7, then not only must my answer, if I obtain one, be a numerical or worded formula, £95 6*s*. 4*d*., perhaps, but also the results of the interim multiplying-operations, dividing-operations, and adding-operations will be numbers. What I say to myself in my head, if I do the sum in my head, will parallel the things that I should write down one after another, if I worked the sum out on paper, and these will be numbers of pounds, shillings, or pence. If asked afterwards whether I had, at a certain stage, said to myself 'Seven twelves are eighty-four, plus two, makes eighty-six' or whether I had in my mind's eye seen the corresponding numerals, or both together, I might recollect just which I had done; and I should not feel irked at the suggestion that I must have done one or the other. Certainly, multiplying does not consist merely in saying numbers aloud or in our heads; but we are ready to allow that it requires this, or some alternative, in the same sort of way as singing a song requires, though it does not reduce to, the uttering of noises. Trying to get the correct answer, unlike just making a guess at it, involves trying to establish checkable intermediate steps, in order to make the correct moves from those steps to the right answer; and these steps, to be checkable, must be formulated.

(c) Some kinds of problems, like those of advocates, debaters, and philosophers, have something in common with the task of composition and something in common with the task of computation. The thinker has, all the time, both to be trying to find out what to say and how to say it, and also to be trying to establish as true what he says. He wants his hearers —including himself—not only to understand what he says but also to accept it, and to accept it perforce. As his task is, in two dimensions, a forensic task, his thinking involves him in producing and canvassing, in however sketchy a manner, words, phrases, and sentences, conclusions, reasons, and rebuttals of objections.

Now if, improvidently, we pick on one of these three special varieties of thinking as our universal model, we shall be tempted to say, as Plato said, that 'in thinking the soul is conversing [or perhaps 'debating'] with herself,' and so postulate that any piece of meditating or pondering whatsoever has got, so to speak, to run on the wheels of words, phrases, and sentences.

Or, if forced by our own reminiscences to allow that sometimes we have thoughts when no wording of these thoughts takes place, we may then be tempted simply to give to the model one extension and postulate that in thinking the soul is *either* conversing with itself *or else* performing some one specific alternative to conversing, such as visualizing things. In either case we are presupposing that thinking, of whatever sort, must, so to speak, employ a concrete apparatus of some specifiable kind or other, linguistic or pictorial or something else. This general presupposition is sometimes formulated in the following way. Just as an Englishman who has become perfectly familiar with the French language may say that he can now think in French, so, and in the same sense of 'in,' he must always think either 'in' his native English or else 'in' some alternative apparatus, like French or visual imagery or algebraical symbols or gestures or something else that he can produce, on demand, from his own resources. The generic term 'symbol' is sometimes used to cover all the postulated vehicles of thinking. It is a psychological necessity, or perhaps even a part of the very concept of thinking, that when thinking occurs, there occur, internally or externally, things or symbols that the thinker thinks in.

It is if we make this presupposition that we are especially embarrassed at being required to tell in retrospect in what symbols (in this awkwardly distended use of the word) we had, for example, the idea that as it was Sunday there might be no petrol available at the next village. For often we cannot recollect any such vehicles being present on the occasion when, as we clearly do recollect, we had that thought.

I want to attack this presupposition. I want to deny that it even makes sense to ask, in the general case, what special sort or sorts of things we think *in*. The very collocation of 'think' with 'in so and so' seems to me factitious, save in our very special case of the Englishman who describes himself as now being able to think in French. So let us clear his case out of the way.

The primary thing that he means when he says that he now thinks in French is that when he has to talk to Frenchmen, he does not any longer have to think out how to say in French what he wants to say. He no longer, for example, has first to say to himself in English what he wants to say, and then to struggle to translate from English into French for the benefit of his French audience. The composition of French remarks is no longer any more difficult for him than the composition of English remarks, that is, it is not difficult at all. But to say that he no longer has to think out how to say things in French has not the slightest tendency to show that all or most of the thoughts that he thinks are now accompanied or 'carried' by the production of French words. It is only to say that *when he is conversing with Frenchmen* he does not have to think about the vehicles of this conversing. When he does have to compose in French he does not have to think *up* French words. But most of the things he thinks about are not matters of French composition, just as most of the things we think about are not matters of English composition. Roughly, he thinks in French when he says what he wants to say in French without any groping or fumbling.

Secondarily, when he says that he now thinks in French, he may also mean that *when* he debates matters with himself he conducts these debates in French without wondering how to put his points in French; and, more generally, that *when* he converses with himself in internal monologue he does this in French without having to consider how to say in French what he wants to say. Even so, to describe him as thinking in French, because what he says to himself he says effortlessly in French, is to put a new strain on the phrase 'thinking in,' under which it did not labour in our primary use of the phrase 'to think in French.' One never does ask it, but *could* one ask a friend who has been deliberating what to do whether he had been deliberating in English? If we did ask him this, I suspect that he would reply that while he had said or half-said a lot of things to himself in English, this had not been any part of his deliberating. He had not deliberated *by means of* saying things to himself, any more than the proof-corrector searches for misprints *by means of* putting marks in the margins of the galley-proof.

But anyhow, what is true of his debatings and conversings, whether with

Frenchmen or with himself, need not be true of his thinkings which are done when no debating or conversing is done. The phrases 'in French' and 'in English' do attach natively to verbs of saying; it does not follow that they attach to verbs of thinking, unless the thinking happens to be thinking what to say or how to say it.

Strained though it may be, save in the one special context, to speak of a person thinking in French or in English, it is worse than strained to speak of him as thinking in, say, mental pictures. Certainly it is true, not of all people, but of many, when thinking about certain sorts of matters, though not of all, that they see things in their mind's eyes, and even that their ability to solve some of their problems is tied up, somehow, with their ability to visualize clearly. Doubtless, some chess-players can think out chess-problems in their heads, if and only if they can visualize chess-situations clearly and steadily.

Consider this case of the would-be solver of a chess-problem. First let us provide him with a chess-board and the requisite chess-men. He disposes the pieces in their proper places and then, with his eyes fixed on the board and his fingers moving piece after piece, he tries to think out the solution to his problem. Are we to say that the thinking that he is doing is done 'in' pieces of ivory or 'in' the experimental moves that he makes with these pieces of ivory? Clearly, there is no place for the word 'in' here. He is thinking *about* the pieces; he is thinking out what they could and could not do or suffer if moved elsewhere or if kept where they are.

But now suppose that we refuse to provide him with a chess-board, so that he has to tackle his task entirely in his head. The chess-problem itself that he has to solve is exactly the same as before; but he is now confronted with an extra set of tasks which he had not had to cope with before. He has, among other things, to remember, at each given moment, exactly where each of the pieces is, whereas previously he just looked and saw where it was. He is like the hostess who can see which of her guests is sitting next to which until the light fails; then she has to remember their positions. This remembering may be preceded by the labour of trying to remember; or she may not have to try. She may just remember. Now if the chess-player has to struggle to remember the positions of his pieces, this struggling could obviously not be described as involving the employment of mental pictures of their positions. He struggles because he cannot yet remember and therefore cannot yet see in his mind's eye how the pieces had been disposed. If in the course of this struggling alternative possible dispositions are pictured, still these, if wrong, have to be scrapped. They are not the vehicles but the boss-shots of the thinking. Conversely, when, after struggling to remember the positions of the pieces, the chess-player does remember, then his seeing them in his mind's eye, if he does do this, is not something by means of which he gets himself to remember. It is the goal, not a vehicle of his struggle to remember. *A fortiori,* if he remembers without having to try to remember, then his mental picture of the positions of the pieces is not something that he thought *in* or *with* or *on,* since he did not have to think at all.

Certainly this chess-player has to *use his memory* in trying to solve the chess-problem in his head, where he had not had to use his memory when he had had the board in front of him. But this is not at all the same thing as to say that he *uses his memory-images* in trying to solve the problem in his head. If we hanker still to reserve some special sense for the phrase 'using images,' this will be very different from the sense of the verb in which we speak of someone using such and such French words when speaking to Frenchmen. That we cannot talk French without using French words is a dull truism; that some people cannot solve chess-problems in their heads without, in some sense, using mental pictures may be true, but it is not a logicians' truism.

So now we seem to be farther off than ever from achieving what we thought that we wanted, namely to nominate some reasonably concrete stuff to be the peculiar apparatus of all of our thinkings.

No singing without noises, no testimonial-writing without ink-marks, no thinking without . . ., but we can nominate no proprietary things or sets of things to fill this gap. Indeed, we have, I hope, become suspicious of the very attempt to assimilate in this way thinking with these other special activities, which do possess their own proprietary implements or materials.

We may be tempted to postpone the evil day by suggesting that thinking differs from singing and testimonial-writing just because its proprietary stuff is a very peculiar stuff, more transparent and more shapeless than jelly-fishes, more scentless than the most scentless gases, and more uncapturable than rainbows. Perhaps its stuff is the stuff that dreams are made of, mental or spiritual stuff, and that is why it slips through our retrospective sieves. But we are soon brought to our senses if we remind ourselves that our own neighbours' very ordinary children, Tommy and Clara, make no more bones about recounting the thoughts that they have had than in recounting the games that they have played or the incidents that they have witnessed. They seem to need no esoteric instructions in order to be able to tell us of the ideas that have come to them or the thinking that they have done. In a way these are the most domestic and everyday sorts of things that there could be. The seeming mysteriousness of thinking derives from some sophisticated theoretical presuppositions, presuppositions which induce us, though only when theorizing, to try to squeeze out of our reminiscences or our introspections some evasive but pervasive drop of something, some psychic trace-element the presence of which, in bafflingly minute doses, is required if thinking is to occur. Yet Tommy and Clara, who were never told of any such psychic trace-element, describe their think- ings in ways which we understand perfectly; nor, when we tell them of the thoughts that crossed Cinderella's mind as she sat among the ashes, do we employ a strange parachemical vocabulary.

Now let us drop, for the time being, the attempt to find a filling or a set of alternative fillings for the gap in the slogan 'No thinking without such and such' and consider a different, though connected, problem.

When a person, who has been for a short or a long time musing or pondering, is asked what he had been thinking about, he can usually, though not quite always, give a seemingly complete and definite answer. All sorts of answers are allowable; for example, that he had been thinking about his father, or about the next General Election, or about the possibility of getting his annual holiday early, or about yesterday's football match, or how to answer a letter. What he has been thinking about may or may not be, or contain, a problem. We can ask him whether he had decided how to answer the letter and if so what his decision was. But his thoughts about yesterday's football match may have been entirely uninterrogative. He was thinking it over, but not trying to think anything out. His thinking termi- nated in no results; it aimed at none. Now though, normally, the thinker can give a seemingly complete and definite answer to the question What had he been thinking about?, he can very often be brought to acknowledge that he had had in mind things which, at the start, it had not occurred to him to mention. To take a simple instance. A rowing enthusiast says that he had been thinking about the Oxford University crew; and if asked bluntly, would deny that he had at that moment been thinking about the Cambridge crew. Yet it might transpire that his thought about the Oxford crew was, or included, the thought that though it was progressing, it was not progressing fast enough. 'Not fast enough for what?' we ask. 'Not fast enough to beat Cambridge next Saturday.' So he had been thinking about the Cambridge crew, only thinking about it in a sort of threshold way. Or I ask a tired visitor from London what he has been thinking about. He says, 'Just about the extraordinary peacefulness of your garden.' If asked, 'Than what do you find it so much more peaceful?' he replies, 'Oh, London, of course.' So in a way he was thinking not only of my garden but of London, though he would not, without special prompting, have said for himself that he had had London in mind at all. Or my visitor says, 'How lovely your roses are,' and then sighs. Why does he sigh? May he not, in a marginal way, be thinking of his dead wife who had been particularly fond of roses? —though he himself would have said, if asked, that he was only thinking about my roses. He does not say to me or to himself, 'Roses—her favourite flower.' But roses are, for him, her favourite flower. The thought of them is an incipient thought of her.

Take one more case. I ask the schoolboy what he is thinking about, and he says that he had been trying to think what 8×17 makes. On further questioning it turns out that his total task is to multiply £9 17s. 4d. by 8, and that at that particular moment he had got to the 17s. So I ask him wheher he had forgotten the 2s. 8d. that he had got when multiplying the 4d. by 8; and now he says that he had not forgotten this; indeed he was keeping the 2s. in mind ready to add to his shillings column. So, in a way, his thought was not totally filled by the problem of multiplying 17×8. The thought of the total multiplication task was, in a controlling though background way, built into his interim, but foreground task of multiplying 17×8. For it was not just 17, but the seventeen shillings of the £9 17s. 4d. that he was then engaged in multiplying by 8. He would have gone on from the shillings to the pounds if I had not interrupted.

It was not that my widowed visitor just *forgot* and had to be reminded that he had been thinking about his wife as well as about the roses, but that his task of telling just what he had had in mind was in some important ways totally unlike the task of trying to recall, say, just how many telephone calls he had made during the morning. The difference between merely thinking how fine these roses are and thinking how she would have admired them is not like the difference between having made eleven and having made twelve telephone calls, namely a difference in the number of happenings to be recorded. Recounting one's thoughts is not like turning back to an earlier page and trying to give an exhaustive inventory of the items one rediscovers there. The question whether or not the Cambridge crew had been in the rowing-enthusiast's mind was not one that he could settle by racking his brains to recollect a bygone fleeting something. In our example it was settled in quite a different way, namely by asking him what the rate of progress of the Oxford crew had seemed to him inadequate for. When he acknowledges that he had been, in a threshold way, thinking of the Cambridge crew, one thing that he does not say is 'Ah yes, your question *reminds* me that the Cambridge crew was in my thoughts after all.' He had not been reminded of a forgotten item but shown how his account of his thought had been an incomplete account. He had failed to indicate part of its internal tenor.

Reporting one's thoughts is not a matter of merely chronicling the items of a procession of quick-fading internal phenomena. If we can pick out any such phenomena and record them, our record of them is not yet a statement of the drift or content of a piece of thinking. The way in which the widower's thinking of the roses was, in a way, thinking about his wife is not that during the time that he was thinking about the roses there occurred one or two very fleeting wafts of recollections of his wife. Such wafts do occur, but it was not them that he was acknowledging when he acknowledged that in thinking of the roses he had been incipiently thinking of his wife.

Rather, he had thought of the roses *as* her favourite flower; in the way in which the rowing-enthusiast had thought of the progress of the Oxford crew *as* insufficient to beat Cambridge; or in the way in which the schoolboy had thought of the 17 that he was multiplying by 8 *as* the 17*s*. to be dealt with after the 4*d*. and before the £9.

What, then, is the virtue of this 'as,' which makes a young man's thought of next Thursday *as* his 21st birthday different from his mother's thought of next Thursday *as* early-closing day for Oxford shops?

We can approach at least a part of the answer in this way. Sometimes we deliberately advise people to think of something *as* so and so. For instance, when giving a child his very first explanation of what a map is, we might tell him to think of the map of Berkshire *as* a photograph taken from an aeroplane very high up over the middle of Berkshire. This may already lead him to expect to find big things showing on the map, like towns, rivers, highroads, and railways, but not very small things like people, motor-cars, or bushes. A little later he enquires, in perplexity, what the contour-lines are which wriggle so conspicuously along and around the Berkshire Downs. We tell him to think of them *as* high-water marks left by the sea, which had risen to drown even the highest parts of the county. This flood, he is to suppose, subsided exactly fifty feet every night, leaving a high-water mark each time. So a person walking along one high-water mark would remain all the time at the same height above the normal level of the sea; and he would all the time be 100 feet higher than someone else who was following the next high-water mark but one below him. Quite likely the child could now work out for himself why the contour-lines are closely packed on the side of a steep hill and widely separated on a gradual incline.

Getting him to think of the map as a photograph taken from very high up, and of the contour-lines as high-water marks makes it natural or at least quite easy for him to think further thoughts for himself. It is to implant the germs of these further thoughts into his initially sterile thoughts about the map. If there was no follow-up, however embryonic and whether in the desired direction or any other, then he had not thought of the map as a photograph or of the contours as high-water marks. To describe someone as thinking of something as so and so is to say of him, at least *inter alia,* that it would be natural or easy for him to follow up this thought in some particular direction. His thinking had those prospects, that trend in it. It should be noticed that what thinking of something as so and so leads naturally or easily into may be subsequent thinkings, but it may equally well be subsequent doings. The golf-professional who tells me to think of my driver not as a sledge-hammer but as a rope with a weight on the end, expects me to cease to bang at the ball and to begin to sweep smoothly

Martin Joos (1907–   )

From *The Five Clocks*

Ballyhough railway station has two clocks which disagree by some six minutes. When one helpful Englishman pointed the fact out to a porter, his reply was 'Faith, sir, if they was to tell the same time, why would we be having two of them?'

NY CLOCKS

more than one kind of English is likely to be in use at the same time ce is a notorious fact. So is sex, for that matter, or the weather. accommodations to those facts are not equally realistic. We have derstood that evolution has so shaped our planet's flora and fauna iculture is best served by fluctuating weather and cyclical seasons. great deal more effort, we are coming to understand that sex is stay and may even have a sort of survival-value—that its seasons agaries may conceivably be essential to the business of being human. ago taught to give weather its highest praise by calling it 'season- e have been learning recently to treat sex with the same respect for he intellectual gain is great, however few may value it. Much some say, is the profit that comes from not sending children into d with useless burdens of guilt.

h-usage guilt-feelings have not yet been noticeably eased by the linguistic scientists, parallel to the work done by the psychiatrists. our custom unhesitatingly and unthinkingly to demand that the language all be set to Central Standard Time. And each normal

e Five Clocks, by Martin Joos, Bloomington, Indiana, Publication 22 of the University Research Center in Anthropology, Folklore, and Linguistics; also the *International Journal of Linguistics,* Vol. 28, No. 2 (1962). Copyright, Martin Joos. Reprinted by arrangement with the author.

through the ball. The parent who gets his child to think of policemen not as enemies but as friends gets him not only to think certain consequential thoughts but also to go to policemen for help when lost.

A person who thinks of something as something is, *ipso facto,* primed to think and do some particular further things; and this particular possible future that his thinking paves the way for needs to be mentioned in the description of the particular content of that thinking—somewhat as the mention of where the canal goes to has to be incorporated in our account of what this adjacent canal-stretch is. Roughly, a thought comprises what it is incipiently, namely what it is the natural vanguard of. Its burthen embodies its natural or easy sequel.

There are other things as well which are, in partly similar ways, constitutionally inceptive. To lather one's chin is to prepare to wield one's razor. Here the vanguard act is an intentional or even deliberate preparation for the future act. We had to learn thus to pave the way for shaving. To brace oneself is to get ready to jump or resist at the next moment; but this inceptive movement is not normally intentional or the result of training; it is instinctive. The tenors that our thoughts possess are similarly sometimes the products of training; but often not. In all cases alike, however, the description of an inceptive act requires the prospective specification of its due or natural sequel. Notice that its due or natural sequel may not actually come about. Having lathered my chin, I may be called to the telephone; and the dog, having braced himself, may be reassured or shot. We must employ the future tense in our description of the inceptive act, but we must hedge this future tense with some 'unlesses.'

At first sight we may suspect the presence of a circularity in the description of something as essentially the foreshadowing of its own succession. But this feature, without any air of circularity, belongs also to our descriptions of promises, precautions, threats and betrothals, and even of nightfalls, thaws and germinations. There could be no complete description of such things which was not proleptic. However, our special case seems to be in a worse plight since I am saying that a piece of thinking of something as something is natively inceptive of, *inter alia,* subsequent thinkings in a way in which a thaw is not the inception of another thaw, or a nightfall the beginning of another nightfall.

So here we are reminded, if not of circles, at least of the verse:

Big fleas have little fleas upon their backs to bite 'em,
Little fleas have lesser fleas and so *ad infinitum.*

But is this reminder disconcerting? Were we not already aware in our bones of just such a feature of thinking, namely that any attempt to catch a particular thought tends to develop into an attempt to catch up with something further? Our story of a particular piece of thinking seems in the nature of the case to terminate in nothing stronger than a semi-colon. It is not incidental to thoughts that they belong to trains of thought.

Now maybe we can begin to see the shape of the answers to both of our two dominant questions. We can begin to see why it is that the narrative of a piece of my thinking cannot be merely the chronicling of actual, monitored happenings 'in my head.' For the content of the thinking comprised its tenor and to describe its particular tenor is prospectively to mention its natural or easy sequels.

But also we can begin to see why we cannot, and do not in our heart of hearts wish to reserve for our thinkings any peculiar concrete stuff, apparatus, or medium, *X*, such that we can say, 'As no singing without noises, so no thinking without *X*.' For adverting to anything whatsoever can be what puts a person, at a particular moment, in mind of something or other. The motorist in the last village but one before home may think of the petrol-station alongside of him *as* being possibly the last place for buying petrol on a Sunday. The widower thinks of my roses that he is gazing at as being of the sort of which she was so fond. The schoolboy thinks of the number 17 that his eye is on as the 17*s*. in the total of £9 17*s*. 4*d*. that he has to multiply by eight. The poet thinks of the word 'annihilating' that crops up in a conversation as a candidate for the gap in his half-composed couplet. The housewife thinks of next Thursday as the day when she will not be able to shop in Oxford after lunch, while her son thinks of it as the day when he comes of age. We could stretch our slogan, if we hanker for a slogan, to read 'No thinking without adverting to something or other, no matter what,' but then it would be as empty as the slogans 'no eating without food,' 'no building without materials' and 'no purchases without commodities.'

However, the very vacuousness of our new slogan 'no thinking without adverting to something or other, no matter what' has a certain tension-relieving effect. From the start we felt, I hope, a gnawing uneasiness at the very programme of treating thinking as a special, indeed a very special activity, special in the way in which singing is one special activity and gardening is a battery of other special activities. For while there certainly are lots of special kinds or brands of thinking, such as computing, sonnet-composing, anagram-solving, philosophizing, and translating, still thinking is not an activity in which we are engaged only when we are *not* singing, writing testimonials, gardening, and so on. Thinking is not a rival occupation to these special occupations, in the sense that our time has to be parcelled out between them and thinking, in the way in which our time does have to be parcelled out between golf and gardening, between testimonial-writing and lecturing, between anagram-solving and chess-playing, and so on. For

we have to be thinking if we are to be singing w— monial, or gardening efficiently. Certainly, we h— sums or anagrams in our heads while singing o— because we had better be thinking how to perfo— singing or lecturing. We had unwittingly sold th— start, when we asked ourselves, in effect, 'Given — certain sort, is what goes to make singing the pr— it is, what is it that, analogously, makes thinking th— that it is?' The verbal noun 'thinking' does not, a— all along, denote a special or proprietary activit— 'singing' does. Thinking is not one department in — that we can ask What line of goods does it pr— goods does it, *ex officio, not* provide? Its proper — ments—that is, there is no particular place which— there are no particular places which are not its prope—

If we had worded our original programme by — and what proprietary apparatus are reserved for t/— should have seen through this question straightawa— use our wits wherever and whenever we should— no field or department of human activity or exp— say 'Here people can use their fingers, their n— their golf-clubs, but not their wits.' Or if we ha— tion by asking 'In what special medium or with— is our use of our wits conducted?,' we should ha— tion too. We swim in water, we sing in noises, w— but using our wits is not a co-ordinate specia— counterpart medium, material, or implements. F— in swimming, singing, hammering, or in anyth— not suggest that the idiom of *using one's wits* i— idiom of *thinking*. There is an element of congra— of someone as having used his wits, an elemen— place, for example, in talking of my widower's— wife's favourite flower. None the less, if we reali— to try to isolate out a proprietary activity of usin— field for it, we realize why it actually was absu— proprietary activity of thinking and a reserved field—

Why do we not require our schools to give se— as they do give separate lessons in computing, t— cricket? The answer is obvious. It is because all — are lessons in thinking. Yet they are not lesso— same time.

American is taught thoroughly, if not to keep accurate time, at least to feel ashamed whenever he notices that a clock of his is out of step with the English Department's tower-clock. Naturally he avoids looking aloft when he can. Then his linguistic guilt hides deep in his subconscious mind and there secretly gnaws away at the underpinnings of his public personality. Freud or Kinsey may have strengthened his private self-respect, but in his social life he is still in uneasy bondage to the gospel according to Webster as expounded by Miss Fidditch.

Shall the porter speak up? Well, it isn't likely to do much good this year. But the porter is a sort of Court Fool and won't lose his job for speaking up once. And if enough of us speak up, travelers may learn to read clocks with more sympathy and self-respect.

The Ballyhough situation was simple. But English, like national languages in general, has five clocks. And the times that they tell are not simply earlier and later; they differ sidewise too, and in several directions. Naturally. A community has a complex structure, with variously differing needs and occasions. How could it scrape along with only one pattern of English usage? (Webster, of course!—Well, . . .)

It would be very little better served with a single range of usages, differing along the length of a single scale. And yet our public theory of English is all laid out along just such a single yardstick. (Webster is one Webster, and Miss Fidditch is his prophet.)

We have not yet learned to speak of English as we speak of the weather and agriculture, and as we are slowly learning to speak of sex and survival. In the school folklore called 'grammar' for lack of effective challenge—a sort of numerology taught in high-schools instead of algebra, an astrology masquerading as astronomy in our colleges—we are bound to speak of English usage only in a simplistic way, like a proper Victorian maiden lady speaking of Men.

Ask a normal citizen to compare 'if they was to tell the same time' with 'if they were to tell the same time' and he will check by Miss Fidditch's tape: 'Bad, fair, good, better, best = Correct.' And that's about all. Oh yes; he will deplore the conditions which prevail, he will mutter that he too has sinned and fallen short of Webster, and he will be worried about his son's English. Then he will wander off into spelling-reform and Communism.

But now if you press him for a program, he will suggest installing a master-clock system. He will promise to speak up in the next P.T.A. meeting for more and better grammar teaching, like they had in Webster's day. What he doesn't know is that he himself has two English-usage clocks as adequately adjusted as any railroadman's watch, for use on different occasions, plus three others that are more or less reliable depending on his experiences and the distances to his horizons. And he will be baffled by your lunacy if you casually say what linguists know: That he built and adjusted those clocks himself, with less help than hindrance from schooling.

What he does know is that his usage varies, as he thinks. The fact is that his several usages do not vary enough to matter, any one of them. They alternate with each other, like his pajamas and overalls and committee-meeting suit, each tailored so as not to bind and so that he finds the pockets without looking. And he has one master-clock to tell him when to change. (Tsk tsk! Mixed metaphor!—Pray for me, Miss F.)

Then, when he happens to notice that the garments differ, he parrots her appraisals of better and worse. Finally he pleads 'No contest,' on the theory that he was surely wrong every time—that correctness is for teachers, who have the word from Webster. (Where did Webster get it from?—Excuse me, I'm busy.)

Bad, fair, good, better, best. Only the best is Correct. No busy man can be Correct. But his wife can. That's what women are for. That's why we have women to teach English and type our letters and go to church for us and discover for us that the English say 'Aren't I?' while we sinfully hunt golf balls in the rough on Sunday, and, when our partner finds two of them, ask 'which is me?' (Webster: colloq.—Professor K of Harvard: I speak colloq myself, and sometimes I write it.)

Only the porter . . . Only a few of us today are aware of the other scales of English usage. It is our business to consciously know about their social utility. We have to say 'consciously,' for, beneath their cant, the members of the community are unconsciously familiar with those other values: that is, in fact, what it means to 'be a member of' a community. The un-aware familiarity is what makes the values effective and gives the individual his profit from them. The kids know that; that's why they don't listen to Miss Fidditch—they have their eye on the main chance. (Where does it say how to sweet-talk in French?—Who cares! She's [He's] American.)

Must usages differ? We might as well ask whether quadrupeds must have four legs and snakes have none. Each question is meaningful—to a believer in Original Sin. A scout from Mars would ask no such questions. He would take each usage as belonging to a current stage in a continuing evolution. And he would not confuse his research with a Golden-Age myth or a Progress theory—nor with a World-is-going-to-the-dogs fallacy either.

His basic research assumption would be: Since usage differences call for efforts to keep them under control, there must be rewards for the efforts. They must have survival-values. Then he would set about tabulating differ-ences, efforts, and values. Rather soon, he would examine how the young advance toward better control and improved chances of survival. Example: 'Hi, Toots!'—'Don't be such a goof!' (Quiet there, Miss F. These are people preparing for examinations.)

Efforts and values are never perfectly in equilibrium. That is why usages change: they are constantly being readjusted to make up for the constant erosion that washes out the profits. In one word, a classical instance of homeostasis—a term which our scout learned at home on Mars from medical research and found useful in describing his native culture. Catabolism and metabolism. When you assume a fixed position, you're dead. Dead as Caesar or a Siberian mammoth. Or Webster.

When too many people had abandoned 'Ain't I?' we promptly used the tar-brush on 'Pleased to meet you.' To a social animal, the question of first importance always is 'What group am I in?' The second question is 'How do I stand within the group?' Only third are the message transactions, namely 'How are things changing within my group?' A poor fourth is 'How's the weather?'—matters of information. Fifth (earlier only for pedants) is 'How does my group rank among other groups?'—with respect to language usage, this is 'correctness.'

Among other things—among a great many others!—the scout from Mars must examine the match-up between the bad-to-best scale of English usage and the parallel scales of occasions, of moods, and of men. It would be foolish to assume in advance that they are just bad-to-best men. (You mean that the Good Guys don't always flaunt Webster and the Bad Guys don't always flout Webster?—Precisely.)

Our scout's report would contain a footnote pointing out that 'bad' is a word also used for an inedible egg, and that 'bad egg' is a personal epithet; also that 'the best butter' occurs in the literature. His chapter on the bad-to-best scale could be a fascinating one. But we have no right to assume that it would be the longest chapter, or the most important one in the scout's view. By trying hard to be as objective as a man from Mars, let's see how close we can come to reconstructing his report.

And Webster?—Complete in his Appendix. But we don't need to reprint it because it's in the Museum of Natural History. Or we could ask Miss Fidditch. We probably will anyhow.

II
HOW MANY CLOCKS?

Here are, in order of importance, four of the usage-scales of native central English:

AGE	STYLE	BREADTH	RESPONSIBILITY
senile	frozen	genteel	best
mature	formal	puristic	better
teenage	consultative	standard	good
child	casual	provincial	fair
baby	intimate	popular	bad

These four scales are essentially independent; relations among them are not identities. (But isn't the best English genteel?—That must be Miss Fidditch talking.)

AGE: The frame within which all other scales develop. Though this is the most important of them all, we shall have very little to say about the age-scale of usage because nothing can be done about it directly, and that little will have to wait to near the end.

STYLE: Here are the five clocks to which we shall principally devote our attention. They may be called 'higher' and 'lower' for convenience in referring to the tabulation; but that doesn't mean anything like relative superiority. More later.

BREADTH: This scale measures breadth of experience and of self-limitation. From popular English up to standard English, your experiences broaden your usages; and from there up to genteel you narrow them again to suit your personality. Nothing further.

RESPONSIBILITY: Here at last is the actual usage-scale nearest to Miss Fidditch's mythical scale of excellence, and we borrow her scale-labels but not her meanings for them, eliminating her favorite synonym 'correct' for the top. More immediately.

Much as linguists hate to admit it, the responsibility scale does exist. It even has considerable though minor importance. Its importance is minor because we use it only in forming social clusters, momentary or lasting. If we have done a good job, the cluster is homogeneous on the responsibility scale, which holds it together as a social group. Then we can forget the responsibility-ratings of the group's members, because we are done using them: they are used only in first forming the group or in adding or dropping members. This responsibility scale needs to be cleared out of the way, to prevent confusion, before we consider the five clocks of style.

The reason why linguists dislike acknowledging the responsibility scale is that any acknowledgement of its existence is customarily taken as an endorsement of the 'quality' theory of usage which they of course reject. That quality theory holds that usages are intrinsically good or bad—that each usage is by itself absolutely good or absolutely bad, under a taboo-rule, without inquiring into what good or evil it performs in real life. For example, 'ain't' and 'hisself' are rated as bad English (or 'not English' to make the condemnation stronger by including a self-contradiction in it);

and every essay at discussing their badness counts as an attempt to introduce poison into the water-supply. (What does Webster say? Well, that settles it, doesn't it? I don't see what good it would do to discuss the matter any further.)

Now those linguists are right to a certain extent. 'Ain't I?' has just as respectable an origin as 'Aren't we?'—and, ultimately, a more respectable origin than 'Aren't I?' as it is pronounced by most of those Americans who use it. Again, in view of everybody's 'Myself, ourselves, yourself, yourselves' the bad minority's 'hisself, theirselves' would be more grammatical if logic governed grammar. Yet the origin and the logic don't matter; here the master rule has been known for centuries: Treason doth never prosper; what's the reason? Why, if it prosper, none dare call it treason. In short, the community's choice of what shall count as the norm and what shall be rated as 'bad' (in general, even by those who use it) apparently is an arbitrary choice, so that usage is never good or bad but thinking makes it so.

What, never? There is more to it than that. There is something about social living that creates a responsibility-scale of usage; and when we have examined the natural basis of that scale, we shall see why the folklore calls it a quality scale.

The community's survival depends on cooperation; and adequate cooperation depends on recognizing the more and the less responsible types of persons around us. We need to identify the natural burden-bearers of the community so that we can give them the responsibility which is heaviest of all: we make them responsible for cooperation itself. Then the majority of us can function carefree in our square and round niches, free of the burden of maintaining the cooperation-net which joins us all. Some few of us have a strong interest in cooperation-nets without much competence in them; we are placed as letter-carriers and writers and legislators and teachers and so on; and for those jobs we are selected by tests which discriminate between interest and talent in the maintenance of cooperation.

In any case, the community places us principally by language-use tests which measure us on the various usage scales. Conversely, each of us selects others. For the present, we are interested in just one scale, namely responsibility—a personality scale and a usage scale running quite accurately parallel to each other.

We start very early learning to use this scale. It would be an exceptionally foolish ten-year-old who trusted a well-groomed sharper in preference to a judge in a bathing-suit. And he selects the more responsible person principally by listening, for the same reason that an employer wants an interview with each job-seeker—an interview for which no handbook is needed, for the oral code is public property.

The oral code for responsible personalities is indeed in part arbitrary, conventional: 'himself,' not 'hisself.' But the convention has a natural base, and in a very simple way. Responsible language does not palter. It is explicit. It commits the speaker. The responsible speaker is under a sort of almost morbid compulsion to leave himself no way out of his commitment. The responsibility-dialect does not mumble; its grammar does not contradict itself; its semantics doesn't weasle. That is its basis; 'himself' and the rest are conventional, but they borrow their strength from the natural basis; they are overlays, but the basis is strong enough to overpower the illogicality of 'himself.'

Miss Fidditch's shibboleths are about half conventional overlays. Did she create them? No; the community did, on the theory that birds of a feather flock together. Through some historical accident—some random fluctuation in the distribution of 'himself' and 'hisself' among members of the community—it happened that 'himself' came to be regarded as relatively more common in the responsibility-dialect. It may not have been actually more common there, but the community at large at least thought it was, and that was enough. Flocking did the rest. Those young people who aspired to responsibilities (perhaps only subconsciously aspired) selected 'himself' (normally without awareness of what they were doing or why), while those who aspired to irresponsible lives selected 'hisself' if it was conventionally available to them.

If it was not, they instead selected effete usages. Vulgarity and effeteness use equivalent signals in our culture. Each supplies its fellowship with passwords. For the community at large, the passwords are signals saying 'No responsibilities wanted!' And we take them at their word—for this is part of our communication-system—the more certainly because the whole code works subconsciously.

Miss Fidditch's mistake is in trying to work out the code consciously and logically, instead of simply listening to what clearly responsible people actually say. Sometimes, however, she does listen; and then if she tries to teach what she has learned, and if her more responsible pupils learn to speak that way, Miss Fidditch is apt to imagine that her teaching is what taught them. That is an illusion. Responsibility earns respect; therefore most people (not all!) try for a step higher on the responsibility scale of English usage: simply to earn the respect of others, even irresponsible persons will try this if they don't feel the danger in it. In any case, that is why usages once labeled 'bad' always dwindle and ultimately vanish. Not because Miss Fidditch banned them! The kids aren't listening to her; they listen to Uncle David who is an aviator and to Dr. Henderson, perhaps also to historical and fictional characters if the school is doing its proper job. Miss Fidditch is convinced that bad English is gaining ground; she is only looking for burglars under the bed; statistics says the opposite, item by item. (Don't cry,

Miss Fidditch! Homeostasis will keep up your supply of bad English, never fear!)

Finally, the community prefers the center of the scale: 'good' usage, not 'best.' It routinely rejects morbidly honest candidates for office, and the best English counts as the disqualification that makes a teacher.

III
INFORMAL CLOCKS

Now for the Five Clocks that will concern us for the rest of this occasion —the five styles duly tabulated and numbered on page 286. With a single exception, there is no law requiring a speaker to confine himself to a single style for one occasion; in general, he is free to shift to another style, perhaps even within the sentence. But normally only two neighboring styles are used alternately, and it is anti-social to shift two or more steps in a single jump, for instance from casual to formal. When the five styles have been separately and comparatively described, the details of shifting will be obvious.

We begin with 'good standard mature consultative style' because the readers of this report are presumably best at home there. The community itself, though its average age is in the 'mature' bracket, is best at home in the completely central 'good standard teenage consultative style,' used for replanning baseball and other matters of moment. To add to the confusion, your reporter is writing good standard mature formal style, with many borrowings from the consultative and casual styles, plus shreds and patches of frozen style placed with honest care.

On the next page there is a long sample of good standard mature consultative style. We know that it is genuine: it was recorded from a telephone line. Here it is copied from *The Structure of English,* by Charles Carpenter Fries (Harcourt, Brace, 1952), with fictitious names used for smoothness instead of giving only initials as in the book. One speaker's words are in italics. Quoting Fries: 'These oral reactions on the hearer's part do not interfere with the continuous flow of utterances of the speaker. They simply serve to give something of the hearer's reaction and to signal the fact that he is listening attentively to the speaker.' In face-to-face consultation, some of these may be silent, consisting of nods and smiles and the like; but it is clear that the audible ones were not invented recently for telephone use, since they can all be documented from earlier printed books. In a lively conversation the total number of listener's insertions, audible and silent together, is likely to be much greater than what we find here, and the audible ones alone perhaps roughly as many as here, that is to say about one every six seconds.

I wanted to tell you one more thing I've been talking with Mr. Da-
2 fis in the purchasing department about our typewriters *yes* that
order went in March seventh however it seems that we are about
4 eighth on the list *I see* we were up about three but it seems that
for that type of typewriter we're about eighth that's for a four-
6 teen-inch carriage with pica type *I see* now he told me that
Royce's have in stock the fourteen-inch carriage typewriters
8 with elite type *oh* and elite type varies sometimes it's quite
small and sometimes it's almost as large as pica *yes I know* he
10 suggested that we go down and get Mrs. Royce and tell her who
we are and that he sent us and try the fourteen-inch typewriters
12 and see if our stencils would work with such type *I see* and if we
can use them to get them right away because they have those in
14 stock and we won't have to wait *that's right* we're short one
typewriter right now as far as having adequate facilities for the
16 staff is concerned *yes* we're short and we want to get rid of
those rentals *that's right* but they are expecting within two weeks
18 or so to be receiving . . . ah . . . to start receiving their orders on
eleven-inch machines with pica type *oh* and of course pica type
20 has always been best for our stencils *yes* but I rather think there
might be a chance that we can work with elite type *well you go*
22 *over and try them and see what they're like and do that as soon*
as you can so that we'll not miss our chance at these

Consultative style is the easiest kind of English to describe, though that
doesn't matter so much because we're not going to write its grammar here.
Still, a few remarks may not be amiss. We see that 'we won't' [14] and 'we'll
not' [23] are not synonymous: in the latter, 'will' is not negatived but only
the following words are, so that the message is 'we'll surely get our chance
at these.' We can see that 'oh' [8, 19] acknowledges receipt of new information, 'I see' [4, 6, 12] certifies that it has been understood, 'yes' [2, 16, 20]
approves the other's understanding of the situation, and 'that's right' [14, 17]
approves the other's decision. Such differences in meaning are so important
in consultation that even face to face the listener's contributions will not remain entirely silent.

The two defining features of consultative style are: (1) The speaker supplies background information—he does not assume that he will be understood without it—such information as 'elite type varies' [8]. (2) The addressee
participates continuously. Because of these two features, consultative style
is our norm for coming to terms with strangers—people who speak our
language but whose personal stock of information may be different.

But treating the listener as a stranger is hard work in the long run; therefore we sooner or later try to form a social group with him. Our most power-

ful device for accomplishing this is the use of casual style. Casual style is for friends, acquaintances, insiders; addressed to a stranger, it serves to make him an insider simply by treating him as an insider. Negatively, there is absence of background information and no reliance on listeners' participation. This is not rudeness; it pays the addressee the compliment of supposing that he will understand without those aids. On the positive side, we have two devices which do the same job directly: (1) ellipsis, and (2) slang, the two defining features of casual style.

The term 'slang' is used here in a strict sense, not in the loose popular sense which makes it a term of condemnation for anything and everything in language which is discountenanced: substandard usage, dialect, cant, jargon, or merely slovenliness. A dictionary definition (in Webster's New International Second Edition) includes 'cant' as one meaning of 'slang' and 'jargon' as a second, both of which we eliminate; the third meaning there is what we will follow: 'Language comprising certain widely current but usually ephemeral terms (especially coined or clipped words, or words used in special senses, or phrases, usually metaphors or similes) having a forced, fantastic, or grotesque meaning, or exhibiting eccentric or extravagant humor or fancy.' Examples: 'leather' is not slang but thieves' cant for 'wallet;' 'to be with it' is not slang but carny jargon; 'to be in the know' was slang in the sixteenth century but is now standard English; 'skiddoo' is dead slang; it is useless to quote live slang, because it is pretty certain to be dead before this page is read.

The purpose of ellipsis and the purpose of slang is the same; but they are opposite in their description and opposite in their history. Ellipsis is a minus feature and is very stable historically; slang is a plus feature and is absolutely unstable. Yet both signify the same: that the addressee, an insider, will understand what not everybody would be able to decipher.

Ellipsis (omission) makes most of the difference between casual grammar and consultative grammar. 'I believe that I can find one' is proper (though not required) in consultative grammar, but casual English requires a shorter form, say 'I believe I can find one' if not the still more elliptical 'Believe I can find one.' All the weak words of English can be omitted at the beginning of a casual sentence: 'Been a good thing if . . .' for 'It would have been a good thing if . . .' and similarly '[A] friend of mine . . .' or '[The] coffee's cold.' Some ellipsis is only phonological: 'Can I help you?' is consultative and 'C'n I help you?' is casual. Modern 'cute' from original 'acute' and 'fence' from 'defence' are two out of many words which originated in casual style and have since been promoted; similarly, 'Thank you' from 'I thank you' has been promoted all the way to formal style, while 'Thanks' from 'Many thanks' or 'Much thanks' (Shakespeare) has been promoted only to consultative. Aside from such little shifts in the tradition, ellipsis is stable: the elliptical expressions in use today can nearly all be found in Shakespeare, for instance 'Thanks.'

As an institution, slang is also ancient; but each individual slang expression is, on the contrary, necessarily unstable. The reason is obvious. Because the utility of any slang expression for classing the addressee as an insider (or excluding an unwanted listener as an outsider) depends on the fact—or at least the polite fiction—that only a minority of the population understands this bit of slang, each slang expression is necessarily ephemeral; for when that fiction has become transparent with age, its purpose is foiled, and then the useless slang is abandoned while new slang has to be created to take its place—not new slang of the same meaning, of course, but just enough new slang to maintain a normal supply. The abandoned slang is then 'dead slang,' a few items of which may still be resurrected as period-pieces for jocular or nostalgic employment, for instance 'kiddo' or 'for crying out loud.' (How awful!—That's life, Miss Fidditch.)

It's what is called 'half-life' in nuclear physics. The half-life of a slang expression is of the order of magnitude of one year, which implies that about one specimen in a thousand will survive for ten years, and thus become tough enough to last indefinitely; example: 'to be in the know.' When slang is created for use in literature, the slang is dignified by such titles as 'trope, simile, metaphor,'—and it is routinely rejected when outworn there also. (I can't believe it.—You don't have to, Miss F.)

Besides these two pattern devices—ellipsis and slang—casual style is marked by an arbitrary list of formulas, all very stable, which are learned individually and used to identify the style for the hearer's convenience. 'Come on!' has been one of these identifiers since before the time of Shakespeare (see The Tempest, line 308); and all this while, every adult native speaker of English to whom it was addressed has unconsciously known that the speaker was using casual style and has reacted accordingly—and the speaker, without knowing why he did it, has used it to procure that reaction. It is all automatic, unconscious, just as the speaker of a falsehood is not aware that his motive for saying 'as a matter of fact' is to label it as false—a Freudian confession which is institutional in English. (I'm sure I never . . . —I believe you!)

Each style has its own list of such conventional formulas, which we may call 'code-labels' because they serve both to carry part of the message and to identify the style. The identifying function of a code-label is uniformly effective; its message-bearing function varies freely from nothing at all to a full message-fraction. Thus 'Come on!' means anything from 'Consider yourself among friends' to 'You're invited;' while 'Come on, cheer up!' means nothing but 'Cheer up because you're among friends.' There is of course a long list of casual code-labels, but 'Come on!' is one of the commonest.

Consultative code-labels include the standard list of listener's insertions 'yes [professorial for *yeah*], yeah, unhunh, that's right, oh, I see, yes I know' and a very few others, plus the 'well' that is used to reverse the rôles between listener and speaker. Another class of consultative code-labels consists of formulas for meeting that fluency problem which casual style evades by never tackling totally new topics; these are skeleton-keys for opening new doors without fumbling for the exact key which formal style will seek out at leisure. In our sample [page 290] these skeleton-keys include the all-purpose noun 'thing' [line 1] for 'item, plan, problem, event, etc.,' the all-purpose preposition 'on' [18] for 'in, for, by, of, concerning, etc.,' and finally the counting-approximaters 'about' [3, 4, 5] and 'or so' [18], both meaning 'approximately' (a formal word). Other consultative code-label skeleton-keys exist, but our sample is enough to show how they work. In line 1, good casual style would have had 'something else' and stiff formal style perhaps 'a situation which has arisen.' A formal jokester may pretend to get a ludicrous picture out of 'I'd like to see you on a typewriter;' the trained social animal simply takes 'on' as a code-label for informal consultation.

Both colloquial styles—consultative and casual—routinely deal in a public sort of information, though differently: casual style takes it for granted and at most alludes to it, consultative style states it as fast as it is needed. Where there happens to be no public information for a while, a casual conversation (among men) lapses into silences and kidding, a consultative one is broken off or adjourned. These adjustments help to show what sort of rôle public information plays in the two colloquial styles: it is essential to them both.

Now in intimate style, this rôle is not merely weakened; rather, it is positively abolished. Intimate speech excludes public information. (Then how can it be language?—Let's see: it's *Miss* Fidditch, isn't it?)

Definition: An intimate utterance pointedly avoids giving the addressee information from outside of the speaker's skin. Example: 'Ready' said in quite a variety of situations, some of them allowing other persons to be present; note that this could be equivalent to either a statement or a question; the manner of saying it will be described in a moment. Another: 'Engh' or 'Cold' said at the family supper-table, but not to tell the speaker's wife that the coffee is cold—as it would tell her after we let Miss Fidditch expand the ellipsis for us: wrongly, for this is not an ellipsis. This tells the speaker's wife nothing about the coffee. How could it! She knows exactly how long since it was hot. If she had had to be told, the casual-style 'Coffee's cold' would have been used instead. After all, they both know the code. The point of any such utterance is simply to remind (hardly 'inform') the addressee of some feeling (unspecified, but that does not matter) inside the speaker's skin. (But I do wish they would speak like human beings!—What else?)

The systematic features of intimate style are two, just as in the other styles: (1) Extraction; (2) Jargon. Both are stable, once the intimate group (normally a pair) has been formed. Extraction has just been illustrated: the speaker extracts a minimum pattern from some conceivable casual sentence. Extraction is not ellipsis. An elliptical sentence still has wording, grammar, and intonation. Intimate extraction employs only part of this triplet. Our printed 'Engh' represents an empty word, one that has no dictionary meaning but serves as a code-label for intimate style. (The parallel word in casual style, spelled 'unh,' has a different vocal quality.) There is, however, a message-meaning; this is conveyed by the intonation, the melody, with which 'Engh' is spoken. The speaker has extracted this intonation from a possible casual sentence, and that is all he uses of the grammatical triplet 'wording, grammar, intonation.' Again, our other example 'Cold' represents the word-identity alone, here spoken in a meaningless monotone; and the same is true of 'Ready.' In these instances, the triplet has been reduced to its first member, as 'Engh' reduced it to its last one, leaving the addressee to fill out the message—or, preferably, to comprehend it as it stands. (I couldn't.—Would you be so kind?)

Once more, this is not rudeness; this pays the addressee the highest compliment possible among mature people. Maturity implies some guardedness in public relations; here there is none, and the speaker is saying so. There is an exact discrimination between the inside and the outside of the speaker's skin; he makes this obvious, and pays the addressee the compliment of implying that she knows him inside and out. (Engh!—It *is* . . . *Miss* Fidditch, isn't it?)

Intimate style tolerates nothing of the system of any other style: no slang, no background information, and so on. Any item of an intimate code that the folklore calls 'slang' is not slang but jargon—it is not ephemeral, but part of the permanent code of this group—it has to be, for intimacy does not tolerate the slang imputation that the addressee needs to be told that she is an insider. The imputations of all other styles are similarly corrosive. Accordingly, intimate codes, or jargons, are severely limited in their use of public vocabulary. Each intimate group must invent its own code. Somehow connected with all this is the cozy fact that language itself can never be a topic in intimate style. Any reaction to grammar, for instance, promptly disrupts intimacy. [S'mother time, M . . . F . . .]

IV

AN INFORMATIVE CLOCK

We return briefly to consultative style. It supplies background information currently, and the listener participates fully. His participation insures that there shall be neither too little nor too much background given. If too little, he will break in to ask for elucidation; if too much, he may say 'yes I know.' The diction is kept in accurate balance with the requirements: the pronunciation is clear but does not clatter, the grammar is complete but for an occasional anacoluthon, the semantics is adequate without fussiness. All is adjusted by instantaneous homeostasis, and the speaker does not compose text more than two or three seconds in advance. He could not in any case, since he must expect the hearer to insert a word or two every six seconds. Being thus entirely automatic, it is the most strictly organized type of language. Its grammar is central to all the possibilities of grammar, and the grammars of all other styles are formed by adding archaisms and other complications to the consultative grammar; the pronunciations of all other styles are most simply described as departures from consultative pronunciation; the meanings of any word which occurs at all in consultative style are basically its consultative meanings, to which each other style adds specific meanings as necessitated by its own function: private meanings in intimate style, slang meanings in casual style, technical meanings in formal style, allusive meanings in frozen style.

Describing formal style by departure from consultative style, the crucial difference is that participation drops out. This is forced whenever the group has grown too large: the insertions then may overlap, causing semantic confusion, or each listener must space his insertions out beyond the biological limit of about thirty seconds; either of these results then causes this or that group-member to withdraw by becoming catatonic or absent, or to begin speaking in formal style and thus to render the others catatonic or absent. This homeostasis, then, either reduces the size of the group so that it may remain consultative or splits the group into one manic speaker and a set of catatonic hearers. A competent manic is able to convert a tête-à-tête into a formal assembly; but normal persons maintain consultation up to a group-size of approximately six, which sets the limits on the size and composition of a 'committee' in the English-speaking sense. Beyond that, parliamentary law is requisite, i.e. a division into active and chair-warming persons.

Non-participation is also forced whenever a speaker is entirely uncertain of the prospective response. Thus conversations between strangers begin in formal style; among urbane strangers in English-speaking cultures, the formal span is only the ceremony of introduction, whose function is to insure that no real business shall be impeded by formality; it then lasts for one consultative speech-span, approximately six seconds. Within a consultation, a similar formal span is instituted whenever embarrassment arises or is imminent. The rupture of consultation is marked either by formal leave-taking or by casual leave-taking; adjournment of consultation is marked by consultative leave-taking, e.g. 'I might not be back for a while.'

Formal style is designed to inform: its dominating character, something which is necessarily ancillary in consultation, incidental in casual discourse, absent in intimacy. The formal code-labels inform each hearer that he is in a formal frame, is not to make insertions but must wait until authorized to speak, and is being given time to plan reactions—as much as half a century. The leading code-label is 'may;' any message requiring either 'might' or 'can' in other styles is suppressed or paraphrased, giving 'May I help you?' and 'We may not see one another for some time,' the consultative equivalent of which was cited previously. We may most economically label an introduction as formal by saying 'May I present Mr. Smith?'—or petrify a child by saying 'No, you may not.' Originally, the well-placed 'may' was as effective as a hat-pin.

Beyond its code-labels, formal style is strictly determined by the absence of participation. This absence infects the speaker also. He may speak as if he were not present, avoiding such allusions to his own existence as 'I, me, mine,' with the possible exception of 'one'—a formal code-label—or 'myself' in desperate situations. The speaker protects both the text and himself from involvement; presumably he will be absent if the roof collapses.

Lacking all personal support, the text must fight its own battles. Form becomes its dominant character. Robbed of personal links to reality, it scorns such other links as the stone painfully kicked to refute an idealist philosopher; instead, it endeavors to employ only logical links, kept entirely within the text, and displays those logical links with sedulous care. The pronunciation is explicit to the point of clattering; the grammar tolerates no ellipsis and cultivates elaborateness; the semantics is fussy. Background information is woven into the text in complex sentences. Exempt from interruption, the text organizes itself into paragraphs; the paragraphs are linked explicitly: thus this is the third of a quadruplet.

Formal text therefore demands advance planning. Consultative speakers never plan more than the current phrase, and are allowed only a limited number of attempts to return to their muttons before abandoning them; the formal speaker has a captive audience, and is under obligation to provide a plan for the whole sentence before he begins uttering it, an outline of the paragraph before introducing it, and a delimitation of field for his whole discourse before he embarks on it. One who does all this currently, keeping the three levels of his planning under continuous control, is correctly said to think on his feet; for clearly it calls for something other than brains, and intelligent persons do not attempt it but instead have the text all composed and written out at leisure.

The defining features of formal style are two: (1) Detachment; (2) Cohesion. One feature, of the highest importance, is retained from the basal styles: intonation. Since the audience hears the text just once, any deficiency in the intonation is dangerous, any major defect is disastrous. Lack of intonation, as in print, is simply a blank check; but false intonation will mulct the listener in triple damages. In the formal frame a native speaker may say 'pine *tree*' with the second word loudest, insisting on an impossible message. The fog of confusion which this spreads over the listeners' attention will render approximately six subsequent words inaudible to them. Meanwhile they must first detect the absurdity of what they plainly heard; second, forget the pseudo-sentence but retain the list of its words in sequence; third, by trial and error construct a plausible sentence from that list. Such listening is known as 'a duty to oneself,' and the monetary cost is deductible in income-tax returns.

V

A FORMATIVE CLOCK

That list of words in sequence is all that is left in frozen style. Punctuation is of very little help towards an adequate intonation, and good frozen style never relies on it. Frozen style—a style for print and for declamation—is defined by the absence of authoritative intonation in the text, as also by the fact that the reader or hearer is not permitted to cross-question the author. Relative to the other styles, these peculiarities clearly are defects in the frozen style, preventing it from functioning as they do. Freed from those other functions, frozen style develops its own functions, by common consent surpassing the others. From the surpassing excellence of good frozen style, our folklore has derived the mistaken theory that it is the ideal of all language.

Is not good writing the highest type of language? Yes, in its own way. But if we approach it through the Grove of Academe, we see nothing but trees labeled 'best' and 'correct' and 'classic' and the rest. It is not possible to discern the nature of excellence in memorable writing from the standpoint that fine printable style is a complex of correct forms and superior formulas. If that were true, it could be learned; the truth is that it can only be invented.

Frozen style can indeed be understood on its own terms, but only if the way is cleared of the prejudice that it does what other discourse does but does it better. To do that, we swiftly approach it twice from the other end of the style scale. Good intimate style fuses two personalities. Good casual syle integrates disparate personalities into a social group which is greater than the sum of its parts, for now the personalities complement each other instead of clashing. Good consultative style produces cooperation without the integration, profiting from the lack of it. Good formal style informs the individual separately, so that his future planning may be the more discriminate.

Good frozen style, finally, lures him into educating himself, so that he may the more confidently act what rôle he chooses.

Each of the latter four does its own work by making a virtue out of necessity—a necessity that springs from its own deficiencies in comparison to one or two basal styles. Personal disparities are over-compensated in social integration by casual devices designed out of the mere fact that one person is not another person. Each lack of shared information is over-compensated in consultation, because two heads are better than one and consultation makes them more than twice as good. Each loss from lack of participation is over-compensated in good formal communication by giving several hours of preparation to one hour of discourse. That makes three.

Frozen style is for people who are to remain social strangers. Our direct compensation for remaining strangers is consultative style. By comparison, frozen style lacks two things, participation and intonation. It gains two things of which this is one: the reader can reread.

Let this word not be misunderstood. Rereading is not re-scanning the print. Re-scanning is the least profitable substitute for rereading, and is best reserved for official documents. Rereading is reconsidering the text. It is best done with the eyes closed. It can be done thousands of miles and thousands of days distant from the printed page.

The reader can reread. In the one fact lies both the writer's opportunity and his danger. If he has not somehow trained himself to his proper task, he will simply lay a fixed message out neatly into sentences, so that they can be fully understood with one re-scanning, so clear and shallow are they. That is only excellent formal style. It will not do the work of even a poor frozen style.

The opportunity is that the writer who is dedicated can enable the rereader to educate himself indefinitely for beyond what the writer put into the text in the first place. The writer only initiates the process; then the rereader carries on from there. What is the writer's part? To rewrite. The writer is a rewriter, or he is no proper writer at all—like Thomas Wolfe. Non-writers have their function too, but that is not what we are concerned with now.

The rewriter is not the man who revises for clarity and force in a message once chosen complete, seeking to clothe it decently. When that is undertaken and well executed, we learn with sorrow that he has not only laid the garment of his thought out handsomely but has laid out the body too. ('Not only' before 'has,' or delete the second 'has.'—Sorry, Miss Fidditch; I will not kill an innocent thought unless you give me a better one.—But that would be clear and correct!—But he's just as dead as if he'd been wrong.)

The rewriter is as one who packs his thought for a long journey. Having packed the garment, he does not merely straighten out the folds and close the paragraph. Instead, he unpacks completely and repacks again. And again; and again and again. Each time, he tucks just one more thought into this or that pocket. When he quits, there are more of them than of words. So many labors of love on a single sentence, that many rewards for the rereader. On the surface, one teasing half-reward; others at successively greater and greater depths, so that each reading finds one more. (Why whatever for?— Reread and see.)

Conceivably those successive depths might be achieved in one writing; but more probably the genius is simply the man who can do the repacking inside his skull. In any case, there must be repacking with more ideas insinuated into the wording. The rewards will lie at successive depths only if they were packed into the text in successive repackings. That is simply the kind of wits we have.

The rereader's wits do not directly reverse the process. The last-packed idea may be the second discovered then, and so on in a sequence that is likely to agree partly with the sequence of packings and partly with the reverse sequence. There is no good reason for preferring either direction. When the rereader reverses the rewriter's sequence, he profits from the harmony between their wits; when he follows it direct, he profits from their disparities; and if he skips a step, he strengthens his wits by the exercise.

Because the present report does not suffer from enough modesty to delay the proceedings, a rewriter's share of the transaction may be illustrated from a parenthesis near the top of page 285. The drafts that can be resurrected ran thus:

Excuse us, please.
Quiet, Miss Fidditch.
Quiet, Miss F; the children are studying.
Quiet there! These are people, studying for exams.
Quiet there, Miss Fidditch. These people are studying.
Quiet there, Miss F. These are people preparing for examinations.

The increasing length bears witness to this writer's amateur standing. Still, there is enough here to make the point. The text is short enough to be read at once as a whole. Then the number of re-scannings can easily be far less than the number of rereadings: each discovery of another meaning counts as one more rereading if there was any delay whatever. Probably this line was reconsidered a good half-dozen times by each rereader among the readers of the page where it is at home. (There! I knew it was obscure!—No comment for the present.)

Next, we must recognize that the rereader has a right to congratulate himself for each new meaning that he finds. There is no essential difference between discovery and invention, and every new thought is compounded and distilled from old memories. To make a centaur, you do need a man and a horse, and yet you are a brave boy when you've done it. The rereader is a creative thinker. He is thoroughly justified in feeling that he has created a half-dozen meanings in reconsidering a text too short to hold them all on its surface. He will feel that; it would be inhuman not to. (Don't you mean 'unhuman' or 'nonhuman?'—'Inhumane' if you say so!)

But—he was lured on into doing it. Definition: Good frozen style is whatever lures the reader on and on through successive inventive discoveries. It is good in the sense that it is a germ and a contagion of good. It starts a process whose continuing is a good thing; it gives momentum to insure the continuing. The reader, rewarded for several successive acts of creative thinking with one reward for each, gets into the swing of it and continues creating more and more meanings to suit his convenience; then he is educating himself.

This is not obscurity in the text, for obscurity breaks off the sequence too early or blocks it from ever starting. This is not clarity, for clarity allows no such sequence to start itself; the reader's own effort must develop the momentum, and the writer's effort can not do it for him. All the writer can do is to repack somewhere between obscurity and clarity.

Fortunately for the dedicated writer, there is a full wide space between the two, within which honest work can achieve respectable small effects like this one every time he tries and where he more or less frequently may make a lucky hit. He need not worry about exactly suiting an imagined reader; after all, what is too much repacking for one prospective reader will be too little for another, and each rewriter gets the audience he deserves. Whether he consciously knows it or not, each writer selects his stable audience by what sorts of things he insinuates and how many of them—not by his surface message. For example, the ninth word of this paragraph will say nothing to one reader, will mean one thing to the next but suggest nothing further, will for a third reader simply add an archaic flavor, will offer an illuminating analogy to a fourth reader, and will start an indefinitely long chain of associations within the fifth. Assuming that the writer is reconciled to having his subconscious select his audience for him—that is to say, assuming that he is mature—the only way he could lose in this transaction is that the fifth man's associations might lead him into a snake-pit of painful memories. But that must happen sooner or later if it can happen at all, and in principle it is independent of the initiating text. The all-human catalog of painful memories is infinite in size and variety, so that no writer can usefully plan to avoid them at all. (I try to tell my pupils not to offend people unnecessarily.—I suppose so.)

Adequately started, the rereader's momentum carries him on—perhaps even for decades—on and on indefinitely far beyond what the writer could decently claim credit for having put into the printed text. Wise writers may discover this fact consciously too, but then they usually keep it a secret: they either have always known or promptly discover that the lay public can't endure to face the truth of the matter and will protect themselves against it by classifying the author's plain statement as a joke or an attempt at obfuscation. Thus Browning on a poem of his earlier years: 'When I wrote that, only God and Robert Browning knew what it meant, and now only God knows.' And Goethe, when asked which of two interpretations of an early poem of his was correct: 'After all, why not?' Some critics know the fact too; but most of them are reluctant to expose it for fear of seeming to be trying to start a new criticism school. (My pupils keep asking me what poems mean.—The guessing is fun, isn't it?)

Therefore, if attention is called, a little later on here, to some possible rereadings of our sample of rewriting, it is not by way of boasting. A writer can at most claim credit for a first push onto an unpredictable path of self-education through rereading and beyond. He deserves neither credit nor blame for what length or turnings that path may develop later. Accordingly, good writers don't have to be perfect; and no man, not even the present reporter, need feel any shame for going to print with an honest day's work. If he has allowed for enough successive rewards to lure some few readers beyond a first reading, he can draw his pay with a clear conscience. (I have some favorite authors that most people don't think much of.—Are they alive? Rewrite and tell them!)

In an obvious sense, consummate formal writing is a waste of time for the reader. When all the writer's own ideas are forced upon the reader, who could protect himself against them only by inattention, no rereading momentum can develop. Apparently everything by Winston Churchill is like that. (My aunt thinks his writing is just wonderful.—So does he.)

No. Good writing is not the perfectly tailored garment of a Personage, perfectly pressed since last he wore it; it is the rumpled suit of a living person, still relaxing from the strain of his labors, its pockets stuffed with trash and with things worth getting at. And each thing gets its value from the finder. (I'll have to think that over.—Good.)

Beside rereading, there is something of its own kind to be called refeeling. When this occurs alone, the text is promptly thrust behind, recoiling from the push it gave, while the refeeler pursues his own nostalgias alone. The style may be speciously like frozen style, but it is not the same thing, as formal style is and is not; indeed, this may be called 'anti-formal' style because it reverses the aims of formal style by subordinating information to involvement. Confusingly, anti-formal style is found in two opposite varieties, namely as emitted by non-writers, like Thomas Wolfe, who simply fill the text with salt tears, and by over-writers, like Franz Kafka and Edgar

Allan Poe, who stew and distill so as to fill it with nothing but ardent spirits. In such case, the reader finds that the ship has sunk with all hands and that he himself is rolling and tumbling, floating alone on a crumbling cask with nothing to drink but rum and sea-water, fit only to inflame his thirst. In one thirsty gulp the unwary reader will utterly drain the text to fill his feelings. Then the cask collapses, the sea is a desert; there is no text left to be reread. One is alone: to re-scan the print, yes, if lust prevails over wisdom; but that will only start up the old lonesome feelings over and over, to go their own road again, a way perchance fascinatingly uncharted —but now it never will be charted, without any text. That is not the way to profit from the second advantage of frozen style: that it can be refelt as well as reread. (But The Raven was lovely!—Do you regress often?)

Yet there is a wise way, an adequate balance of rereading and refeeling. This comes about when the text and feelings are first not too far from equally worth reconsidering; then the reader promptly brings them into balance; then their double pursuit never abandons either the one or the other. This double process is initiated in the adequate reader by genuine poetry and by dedicated prose.

Only by virtue of this balance is it possible for the pursuit of feelings to transcend both crude facts and raw lust and go on into another country: wisdom. The reason is that we are not only thinkers but feeling thinkers, not only animals but speaking animals. Our kind of wisdom implicates and is implicated by text, and likewise implicates and is implicated by feelings. Feelings and text are inseparable in human wisdom. Not just the text first seen in print or heard, and the feelings first rousing themselves then, but also—and rather—the continuations created by one who refeels and rereads them together in their indissoluble marriage. And this wisdom is the esthetic of literature.

Definition: Literature is that text which the community insists on having repeated from time to time intact. It is created in its success. When the community refuses to reread and refeel a composition, it is not a literary text; it remains a draft. (We must wait and see!—See if we want to reread it.)

What intactness must be is clear. It is whatever constancy in the text preserves its marriage with the community feeling for it. Diverging versions —of text, of community feeling, of personal self-placement—divide and unite genres and also sub-communities. In a stable and evolving culture, the balance between division and union keeps all the entities healthy. (Homeostasis?—After all, why not?)

In unwritten literatures, as the culture evolves through the generations and the catastrophes, feelings evolve under that law continuously. When the feelings drift right along with the culture, the text keeps in step by moderniz-ing itself continuously; example: any medieval ballad of Scottish border tragedy and its modern versions referring to feuds in our eastern mountains. (I don't know why, but I like them.—You don't need to, and I'm glad.)

When the values drift down certain slopes to occupy swampy areas con-tinuously depopulated by the disintegration of texts, the text becomes vulgar and less stable; example: any Boccaccio's tale and the immensely numerous and variable anecdotes of today stemming therefrom. (I try not to listen. —So you do hear them? Good: there's vitamins in them—they grow in rich muck.)

When the values similarly drift upward on certain slopes to occupy up-lands repeatedly depopulated by the disintegration of feelings, the text be-comes constitutional and more stable; example: any sacred book. Then that sub-community which feels able to follow the rising feelings becomes smaller and develops a more intense pride in the possession of the mystery—which swiftly completes the alienation from the community feeling norm: the text is now hieratic and forever fixed. (How long is that?—While the com-munity is intact.)

When, finally—and this fourth case joins with the first—the feelings diverge sidewise instead of down or up, the text becomes obsolete and vanishes, as a whole, through lack of demand for its intact repetition; ex-ample: any ancient hero-tale which didn't happen to be written down in time. (The Mabinogion!—What there's left of it.)

Then the disintegrating text is treated as a grab-bag of fragments, of all sizes down to single words and even shapes of words, to be patched into and onto any tale apt to be adorned by them. When patched onto, they give at least two layers of depth at once, to start the rereading and refeeling process and to teach writers what depth may be; and by appealing to nostalgias they provide the requisite first surface values. (I'm just in love with old English ballads.—Right you are.)

Now the community is free to reread and refeel the well-patched text into an above-average status with respect to sufficient sub-community norms of feeling; then it is classical; examples: Icelandic family sagas and the Paul Bunyan cycle. (I read a Paul Bunyan collection recently, but I think there are some fakes in it.—You can tell, can't you!)

Description amounting to a definition: Classical text is that text which has been spun from a thread of feeling, woven close to a community pattern of feeling, tailored to suit rereadings of men and events, patched with pieces that would not have been taken while the brands were still visible, and worn long enough to prove that it will wear. (Why isn't that your five clocks?—Come to think of it, you're right! Thank you, Miss Fidditch, I mean Candida, and come home: all is forgiven.)

When a next-succeeding text is made in this way, the thread and tissue of actual feelings must sew and piece it. This living material is apt to form the most cherished parts for the time being. Cherishing them makes them hardy, and they can survive to achieve their second life in the next fragmentation, when the former fragments have been discarded as text and are gone to the pulping-mill. (Linen paper?—Bleached rag body, fit for any writing: semantics, grammar, phonology.)

And so on forever and ever, with never more need to invent a totally new tale than to make a man in a laboratory. The whole process is automatic. Communities have always found it easier to maintain literature than factual history, and the most stable texts referring to actual men and events are always the mythical texts like the patched-up tale of George Washington and his cherry-tree. (I keep trying to get my students to be original.—Why how do you do, Miss Frankenstein!)

The definition again: Literature is that text which the community insists on having repeated from time to time intact, and the word 'intact' has just been reread. It is the key word here. It seems to answer to some instinct or other, for each child, once he is old enough to follow a tale at all, insists that repetitions must occur and must occur in the identical wording. It is as if the child was born knowing what mature people imagine they found out by developing a taste for classical literature: that self-education best starts out repeatedly from the identical text. But this coincidence ought not to surprise us. Anthropologists, by analysing many . . . (That manic is here again!—Sorry; thank you.)

With the parallel growth of printing and of monster nations, a text can survive on paper if only one person in a thousand buys a copy once in his lifetime. Then arithmetic says that there could be a thousand literary genres in a single nation. But the most popular genre, what with advertising and all that—in ancient times already the varying choices of hearers and the reputation of this or that literary cloth or tailor—is sure to claim some large fraction of the market; then the next one can claim a large fraction of the remainder, and on on until the residue will not be large enough to pay for printing or for a minstrel's supper. Today, the result is something like ten genres: the comic books for one, Readers Digest for another, and so on. (I prefer . . . —Of course: we all do.)

Let us pick a genre at random, then, and get on with it. We go back to the point that the text is to be unfrozen by reconsidering it; a text that does not require unfreezing is not in frozen style and we need not consider it, any more than a reader will reconsider it. (I hope the random choice appeals to me.—We aim to please, Candida.)

If a man who reads Hamlet a hundred times is a more faithful devotee of literature than one who reads Hamlet ten times, then the narratives of baseball games claim one of the largest bodies of rereaders intensely devoted to literature; for they insist that the texts must read so nearly alike that one who has let slip a few random facts will glance at the date to make sure it isn't yesterday's paper. It is clear that one profits thrillingly from the thousandth departure from the same text. (You can't be serious!—How do you know I can't?)

Baseball is a highly literary game. Its rereader, knowing that the players need not be superlative athletes as in tennis or soccer, feels no bar to identifying with them—a necessity of literature. The rules are intricate to the point of inscrutability; the events are various enough to simulate the complexity of life itself. Then our normal reluctance to face complexities can equalize the comprehensions of life and of baseball, facilitating the just balance of text and feelings for continuing joint reconsideration: by definition, then, baseball text is dedicated prose. The lexicon is rich and strictly organized, yet with ample room for tropes—which are not slang because the business is known to be serious. The same event may be narrated with emmense variety, the same patch of text will cover an infinite number of events—for who can doubt that baseball will endure as long as apple pie? (How long is that?—Same answer.)

Then since it doesn't matter whether we take a baseball text or any other sample of frozen style, we return to page 299. We have seen what the rewriting process looks like as factual history; now how about a literary myth to clothe it? (Why not the truth, the whole . . . —What is truth?)

Here goes, then. Suppose the writer has chosen a message; how can he compensate for the absence of intonation if nothing more? In principle, there are two separate methods, though in practice they are routinely combined. One method is to choose and arrange words that will do their work without relying on intonation; and the other is to force an adequate intonation. And remember that these methods, combined or separately, must accomplish the rewriter's task: packing several ideas down and down, where they can be discovered later and later. (I'm holding my breath.—Keep your fingers crossed too, Candida.)

Take the word 'preparing.' First its value independent of intonation, a value or values which may emerge sooner or later as the rereader experiments with the text and feelings. On those grounds, and assuming, as the writer must, that the rereader is his own twin, the word 'preparing' was chosen for two sorts of effects. For one thing, it would be more persuasive to our hypothetical Miss F than 'studying' or perhaps any other word that might have suited the dramatic occasion; this may lure the reader into reconsidering his image of Miss F and what makes her tick, a reconsidering which may be renewed as he comes to think of her and of her sisters either on real-life occasions or on literary ones, again and again into the indefinite future. For another thing, it was intended to lure the reader into side-slips, such as thinking of 'preparation for living' as the P.T.A. calls it, then into reconsidering the future lives of young members of one's own family, specifically perhaps from the amusing departure of thinking what an 'examination' might be in that context—a proposal of marriage—trying for a job where 'Toots' would disqualify—selecting a girl who 'doesn't criticize' (forming a group that will be homogeneous on the responsibility scale) —choosing an ambitious husband—and so on and on; and then departing again, from any link, down other association-chains. If some reader of that text or of this paragraph calls this the main message and calls the other one the side-slips, the writer will be the last man to object. (Do you mean to say that writers don't know what they're saying?—Yes;)

Second, the contribution of 'preparing' toward forcing an adequate intonation. The word 'people' had been chosen previously; now the problem was to prevent its being taken as a synonym for 'children.' The obvious solution is to not only make it loud, which English grammar otherwise does already, but leave it marked with a pregnant pause—a pause which says that the preceding word is to be taken in its most intense meanings. Such a pause is an English comma-pause; now the problem is to force one. (Note the word 'English' here; this sort of transaction is a large part of what we mean when we say 'literature is untranslatable.') Now listen to the sequence 'people preparing.' It contains four successive syllables beginning with [p]. (Shade of Macaulay!—I hope he's as happy wherever he's at home.) Again, in the middle there is the dark English [l] sound. Now a series of four [p] syllables in this English rhythm will force a pause midway; and then the dark [l] will force the dipping intonation which makes this an English comma-pause. This comma-pause, finally, makes 'people' pregnant, as required by the conditions of our whole problem. (You can't mean you knew you were doing all that!—How should I know what I can mean?)

A comma there is [,] now no longer needed. There is no great harm in printing the comma in prose; but a poet would be justified in striking it out in galley-proof, with the same reason as for not using italics. Simply printing the comma without having forced the pause by the wording is a surrender in ignominious defeat. If only shallow wordings, or wordings which will not force a useful intonation, can be found for the first message thought of, the writer must start all over again, hoping to hit upon another message of greater promise. (What's the matter? Don't you . . . —You mean to say that writers don't care what they say just so they say at least two things at once? Why, that's . . . Oh, never mind; I think I'll just take an aspirin and . . .)

The writer invites defeat whenever he takes on the double burden of placing a certain message complete within a certain span of text. Postponement is wiser, at least for the most important messages; for then they will invade the text all along meanwhile, pervading its suppressions and ambiguities with a tincture of expectancy. It would be hard to accomplish that by plan; it is easy to let it happen: just postpone, and it happens anyhow. (Good writing can't be planned?—Believe The Raven if you like, but not Poe's essay on it!)

Trivialities can be planned, for instance the question that elicited the answer 'Yes;' not long ago, signifying: (1) They know what they are saying. (2) I mean they don't know. (3) You have asked a dear sweet four-year-old's unanswerable question; I will answer accordingly and hope you'll be content and go away to play. (I like that!—Thank you.)

A more complex example is the answer to a more recent question, designed to be entirely at the mercy of the reader's intonation so that it can be taken absolutely any way he likes. At least eight ways of taking it are given by choice of accented syllable; in the printed versions here, the chosen word is italicized without meaning over-emphasis—simply to locate the choice for the reader:

How should I know what I can *mean* when I don't even know . . .
How should I know what I *can* mean unless I try?
How should I know what *I* can mean when I don't know what . . .
How should I know *what* I can mean—quite a lot so far!
How should I *know* what I can mean when I feel I must guess?
How should *I* know what I can mean—ask the experts!
How *should* I know what I can mean if not this way?
How should I know what I can mean? You shall teach me.

Now multiply by two, because it was either 'mean in the text under consideration' or else 'mean during the present reconsideration;' that makes 16. Then pick a number and multiply by that, since not all fluent continuations have been printed here, and again because some continuations may also be ambiguous. (Pretty vague!—Would you recognize vagueness in a . . . no; sorry; that was rude of me.)

No, this is not vagueness. To be vague is to be rude; and this is not rudeness. It is, indeed, exactly what was called 'not rudeness' in considering the two familiar styles. This ambiguity is the special politeness of frozen style. The rewriter does not force the reader to swallow a single message. (Ambiguity again! Aw, I give up!—Come on; relax and enjoy it.)

This Bluebeard has told the reader exactly the same thing as her mother must have told her—to open any door but one in the sprawling castle he has provided for her. If instead he had turned her out to forage for herself during his absence, that would have been vagueness, that would have been rudeness. (Bluebeard—and Mr. Rochester!—Fine! Reread more!)

The rewriter treats the rereader as one who is equally human; he deserves to be paid in the same coin. He feels, as the reader must, that we can understand only what we can say. The only messages a literary writer can possibly put over, in any case, are those inventively discovered by the reader. In his most broadly ambiguous text, he is at his most thorough; he is most mindful of his duty when he gives each rereader perfect freedom to create the most profitable messages. (But it makes me feel so insecure!—How do you think I feel?)

His other duty—in the sense that it is a politician's first duty to get himself elected—is to provide the first allurements. He need not always provide equally many of them: certain readers profit most when they must even break into the castle before they will wander in it. From that to the opposite extreme—those who want only surface gold, and wouldn't do a day's digging themselves for a million—the readers are spread out in a broad spectrum. The writer can choose his reader-companions along the whole length of this responsibility-scale, as we always form our social groups. (I try so hard, and . . . —Knock at some other door, Candida.)

But there is no use having a scale unless you know which way is up. It is your reporter's choice to say that the top is where the text and the feelings can be made, in an adequate reader, equally worth reconsidering, and the total depth is as much as a lifetime of reconsidering needs. The Gettysburg Address is deep enough; and Robert Frost will do. And he'll do and he'll do. How much more, this respondent has not yet lived long enough to know. (Then. . . ? —I hope you're as young as you look right now, Candy.)

Now there was that question of good literary form. Let's take it as an honest question and suppose that 'fine writing' was not meant. The answer is that there is no such thing as good literary form; there is only literary good form. It is all a question of politeness. (Oh . . . Thank you!)

Good form is that behavior which makes your partner feel at home; that's why literature is about people and the best literature is all about people. The ceremony of introduction must signal to the reader what kind of house and what kind of company he is getting into. And thereafter he is not to be treated like one who has wandered into the wrong house and company by mistake. Unless you choose for your house-guests only such persons as can feel at home in a practical joker's house. (—You're welcome.)

Tell him 'black tie' or 'sport clothes' when you are inviting him; introduce him to a company who are reasonably well assorted among themselves, and don't replace them with a different set overnight so that he sees only unplaceable strangers at breakfast. Since you are a member of the community, you'll know what to do. (Oh, I do hope so . . . —Come on, we're all with you.)

Definition: Literary good form is whatever keeps the reader feeling at home. More later. (Oh, wait a minute! May I understand that correct spelling is good form?—You might. You may if you can. I'm inclined to feel so myself.—

AIDS TO STUDY

The five clocks to which Professor Joos's title refers are, of course, the five sorts of style which he lists at the beginning of section II—different styles which different people use on different occasions. The other usage-scales, which he lists under 'age,' 'breadth,' and 'responsibility' are not, he warns us, to be taken as simply equivalent labels. And it is very important to heed that warning. In other words, if we think the best English is genteel, frozen, and senile, we will misunderstand this selection pretty badly. Intimate style is by no means limited to babyhood, as Professor Joos points out in section III; genteel English is not necessarily the best, though Miss Fidditch assumes it must be.

Miss Fidditch, a sort of benighted schoolmarm, represents the view that there is but one measure of language, the measure of 'correctness,' which always applies to all people and all occasions. This is a view which many contemporary Americans more or less hold (though, as Professor Joos points out, they really know better). Such people wish they had learned their 'grammar' in school, and insist that their children be taught it—or, at least, so they say. But their language does not square with their notions about language.

What Professor Joos suggests is that we look at our language with the objectivity of a visitor from Mars. Such a visitor might observe that our language varies with the age of speakers, in the purpose or style of the speakers, in the breadth of experience it reflects, and in the social responsibility it assumes. He would not assume that any distinctions he found under any of these heads were necessarily good or bad in any ultimate sense. Once delivered of the notion that language is 'good' or 'bad' in an ultimate sense, we can look at the various ways we use language sensibly, and perhaps with profit.